D0845194

BURIED by THE TIMES

Buried by The Times: The Holocaust and America's Most Important Newspaper is an in-depth look at how the *New York Times* failed in its coverage of the fate of European Jews from 1939 to 1945. It examines the many decisions that were made up and down the chain of command at the *Times* – decisions that ultimately resulted in the minimizing and misunderstanding of modern history's worst genocide. The fascinating and tragic narrative of *Buried by The Times* is unfolded by Laurel Leff, a veteran journalist and professor of journalism. She recounts how personal relationships at the newspaper, the assimilationist tendencies of the *Times'* Jewish owner, and the ethos of mid-century America all led the *Times* to consistently downplay news of the Holocaust. It recalls in precise detail how news of the Nazis' "Final Solution" was hidden from *Times* readers and – because of the newspaper's profound influence on other media – from the larger American public. *Buried by The Times* is thus required reading for anyone interested in the Holocaust and America's response, as well as for anyone curious about how journalists determine what is newsworthy.

Laurel Leff has been a faculty member at Northeastern University since 1996. Prior to her university appointment, she was a professional journalist for 18 years, reporting for the *Wall Street Journal* and the *Miami Herald.* She also served as an editor for American Lawyer Media and the *Hartford Courant.*

Advance Praise:

"Laurel Leff has written an exceptional study of one of the darkest failures of the *New York Times* – its non-coverage of the Holocaust during World War II. How could the best newspaper in the United States, perhaps in the world, underestimate and underreport the mass killing of more than 6,000,000 Jews? Read this book, which provides answers and in the process stands tall in scholarship, style, and importance."

– Marvin Kalb, Senior Fellow at Harvard's Shorenstein Center on the Press, Politics and Public Policy

"This is the best book yet about American media coverage of the Holocaust, as well as an extremely important contribution to our understanding of America's response to the mass murder of the Jews."

– David S. Wyman, author of *The Abandonment of the Jews: America and the Holocaust*

"This important book answers – in a compelling fashion – some of the questions which have long been asked about the *New York Times*' coverage of the Holocaust. Probing far behind the headlines, Leff tells the fascinating story of how the Sulzberger family was rescuing its relatives from Germany at the same time that it was burying the story of the Holocaust in the inner recesses of the paper."

– Deborah E. Lipstadt, author of *Beyond Belief: The American Press and the Coming of the Holocaust*

"Laurel Leff has written an engrossing and important book about the abject failure of the world's most influential newspaper, the *New York Times*, to report on the Holocaust that its owner and key figures knew was occurring. Her book tells us much about America at the time, the level of anti-Semitism, and the assimilationist desire of the Jewish owner of the *Times* to avoid stressing the unique Jewish nature of the genocide. It is part and parcel with the same mindset of the Roosevelt Administration. One can only wonder in great sorrow at how many lives might have been saved if the nation's and the world's conscience had been touched by full and complete coverage by the *Times* of what remains the greatest crime in world history."

– Stuart E. Eizenstat, a former senior official in the Clinton Administration and the Special Representative of President Clinton on Holocaust-Era Issues, author of *Imperfect Justice: Looted Assets, Slave Labor and the Unfinished Business of World War II*

Buried by The Times

The Holocaust and America's Most Important Newspaper

Laurel Leff
Northeastern University

CAMBRIDGE UNIVERSITY PRESS
Cambridge, New York, Melbourne, Madrid, Cape Town, Singapore, São Paulo

Cambridge University Press
40 West 20th Street, New York, NY 10011-4211, USA

www.cambridge.org
Information on this title: www.cambridge.org/9780521812870

First published 2005
Reprinted 2005

Printed in the United States of America

A catalog record for this publication is available from the British Library.

Library of Congress Cataloging in Publication Data

Leff, Laurel, 1957–

Buried by the Times : the Holocaust and America's most important newspaper /
Laurel Leff.

p. cm.

Includes bibliographical references and index.

ISBN 0-521-81287-9 (hardback)

1. Holocaust, Jewish (1939-1945) – Press coverage – United States. 2. World War, 1939–1945 – Press coverage – United States. 3. New York Times Company. 4. Journalism – Social aspects – United States. I. Title.

D804.7.P73L44 2005
070.4′499405318 – dc22 2004018271

ISBN–13 978-0-521-81287-0 hardback
ISBN–10 0-521-81287-9 hardback

Dedicated to the Memory of

Sarai K. Ribicoff
1957–1980

and

Ricardo Hunter Garcia
1957–2004

Contents

Acknowledgments

I learned to be an editor by working with great ones: John McPhee at Princeton University; William Blundell and Byron Calame at the *Wall Street Journal*; Matthew Walsh and Edward Wasserman at the *Miami Herald*; Steven Brill, Eric Effron, Julie Lipkin, James Lyons, and Edward Wasserman at American Lawyer Media; and David Fink, Pamela Luecke and Lawrence Roberts at the *Hartford Courant*. I also had the fortune of working with a great editor on this book, Andrew Beck of Cambridge University Press, who praised, prodded, and improved in appropriate measure.

During my years teaching at Northeastern University in Boston, I have had a number of talented and inspiring graduate students, some of whom helped in researching this book. Among them are Lisa Eramo, Sarah McDonald, Nathan Fox, Hollie Gowen, Robert Greene, and most of all, Karen Fischer of Germany and Jacques Maes of France, who not only provided invaluable assistance, but who also exemplified the best of a generation of Europeans able to learn from the past. Among the many archivists who assisted me, Lora Korbut at The New York Times Company Archives stood out for her cheerfulness and her willingness to help me make full use of that priceless resource. In conducting my research, I received financial support from the Memorial Foundation for Jewish Culture and from Northeastern University's Research and Scholarly Development Fund.

Although only a few people were available to be interviewed for this book, they more than made up for their small number by their generosity in terms of time and insights. They include Clark Abt, Neil MacNeil, Jr., Margarete Midas Meyers, Marylea Meyersohn, Ruth Nussbaum, Daniel Schwarz, Louis Shub, and Jacob Trobe. In addition, Eli and Shoshanna Eliat and Otto and Gizella Heda helped me understand my family's involvement in the greater catastrophe of the Holocaust.

Several people encountered early incarnations of this book and offered encouragement when it was most needed: Nicholas Daniloff, Colette Fox, Debra Kaufman, Ada G. Leff, Ernest Leff, Thelma Magun, Bonita Miller, Eve Paul, Lawrence Roberts, James R. Ross, Vicki Schultz, Judyth Singer, Avi Soifer, Cassie Solomon-Gillis, Jerry Sontag, Sarah Tomlinson, Gillian Whitman, and my father-in-law, Robert D. Paul, who was the first person to read the entire manuscript and who sadly passed away before it was published. Still others devoted many hours to making this a better book through their penetrating criticisms: Nathan Fox, Ricardo Hunter Garcia, Julie Lipkin, Rafael Medoff, and Jeremy Paul, my best critic and best friend.

My children gave me hope during what was often a dark and disturbing endeavor: Jason Paul, through his dedication to tikkun olam (repairing the world), and Russell Paul, through his determination to recognize the best in others.

A final note in the interest of disclosure and remembrance. On June 26, 1942, the *New York Times* published a two-paragraph story on page five reporting that half of Slovakia's estimated 100,000 Jews had been sent to ghettos in Poland and Russia. Among them were my great aunt and uncle, Anna and Jacob Heda; their daughter, Vilma Kaufmann; my great aunt and uncle, Rudolfina and Armin Grunmann; and their 13-year-old daughter, Judit. Only Vilma, who was in Auschwitz and Bergen-Belsen, survived.

Note Abbreviations

Archives

AJA	American Jewish Archives
AJHS	American Jewish Historical Society
BU	Brandeis University
CAHJP	Central Archives for the History of the Jewish People
CU	Columbia University
CZA	Central Zionist Archives
FDRL	Franklin D. Roosevelt Library
HI	Hoover Institution
HU	Harvard University
JTS	Jewish Theological Seminary
LC	Library of Congress
NA	National Archives
NYTCA	New York Times Company Archives
PU	Princeton University
WSHS	Wisconsin State Historical Society
YIVO	Yiddish Scientific Institute
YU	Yale University

Collections

ACJ	American Council for Judaism
AHS	Arthur Hays Sulzberger
AK	Arthur Krock
AS	Abba Hillel Silver
BB	Berlin Bureau
BGR	Bernard G. Richards

BV	Bernard Valery
CH	Cordell Hull
CLS	Cyrus L. Sulzberger
CM	Charles Merz
DB	Daniel Brigham
DN	David Niles
EK	Eugen Kovacs
ELJ	Edwin L. James
EPS	Ernest and Paul Sulzberger
FDR	Franklin D. Roosevelt
FF	Felix Frankfurter
FMS	Fred M. Sulzberger
FTB	Frederick T. Birchall
GHA	Gaston H. Archaumbault
JGM	James G. McDonald
JJ	Jews and Judaism
JLM	Judah L. Magnes
JM	Julian Meltzer
JML	Joseph M. Levy
JSS	Jules S. Sauerwein
JTA	Jewish Telegraphic Agency
LCR	Leo C. Rosten
MB	Moscow Bureau
MSL	Morris S. Lazaron
NM	Neil MacNeil
OWI	Office of War Information
PZ	Palestine and Zionism
RB	Ray Brock
RD	Raymond Daniell
RM	Raymond McCaw
SSW	Stephen S. Wise
SW	Sumner Welles
WRB	War Refugee Board

Other

NYHT	*New York Herald Tribune*
NYT	*New York Times*

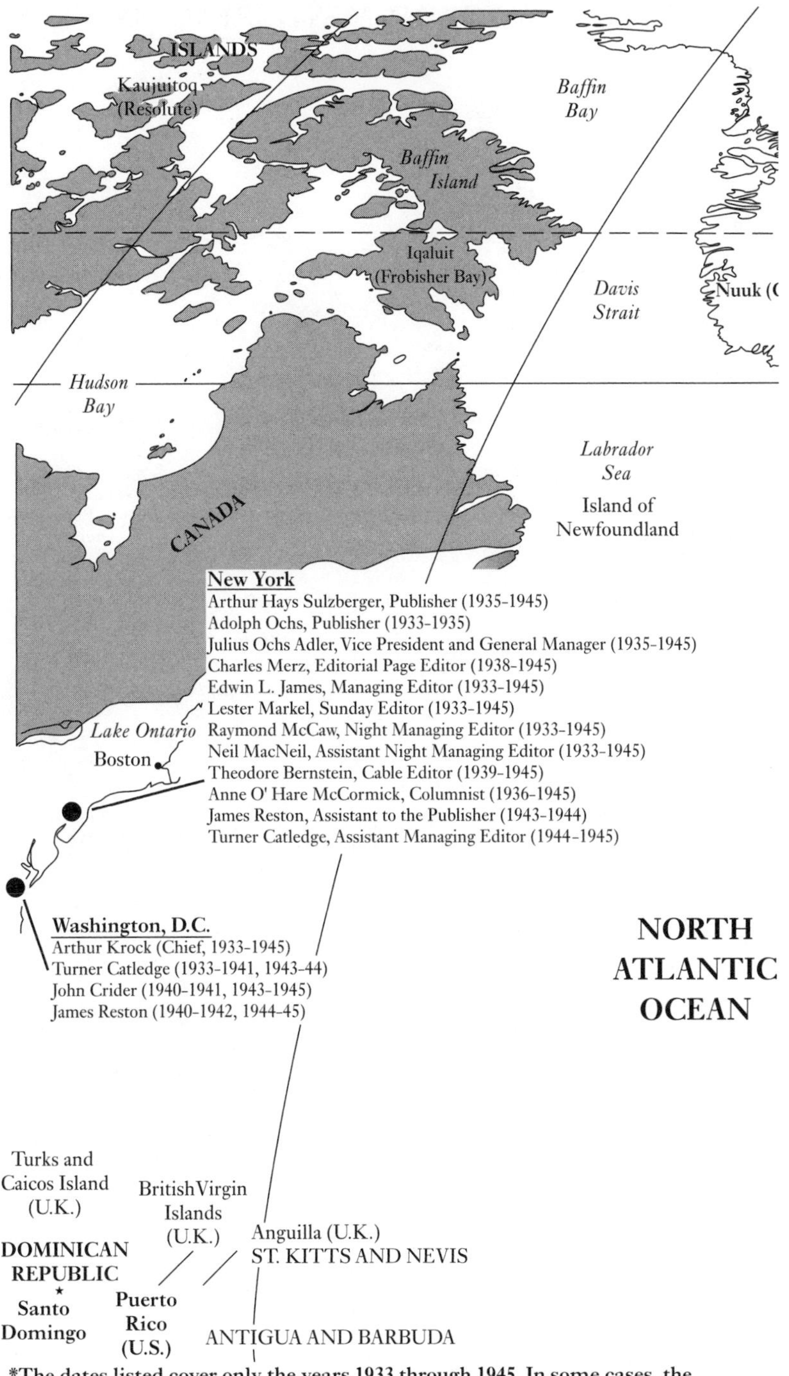

***The dates listed cover only the years 1933 through 1945. In some cases, the journalists held their positions before and/or after this time period. They also may have held other positions with the *Times*. In addition, some reporters left these bureaus for extended periods either to cover combat or to travel throughout a region.**

SELECTED NEW YORK TIMES BUREAUS 1933-1945*

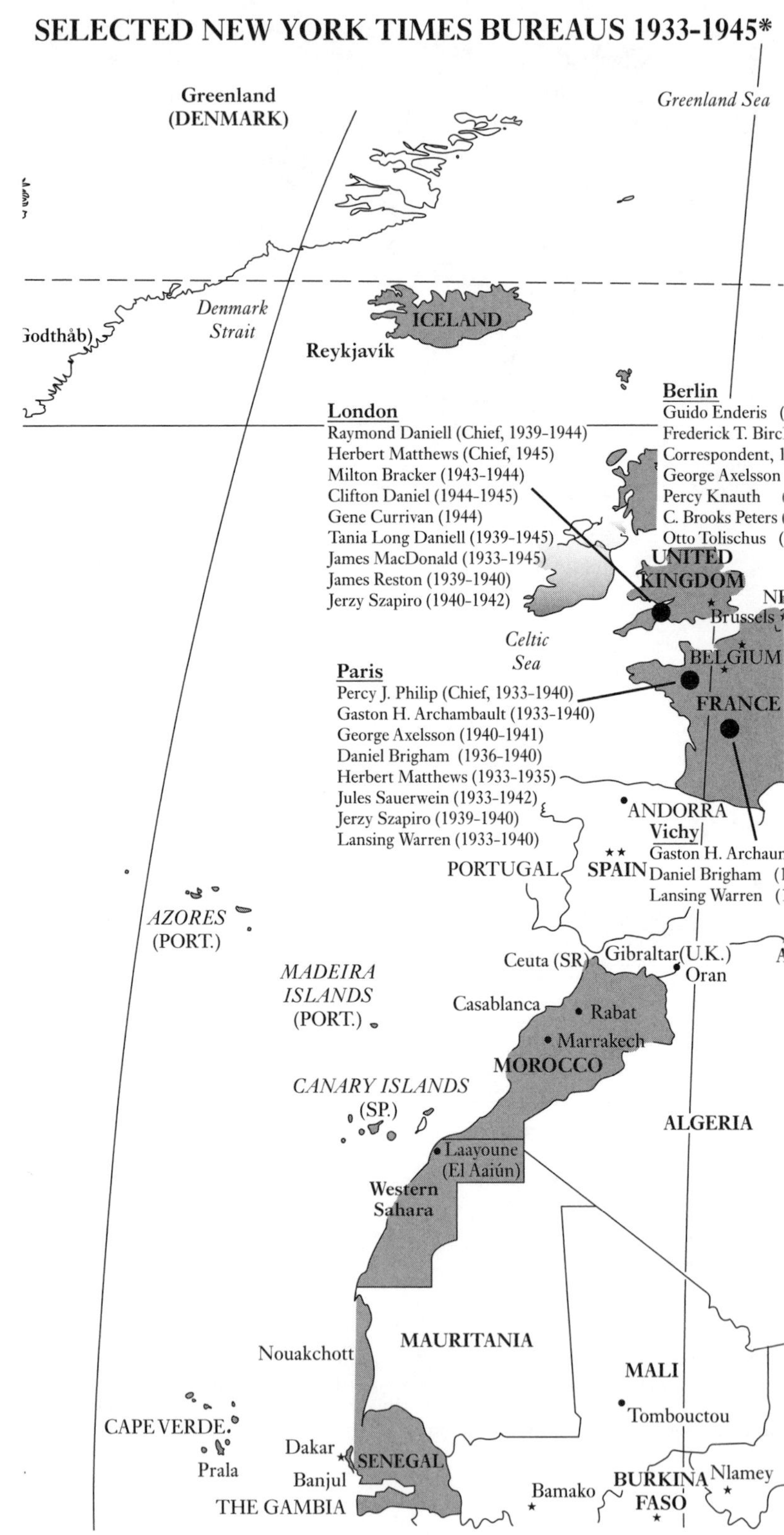

Greenland
(DENMARK)
Greenland Sea
Denmark
Strait
ICELAND
Reykjavík
Berlin
Guido Enderis
Frederick T. Birc
Correspondent,
George Axelsson
Percy Knauth
C. Brooks Peters
Otto Tolischus
London
Raymond Daniell (Chief, 1939-1944)
Herbert Matthews (Chief, 1945)
Milton Bracker (1943-1944)
Clifton Daniel (1944-1945)
Gene Currivan (1944)
Tania Long Daniell (1939-1945)
James MacDonald (1933-1945)
James Reston (1939-1940)
Jerzy Szapiro (1940-1942)
UNITED
KINGDOM
Brussels
Celtic
Sea
BELGIUM
Paris
Percy J. Philip (Chief, 1933-1940)
Gaston H. Archambault (1933-1940)
George Axelsson (1940-1941)
Daniel Brigham (1936-1940)
Herbert Matthews (1933-1935)
Jules Sauerwein (1933-1942)
Jerzy Szapiro (1939-1940)
Lansing Warren (1933-1940)
FRANCE
ANDORRA
Vichy
Gaston H. Archaur
Daniel Brigham
Lansing Warren
PORTUGAL
SPAIN
AZORES
(PORT.)
Ceuta (SP.)
Gibraltar(U.K.)
Oran
MADEIRA
ISLANDS
(PORT.)
Casablanca
Rabat
Marrakech
MOROCCO
CANARY ISLANDS
(SP.)
ALGERIA
Laayoune
(El Aaiún)
Western
Sahara
MAURITANIA
Nouakchott
MALI
Tombouctou
CAPE VERDE
Prala
Dakar
SENEGAL
Banjul
THE GAMBIA
Bamako
BURKINA
FASO
Nlamey

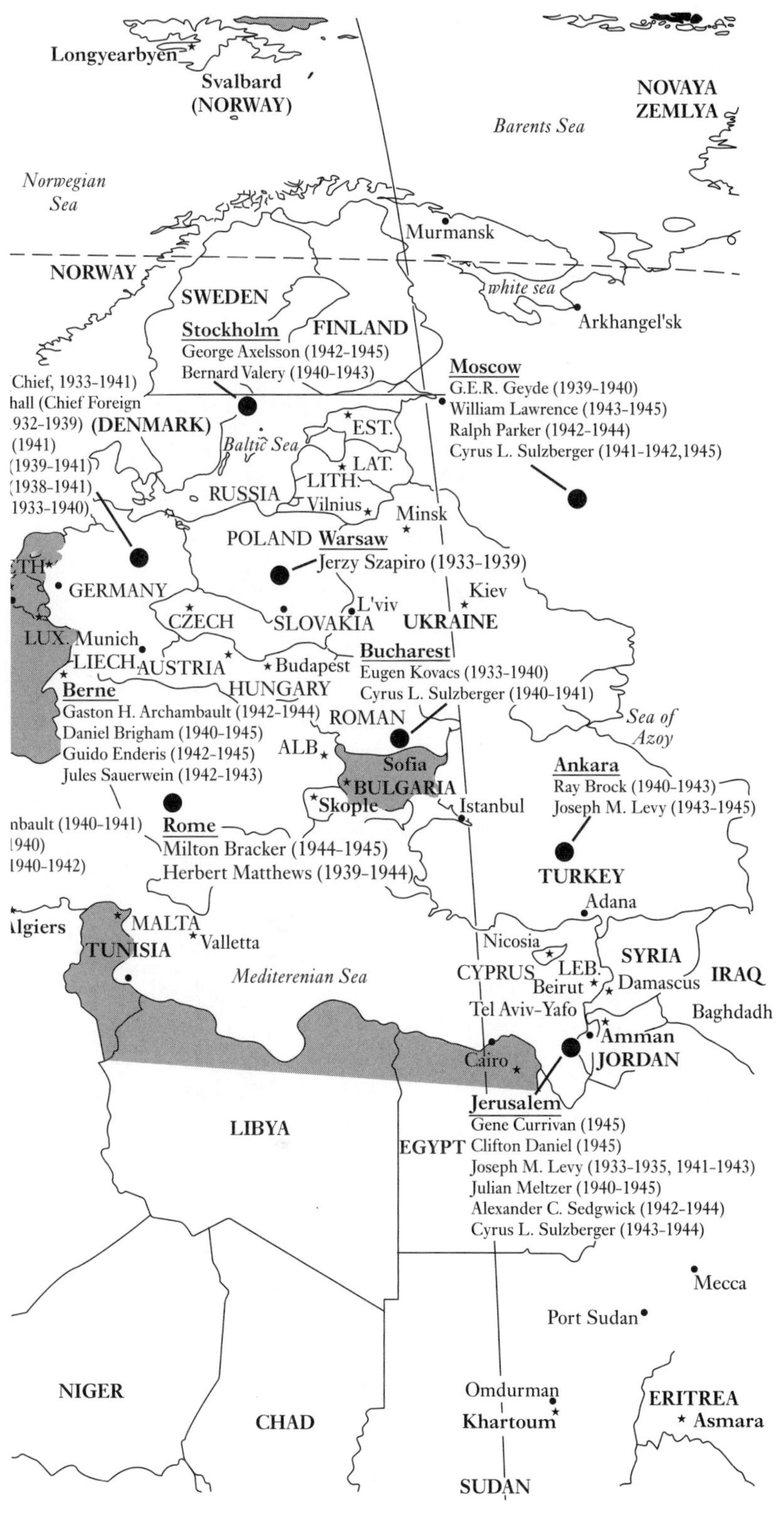

Longyearbyen
Svalbard
(NORWAY)
NOVAYA
ZEMLYA
Barents Sea
Norwegian
Sea
Murmansk
NORWAY
SWEDEN
white sea
Arkhangel'sk
Stockholm
FINLAND
George Axelsson (1942-1945)
Bernard Valery (1940-1943)
Moscow
G.E.R. Geyde (1939-1940)
William Lawrence (1943-1945)
Ralph Parker (1942-1944)
Cyrus L. Sulzberger (1941-1942,1945)
Chief, 1933-1941)
hall (Chief Foreign
932-1939)
(DENMARK)
(1941)
(1939-1941)
(1938-1941)
1933-1940)
EST.
Baltic Sea
LAT.
LITH.
RUSSIA
Vilnius
Minsk
POLAND
Warsaw
Jerzy Szapiro (1933-1939)
GERMANY
Kiev
L'viv
CZECH
SLOVAKIA
UKRAINE
LUX.
Munich
LIECH.
AUSTRIA
Budapest
Bucharest
Eugen Kovacs (1933-1940)
Cyrus L. Sulzberger (1940-1941)
HUNGARY
Berne
Gaston H. Archambault (1942-1944)
Daniel Brigham (1940-1945)
Guido Enderis (1942-1945)
Jules Sauerwein (1942-1943)
ROMAN
Sea of
Azoy
ALB.
Sofia
BULGARIA
Ankara
Ray Brock (1940-1943)
Joseph M. Levy (1943-1945)
Skople
Istanbul
nbault (1940-1941)
1940)
1940-1942)
Rome
Milton Bracker (1944-1945)
Herbert Matthews (1939-1944)
TURKEY
Adana
lgiers
MALTA
Valletta
TUNISIA
Nicosia
SYRIA
CYPRUS
LEB.
IRAQ
Mediterenian Sea
Beirut
Damascus
Tel Aviv-Yafo
Baghdadh
Amman
JORDAN
Cairo
Jerusalem
Gene Currivan (1945)
Clifton Daniel (1945)
Joseph M. Levy (1933-1935, 1941-1943)
Julian Meltzer (1940-1945)
Alexander C. Sedgwick (1942-1944)
Cyrus L. Sulzberger (1943-1944)
LIBYA
EGYPT
Mecca
Port Sudan
NIGER
Omdurman
ERITREA
CHAD
Khartoum
Asmara
SUDAN

SULZBERGER/OCHS GENEOLOGY

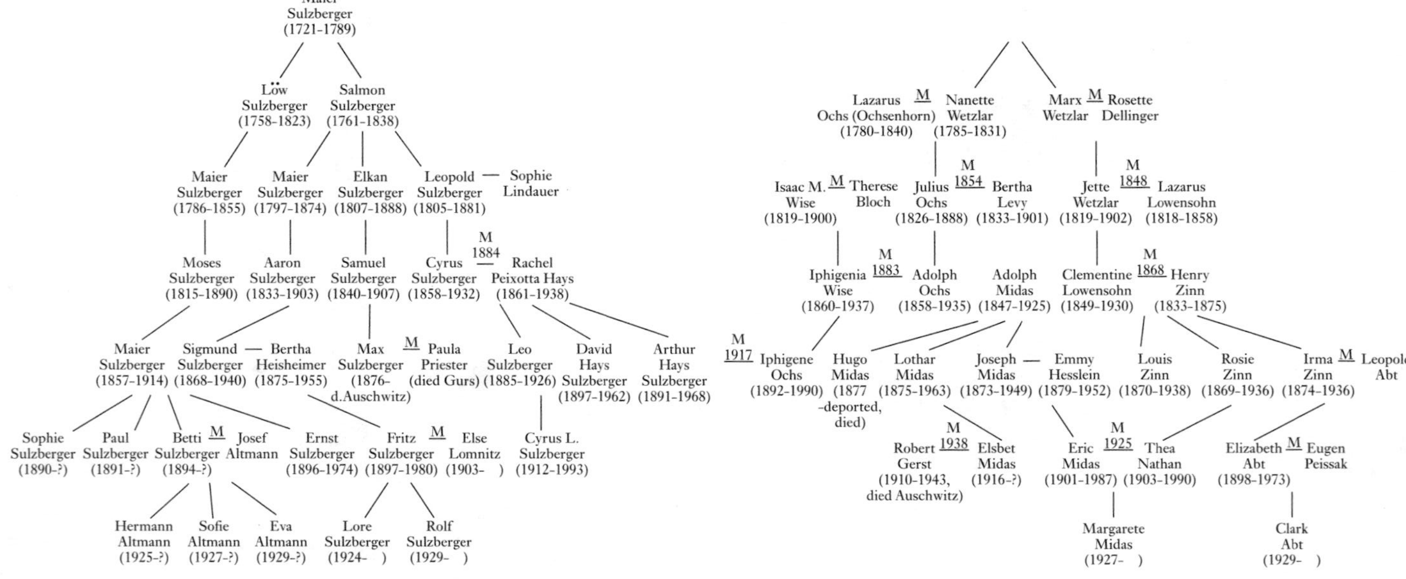

Introduction

"Last Voice from the Abyss"

MARCH 2, 1944 was a typical news day – that is, if any day could be considered typical in the midst of a world war. The pivotal battles of Britain, El Alamein, and Stalingrad were in the past, the Normandy invasion was 3 months in the future. On the *New York Times*' front page, the Allies were holding off a German drive near Anzio in Italy, while the Red Army was making steady progress retaking parts of the Soviet Union seized at the war's outset. On the inside pages of the newspaper, the War Manpower Commission was establishing veteran information and service centers in New York State. West Point was continuing its unbeaten streak in basketball, clobbering Maryland 85 to 22. The stock market was regaining ground it had lost in the previous session. "The Bridge of San Luis Rey" was starting a run at the Capitol Theater. Hungarian hot slaw with leeks and cabbage was the featured recipe.

On page four, amid 13 other stories, appeared a five-paragraph item with a London dateline. The first two paragraphs described the House of Commons' decision to appropriate 50,000 pounds to help fund the Inter-Governmental Committee on Refugees. Then came these paragraphs:

> During the discussion, S. S. Silverman, Labor member, read a report from the Jewish National Committee operating somewhere in Poland, saying:
>
> 'Last month we still reckoned the number of Jews in the whole territory of Poland as from 250,000 to 300,000. In a few weeks no more than 50,000 of us will remain. In our last moment before death, the remnants of Polish Jewry appeal for help to the whole world. May this, perhaps our last voice from the abyss, reach the ears of the whole world.'

Without skipping a beat, the story continued: "The Commons also approved an installment of 3,863 pounds to help the International Red Cross open an office in Shanghai. . . ".

The journalists at the *New York Times* did not respond to that anguished cry[i] – not the London correspondent who filed it, or the cable editor who read it, or the copy reader who edited it, or the night news editor who determined its placement, or the managing editor who signed off on it, or the publisher who had ultimate responsibility for the newspaper in which it appeared. One-quarter of a million people were about to die, 3 million were already dead. Yet, no one at the *New York Times* said, "This is not routine. This is a catastrophe. Perhaps we can not stop it, but we can lay bare the horror. We can move this story from page four to page one. We can give it a headline that befits the tragedy. We can write a forceful editorial today and tomorrow and the next day. We can recall the calamity in Sunday's week in review. We can help our readers understand the pain, the panic, the powerlessness of a people about to be exterminated."

But no one at the *Times* did, not on that day or any of the 2,076 days of the European war. As a result, the "last voice from the abyss" never reached "the ears of the whole world." It was smothered by the hundreds of other words in the page four story, the thousands of words in the March 2 edition, and the millions of words published in all the *Times* editions throughout the war.

For March 2, 1944 was typical in more ways than one. From the start of the war in Europe on September 1, 1939 to its end nearly 6 years later, the *New York Times* and other mass media treated the persecution and ultimately the annihilation of the Jews of Europe as a secondary story. They reported it. In fact, from September 1939 through May 1945, the *Times* published 1,186 stories about what was happening to the Jews of Europe, or an average of 17 stories per month.[1] But the story never received the continuous attention or prominent play that a story about the unprecedented attempt to wipe out an entire people deserved. The story of the Holocaust[ii] – meaning articles that focused on the discrimination, deportation, and destruction of the Jews – made the *Times* front page just

[i] The Jewish National Committee's full report, which reached the West, was more than a general cry of pain. The committee wanted the U.S. government to loan or donate dollars to the Polish government in London, which had agreed to spend 5 million pounds to help Jews in Poland live as gentiles or organize their escape to Hungary. Goldmann to Pehle, 3/23/44, WRB Collection, Box 50, FDRL.

[ii] Journalists at the time did not use the term "Holocaust," although, as is seen, the word did begin to creep into the language, without a capital, during the war. The word is used here and in the conclusion as shorthand, but not in other chapters that describe journalists' contemporaneous understanding.

26 times, and only in six of those stories were Jews identified on the front as the primary victims. Never did page one stories appear back to back, nor did one follow another over a span of a few days. Not once did the story lead the paper, meaning appear in the right-hand column reserved for the day's most important news – not even when the concentration camps were liberated at the end of the war. When the Holocaust made the *Times* front page, the stories obscured the fact that most of the victims were Jews, referring to them instead as refugees or persecuted minorities. In addition, the *Times* only intermittently and timidly editorialized about the extermination of the Jews, and the paper rarely highlighted it in either the News of the Week in Review or the magazine section.

The *New York Times* did not downplay the Holocaust because it lacked the information to play it up. It is true that news of the destruction of the Jews did not flow unfettered to the West. Once the war started, journalists could not report at all in much of occupied Europe, and the Germans made a concerted effort to conceal at least the final stages of their campaign against the Jews. Even before the war, foreign correspondents faced hostile governments, particularly in Germany and Russia, brutal working conditions and transmission methods that were expensive and erratic. Yet enough information reached Allied and exile governments, and Jewish and other relief organizations,[2] that the punctilious wartime reader of the *New York Times* would have had a good idea of what was happening to Europe's Jews as it was happening. The *Times* described the propagation of anti-Semitic laws in German allied countries; death from disease and starvation of hundreds of thousands in ghettos and labor camps in Eastern and Western Europe; and mass executions in the Soviet Union and mass gassings in Auschwitz, Treblinka, and Maidanek. The *Times* also indicated that these were not isolated incidents, but part of Germany's attempt to find a solution to Europe's "Jewish problem," which from 1942 on was the Final Solution, a systematic campaign to kill all the Jews in Europe.

Nor did the *New York Times* downplay the Holocaust primarily because it doubted the veracity of the information it received. In trying to explain why the *New York Times* put a story about the murder of 1 million people on page seven, Walter Laqueur in *The Terrible Secret: Suppression of the Truth About Hitler's 'Final Solution,'* encapsulates this view.

> If it was true that a million people had been killed this clearly should have been front page news; it did not, after all, happen every day. If it was not true, the story should

not have been published at all. Since they [*Times* editors] were not certain they opted for a compromise; to publish, but not in a conspicuous place. Thus it was implied the paper had reservations about the report: quite likely the stories contained some truth, but probably it was exaggerated.[3]

But the *Times* stories, including the one Laqueur cited, do not read as if the editors did not believe them. For the most part, they were detailed accounts of specific recent events attributed to "reliable sources," or from authoritative sources such as the German and other Axis governments, Allied and exile governments, Jewish organizations, and, occasionally, eyewitnesses and first-hand observations. In a handful of instances, the stories stated explicitly that the information could not be confirmed, which suggests that in the 1,000-plus other stories it could be. Furthermore, in other contexts, the *Times* put stories it acknowledged contained information that could not be confirmed on the front page.[4] In addition, *Times* editorials, few as they may have been, stated directly that millions of Jews were being murdered in a systematic campaign. If the *Times* editors did not trust the reports, it is unlikely they would have written about them as established fact on the editorial page.

Most tellingly, the *Times* continued to put stories about the Holocaust inside the paper even after doubts about their authenticity evaporated. Most scholars agree that the truth of the Holocaust was established when the 11 Allied governments confirmed the Final Solution in December 1942.[5] But there is no discernible change in the *Times* coverage after that. Considering all the wartime stories about Jews, the paper printed six such front-page stories in 1940, seven in 1941, nine in 1942, and seven again in 1943. Only in 1944 did the number climb to 12 front-page stories. Nor did the total number of stories printed jump once the extermination campaign was verified. The *Times* printed 240 stories about what was happening to the Jews in 1940, 207 in 1941, 139 in 1942, 186 in 1943, and 197 in 1944. It was not a failure of information, but what historian Henry L. Feingold calls "a failure of mind" that kept the story off the front page.[6]

This book seeks to explain how that could have happened, how a newspaper like the *New York Times* could have been presented with the facts of genocide, and yet have missed – or dismissed – their significance. In doing so, it serves as a case study of how difficult it is for a group the press has identified as "the other," as being outside it and its audience's sphere of concern, to receive adequate media attention no matter the extent of the catastrophe. The book thus has resonance for contemporary journalists grappling with other tragedies far from American shores, whether AIDS in Africa or human rights abuses in China.

The book asks: What was it about prevailing press standards and the policies and personalities at the *Times* that led the nation's most important newspaper to discount one of the century's most important news stories? Both avenues of inquiry are essential. The *Times* did not stand alone either in reporting the destruction of European Jewry or in understating its significance, as Deborah Lipstadt reveals in her important book, *Beyond Belief: The American Press and the Coming of the Holocaust 1933–1945*. "By the later stages of the war virtually every major American daily had acknowledged that many people, Jews in particular, were being murdered," Lipstadt concludes (p. 275). "They lamented what was happening, condemned the perpetrators, and then returned to their practice of burying the information." Similar patterns can be found in radio broadcasts,[7] magazines, and the Protestant and liberal Catholic press.[8] The Jewish press' treatment of the Holocaust was more extensive and prominent.[9]

The *Times* was unique, however, in the comprehensiveness of its coverage and the extent of its influence among American opinion makers. Because of its longtime commitment to international affairs, its willingness to sacrifice advertising rather than articles in the face of a newsprint crunch, and its substantial Jewish readership, the *Times* was able to obtain and publish more news about what was happening to the Jews than other mainstream newspapers. The way the *Times* published that news also had a disproportionate impact on both policy makers and fellow journalists who considered it the newspaper of record. That the *Times* was owned by Jews of German ancestry, who would seemingly be more sensitive to the plight of their European brethren, further magnified the *Times*' critical role in shaping contemporaneous coverage of the Holocaust. The *Times*' judgment that the murder of millions of Jews was a relatively unimportant story reverberated among other journalists trying to assess the news, among Jewish groups trying to arouse public opinion, and among government leaders trying to decide on an American response.

In making that judgment, the *Times*, along with the rest of the mainstream American press, was influenced by overarching journalistic standards and cultural assumptions. Several have been offered to explain the almost universal treatment of the extermination of the Jews as an inside story.[10]

- The overwhelming demands of covering a world war dwarfed all other considerations, consuming news organizations' resources and journalists' mental energies. The war also produced global carnage on an unimaginable scale, making it harder to recognize the suffering of one minority group. Diffuse Jewish organizations with a divided message and exile governments with their own agendas could not hope to grab the attention of a preoccupied press.
- World War I's fake atrocity stories bred skepticism about death factories and mass gassings, especially among hard-bitten editors who had been young journalists during the war two decades earlier. Both sides' use of atrocities for propaganda purposes during the just-completed Spanish Civil War reinforced those doubts.[11] Plus, journalists were willing to indulge their doubts because the alternative meant accepting information "too terrible to be believed."
- Afraid that too much attention would alienate Americans loath to fight a war to save the Jews, the U.S. government was quiet on the subject. Because the press corps defined news largely as what the government said or did, the fact that the U.S. government said and did little about European Jews meant their plight was, by definition, not important news. In addition, there was no consensus on what the government could do to help Jews trapped behind enemy lines – save winning the war.

All these reasons help explain why the press downplayed news of the Holocaust. But there were countervailing currents: information that challenged prevailing assumptions, values that suggested different assessments, and voices that urged an alternative outcome. Although the war was the dominant news, it need not have been, and was not, the only front-page news. The *New York Times* printed between 12 and 15 front-page stories every day. Fewer than half of these typically concerned the war. Attention to war news therefore does not fully explain the simultaneous downplaying of the Holocaust. Nor does the extent of the global carnage. Although the war resulted in millions of deaths, including the loss of millions of civilians, it became evident halfway through that the murder of Jews was not just "collateral damage." As many *inside* news stories indicated, the Jews alone were singled out for complete eradication in a systematic and purposeful program. The *Times*' first story on the Nazi extermination campaign, which described it as "the greatest mass slaughter in history," appeared on page five, tacked onto the bottom of a column of stories.[12] Yet, the deaths of other civilians, often fewer than 100, regularly appeared on the front page.[13] Some Jewish leaders recognized this discrepancy and urged the press to pay more attention to the plight of the Jews.

Although World War I and other atrocity stories led some World War II journalists to doubt news of mass slaughter, others, particularly those reporting from the field, relinquished their skepticism. In fact, many journalists *at the time* were acutely conscious of how the events they were reporting differed from those in the previous war. "Since World War I[,] stories of child victims of German brutality have been received with a certain skepticism," wrote *Times*' Moscow correspondent Ralph Parker in 1942 in just one of many such statements. "What [your correspondent saw at a Moscow hospital] and what the children told him convinced him that there had been no exaggeration by the Russians about German behavior on their territory."[14] Rather than be duped by misplaced skepticism, journalists offered straightforward acknowledgment of the doubts implanted by the earlier war's propaganda and used such acknowledgment to reinforce the truth of current outrages. Similarly, journalists often admitted that the news they were reporting was "too terrible to be believed," yet insisted it should be believed nonetheless. Direct refutations of the possibility of deception or exaggeration, however, did not move these stories to the front page.

Whereas the government influenced press coverage of the Holocaust, U.S. policy did not dictate it. The government did not censor news of the Holocaust, and in only a few cases literally suppressed it. The press had the information and was free to exercise its own judgment about its importance. Even during wartime, the press occasionally challenged the government's priorities, and some journalists challenged the government's policies toward the Jews. Nor was the government a monolith of neglect. Although some administration officials believed that too much attention to the Jews would alienate Americans, others did not and effectively used public pressure. Similarly, although some government officials insisted that winning the war was the only way to save the Jews, others argued that winning the war would prove futile if, at war's end, there were no Jews left to save. That few options existed for saving many Jews, and none for saving most Jews, unquestionably affected the public debate, making it harder to mobilize thousands of citizens or move an intransigent bureaucracy. Yet the lack of clear-cut solutions probably played less of a role in decisions about whether a story should appear on the front page. As Deborah Lipstadt points out in *Beyond Belief* (p. 239): "[T]he press does not decide how it will treat a story on the basis of whether attention to a topic will effect a change in policy. The press pays attention to those stories it considers significant."

So, at the time, not merely in retrospect, a swirl of information about the Holocaust flowed to journalists, who assessed it in a variety of ways. The surface currents pushed journalists to conclude that the persecution of the Jews was neither "distinct" nor "particularly salient," as Peter Novick puts it in *The Holocaust in American Life* (p. 29). As he observes, the murder of European Jewry "was just one among the countless dimensions of a conflict that was consuming the lives of tens of millions around the globe." But there were also undercurrents that suggested the mass murder of Jews was distinct in its scope, aim, and methods, and salient as a supreme violation of bedrock assumptions about Western civilization. Those undercurrents reached the American press, and, from time to time, rose to the surface, sending ripples through the dominant way of understanding events, and even threatening to reverse the waves. Yet, the tide was too strong; the unique suffering of the Jews never fully broke through to public consciousness during the war or for years afterward.

The acknowledgment that one interpretive framework – perceiving the mass murder of Jews as a minor part of a worldwide conflagration – dominated Americans' contemporaneous knowledge of the Holocaust should be the start of the inquiry, not its end. A clash of information, values, and understandings occurred within American news organizations – as it did within the Roosevelt Administration and within the Jewish community. (The latter two struggles have been extensively chronicled with diverging conclusions.) How and why did one perspective come to prevail over others within the press? What information exactly was available to journalists? Who provided it, when, and in what form? What pressure did the government and Jewish groups apply to influence the presentation of this information? What internal factors affected news judgments about its reliability and significance? How did all these factors interact to produce a framework that did not recognize the distinctiveness or importance of the Holocaust?

One of the best ways to seek answers to these questions is by looking at how events played out within one institution. The reason for a singular focus is simple: that is how the news is made. Global economic, political, and social forces shape news production. Deep-seated professional and cultural traditions play a part. But so do the idiosyncrasies of an individual newsroom. A publisher's particular sensitivity, a managing editor's preference for evenings at home, a nighttime editor's religious orientation, and a reporter's gambling habit can be as important in determining the contents of tomorrow's paper as the need to attain a particular profit margin or maintain the appearance of objectivity. Only by unearthing those predilections – not to mention who hates whom and who wants whose job – is it possible to understand how news is manufactured.

In that sense, a close look at the *Times* serves to reveal both the general journalistic culture and the particular circumstances at the *Times* that led the Holocaust to be considered a secondary story. The *Times* merits special scrutiny in this case for reasons that go beyond methodology. No American newspaper was better positioned to highlight the Holocaust than the *Times*, and no American newspaper so influenced public discourse by its failure to do so. The first reason makes the *Times*' failure more puzzling, the second more devastating.

The *Times* unquestionably was at the pinnacle of 1940s American journalism. "What Harvard is to U.S. education, what the House of Morgan has been to U.S. finance, *The New York Times* is to U.S. journalism," *Time* magazine declared on April 12, 1943. Nothing distinguished the *Times* more than its "far-flung staff of foreign correspondents, certainly the best in the U.S., perhaps in the world." The *Times* made more of a commitment to foreign news than any other American newspaper. At the outbreak of World War II, the *Times* had more than 30 correspondents in Europe, including ones stationed in such out-of-the-way capitals as Bratislava, Sofia, and Istanbul.[15] In contrast, the *Washington Post* had one reporter doubling at the White House and the State Department.[16] The *New York Herald Tribune* had a similar interest in international news, but fewer reporters in the field and far less space dedicated to its coverage.[17] In 1941, the *Times* was awarded a Pulitzer Prize for "the public educational value of its foreign news report." The "precedent-setting" prize was made for "a supreme journalistic achievement."[18]

Unlike its competitors, the *Times* also maintained its commitment to provide complete news despite a wartime newsprint crunch. It printed more war news than any other paper, averaging 125,000 words an issue and turning away advertisements in the process – a fact that the *Times* repeatedly trumpeted on its front page.[19] "In America no other journal approaches it in the volume of news and coverage of the world," a book of press criticism concluded in 1944.[20] The *Times*' reach probably accounts for Lipstadt's conclusion that its coverage was "relatively good" compared with other daily newspapers, particularly in its comprehensiveness.[21] David Wyman also concludes in *The Abandonment of the Jews* (p. 62) that "the *Times* provided by far the most complete American press coverage of Holocaust events."

In addition, the *Times* could not claim, as other papers might have, that its readers were not interested in the fate of foreign Jews while their sons were dying in foreign lands. Half the Jews in America lived in the New York metropolitan area in the 1940s and a growing number of them read the *Times*.[22] Many of them were first- and second-generation Jews from Eastern Europe whose brothers and sisters, mothers and fathers, were being marched into gas chambers. One American woman, who had learned in early 1944 that her husband was in Bergen-Belsen, began scouring the *Times* for stories about the treatment of Jews in Germany and the occupied countries, cutting out any *Times* articles she found. When she died nearly six decades later, her family discovered the clippings stored in several shoeboxes in her attic.[23] Samuel Halperin describes the position of American Jewry at the end of the war. "An appreciable number of American Jews, possibly a majority, had lost close relatives in the holocaust. Few American Jewish families had not suffered a loss of a friend or, at least, the personal knowledge of one of the murdered victims. The American Jewish community, with its strong Old World ties, suddenly was wrenched loose of its loved ones."[24]

If the *Times* was better positioned – via its resources and readership – to highlight the Holocaust than any other newspaper, its coverage was also most likely to influence the national discourse. In 1944, the *Saturday Evening Post* described the *Times* as as close to a national newspaper as the United States had. One-quarter of its 440,000 weekday readers and half its 805,000 Sunday readers came from outside the New York area.[25] The New York Times syndicate also sent *Times* articles to 525 newspapers, including such important papers as the *Detroit Free Press*, *Chicago Tribune*, the *Denver Post*, the *Los Angeles Times*, and the *San Francisco Chronicle*.[26] More important than how many people read *Times* articles was who read them. "[T]he *New York Times* is probably America's most influential news organ because it is read by the nation's most influential people as their primary source of information," J. J. Goldberg explains.[27] The *Times*' "position of unique authority," as Isaiah Berlin put it, was even more widely accepted in the 1940s.[28] Files of the Office of War Information, the Office of Strategic Services, the World Jewish Congress, and the Secretary of the Treasury, to name just a few, bulge with clippings from the *New York Times*; no other newspaper comes close.[29]

Members of different branches of the U.S. government attested to its importance. Secretary of State Cordell Hull described the *Times* as performing a "magnificent public service" in "providing the American people with the knowledge necessary for the formulation of responsible judgment," especially "in the field of foreign relations."[30] Supreme Court Justice Felix Frankfurter probably provided the strongest testament to the *Times* as "quite distinct from all other newspapers." Frankfurter said he regarded it as "a public institution with as much public responsibility as any public official owes the nation." He went so far as to conclude that it was a "quasi-judicial agency." Frankfurter explained: "In my conception The Times is nearer to the function of the courts than that of the other two branches of government."[31]

Foreign governments too looked to the *Times*. Public relations expert Albert Lasker concluded that they tended to judge American public opinion based on editorial comment in the *New York Times* and the *New York Herald Tribune*.[32] In organizing its public relations effort during the war, the Polish exile government's Information Center directed that the "closest possible contact" should be established with "American correspondents in London, at least" of the *Times*, and described the *Times* as a "powerful organ of American opinion."[33] Even Pope Pius XII was a "careful reader of the foreign press in general and *The New York Times* in particular."[34]

The *Times*' influence among fellow journalists was stronger still. Polls of American journalists consistently established the *Times*' preeminence. A poll of 200 correspondents in 1939 found that 100% of them read the *Times*,[35] and one 2 years earlier concluded that "the 'angle'" the *Times* takes on a story affects "the news-dispatches of correspondents for journals all over the United States."[36] In a 1944 survey, Washington correspondents concluded by more than five to one that the *Times* was the nation's most reliable and comprehensive newspaper.[37] Arnold Beichman, a reporter for *PM*, a New York City daily published in the 1940s, attested to the *Times*' influence. "*PM* was called an eight cent paper, you know why? The *Times* cost three cents and *PM* cost a nickel but everybody knew that if you wanted to get all the news, you had to read the *New York Times* as well,"

Beichman said. "What it symbolizes is the tremendous importance that the *New York Times* had. It didn't happen if it wasn't in the *Times*."[38] The respected former editor of *The Nation*, Oswald Garrison Villard, wrote of the *Times* in a 1944 book of press criticism: "No important journalist can possibly do without it, and it has literally made itself indispensable to anyone who desires to be thoroughly informed as to what is happening on this globe. To miss even an issue is a detriment to all who deal with foreign affairs."[39]

One final factor likely magnified the *Times*' already considerable influence on this issue: the *Times* was owned by a Jewish family of German ancestry. "It is possible that editors [of other newspapers] took a cue from the *New York Times*," David Wyman postulates in explaining why the mass media generally failed to draw attention to the extermination of the Jews. "Other newspapers recognized the *Times*' guidance in foreign news policy. A perception that the Jewish-owned *Times* did not think the massive killing of Jews was worth emphasizing could have influenced other newspapers."[40] Although there is no direct evidence to prove it, it is likely that other newspapers did not highlight the Holocaust at least partly because the *New York Times* did not. After much thought about "why a story like this did not get played by the establishment press," liberal journalist Max Lerner concluded that "one answer . . . is the hypersensitivity of *The New York Times* because of its Jewish ownership."[41]

The *Times*' Jewish ownership had another important effect on the coverage. Because of its Jewish leadership, the *Times* was less likely than other news organizations to miss what was happening to the Jews, but more likely to dismiss its significance. The *Times* was less likely to miss such stories for two reasons. First, the family's personal ties to German Jews and its deep, if not always amicable, involvement with the American Jewish community meant the *Times* had greater access to information about the fate of the Jews. Second, the *Times*' owners created an institution that was particularly attuned to stories involving Jews. Widespread anti-Semitism led even successful Jews to feel insecure about the position of Jews in American society and therefore to fret about how their co-religionists were portrayed. Since the *Times* had come under Jewish ownership at the turn of the twentieth century, its managers had communicated those concerns to the paper's journalists. Although the newspaper was the product of a complex interaction between reporters, editors, and the business staff, the owners set the tone. Their concerns about how Jews were depicted led "within the institution to a sensitivity to Semitism."[42] The rise of Hitler only heightened that sensitivity. It put Jews in the news and the *Times* itself came under attack from the Hitler regime for its Jewish ownership. Coupled with the newspaper's commitment to foreign news and its Jewish audience, the *New York Times* was not likely to completely lose sight of the plight of Jews, even in the midst of a worldwide conflagration.

Yet, if its Jewish ownership meant the *Times* recognized what was happening to European Jews, it also made the newspaper more hesitant to highlight it. Before the war, isolationists' claims that the Jews would lure America into war to help their persecuted brethren made some American Jews reluctant to engage in what might be perceived as special pleading. Those concerns only grew once America went to war. Assimilated Jews in particular did not want to be seen as emphasizing Jewish suffering while all freedom-loving peoples were fighting and dying for democracy. The *Times*' owners were not immune to those fears. As they advocated that the U.S. government adopt a strong interventionist policy toward Hitler in the late 1930s, they deliberately downplayed the plight of the German Jews. Sensitive to charges of dual loyalties once the war began, they were particularly eager to be seen as good Americans adhering to the government line.

In the case of *Times* publisher Arthur Hays Sulzberger, concerns about special pleading and dual loyalties were not purely a pragmatic calculation. They also reflected a deeply felt religious and philosophical belief that made Sulzberger resistant to changing his views in the light of changing circumstances. Being Jewish was solely a religious, not a racial or ethnic orientation, he maintained, that carried with it no special obligation to help fellow Jews. As anti-Semitism intensified in Germany, and to a lesser extent in America, he protested – a bit too vigorously perhaps – that Jews were just like any other citizen. They should not be persecuted as Jews, but they should not be rescued as Jews either. In fact, American Jews who helped other Jews because they were Jews threatened to undercut their position as Americans, Sulzberger believed. The *Times* publisher thus was philosophically opposed to emphasizing the unique plight of the Jews in occupied Europe, a conviction that at least partially explains the *Times*' tendency to place stories about Jews inside the paper, and to universalize their plight in editorials and front-page stories.

Sulzberger's involvement with the American Jewish community also led him to be less inclined to emphasize the Jews' fate. His antipathy for Jewish leaders in the United States and Palestine tempered somewhat his sympathy for persecuted Jews in Europe. He had long opposed a Jewish homeland on religious grounds; if Jews were not a people, they could not possibly form a state, Sulzberger reasoned. During the war, his opposition grew, based on fears that agitation for a Jewish state in Palestine would drive the Arabs into the Nazi Axis, just as traditional Jewish leaders rallied around Palestine as the best possible haven for their tortured brethren. The disagreement drew the publisher into fierce, public fights with American Jewry's top leaders that colored his views not only of their activities on behalf of a Jewish state, but also of other efforts on behalf of European Jews. The *Times* editors and reporters understood the sensitivities of the organization they worked for and often deferred to the publisher on issues involving Jews – or sometimes to what they assumed the publisher's position to be. In a few cases, the editors or reporters were Jews themselves with similar concerns.

So the *Times*, more than most American newspapers, was in touch with the undercurrents of information about the unique suffering of the Jews, which accounts for its 1,000-plus stories on the Final Solution's steady progress. Yet, the *Times* had its own reasons for submerging that information.[iii] Stories on the Jews' plight only emerged from inside the paper if some other authority – the president, the Pope, the secretary of state – issued a statement lamenting it. In those instances, the *Times* could not be accused of special pleading on behalf of Jews; the newspaper was simply reporting what the president, the Pope, or the secretary of state had to say about Jews. The *Times* would document what was happening to the Jews in inside news stories, but it would not take the lead in alerting the world to European Jews' ongoing destruction.[iv]

Because of the *Times*' unique position of influence among American opinion makers, this reticence had wider ramifications. Scholars looking into the role of bystanders to the Holocaust – those who knew of but were not directly involved in the extermination of the Jews – have identified a gap between the information that was available to witnessing nations and

[iii] As is seen, the *Herald Tribune*'s Protestant owners were more willing to run stories about the extermination of the Jews on the front page.

[iv] The *Times* has taken the lead on many important stories, ranging from its skeptical reports on the speculative stock market of the 1920s to its sustained coverage of the civil rights movement and its early criticism of the war in Vietnam. See Susan E. Tifft and Alex S. Jones, *The Trust: The Private and Powerful Family Behind The New York Times*, Boston: Little Brown & Co. (1999), and Gay Talese, *The Kingdom and the Power*, New York: Ballantine Publishing Group (1971).

groups, and their response to that information. The general apathy and inaction that greeted the news suggests that bystanders encountered the facts but did not fully grasp their meaning. The way the press in general and the *Times* in particular presented the facts played an important role in creating the gap between information and action. The *Times* supplied the information in isolated, inside stories but did almost nothing to help readers understand its importance. The few hundred words about the Holocaust the *Times* published every couple of days were hard to find amidst a million other words. So *Times* readers, whether ordinary citizens or opinion makers, could legitimately have claimed not to know, or at least not to have understood, what was happening to the Jews. A generally ignorant American public made it easier for government leaders to take action – or not – without having to worry about the possible response. As a result, the *Times* contributed to the conditions that led to inaction even in the face of considerable information.

That does not mean millions of Jews, or even thousands of Jews, would have been saved had the *Times* acted differently. Whether a different response by the *Times* would have produced a different reaction by other bystanders is impossible to say. The *Times* could have highlighted the Holocaust on its front page, and the rest of the press could have continued to discount it as the "special pleading" of a Jewish institution. The press could have devoted more attention to the plight of the Jews, and the American public could have been unmoved, or even alienated, as some feared. The public could have been moved, but the Allied governments could have resisted pressure for a rescue strategy other than the one they already employed – winning the war as soon as possible. The Allies could have been committed to rescue and still not have succeeded. Indeed, the Nazis' determination to kill all the Jews and their control of much of Europe for most of the war meant that millions of Jews would have died even if the Allies had mounted determined rescue efforts.

What is certain, however, is that those possibilities were never truly tested. The way the *Times* and the rest of the mass media told the story of the Holocaust engendered no chance of arousing public opinion. It is also clear that had the *Times* and other news organizations decided that the extermination of the Jews was important, they could have and should have highlighted it, regardless of whether it would have saved lives. The press' responsibility was not necessarily to affect government policy. Rather, the press' responsibility was to harness the flood of information it received about the war – about battles, about strategy, about industrial capacities, and about civilian casualties – and to channel the most critical news to the public. As just one among multitudes of actors, many with far more power than itself, the press alone could not have altered the currents of public discourse that swamped the news of the Jews' destruction, and certainly a single newspaper could not have accomplished that. Still, the *Times* had an obligation to do more than be swept along with the tide. The journalist's job was to determine what the public needed to know – even if the information lurked beneath the surface and the government preferred it to remain there – and then to ensure the information reached newspaper readers in a way they could absorb. If the systematic campaign to annihilate European Jewry was a critical story, it should have been on the front page, regardless of whether Jews could have been rescued as a result.

But the *Times* never acknowledged that the mass murder of Jews, *because they were Jews*, was something its readers needed to know. The *Times* never treated the news of the Holocaust as important – or at least as important as, say, informing motorists to visit the Office of Price Administration if they did not have their automobile registration number and state written on their gasoline ration coupons. A story about that possible bureaucratic snafu appeared on the front page on March 2, 1944, the same day that the "last voice from the abyss" was relegated to page four.

PART I

1933–1941

I

"Not a Jewish Problem"

The Publisher's Perspective on the Nazis' Rise and the Refugee Crisis

SITTING in his office on 43rd Street in November 1939, *New York Times* Managing Editor Edwin L. James knew that the letter on his desk raised a charged but peripheral issue. A reader had written wanting to know why the *Times* had not carried a particular report from the Jewish Telegraphic Agency (JTA), a wire service for Jewish news. The JTA had reported from newly occupied Poland that the Germans were demanding that a Jewish council in Lodz provide its soldiers with "100 young Jewish girls, the object being to quench their desires." James understood Europe as well as anyone at the *Times*, having covered what would now be called the First World War and having remained on the continent for the following 13 years. So he knew the report was not important in terms of the almost 3-month-old world war: the Germans had easily subdued Poland weeks ago. It was not even central to the emerging picture of what was happening to the Jews there. The main story, as the *Times* reported it, was the deportation of thousands of Jews from Czechoslovakia, Austria, and Germany to a "reservation" near Lublin. But given the subject and knowing his boss, James believed he had better run the JTA report past him.

James' boss was Arthur Hays Sulzberger, the *Times*' publisher and representative of the family that had owned the newspaper for four decades. The 48-year-old Sulzberger ran both the business and the editorial operations of the most important newspaper in the United States, arguably in the world. A trim 5 foot, 10 inches, with blue eyes, graying hair, and regular features, Sulzberger presided over a corporation with unparalleled influence in Washington, DC, and other world capitals. Every weekday, the *Times* reached 485,000 people, carried 37,000 lines of advertising, and printed more than 100,000 words in news copy. On Sundays, those numbers nearly doubled. With the *Times* recovering financially from the Depression – its total advertising lines at 21.2 million were still two-thirds of what they had been in 1929 – and gearing up to cover what would surely be a long, bloody war, Sulzberger had a lot on his mind. Still, James, who had worked for the *Times* for 24 years, 8 years as managing editor, knew that when it came to Jewish news it was best to inform Sulzberger, no matter how insignificant the item might seem. The managing editor had already asked his Berlin bureau chief to check on the JTA report. The bureau chief had promptly wired back that not only was the charge "flatly denied but [it has also been] designated [a] stupid canard" because of the Nazis' "racial defilement legislation," meaning the laws that made it a crime for Aryans to have sex with Jews. The laws, the bureau chief pointed out, were rigorously enforced in "army as elsewhere." Given the improbability of the report, James asked in a memo to Sulzberger what should he tell the letter writer?[1]

How to handle news involving Jews – whether a Hadassah meeting in Brooklyn or Jewish council directives in Lodz – had long been a touchy subject for Sulzberger and the *New York Times*. Ever since his father-in-law, Adolph Ochs, the son of German Jewish immigrants, bought the *Times* in 1896, *Times'* management had worried that the publication would be perceived as a Jewish newspaper. With objectivity as a *Times* hallmark, any suggestion that the paper might be partial to one group or another was sure to raise the hackles of its publisher. That the bias might favor a socially marginal group to which the owners belonged made the charge even more infuriating – and potentially damaging. Like his father-in-law who preceded him as publisher and his son who would succeed him, Sulzberger always maintained that being a Jew and being a journalist had nothing to do with one another. He excoriated anyone who so much as hinted that the religion of its owners affected the news in the *Times*. Even the mention of a "Jewish market" in the newspaper industry would lead Sulzberger to blast a trade publication for printing something "that might just as well have emanated from Berlin." Yet, Sulzberger understood that not everyone was as enlightened as he. So he had to be vigilant about how Jews were portrayed in the pages of the *Times*, and how the *Times* was portrayed in relation to Jews. At the same time, Sulzberger recognized the *Times* had a large and devoted Jewish audience, who were equally attentive to any slights or oversights in the paper's coverage. "I cannot tell you what difficulty we have in getting the publicity we need in the pages of the *Times*," Rabbi Stephen S. Wise, an important Jewish leader who would cross swords often with Sulzberger during the war, complained. "The Times seems to consider nothing as news which originates from and through Jews."[2] If other publishers worried about appearing neutral with respect to Republicans or Democrats, business or labor, the Dodgers or the Giants, Sulzberger worried about the Jews.

Until the 1930s, complaints arose regarding issues such as too much attention to Jews on the obituary page, too little on the society page; too much coverage of meetings of Jewish organizations, too little of poverty on the Lower East Side. For the last 6 years, however, since Adolf Hitler assumed power in Germany, the relationship between the paper's Jewish ownership and its news coverage had been elevated from an irritant to a dominant issue. The Nazi regime's persecution of the Jews was important news that demanded extensive coverage in the nation's preeminent newspaper. Yet, Hitler's ranting about a worldwide Jewish conspiracy of international bankers and media moguls implicated the *Times* and impugned its coverage.[3] In 1933, soon after Hitler became chancellor, a German newspaper accused the *Times*' "Jewish publisher, an immigrant from Germany" of "incendiary action against Germany" by printing false reports of atrocities during the First World War. The *Times* was also singled out for its coverage of Hitler's regime, the charge being of "habitual biased suppression," as the Berlin reporter translated the German in his cable to New York.[i] Three years later, the anti-Semitic German newspaper, *Der Stuermer*, published a picture of Ochs accompanied by "scurrilous references [to] his origin personality career," as Berlin Bureau Chief Guido Enderis put it in a cable to James alerting him to the publication. The article also described Ochs, in Enderis' cable translation, as "one activest foes" of Germany, even though Ochs had been dead for more than a year.[4] The *Times*' Vienna correspondent had sent the same article straight to Sulzberger.[5] Even readers at home were suspicious of the *Times'* Jewish connection. "In spite of what you and the rest of the 'Jewish Press' think and say Germany will go on, as she has the past year under Hitler, to again become a great Nation," read one letter the *Times* received but never published. "The German people are an honest, decent, upright, hard working people and have whatever else it takes to build up a fine nation. Can you

[i] Like most foreign correspondents communicating with the home office, the *New York Times* reporters used "cablese." Because journalists were charged for each word used in a cable, they adopted a peculiar shorthand devoid of punctuation and articles and full of its own terminology.

say as much for the Jews?"[6] In that atmosphere, Sulzberger considered it even more important that the *Times* be scrupulous in its handling of news involving Jews. Those who worked for him, like James, knew it.

So, in November 1939, it was not surprising that the managing editor would seek his boss's guidance on how to respond to the latest twist in the news about the Jews in Poland. The German occupation of Austria the previous year, then Czechoslovakia in March and Poland in September, had more than quadrupled the number of Jews under Nazi control to 4 million. Yet, as Sulzberger received the memo from James, he was confident he could make decisions during what would turn out to be the next 6 years of war as he had during the previous 6 years. Because he was a Jew, Sulzberger would be certain that none of his decisions was based on that fact. The *Times* could, indeed should, report what was happening to the Jews, but it would not treat them differently than other groups. There would be no special attention, no special sensitivity, no special pleading. If anything, Sulzberger would use his position to persuade both Jews and non-Jews that no matter what Adolf Hitler said, Jews were exactly like everybody else. As World War II began, that was Sulzberger's mission – some would say, his obsession.

Sulzberger's sensitivity over Jews' treatment in the *Times* was at least partly a response to the pervasive anti-Semitism of American society.[7] Like most Jews of his generation, he had come face-to-face with discrimination. From being called a "sheeny" as a child to being turned away from a Cape Cod resort as a young family man, Sulzberger had had "an education in prejudice."[8] In a less direct sense, he knew that anti-Semitism was a potent force, particularly in Depression-era America. The popularity of Father Charles Coughlin's radio show and the Nazi-supporting German-American Bund attested to that. While traveling the United States in 1938 to gauge public opinion, Sulzberger tried to sniff out hostility toward Jews. "Anti-Semitism is difficult for a Jew to check up on," he wrote en route the Santa Fe Chief to his friend, Treasury Secretary Henry Morgenthau, Jr. "I have the feeling however that it is following the normal course of bad times which is when it always flourishes."[9] At least on some level, he worried that if the *Times* was perceived as a Jewish newspaper it might alienate the Protestant establishment that had embraced the newspaper for its thoroughness and dispassion, or that a Jewish *Times* might aggravate anti-Semitism by serving as a reminder of Jews' power in American society. So he took steps to minimize that perception. Some reporters found that the

Times had substituted initials in their bylines for "too Jewish-sounding" first names, such as Abraham. Jews did not hold the *Times*' most visible editorial positions, managing editor and editorial page editor, and top Jewish contenders for those posts believed, as is discussed later, that their religion stood in the way of further advancement.[10]

Yet, Sulzberger did not respond to the prejudice of the surrounding society by shunning all things Jewish. He never attempted to conceal his religion, and, unlike other prominent American journalists, most notably Walter Lippmann, he did not cut himself off from the Jewish community.[11] He belonged to four synagogues, and served on the board of the Jewish Theological Seminary and as a member of the executive committee of the Union of American Hebrew Congregations. Even within the *Times*, Sulzberger's attitude was ambivalent. He never issued an edict banning "too Jewish sounding names." In fact, Meyer Berger's and Joseph M. Levy's names appeared just like that in their bylines, whereas A. R. Parker, G. E. R. Geyde, W. H. Lawrence, and countless other non-Jewish *Times* reporters used initials in theirs.[12] In 1939, a Jew had yet to be appointed to the *Times'* top editorial posts, but Sulzberger had reasons, other than religion, for not giving the jobs to Jewish candidates. Jews did hold key news positions, including Sunday Editor Lester Markel, Cable Editor Theodore Bernstein, and Washington Bureau Chief Arthur Krock. The *Times* Executive Committee, which met every few months to set policy, included two Jews, Markel and Krock, and two non-Jews, James and Editorial Page Editor Charles Merz, along with Sulzberger. If Sulzberger was motivated solely by fears of an anti-Semitic response, he would have sundered altogether his ties to Judaism. That he did not do.

As much as Sulzberger's concerns stemmed from his precarious position as a Jew navigating the difficult terrain of mid-century America, they also were the result of his sense of himself as a Jew and an American. Indeed, his greatest fear of "being continually classified" with other Jews, including less-educated, more recent immigrants, was that it would lead gentile Americans to misjudge his own lineage. "A vulgar Christian is merely someone who does not concern me – a vulgar Jew is a direct charge upon me," he wrote in 1930 in a private essay. "I am being judged with him according to the standards of my fellow Americans."[13]

Sulzberger knew he was no "vulgar" Jew, having descended from distinguished families on both parents' sides. His father's ancestors had been rabbis and cantors in Germany, many of whom, including his grandfather and grandmother, had emigrated to the United States in the middle of the nineteenth century. Once here, his forefathers became judges and leaders of important Jewish institutions, such as the American Jewish Committee and the Jewish Theological Seminary. His own father, Cyrus L. Sulzberger, a cotton merchant, had been deeply involved in Jewish philanthropic organizations. He had funded two Jewish publications and helped establish the Industrial Removal Office, which relocated Jewish immigrants to areas outside New York. His mother, Rachel Peixotto Hays, traced her lineage to Jews who had first come to the United States in 1700 from Spain, Portugal, and the Netherlands. An ancestor had been a captain in the Revolutionary Army, which had enabled his mother to join the Daughters of the American Revolution and he, the Sons of the American Revolution. Among the Hays relatives were the first police chief of New York City, a founding member of the New York Stock Exchange, and rabbis at the famed synagogue in Newport, Rhode Island, the nation's oldest Jewish congregation. The family's pedigree was so impeccable that the family considered it beneath Rachel Hays to marry the German Jew, Cyrus Sulzberger.[14]

Their son, who was born in 1891 – one of five children, three of whom survived childhood – took delight in both aspects of his heritage. "To America came those who sought a new life and among them, very early in the procession, came my forebears," he once wrote. "In all the wars of America, and in the making of its laws, they played an honorable part. No one could say to them, you are a stranger here. No one could say, you do not belong. Judaism and Americanism never came into conflict. Their only association was that by being a good Jew just as by being a good Methodist or Catholic one became a better American." Years later, he would bridle at the suggestion that a Jewish state in Palestine would deepen the roots of American Jews, noting that his ancestors came to the United States "in the seventeenth century and my roots in America are deep enough."[15]

Rachel and Cyrus Sulzberger brought him up to be a good American and a good Jew. Although not particularly religious themselves, his parents "decided to bring us up observantly and let us decide for ourselves," their middle son wrote to his own children. The family held regular Sabbath dinners, where his father said prayers over the wine and challah, his mother lit candles, and their sons, even as adults, were expected to attend. As a child, Arthur Sulzberger studied the Bible and Hebrew. At 13, he was a bar mitzvah and read his Torah portion, even though it was not the custom in his family's Reform congregation. As an adult, Sulzberger did not attend synagogue regularly, despite his multiple memberships. But as his wife recalled, he "always fasted on Yom Kippur" and "neither of us ever really drifted away from the faith."[16]

If Judaism was his faith, however, assimilation was Sulzberger's religion. Like most American Jews whose families had emigrated to the United States from Germany before the twentieth century, he was a Reform Jew. This meant he continued to worship as a Jew but without obeying many of the faith's demanding commandments, such as observance of the Sabbath or the laws of Kosher. He also was willing to celebrate Christmas and skip a Passover seder or two. Like many Reform Jews at the turn of the twentieth century, his family was prosperous and well integrated into American society. The elder Sulzbergers lived comfortably on Manhattan's Upper West Side, and Arthur and his two brothers traveled abroad and attended the best private schools. Arthur graduated from Horace Mann School and Columbia University. Unlike most Reform Jews, however, Sulzberger approached Jews' integration into American life with missionary zeal. For that, he owed not the family he was born into, but the one he married into – that of the celebrated rabbi, Isaac M. Wise.

Isaac Wise was a towering figure in Reform Judaism. Born in 1819 in Steingrub, Bohemia, Wise immigrated to the United States in 1846, eventually settling in Cincinnati. His influence reached far beyond his Ohio congregation. He is considered the architect of all American Reform's major institutions, founding the first association of Reform congregations (the Union of American Hebrew Congregations in 1873), the first organization of Reform rabbis (the Central Conference of American Rabbis in 1889), and the first permanent rabbinical school in America, Hebrew Union College.[17]

Wise's brand of Reform Judaism differs from the contemporary version, so much so that it is now referred to as Classical Reform Judaism. The biggest difference: Wise's rejection of the idea of Jews as a people. In Wise's formulation, after the destruction of the Second Temple in 70 C.E. and the dispersal of Jews throughout the world, Jews ceased to be a nation and became solely adherents of a religion. Wise believed that Jews could become just like the people they found themselves living among. They could be good Germans, or good Russians, or good Americans, who differed from their fellow citizens only in how and where they worshipped. Not only could they, but, in Wise's version of Reform Judaism, they should. The Jews, he believed, had a special mission. Blessed with the perspective of outsiders and the adaptability of insiders, Jews were to champion the principles of the Enlightenment. They were to teach their fellow countrymen the evil of divisions based on race, blood, territory, or language. Nowhere was this easier, or more imperative, Wise believed, than in the United States, whose government was already in accord with Mosaic ideals of morality. Or as the Union of American Hebrew Congregations stated in an 1898 resolution: "America is our Zion."[18]

Wise and his followers, therefore, did not support the Zion pushed by other American Jews beginning at the turn of the twentieth century – a Jewish state in what was first the Ottoman and then the British colony of Palestine. To Wise, Zionism was both foolish and dangerous. If Jews were not a people, it was folly to believe they could constitute a state. Even the effort to create such a state posed a danger. In "unenlightened" countries such as Russia, it would reinforce the perception of Jews as foreigners. In "enlightened countries" such as the United States, it would slow the integration of new Jewish immigrants and impugn the loyalty of all Jews. So Wise and the institutions he founded opposed Zionism in all its manifestations. When he died in 1900, the bulk of American Jews adhered to these Reform principles. During the first few decades of the twentieth century, that would change, as more Eastern European Jews settled in America. Even Reform Judaism began to change. But Wise's family, most prominently his son-in-law and grandson-in-law, remained true to his principles.

Wise had been dead for almost two decades when Arthur Sulzberger married the rabbi's granddaughter, Iphigene Ochs, in 1917. Iphigene was the only child of Adolph Ochs and Wise's daughter, Iphigenia. Adolph Ochs embraced his father-in-law's brand of Reform. Although a son-in-law, he quickly became the "the family pattern maker after Isaac M. Wise."[19] The pattern was to accept Judaism as a religion and nothing more. "Religion is all I stand for as a Jew," Ochs said in a 1925 address to mark a synagogue's construction. "I know nothing else, no other definition for a Jew except religion." He supported the institutions Wise had founded, including Hebrew Union College. Ochs opposed all Jewish organizations whose mission was not strictly religious, even the Reform-led American Jewish Committee. So he refused to support the committee's campaign to help Jews in European war zones during the First World War, he protested the name and Jewish-only subscriber base of the Jewish Fund for the Relief of Distressed Jews, and fought against a national home for Jews.[20]

Ochs' son-in-law and successor would be equally entranced by the Wise approach to Judaism. From his father, Sulzberger acquired a sentimental attachment to certain Jewish rituals and institutions, but from his in-laws he acquired what he referred to as a "splendid philosophy."[21] When he explained why he was not a Zionist in 1934, Sulzberger sounded like his grandfather-in-law in 1894:

> I am a non Zionist because the Jew, in seeking a homeland of his own, seems to me to be giving up something of infinitely greater value to the world. Here is a people of perfect loyalty to the countries of their birth who nonetheless by reason of infinite complexity are able to see across their chauvinist boundary lines and view with understanding those who talk other tongues than their own. The crying need of the world these days seems to me to be an enlarging of this outlook and I look askance at any movement which assists in making the peacemaker among nations merely a national warrior.[22]

That philosophy provided a guiding spirit for Sulzberger's private and public life. As a student at Columbia University, he refused to join a Jewish fraternity because he would not "admit that religion was a basis for social contact." He stuck to that position four decades later, rebuffing the fraternity's offer to make him an honorary member.[23] (Arthur and Iphigene did support the rabbi who served as "Jewish adviser" to the university, but solely because he understood "the problem of the Jewish youths who come from orthodox and foreign homes, and who need to be taught the principles of this country and made to abandon their ghetto thinking." Plus, the rabbi came "from a Philadelphia family which has been in this country since Revolutionary days."[24])

Arthur Sulzberger also refused to join the American Jewish Committee, even though it had been formed by and for men of his class and background. In fact, his cousins Cyrus Adler and Mayer Sulzberger were among the committee's founders and both served as its president. His brother, David, was on its executive committee during the 1940s. "I do not feel the ties which cause the group of high-minded men who compose its executive committee to watch the interests of the Jew as they do," Arthur Sulzberger wrote.[25] In 1938, he opposed Roosevelt's nomination of Felix Frankfurter to the U.S. Supreme Court, not, as has been frequently portrayed, because he feared that the appointment of a Jew to such an important position would incite anti-Semitism.[26] Instead, Sulzberger worried that appointing a Jew to replace another Jew, Benjamin Cardozo, "would make it appear as if a particular religion had a lien on a certain seat."[27]

Jews could hold positions of influence, he maintained, as long as they did not hold those positions because they were Jews or act as Jews once they held them.

Some of Sulzberger's contemporaries, from leaders of Jewish organizations to Frankfurter himself, suspected that the publisher's supposed devotion to a high-minded philosophy actually masked a deep sense of insecurity, that his heated insistence that Jews were no different than anyone else concealed neurotic fears that they were – and thus he was – actually worse.[28] Whatever his psychological motives, Sulzberger's belief that he was acting out of principle, not pragmatism, had its own consequences. It led him to be more willing to take extreme positions, and less willing to shake them, as catastrophe enveloped the Jews.

Until the 1930s, Jews had not been one of the *Times*' top news concerns. In the first decades of the century, *Times* readers tended to be concentrated among the Protestant uppercrust. True, the *Times* circulation area included almost 3 million Jews, nearly half the Jews in America, but they preferred the *New York Post* or Yiddish-language papers. Occasionally, news from abroad would flare up, such as the murder of dozens of Russian Jews in the Kishniev massacre in 1903. Or a gruesome crime might heighten anti-Semitism, such as the murder of a 13-year-old girl in Georgia that led to the 1915 lynching of the Jewish Leo Frank, or the trial of two Jews, Nathan Leopold and Richard Loeb, for the 1924 "thrill" murder of a 14-year-old boy in Chicago. For the most part, however, Jews were not important to the *Times* as readers or as subjects. That changed in the century's fourth decade. First- and second-generation Jews increasingly turned to the *Times* for its comprehensive, straightforward approach to news. At the same time, the rise of Adolf Hitler put their European brothers and sisters at the center of world events.

The Nazi Party in Germany grew steadily in the 1920s and early 1930s. By 1932, it had the largest bloc in the German legislature, the Reichstag, and by the following January, its leader, Adolf Hitler, had been appointed chancellor. Hitler moved quickly to consolidate power, suspending civil liberties, taking over state governments, and persuading the Reichstag to let him govern without consultation. From the beginning, anti-Semitism was central to Hitler's actions. Within 2 months of his appointment as chancellor, the Nazi Party announced a boycott of Jewish businesses throughout the country. The government expelled Jews from key positions and sent many to concentration camps.

Ochs was still the *Times* publisher when Hitler started his march to power. The news from Germany was distressing to the man whose parents had both been born in Bavaria. "From Germany his parents had brought and had taught to him as a child a great store of legend and tradition, most of it kindly, much of it merry, all of it charming," Ochs' biographer Gerald Johnson wrote.[29] Ochs' connections to Germany were more than folklore. He visited often and retained close ties to the members of his father's family who had remained there. In 1930, he traveled to Germany, stopping at the *Times* Berlin bureau and visiting his father's hometown of Furth, where Jews had resided for almost 500 years. The town had 2,300 Jewish inhabitants, including future U.S. Secretary of State Henry Kissinger, and a host of Jewish institutions, including seven synagogues, a hospital, an orphanage, and an elderly people's home. Ochs posed for a snapshot in front of the house where his father, Julius Ochs, had lived. He saw the deteriorating Jewish cemetery, with the gravestones of his forefathers bearing inscriptions in German and Hebrew. The sight moved Ochs to ask his second cousin, Louis Zinn, a toy manufacturer who lived in nearby Nuremberg, to help him refurbish the cemetery.[30]

Ochs never had a chance to carry out his project. Within a few years of his trip, more than Jewish cemeteries were imperiled. Hitler's rise shook Ochs. "Toward the end of 1933 Ochs seldom appeared in public. He was now broken mentally as well as physically," wrote *Times* reporter Meyer Berger. "The spread of intolerance, the ever more melancholy cast of the international situation, the country's slow and painful drag from the depression's pit were too great a burden for his years to cast off. The spread of Hitler's power became his nightmare." He died in April 1935.[31]

Control of the *Times* passed to his son-in-law, just as control of Germany was passing to Hitler – a correspondence that Sulzberger noted. "Mr. Ochs was ill for about two years before his death so it is fair to say that, from the time Hitler came into power in 1933, I was in charge."[32] Sulzberger presided over a newspaper trying to come to grips with the rise of Nazism and Hitler's treatment of the Jews. The *Times*' chief European correspondent, Frederick Birchall, put it succinctly in a May 1935 dispatch from Berlin: "So long as National Socialism lasts, there will be no future for German-born or for alien-born Jews in Germany."[33] Birchall's assessment preceded the enshrining of anti-Semitism in the notorious Nuremberg laws. The laws, which were adopted in September 1935, defined anyone with a single Jewish grandparent as a Jew and officially disenfranchised them. The laws prevented Jews from working for the government, serving in the army, marrying or having sexual relations with Aryans, or hiring female non-Jewish domestic help. Soon, Jews were barred from all professions and trades, forbidden to enter restaurants, theaters, museums, and beaches, or to sit on certain park benches. Their property was confiscated and a huge tax was imposed.

Watching from the United States, Sulzberger was appalled by Germany's treatment of the Jews, especially its biological basis. But he did not respond, at least visibly, as if his people – or any people for that matter – were being persecuted. If anything, Hitler's assumption that Jews were a race pushed Sulzberger to deny it more strenuously and to insist more vigorously that Jews not be treated as a group in the pages of the *Times* or in public policy. The *Times* was already careful about how it referred to Jews, adopting, at the urging of the Anti-Defamation League, complicated rules that deemed it appropriate to use "Jew" when "applied to the whole body of Israel," but not appropriate when used as an adjective ("Jew boys") or as a verb ("to Jew down").[34] As publisher, Sulzberger tightened those rules. "After a great deal of effort," he convinced his editors not to use the word Jew as the "common denominator" for all activities in which Jews participate. "Thus, when the American Jewish Congress meets our headline does not say 'Jews Meet' but emphasizes the fact that it is the Congress," he wrote. "When the Zionists meet it is not Jews, but Zionists."[35]

Sulzberger was not wholly successful in this endeavor, however. Sulzberger complained to his Washington bureau chief that "every other word was Jewish" in a story about the funeral of B. Charney Vladek, an American labor leader. Arthur Krock replied: "This [that Jews are a racial entity, not a religious community] is the general American attitude, the basis of some social policy, and abroad in dictatorships it is the basis of political and economic policy. You and Mr. Ochs dispute and resist that. But, if I am right about the Vladek funeral, the point continues to get nowhere."[36]

Yet, Sulzberger trumpeted the point incessantly and made it central to his newspaper's response to the Nazi menace. Sulzberger's position was consistent. He was adamantly opposed to Hitler's persecution of the Jews, but he was equally adamant that Jews do nothing special to help other Jews. In this he differed even from the old guard German-Jewish elite, who preferred a strategy of accommodation to activism, but still assumed Jews should assist their fellow Jews. When Jewish groups organized a boycott of German goods, Sulzberger opposed it, as did the American Jewish Committee. But the Committee's stance was tactical, fearing a backlash on the part of the American public.[37] Sulzberger's position was, at least in his own words, philosophical. "In doing what I can to help distressed German and Austrian Jews, I must act as an American and not as a Jew," he wrote in 1938. "As a Jew, in my judgment, I have no right to cross national boundary lines in a manner which may involve nationalism."[38]

The *Times* editorial page served as a showcase for Sulzberger's views. After Ochs died, his son-in-law hesitated to change too much, too quickly at the *Times*, but the editorial page was one place where he was eager to depart from the Ochs era. His father-in-law believed "*Times* editorials should be expository rather than anything else," Sulzberger explained, and Ochs' "editorial page rarely took a position." According to Sulzberger, he changed that. "We took positions, and we took them as hard as we could," he said.[39] Even before Ochs' death, Sulzberger had brought on board an editorial writer with whom he had a particular affinity. Just 2 years younger than Sulzberger and Yale educated, Charles Merz had been at the *New Republic* where he became known for writing a 1920 article with Walter Lippmann attacking the *New York Times*' coverage of the Soviet Union. Merz followed Lippmann to Pulitzer's New York *World*, where Lippmann headed the editorial page and Merz was one of the page's staff writers. When the *World* folded in 1931, Sulzberger recommended to Ochs that he hire Merz rather than his boss, who by then was renowned as a columnist and intellectual. Sulzberger considered Lippmann "not a good executive, not an organizer – nor could he, I think, serve well under other people."[40] Ochs hired Merz.

Seven years later, in November 1938, Sulzberger named Merz editorial director, a decision he never regretted. On the occasion of Merz's twenty fifth anniversary with the paper, Sulzberger noted the often "delicate" relationship between a publisher and his editor: "No editor worth his salt would write or cause to have written that in which he does not believe. And no publisher could permit his own responsibility to be taken from him." That was never an issue between Merz and Sulzberger, the publisher said, because they were in "complete harmony," without even engaging in "serious discussions of policy." Instead, Sulzberger and his editorial page editor vacationed together, did jigsaw and crossword puzzles, and played backgammon, Chinese checkers, gin, and canasta.[41]

"It is a pleasant thing to be able to record that he [Merz] and I never differed on a fundamental policy involving The *New York Times*," Sulzberger wrote to playwright Robert Sherwood.[42]

Others at the *Times* understood their closeness. "They thought alike, they talked alike," said Daniel Schwarz, who started at the *Times* in 1929 and eventually became its Sunday editor. "Sulzberger had complete confidence in Merz and Merz had complete confidence in Sulzberger. Sulzberger wouldn't have to say to Merz what he should do and not do. They could have talked about it while playing cards. They would have traded feelings about it. But nothing had to be told."[43] On the rare occasions that Merz was not sure what Sulzberger wanted, he would ask, especially about sticky Jewish issues. Late in the war, when the leader of a Zionist organization celebrated his anniversary as president of the group, Merz wanted to check with the publisher on the paper's position. "We can readily prepare such an editorial if it is a good thing for us to publish," he wrote, "but I think Mr. Sulzberger's opinion on that point ought to be the decisive factor."[44]

Before Sulzberger became publisher, the *Times* editorial page had already made one important decision – it banned letters to the editor on the rise of Nazism in Germany. Sulzberger maintained the prohibition even as the pace of Hitler's outrages and corresponding letters quickened. The officially stated reason was that the paper received too many such letters,[45] but the real reason seemed to be they would open the door to commentary on the situation of Germany's Jews. "I was in favor of lifting the lid on German letters if they related to the general political situation, but this one is on the Jewish angle and none other," Managing Editor James explained in a memo to Sulzberger. The letter did not run. The *Times* wanted neither to publish anti-Semitic letters – of which it received plenty – nor open itself up to the charge that as a newspaper owned by Jews it would not publish them. The *Times* had to be receptive to "both sides of any issue," Sulzberger explained; it had decided not to run contributions attacking anti-Semitism to avoid having to "give this opportunity to those who might urge the extension of anti-Semitism."[46]

Early in Sulzberger's tenure as publisher, an issue arose that he could not bury the way he had anti-Semitic letters to the editor. One of the world's most pressing problems was the hundreds of thousands of desperate Jewish refugees seeking to flee first Germany and then Austria and Czechoslovakia, but finding they had nowhere to go. Deprived of all political rights and most economic resources, subject to wanton violence and random arrests, Jews scrambled to leave Nazi-controlled lands. The situation became more dire after Kristallnacht in November 1938. Bands of Nazi thugs, encouraged by the German government, rampaged through the country, burning synagogues, destroying Jewish businesses, and beating Jews. In Furth, Adolph Ochs' ancestral hometown, the main synagogue was burnt to the ground and 132 Jewish men were sent to the Dachau concentration camp. The steady stream of hopeful émigrés became a torrent. Still reeling from the decade-long economic depression, however, most countries, including the United States, were willing to take only a tiny proportion of those frantic to leave. American popular sentiment, fanned by anti-Semitism, weighed heavily against admitting immigrants who could usurp jobs, import foreign ideologies, and drag America into war. Even many American Jews, worried that an influx of foreign Jews could spark an anti-Semitic backlash, opposed liberalizing immigration policy.

As publisher of the *Times*, Sulzberger had to take an editorial stand. But Sulzberger was determined that the stance would not be – could not be – perceived as influenced by his religion. Sulzberger was so insistent that the refugee problem not be identified with Jews that he forced James G. McDonald, the former League of Nations' High Commissioner for Refugees who was just about to join the *New York Times* editorial board, to refuse an award from the Jewish Forum for promoting the welfare of the Jewish people and humanity. In instructing McDonald to decline the award, Sulzberger suggested that McDonald point out that his effort "has been to draw international attention to the fact that this is not a Jewish problem but a general one; that to accord you the honor which they proposed would again contribute to placing the emphasis upon the Jewish side of the question."[47]

Times editorials never emphasized the Jewish side of the question. Even though the majority of people hounding embassies for visas and boarding rickety boats for uncertain destinations were Jews, *Times* editorials maintained throughout the 1930s that the refugee crisis was not particularly a Jewish problem.[48] "The problem posed by the German refugees constitutes a test of civilization itself," a July 22, 1939 editorial (p. 14) explained. "It has nothing to do with race or creed. It is not a Jewish problem or a Gentile problem. It does not belong to Europe or to America. It is the problem of mankind." Viewing German refugees as mankind's problem, not America's, *Times* editorials pushed for an international solution rather than unilateral action on the part of the United States. That meant the United States should not lift its immigration quotas, which restricted Germany and Austria to a combined 27,360 people per year. Because of the strict policies of American consulates, even those annual quotas often went unfilled. Only once did the *Times* advocate loosening the restrictions; the paper supported Senator Robert Wagner of New York's plan to bring 10,000 German-born children here. But even then the *Times* was careful to point out in its sole editorial that the children would be "of every race and creed."[49] The bill died in committee, and the mostly Jewish children who would have entered the United States never came.

Both behind the scenes and in the pages of the *Times*, however, Sulzberger did support a number of efforts to resettle Jews, although again he was careful not to highlight their religious identity. "The wise course, he thought, was to help the refugees find new homes in countries where they would be welcome," his wife wrote. So he searched for welcoming locations, from South West Africa, to Costa Rica, to a Soviet colony in Biro Bidjan.[50] "He put particular stock in the idea of settling Jews in Northern Australia and, when that failed, in the Dominican Republic," Iphigene said.[51] The pages of the *New York Times* served as an outlet to push the latter project, what is now viewed as an "inconsequential settlement in Santo Domingo."[52] Between October 1939 and March 1941, when immigration from Europe effectively ended, the *Times* ran 23 stories and three editorials about this settlement where just 159 Jews settled.[53] In full-page photo spreads, the paper presented the settlement as idyllic. Handsome young men and women without discernible Jewish traits – one girl was described as "from Spain," whereas another, wearing an old-fashioned German frock, was a "Tyrolean girl" – lived in tidy houses with porches, surrounded by palm trees and beautiful beaches.[54]

At the same time he was insisting that American Jews bore no special burden in the refugee crisis, Sulzberger knew all too well that they did. Since the mid-1930s, he and his wife had been receiving plaintive letters from relatives in Germany. "The uncertainty of what will happen to us in Germany, the moral pressure of which we all are subjected – all these things are such compelling reasons that I take the liberty of appealing to you," wrote Fritz Sulzberger, a prosperous 41-year-old doctor living in Bruchsal with his wife and two children. After noticing the publisher's name in a Jewish paper in 1937, Fritz's father, Sigmund, had begun the correspondence by sending Arthur a family genealogy dating back to 1525. Sigmund and Arthur had a great-grandfather, Salmon Sulzberger of Heidelshem, in common.[55] That was enough to prompt Sigmund's son to plead for help in immigrating to America; even within the strict country-by-country quotas, refugees needed an affidavit from an American promising financial support.

The Ochs family in southern Germany did not need to reestablish ties to their prominent relatives in New York; they had been maintained for more than a century. When the American branch of the family traveled abroad, they would often visit the German relatives or meet them at posh European resorts. In the mid-1930s, Arthur Sulzberger sent his chief foreign correspondent, Frederick Birchall, to check on Iphigene's cousins. Birchall became enough of a fixture in their homes in Furth and Cologne that the children referred to him as "Uncle Birchie." Margarete Midas Meyer recalled "Uncle Birchie" making frequent visits to Furth, taking her to Berlin's best restaurant and to the zoo, and sending her postcards from the exotic places he traveled as a correspondent. Birchall conveyed to the German relatives that the Sulzbergers were willing to help them immigrate. Assimilated and well-to-do, they resisted at first.[56] That changed in March 1938. "We cannot bear it any longer," Thea Midas of Furth wrote her third cousin, Iphigene Sulzberger. "I don't want to see my husband shot down neither as a soldier nor as hostage. The difficulties increased during the last half year in an unexpected manner and even my husband is now decided to go away – late, but not too late, we hope."[57]

It was not too late for Midas, her husband, Erich, and daughter, Margarete. The Sulzbergers promptly signed an affidavit, the receipt of which Erich Midas acknowledged in his first letter typed on "my new American typewriter" ("I beg you to excuse both the fault in type-writing and in English."): "I am shure [sic] that we lose 90 percent of our fortune, but all three we are happy to come to a new land, where our Margarete can live as a free and joyful child."[58] It was too late, however, for Louis Zinn, Midas' uncle and the cousin Adolph Ochs had asked to help him restore the family cemetery in Furth. Zinn, who was imprisoned by the Nazis in 1936, committed suicide after his release. "He has won the better lot," Thea Midas wrote her cousin in her first letter begging for help, "we others have still to live and struggle."

In her memoirs, Iphigene Sulzberger recalled that she and her husband "received a flood of letters from German Jews claiming to be blood relations." So many inquiries reached Arthur that when someone wrote inquiring about Fritz Sulzberger, he could not remember to which Dr. Sulzberger the writer referred. But "Arthur and I couldn't see our way clear to vouching for complete strangers," Iphigene wrote. "We rationalized our reluctance by saying that the situation wasn't as bad as people said, and we put the letters aside. Ever since then, I have wished we had taken the chance. I wish I had signed for them all – I wish to God I had." Still, Iphigene recalled in rosy terms the assistance she and her husband did provide to their German relations. "As the various families arrived, we gave them money so they could get themselves settled," she wrote. "When they got on their feet, every one of them reimbursed us, down to the last penny. We didn't want the money back, but they insisted on it. They were a wonderful group of people, and many of them made a great success of their lives."[59]

The relationships, however, were more complicated than Iphigene let on. Understandably, the Sulzbergers found it trying to be constantly tugged at by desperate people. At times, they responded with great generosity. At other times, they did not. With his cousin Fritz, Arthur was reticent initially. In March 1938, he flatly told the internist that he could not find him a job and advised him to stay in Germany. When Fritz decided to emigrate anyway after Jewish doctors were prohibited from practicing medicine, Arthur refused to intervene with the American consul. Fritz and his family had secured affidavits from someone else, but Fritz wanted the publisher to send a personal letter of recommendation to the consulate besieged by visa applications because "your personality is known and your word counts for much." Arthur would not. "Because of my position with The New York Times I have made it a rule not to ask any special consideration or favor from men in public office," he explained, although he broke this stricture repeatedly. Arthur was decidedly antsy when Fritz broached the possibility that Arthur should care for Fritz's 14-year-old daughter and 8-year-old son. Yet, when Fritz arrived in New York with his family the following year, Arthur provided contacts that eventually enabled the doctor to establish a practice in Southbridge, Massachusetts. Arthur even paid for Fritz's daughter, Lore, to go to summer camp.[60] Most important, Arthur would later be instrumental in trying to save Fritz's mother who had been left behind in Baden.

Iphigene sent a secretary in a taxi to greet the Midases when they arrived on the *S.S. Bremen* on October 12, 1938, and to ferry them to a boarding house on the West Side. Arthur helped Erich Midas, who had studied law in Germany and spoke five languages, to get a job with Kimberly-Clark Co. in upstate New York. The *Times* and Kimberly-Clark were joint owners of a paper plant. The family then supported themselves. But others became an emotional drain and a financial inconvenience. Iphigene and her cousin, Julius Ochs Adler, who was general manager of the New York Times Co., each sent $50 a month to support another Furth cousin, Elizabeth Abt-Peissak, her husband, Eugen, and their son, Claus, who had emigrated in 1936. Adler had signed the Peissaks' affidavits. Iphigene provided them with an "advance" of $2,500 when they arrived and provided additional advances of $1,500 from time to time. But the careful accounting makes clear that the advances were considered loans that the American relatives expected would be repaid. At the end of the war, Adler wrote a testy letter to Eugen Peissak, whom Elizabeth divorced in 1939, asking for $4,250. It is not clear whether the amount was ever paid.[61] Arthur himself seemed to want no part of Eugen, whom he later described as "a no-good." Peissak lost a job at the Parke-Benet art gallery that Sulzberger had gotten for him when he refused to move furniture. Sulzberger later would not help him make contacts to finance an antique business. Sulzberger did take pride in the fact that their son, who later Americanized his first name to Clark and used his mother's maiden name, Abt, became a highly successful political scientist working for military contractors and founded an important Cambridge consulting firm.[62]

Sulzberger had an even more strained relationship with another distant family member. In 1936, Sulzberger sponsored Ernest Sulzberger, his 40-year-old third cousin (Arthur's great-great-grandfather, Maier Sulzberger, was Ernest's great-great-great grandfather[63]), and his family to immigrate to the United States. As soon as Ernest arrived in the States, he began to lobby his cousin Arthur to help his sister and brother in Germany. In 1938, he went to Sulzberger's office to beg the publisher to do something for his older brother Paul, a successful 47-year-old attorney who was then in a concentration camp, and his family. "He wanted me to sign an affidavit to help bring them over to this country, but I told him very frankly that I was unable to do anything further, that I had already signed more than I should," Sulzberger wrote to his sister-in-law Beatrice Sulzberger, whom he asked to sign the affidavit instead. Her reply is not preserved, but Paul Sulzberger did not immigrate to the United States.

A month later, an increasingly distraught Ernest wrote to Arthur, this time about his older sister, Betti, her husband, Josef Altmann, and their three children, ranging in age from 8 to 13. "Now I appeal to you for the last time to sign an affidavit for my sister and her family so that they may be admitted to this country of liberty. You know also that this affidavit is a formal procedure. I claim no direct relationship to you, but one thing I like to tell you, that our grandfathers were related, but only your branch had the luck to come to this wonderful country." Sulzberger would not sign the affidavits. "I cannot agree with you that the procedure is strictly formal. By signing the affidavits I make myself responsible for those persons here, and I have already assumed such responsibility already in so many cases that I am unable to do so again," Arthur Sulzberger wrote. "I fully sympathize with the effort you are making in your family's behalf, but I have the right to expect understanding on your part that my present refusal is not made without heart or without comprehension. It is, however, beyond my means to do anymore." (Sulzberger eventually signed affidavits for four more people.) Eight days later, Sulzberger received the following radiogram from Wiesbaden: "dear mister sulzberger our brother ernest sulzberger has already spoken with you and we hope with great confidence that you will have the great kindness to give us a affidavit. we hope of your favourable cable." It was signed "yours sincerely altmann sulzberger." Arthur apparently remained unmoved.[ii]

Ernest Sulzberger then renewed his efforts on behalf of his brother, who had recently been released after 9 months in a concentration camp. He wanted the publisher to provide an introduction to Rabbi Stephen S. Wise, head of the American Jewish Congress, whom he believed might be able to help Paul. This time Arthur Sulzberger had his assistant send a curt note explaining that the publisher's "acquaintance with Wise is non-existent" and suggesting that Ernest Sulzberger get in touch with another cousin, Judge Myron Sulzberger. Paul Sulzberger eventually emigrated to Palestine and, in 1941, sought Arthur's support for a drive to seek reparations from Germany for the Jewish community. Arthur turned him down on the theory that the "Germans of Jewish faith" did not have greater claims than those of other faiths or nationalities.[64]

[ii] According to Aktives Museum Spiegelgasse in Wiesbaden, the family received visas to emigrate to the United States on March 15, 1939, but it could not be determined whether the Altmanns ever arrived in America.

Clark Abt has a theory about why the Sulzberger/Ochs family treated some refugees more sympathetically than others. Abt's grandfather, Leopold Abt, who was married to Adolph Ochs' second cousin Irma, was a Munich businessman who had grown wealthy supplying grain to the German Army during the First World War. "The affluence and power and status of my grandfather in Munich was comparable to Julius Adler in New York," Abt said. Leopold Abt had hosted Adler and Ochs in Munich before the first war. When the elder Abts escaped to Zurich, Sulzberger had Birchall help them settle in and sent the *Times*' Geneva correspondent to check on Leopold shortly after his wife died to "let him feel there is someone in the world who is standing by him at this time." To Abt, this reflected "reciprocity of generosity." The elder Abts "were not poor relations begging for a handout." That generosity extended to their daughter, Elizabeth, for whom Adler helped obtain a visa to leave Great Britain for the United States. Her husband was not of the same status, or as his son, Clark, put it "work ethic."[65]

In private, Arthur Sulzberger proved willing to help refugees he did not know. When AP Berlin correspondent Louis Lochner wrote Sulzberger asking him to sponsor an advertising executive, Walter Pelz, and his wife, Edith, the publisher agreed. The grateful Pelzes sent Sulzberger a gift every year on the anniversary of their 1941 arrival in the States.[66] Sulzberger also signed an affidavit for Isidor Kirschroth, a 19-year-old from Westphalia. He was attending Gross Breesen, a farm school to train young people who wanted to immigrate to any country but Palestine. Kirschroth was all set to immigrate to a Virginia farm, when Sulzberger was informed that Gross Breesen was "terribly demolished" during Kristallnacht. The boys had been imprisoned in concentration camps and their affidavits had been destroyed, the sponsoring agency told Sulzberger. He signed another affidavit and Kirschroth emigrated.[67]

He was not, however, willing to have these gestures become public. That led to a strict rule in dealing with refugees: any help Sulzberger provided could not involve the *Times*. "I regret . . . that it will not be possible to find a place for you on The New York Times," Arthur Sulzberger wrote Ernest Sulzberger who had requested a job shortly after his arrival. Once the war started and the wine importing company that had employed him as a bookkeeper shut down, Ernest again appealed to his cousin to "give me a chance in your concern." Ernest, who had been the manager of a 3,000 acre farm in Germany, would take any job. "If there is no opening in the office, I wouldn't hesitate to do any kind of work, for instance as packer, or in receiving and shipping department or other manual work," Ernest Sulzberger wrote. Apparently no longer willing to communicate with his persistent cousin, Sulzberger had his assistant arrange with the National Refugee Service to get Ernest into a baker training program. Arthur Sulzberger paid $360 toward maintenance of the family for 6 months in 1941.[68]

Sulzberger was as unrelenting with Albert Einstein and his own brother. When the famed Jewish physicist, who had himself immigrated 2 years earlier, asked the *Times* publisher to hire Alfred Kerr, a renowned Berlin critic, Sulzberger refused. "I am certain that upon reflection you will appreciate how unwise it would be for us to accept political articles from a German refugee," Sulzberger wrote in 1934. He was no more receptive to his brother's appeal. Shortly after Einstein's request, David Hays Sulzberger, who worked with the Jewish Social Services Association, wanted to send "five or six men who have been connected to newspapers" to the *Times* as possible hires. Arthur attached a copy of his letter to Einstein with a note: "I'm afraid there is nothing doing." Perhaps fearing that he had been too abrupt with his brother, who was 6 years his junior, Arthur Sulzberger followed up with the suggestion that David write to Victor Ridder of the *Staats-Zeitung*. "He is in touch with the German press throughout the country and undoubtedly has some Jew well up in his employ here in New York who might function for you." An obviously perturbed David Sulzberger replied: "I have no doubt that Mr. Victor Ridder and his 'well up' Jew are estimable gentlemen, but I don't know them. I suppose you had some good reason for not offering to fix it with Ridder, but whatever this reason was, won't you reconsider it?" Noting that David's letter had "been bothering me," Sulzberger then tried to explain. "I am in the unfortunate position of being able to give jobs to people who apply provided I want to do so. That instantly puts me at a handicap in talking with them, as you must realize. Without my again emphasizing it that we have a special problem which we cannot at any time afford to ignore."[69]

Sulzberger never identified "the special problem," but it is hardly a stretch to conclude it was the family's Judaism. A year later, in 1935, he refused to host a dinner to raise funds for a "university in exile" at the New School for Social Research made up of refugee academics. As he explained in a letter to Ira Hirschmann, a Bloomingdale's executive who had asked him to host the dinner, he had to "keep myself disassociated from active participation in any movement which springs from the oppression of the

Jews in Germany. Only in this way can the unprejudiced and unbiased position of The Times be understood." Sulzberger did donate $250, and promised another $250 in 1936.[70]

Even before the war started in September, 1939 proved a momentous year for Europe's Jews. The Germans' goal in the 1930s had been to eliminate Jews from Europe, not eliminate them period. Given the requirement that Jews leave behind whatever resources they had and the hostility of other nations to penniless refugees, it was not at all clear how this could be accomplished. By 1939, Germany had more Jews it was trying to get rid of, and fewer places that would take them. In January, Hjalmar Schacht, president of the Reichsbank, hatched what would turn out to be one of the last "solutions" to the "Jewish problem" short of the Final Solution. In January, Schacht proposed that the world's Jews, under the auspices of western governments, make a huge loan to Germany to finance Jewish emigration, help expand German exports, and provide Germany with desperately needed foreign exchange. Schacht began negotiations with George Rublee, director of the Intergovernmental Committee on Refugees, an organization formed by western governments, including the United States and Great Britain.

The *Times* featured the negotiations prominently, publishing six front-page stories in January and February. (When the plan fizzled, the *Times* never directly informed its readers, only noting on the obituary page that an official had told a Hebrew Immigration Aid Society convention that the plan was now hopeless.[71]) Schacht was soon removed from the Reichsbank, but the two sides reached an agreement. Some American Jews, however, opposed the plan that would have allowed 150,000 young Jews to leave in the first year. U.S. State Department officials assumed Arthur Sulzberger was one of the leaders of the opposition because of his well-known hostility to any plan that singled out Jews for assistance. It was even suggested that Rublee talk to Sulzberger to try to straighten him out.[72]

The opposition to the Schacht-Rublee proposal turned out to be more widespread than the State Department had initially assumed, and the plan never reached fruition. What role, if any, Sulzberger played in the opposition, is not clear. State Department officials were right about one thing though – Sulzberger did oppose the agreement. The publisher worried that acceptance of the plan would encourage other Central European countries to export their Jews in exchange for currency. "The news of the last two days surely indicates that the problem is swelling to such an extent that it cannot be solved by soft heartedness," Sulzberger explained in a confidential letter written in March to New York Governor Herbert Lehman.[73] The news of the last 2 days was Germany's seizure of Czechoslovakia, which added another 400,000 Jews to the Reich and to the refugee problem.

As the number of refugees grew, Sulzberger supported the partial closure of an escape hatch – the one to Palestine. Like his father-in-law and grandfather-in-law, Sulzberger opposed Zionism for religious and political reasons, but he also had a deep, personal dislike for the place. His antipathy only grew worse after he visited in 1937. "I have traveled pretty well over the face of the earth, but never have I felt so much a foreigner as in this Holy Land," he wrote in an unpublished essay. "In Palestine I was told by every act, every thought and every gesture, 'You are one of these people – you are a foreigner in America – here you belong'.... If there was to be any emotional conflict between America as my land and this as my land I must choose America, even if that were to mean that I can no longer be a Jew."[74]

The fact that Palestine, which was inhabited by Arabs and Jews and controlled by the British, had become an important refuge for Jews fleeing the Nazis, did not change his mind. After his 1937 trip, he advocated "compromise" with the Arabs. He argued that the Jewish population, which was then 30% of those living in Palestine, be allowed to increase to 40%, or 30,000 per year for 10 years. Unrestricted immigration, however, "would be the height of folly," encouraging Jews from Poland and Rumania to immigrate. "Countries with large Jewish populations must be made to realize that they face only the alternative of living with their Jews, or killing them spiritually or physically," he wrote.[75]

Even in 1939, when the idea of killing Jews "physically" seemed less hypothetical, Sulzberger stuck to his position that Palestine was not a worthy haven. He would not contribute to any organization that benefited Zionism, even indirectly. (One exception was Hebrew University in Jerusalem, which he supported grudgingly and only because of his father's attachment.[76]) When Governor Lehman asked him to serve as chairman of the Publishers' Division of the United Jewish Appeal (UJA), he refused because of the UJA's support for Palestine. "I have never given a penny to Palestine," he wrote, "and at the present moment I am not prepared to alter that attitude despite the stress of the present emergency."[77] At the end of 1939, he also would not contribute to the American Jewish Joint Distribution Committee, the leading Jewish overseas relief organization, for similar reasons. His charity of choice – the National Missions of the Presbyterian Church, to which he contributed $500.[78]

So, in May 1939, when the British proposed a "White Paper" that would restrict Jewish immigration to Palestine to 15,000 per year for the next 5 years, Sulzberger endorsed it. On the news pages, the *Times* highlighted British plans to provide a haven for Jews in Guinea – which never came to be – and played down the new limits on Palestine immigration. On the editorial page, the *Times* applauded the restrictions. "The pressure on Palestine is now so great that immigration has to be strictly regulated to save the homeland itself from overpopulation as well as from an increasingly violent resistance on the part of the Arabs," the *Times* wrote.[79] The Jewish press, in one of the first of what would be many attacks on the *Times*, took note of this "stabbing in the back," as *The Reconstructionist* put it in a June 16, 1939 editorial.

Another crisis loomed in May. For months, items of a paragraph or two had appeared in the *Times* about groups of refugees sent back to Europe after Uruguay or Venezuela or Argentina had turned them away.[80] On May 28, the *Times* carried a six-paragraph item on page 15 about 700 Jewish refugees aboard a Hamburg-American liner, the *St. Louis*, waiting for permission to land in Havana. Within 5 days, the story of the *St. Louis*, now with the accurate figure of more than 900 Jewish refugees aboard, would be on the *Times*' front page and on its way to becoming a lasting symbol of the refugee crisis. The refugees, whose Cuban visas had been retroactively declared invalid, spent 9 days adrift off the Cuban and American coasts. At one point, boats filled with relatives and friends circled the *St. Louis*, according to a *Times* story. "The *St. Louis*'s passengers, many sobbing despairingly, lined the rail and talked with those in the surrounding boats, some of whom remained several hours."[81] Finally, on June 6, the ship sailed back to Europe, most of its passengers to take what turned out to be temporary refuge in the Netherlands, Belgium, France, and Denmark. Germany occupied those countries within a year. Two hundred and eighty eight passengers found more permanent refuge in Great Britain.

Sulzberger's response to the *St. Louis* is not recorded, except indirectly on the *Times* editorial page. The *Times* wrote movingly of the *St. Louis* "as the saddest ship afloat" and noted that "no plague ship ever received a sorrier welcome." The refugees, the editorial noted, "could even see the shimmering towers of Miami rising from the sea, but for them they were only the battlements of another forbidden city." Yet, those powerful words came too late to matter. Tellingly, the editorial appeared on June 8, 11 days after the *St. Louis* first become a news story and 2 days after the ship set sail for Europe. The *Times* did not weigh in at all as the ship's fate was being decided. Nor was the editorial given prominent display, appearing as the fourth of five editorials the *Times* ran that day. The editorial also may have been more important for what it did not say, than for what it did. It did not mention that the refugees were Jews – although all but six were, and even the *Times'* news stories clearly identified them as such. It did not call on the U.S. government to admit the refugees, it only suggested that Cuba give them a temporary haven – after it had already refused to do so. In its next-day editorial, the only other one on the subject and the fifth of six editorials on the page, the *Times* was even more cautious. It refused to lay blame, except on a "dictatorship which offers scapegoats as a substitute for justice." The editorial again omitted that the refugees were Jews, going out of the way to minimize that fact. "For any one who believes that human beings have rights as human beings, the family names or religious preferences of these unhappy pilgrims will not figure. It is decency and justice that are being persecuted – not a race, a nationality or a faith."[82]

The *St. Louis* was just one of many ships; its passengers hundreds of the hundreds of thousands trying to find refuge. During those few weeks in May and June of 1939, the *Times* reported, although less prominently, the fate of other such ships.[83] The *Times* also reported the fate of the millions who remained trapped in Europe. In Vienna, 200,000 Jews lived "as an alien and outcast mass" who were "being driven from many apartments and forced to live outside the city or in overcrowded rooms within in it" and were "on the verge of starvation."[84] At Zbaszyn, the Gestapo drove several hundred Jews across the border into Poland, while another 20,000 were warned they would be next.[85] In the "Reich Protectorate for Bohemia and Moravia," part of what had been Czechoslovakia, Jews were required to register themselves and all their property, including "valuable pictures and finery," by July 31.[86] In Germany itself, Jews were relegated to "a ghetto from whence the able-bodied men are fetched for enforced labor in the factories or State projects." They had "but one thought and one hope: emigration."[87] Among those waiting for that hope to be realized were Bertha Sulzberger, Fritz's 68-year-old mother, in Baden, and Erich Midas' parents, Joseph and Emilie, in Furth.

In mid-August 1939, Arthur Sulzberger visited Germany and had an "unforgettable three hours' talk" with Leo Baeck, the chief rabbi of Berlin.[88] Soon, even more would be expected of Baeck as he sought to protect Germany's Jews during wartime. On September 1, Germany invaded Poland and the fate of the Jews, which seemed as bleak as it could be, grew even darker. Again, Sulzberger's *Times* provided a relatively thorough account, if not a thundering indictment, of what was happening to the Jews. Just 2 weeks after the invasion, the *Times* reported that a "'solution of the Jewish problem' in Poland is on the German-Polish agenda."[89] The *Times* noted that with 3 million Jews in Poland, the largest number in any European nation and the second largest in the world, the implications of such a solution, "were it carried out on the German model are ominous." What form that solution would take became clearer when the *Times* reported that Hitler was considering a Jewish reservation within the Polish state to be modeled after American Indian reservations.[90]

Two weeks later the first of what would eventually be nearly a million non-Polish Jews were on their way to Poland, and the *Times* published the first of what would be dozens of stories on these deportations. "Two thousand Vienna Jews are en route to a 'reservation' near Lublin, Poland between the Nazi and Soviet spheres of influence, it was learned tonight," the *Times* reported. "It was understood that this was the first of a series of mass migrations that eventually may include all Austrian, or possibly all German Jews." Jews from what had been Czechoslovakia soon followed, the *Times* reported in a succession of stories.[91]

The news filtering to Germany of conditions in Poland "was anything but reassuring to German Jews," the *Times* Berlin bureau reported. By mid-November 1939, the *Times* reported that the Gestapo had "dumped nearly 40,000 Jews" in the Lublin area "without any means of subsistence and with the prospect of having to meet the hard Winter conditions prevailing in the area without sufficient clothes or housing.... The object evidently is not to settle the Jews but to expose them to the peril of painful death from cold and famine." The Jews already in Poland faced an equally difficult time. That same day, the *Times* announced the first move to close off the Warsaw ghetto, which would ultimately imprison 500,000 Jews. "Barricades patrolled by armed guards cut off Warsaw's ghetto from the rest of the city today [November 19], all Jews being strictly confined to this district," the *Times* reported. Two weeks earlier, the *Times* reported that Jews' property was being confiscated in Lodz and other West Poland towns, pogroms were taking place in Kaluszyn, Lukow, and Pultusk, and that "a 'specialist' from the Dachau concentration camp" was arriving to set up a camp for Jews.[92]

All this news was reported inside the paper, often in stories that consisted of just a few paragraphs. Yet, there was little war news competing for journalists' attention. Things were so quiet that the *Times* ran a story with the headline: "38 war reporters in search of a war." Nor did the *Times* editorial page chime in with denunciations of the Germans' treatment of the Jews. In November, it ran two editorials condemning the Nazis' actions in Poland, but never mentioned Jews.[93]

Amidst the frightening rumbles from Poland about what was happening to the Jews, only one item seemed to arouse Sulzberger: President Franklin D. Roosevelt's reference to the "Jewish race" in a statement at a meeting of the Intergovernmental Committee on Refugees. Sulzberger knew to whom he could complain. Treasury Secretary Henry Morgenthau, Jr. was of a similar German Jewish lineage and was a childhood playmate of his wife. Sulzberger and Morgenthau had become friendly as adults. Both were senior members of the "Poker & Pretzel Club," an informal group that got together to play and eat. In their respective roles as publisher and treasury secretary, however, they tried not to invoke their friendship too often. When *Fortune* did a story on Morgenthau right after he assumed his cabinet post in 1934, the magazine interviewed Sulzberger, who wrote his friend of his unhappiness. "Seriously, though, I am a little disturbed at the way in which you, the Jews and the *Times* are linked together," Sulzberger said. "I tried to steer *Fortune* away from it when I refused to comply with their request for one of my pictures to use in the article."[94]

But the President's remark about the Jewish race was one of those rare occasions when Sulzberger did make use of his friendship with Morgenthau. He wrote the treasury secretary an impassioned letter. "Any anthropologist will, I believe, destroy the theory that there is such a thing as the Jewish race," he wrote Morgenthau the day FDR's statement appeared in the *Times*.

> I would argue further that the Jews are not a people.... It seems to me that a people is a group having common ideals, common interests.... Certainly there is no such common denominator between the poor unfortunate Jew now being driven around what was recently Poland, and let us say, Mr. [Leslie] Hore-Belisha [Britain's Jewish secretary of state for war] or myself. In Poland this Jew is a part of a recognized minority. Mr. Hore-Belisha and I, fortunately, are in no such category....
>
> All of this is relatively unimportant in a world that has as many problems as exist today; yet I am confident that unless the people of good will – and I count the President high on that list – exercise great care in choosing their words in defining this particular problem, they may all too unwittingly help to play Hitler's game.[95]

Two months later, Sulzberger would delight in the fact that his letter apparently produced results. After having lunched with the President at the White House on "very good oyster stew," Sulzberger chatted amiably with Roosevelt about the refugee problem and possible settlements on the East Slope of the Andes, among other places. (FDR shared Sulzberger's penchant for far-flung settlement schemes.) During their conversation, the President referred to "those of the Jewish faith," rather than Jewish race. Sulzberger took credit for this linguistic conversion.[96]

A month later, Managing Editor James' memo looking for guidance on the JTA report of German demands for Jewish girls came across Sulzberger's desk. It was the first time during the war that Sulzberger would be asked directly how to handle news about Jews, as well as the possible fallout from the Jewish community. It was not a hard decision. Sulzberger had never liked the JTA. He found the idea of "Jewish news" offensive and the service untrustworthy. He had pressed his father-in-law to end the *Times* subscription early in the decade, but Ochs had held on out of loyalty to the JTA staff and editorial board, many of whom were fellow members of the German-Jewish elite. As publisher, Sulzberger threatened several times to cut off the service, even though it cost just a few hundred dollars per year.[97] Passionate entreaties from the JTA's editor saved the subscription for a time, but finally in 1937, the *Times* stopped receiving the JTA. From the JTA's point of view, the problem was that after 1933, the *Times*, like other newspapers, was as hesitant to receive news from "a partisan (Jewish) source" as it was to become part of "Nazi anti-Jewish propaganda." "Organs like the New York Times insisted that their reports on 'controversial' subjects had to come through 'neutral' channels," JTA editor Jacob Landau wrote to his board explaining the *Times*' decision to drop the service. Other New York newspapers, including the *Post* and the *Herald Tribune*, continued to subscribe and "give prominent display to J.T.A. news."[98]

Thus, the *Times* could not print the Lodz story because it had not gotten it, and it would miss JTA news throughout the war. Nor would it publish the story now that a distressed reader had called attention to it. James considered his Berlin bureau chief's reply that the law prohibited sex between Jews and Aryans to "settle the matter." His question for Sulzberger was whether his reply to the reader should "say or intimate that the JTA was inaccurate." Do not print the story, Sulzberger advised, and do not impugn the JTA directly either. "I should assure him that we checked and that our people discount the story," Sulzberger scrawled on James' memo. James did just that.

The JTA, however, would not let the matter drop there. In mid-January, it transmitted another story about a similar request for Jewish girls this time of the Warsaw Jewish Community Council and appended a five-page affidavit from Dr. Henryk Szoszkes, a banker and council member who had recently escaped from Warsaw. The JTA pleaded with the *Times* to run a story based on Szoszkes' affidavit even though it did not subscribe to the service, but to no avail.[99]

Dr. Szoszkes would prove to be an important, reliable source on the condition of Polish Jews throughout the war for Jewish organizations, and even the *Times* upon occasion. The incident, although minor on its own terms, would exemplify the *Times* sensitivity over news about Jews throughout the next 6 years.

It revealed something about the *Times*' publisher as well. At the same time he was discounting the value of Jewish news and the agency that provided it, Sulzberger was writing to JTA editor Landau asking for "confidential status reports" on the condition of Jews in Germany. The JTA provided them.[100]

2

"This Here Is Germany"

Reporting from the Berlin Bureau

IN 1940, Arthur Sulzberger received his first warning that Europe's Jews faced horrors far worse than anything yet imagined. A young rabbi who had arrived from Berlin just 3 days earlier came to Sulzberger's office in August bearing alarming news. Germany planned to send more than 4 million European Jews to the island of Madagascar, Max Nussbaum told the publisher.[i] After meeting with Nussbaum a second time on September 11, Sulzberger called Henry Morgenthau. He urged Morgenthau to meet with the rabbi as soon as possible. "He's a most attractive looking fellow and taught himself English which he speaks remarkably well," Sulzberger said in a telephone conversation that Morgenthau recorded, "and I thought his story was sufficiently dramatic and some of the things that he had to say of what the Gestapo had told him as to the ultimate plans for the Jews there, if you were to hear it and if you're as much impressed, to pass him on to higher ups." Sulzberger even told Morgenthau that he would pay for Nussbaum and his wife, Ruth, to travel to Washington, DC. Morgenthau agreed to see him at 9 the next morning.[1]

The Nussbaums met with Morgenthau, who promised to relate what he heard to members of the Cabinet and the president. The treasury secretary discouraged the Nussbaums from publicizing the Madagascar news. Morgenthau said such news would "upset [American Jews] profoundly, at a time when one ought to strengthen their position and their morale." The war news had been discouraging that summer, with Germany easily consolidating control over the countries it had invaded in the spring and launching its air attack on Great Britain. Morgenthau asked Nussbaum "to convey his opinion to Mr. Sulzberger." Sulzberger also arranged for the

[i] Nussbaum's information about the Madagascar scheme was accurate, although the plan was derailed by Britain's capture of the island.

Nussbaums to meet with Arthur Krock of the *Times* Washington bureau while they were in DC. Krock said he would write an article for the *Times* Sunday magazine.[2] Nussbaum then prepared a written statement, which former ambassador and *Times* editorial writer James McDonald gave to Felix Frankfurter with the suggestion that he share it with his Supreme Court colleague and fellow Jew, Louis D. Brandeis.[3, ii]

Yet, although Sulzberger took Nussbaum's news seriously enough to ensure his information reached the highest levels of the U.S. government, it no more affected the *Times*' coverage of the Jews than did the backdoor reports the JTA had provided Sulzberger years earlier. The *Times* never printed a word about the Madagascar plan, or Nussbaum's other concern, German Jews' difficulty in getting U.S. visas. Despite his promise, Krock never wrote an article for the *Times* magazine. Nor did this information, or a stream of reports about the steadily worsening situation of Europe's Jews, change the *Times*' approach. Throughout 1940 and 1941, as the war escalated to include almost every country on the European continent, Sulzberger and his editors continued to present what was happening to the Jews as a secondary story that accordingly was to be covered by second-string reporters. Nor did it push Sulzberger to beef up the primary news bureau that would for the next 2 years report on the fate of the remaining Jews in the Reich.

The Berlin bureau had been a problem for the *Times* ever since Hitler had come to power. Covering Nazi Germany was difficult for all foreign correspondents. The government strictly censored radio reports. Although newspaper stories were rarely banned and reporters could circumnavigate the possibility by phoning their stories to other European bureaus (the *Times* frequently relied on London or Paris), the Germans employed other methods to keep reporters in line. For one thing, the government tightly controlled information. Dissidents willing to buck the party line were so few that the *Times* was compelled to violate its own ethical guidelines to pay for tips. In 1935, the Berlin bureau was allowed to charge up to

[ii] Soon after their Washington meetings, the Nussbaums moved to Oklahoma, where Stephen S. Wise had arranged for Max to lead a congregation. The next year, they headed to Los Angeles. Max Nussbaum became the celebrated rabbi of Temple Israel of Hollywood who converted Marilyn Monroe, Elizabeth Taylor, and Sammy Davis, Jr., to Judaism.

100 marks monthly for "'expenses'" in acquiring information. The cost went up the following year. In 1936, the *Times* had at least three informants on its payroll, referred to only as "Herrs A, B, and C," who were each earning 100 marks a month. "Our work in Germany is becoming more and more a matter of obtaining information confidentially," a *Times* correspondent wrote to Managing Editor James. "I know this contravenes every rule of civilized business, but what would you do? This here is Germany."[4]

When information managed to leak through the almost impenetrable German bureaucracy and find its way into print, officials would harangue and threaten the offending reporters. *Times* correspondents remembered being summoned to the foreign office or the propaganda ministry to be "chewed out" for something in a dispatch.[5] Associated Press reporter Louis Lochner said the officials would deliberately keep reporters waiting to "humiliate you" and then they would "put you through the wringer to harass you and also then to make you feel small."[6] If the government really did not like what reporters had written, it would refuse to distribute their newspaper. A *Times* reporter informed the home office in 1935 that the Nazi regime daily banned a half dozen British and French newspapers, a number he expected to increase and to include the *Times*.[7] Nor did the government hesitate to use its most serious and effective tool – denying journalists a reentry visa after an out-of-the-country vacation, or simply kicking them out of Germany for good.

Frederick Birchall, considered "the preeminent *Times* chronicler of the Nazi scene,"[8] summarized the hardships Berlin reporters faced. "The strain of constantly fighting a hostile regime, of being continuously under its suspicion and of countering the innumerable moves it is always initiating to hamper truthful presentation of facts, has been more than ordinarily trying for the men who have to live here all the time and whose jobs are dependent upon their striking a nice balance between telling the truth and retaining the toleration of the authorities." *Times* correspondents felt the burden even more acutely than other journalists. "It has been especially trying in the case of this bureau which from the beginning has been the central target of official dislike because of its ownership," Birchall explained.[9] Along with the German government's antipathy, the *Times*' Jewish ownership also provoked extra scrutiny from American Jews. Sulzberger needed correspondents in Berlin who understood the paper's delicate balancing act. He found one in Birchall.

A short Englishman with a bald head, a red Vandyke beard that stuck straight out, and a loud voice, Birchall had been with the *Times* since 1905 and had served as the *Times* acting managing editor from 1926 to the end of 1931. Even with the designation "acting," Birchall was exceptionally dedicated, working half the night to detect errors in the page proofs of the next day's paper. He sometimes slept in a room down the hall from his office and, should a big story break, reappeared in the newsroom in pajamas, carpet slippers, and a bathrobe.[10] Impressed by his commitment, Sulzberger had wanted to remove the "acting" from Birchall's title upon assuming control of the *Times* in the early 1930s, but he hesitated to give a foreigner such a critical editorial position. So Sulzberger offered Birchall the job on the condition that he become a U.S. citizen. Birchall, who was exceptionally loyal, to employer *and* country, refused. He suggested the position go to James, which it did.[11]

Birchall, already in his sixties, instead took on a job that, as Hitler came to power, would be draining even for a much younger reporter. He became the *Times* chief foreign correspondent, traveling throughout Europe but concentrating on Germany. Birchall realized the sensitivity of his position as soon as he arrived in Germany to cover the new regime. The criticism, however, did not come from Nazis, but from Jews. Birchall got into trouble with his boss for a radio broadcast that Jewish groups criticized as an attempt to whitewash Hitler.[12] In March 1933, shortly after Hitler became chancellor and in the midst of the Nazi Party's boycott of Jewish businesses, Birchall stated on CBS radio that Germany had no plans to engage in "slaughter of the enemies or racial oppression in any vital degree." Instead, predicting "prosperity and peace," he assured listeners that German violence "was spent."[13]

Sulzberger told his chief foreign correspondent that he knew "by reason of the censorship the talk had to be more temperate than the splendid articles you have been sending us." Still, Sulzberger considered it "unwise" for Birchall to have spoken on the radio because his statements "were susceptible of the interpretation that you were speaking in defense of what has been taking place in Germany." Birchall replied that he knew Hitler "really desired to stop this racketeering and was about to take action, so it seemed to me that a little cheery optimism might be well based." When his prediction that Hitler would stop the Nazi Party boycott of Jewish stores did not pan out, Birchall had a ready explanation for Sulzberger. Birchall maintained that he had not read Hitler wrong. "The fact is that this movement has got away from Hitler," he told Sulzberger. "Its mouthpiece is now Goering, not the new Chancellor and Hitler dare not stop him. He even has to play along with him as far as he can."[14]

Although Birchall never quite abandoned this perception of a bureaucratic war between Nazi "moderates," such as Hitler, and Nazi extremists,[15] he lost hope for "prosperity and peace." By the following year, he was attacking anyone who suggested economic restraints on Jews were only temporary. When Birchall learned U.S. Ambassador to Germany William Dodd had been the source for a *Times* story out of the Washington bureau implying "modification of Jewish rigors here," he snapped: "All I can say is that Dodd was not acting in good faith, because he knowed[sic] damned well that, whatever he would like to believe, there is no let-up here and will be none in the economic restrictions against the Jews."[16]

Birchall soon came to be considered such a tough observer of Germany that the press critic George Seldes, who rarely had kind words for the *Times*, concluded: "None but Nazis have found fault with a single word or line in the Birchall dispatches."[17] Sulzberger's faith in Birchall was rewarded when the foreign correspondent won the 1934 Pulitzer Prize for his reporting from Germany. "Knowing me as you do, you must have realized the problem which the news from Germany presented and the worries that were associated with it," Sulzberger wrote in congratulating "Mr. Birchall" on the award. (Despite their years working together, they maintained the formality of addressing each other as "Mr. Birchall" and "Mr. Sulzberger.") The prize conferred "a stamp of public approval" upon the *Times*' German reporting, Sulzberger continued, so that "one very big burden is now lifted."[18]

The *Times* still had plenty of burdens, and Birchall, who served as the publisher's eyes and ears in Germany, bore many of them. In addition to his reporting duties, he watched over the assorted Ochs relatives in Germany and worried about the *Times*' business interests in the Reich. In 1934, the worry was over the portion of the *Times*' World Wide Photo distribution service that was incorporated in Germany. The *Times* soon discovered that it would have to make compromises if it wanted to keep the business running. Birchall suggested to Sulzberger that the *Times*, after being invited to advertise by *Voelkischer Beobachter*, should take out an ad for 275 marks in the Nazi Party organ. "Its inclusion gives us the cachet of being in the party's good books," Birchall explained, and *Voelkischer* spent 1,000 marks weekly for World Wide's photos so "we ought to reciprocate."[19]

Birchall also seemed willing to tolerate a Nazi shopcell in World Wide Photo's workroom. Under German law, any company with more than 20 employees had to permit such a cell if an employee demanded it; two World Wide employees had, a photographic printer and "family man," and a filer, who was known as a "steady, reputable worker." Birchall tried to make the best of it in a letter to *Times* business manager, Julius Ochs Adler, likening the Nazi cell to "the *Times* chapel in our composing room at home." Birchall said he recalled the chapel as "sometimes a nuisance and at others a convenience. Anyway, we have to get along with it. It is the same here." On May Day 1934, World Wide Photos' employees marched with other German workers "to demonstrate their rejoicing that God has given to us Adolf Hitler and the Nazi movement." Even the newsroom was not exempt from Nazi symbolism. That same year, the owners of the building at 28–29 Kochstrasse that housed the bureau and bore the moniker, *The New York Times*, in big golden letters, decided to add another symbol to its facade: a huge Nazi flag with a swastika that flew to the left of the *Times* sign and right under Birchall's office window.[20]

Within a year, however, the impositions on its business became more than the *Times* could take. The German government had made it impossible to employ Jewish photographers by refusing to issue them the licenses that were required to do business. Because Birchall considered the most capable news photographers in Germany to be Jews, the *Times* tried to work around the restrictions. It hired "Aryan camouflages" for the Jewish picture editor and the manager, Julius Bolgar. The "camouflages" assumed the titles and negotiated with the authorities, while the Jews did the work. When the picture editor's camouflage quit, Birchall advised "engaging Bolgar's Aryan" to be the picture editor, too, at 500 hundred marks monthly. But Birchall doubted the subterfuge would work for long. "The authorities are undoubtedly 'after us' and are now watching us closely," he warned.

So closely that a few days after Birchall's admonition, the Germans kicked the Hungarian-born Bolgar out of the country. Birchall then advised Sulzberger to close the Berlin picture service whose German market had shrunk due to an "unofficial" but nonetheless effective boycott. Birchall attributed the sales drop to the paper's Jewish ownership and its unfriendly attitude toward the regime in Germany. "To put it plainly, if we are to continue to do business in Germany it must be in accordance with the Nazi rules – that is as an Aryan outfit . . . I do not think personally that it is worth while under these conditions. Personally they are abhorrent to every principle I hold and I am quite sure how you personally will feel about it." Sulzberger took his advice. Within 5 months, the *Times* closed World Wide Photos in Berlin.[21]

Birchall's concerns in Berlin were not just about the *Times'* business operation. Another problem was its bureau chief, Guido Enderis. The Swiss-born Enderis, who joined the *Times* in 1928, had limited journalistic abilities and excessive German sympathies, as even his editors admitted. The *Times*, like other American newspapers, tended to hire reporters for its Berlin bureau who knew the language and understood the country.[22] Familiarity often bred affinity, however, particularly among reporters who had been stationed there a long time. Enderis, who turned 60 as Hitler came to power, certainly fit that mold. The reporter, who invariably wore a gaudy suit with a loud red tie, had been a Berlin correspondent since before the First World War. In fact, Enderis, who was then working for the Associated Press, had been one of the only American correspondents allowed to remain in Germany during the war. His continued residence in Berlin had raised eyebrows at the time, particularly because, although technically interned, he had been allowed to live in the luxurious Adlon Hotel. (Enderis liked the Adlon so much that he was still living there when the next world war broke out.) Questions about his World War I sympathies did not prevent the *Times* from hiring him a decade later to lead its German news operation.

Almost as soon as he became chief foreign correspondent, Birchall was dispatched to Berlin where he concluded that Enderis was responsible for most of the bureau's deficiencies. Yet, Birchall did not recommend replacing Enderis, whose knowledge of Germany made him the "Dean of Berlin Correspondents," and who did a commendable job of holding down the bureau's expenses. Birchall advised Sulzberger to retain Enderis as bureau chief, but to put "a younger, more enterprising and picturesque man in just below him."[23]

That man turned out to be Otto Tolischus. Like Enderis, Tolischus had long-standing ties to Germany. He had been born there in 1890 and had immigrated to the United States with his family at the age of 17. After working in factories in Syracuse and Trenton preparing for college, he entered the Columbia School of Journalism, graduating in 1916. He served in the American military during the First World War and was scheduled to ship to France when the Armistice was signed. After stints in Berlin for two wire services and in London as head of the International News Services' office there, Tolischus joined the *Times* staff early in 1933. "Complicated, profound, studious, with a fine penchant for getting at the bottom of things," is how famed Berlin correspondent William Shirer described Tolischus.[24]

For most of the prewar years, the triumvirate of Birchall, Enderis, and Tolischus provided the bulk of the *Times* news out of Germany. A few other reporters came and went, and the *Times* had stringers in Hamburg, Frankfurt, and Munich. Robert Crozier Long wrote financial articles until his death in 1938, whereupon the *Times* hired a young reporter, C. Brooks Peters. Sulzberger had already vetoed Enderis' request for a "fourth man" before Long's death, explaining to James: "The line I have drawn on your note is a picture of the business curve. Until it changes I think we will have to limp along in Berlin as best we can." After Long's death, Tolischus was expected to pick up some of the slack, writing financial articles for which he requested additional compensation. Responding to a question from New York about whether the articles had been written on office time, Tolischus grumbled: "I don't know what office time is supposed to be. In practice I find myself working between 8 and 15 hours a day, seven days a week."[25]

With Tolischus and Enderis stationed in Berlin, and Birchall making frequent extended visits, *Times* management seemingly had the balance it wanted. Birchall and Tolischus played the role of bad cop, writing critical articles about the regime, whereas Enderis was the good cop, soothing any ruffled feathers. His bosses had no illusions about Enderis' role or his sympathies. Within a few months of the Nazis assuming power, Enderis phoned Birchall to advocate changes in the *Times* Berlin organization. The bureau chief wanted the *Times* operation, particularly its World Wide Photo subsidiary, to become more compatible with the new regime. According to Birchall, who promptly wrote Sulzberger about the bureau chief's recommendations, Enderis wanted the *Times* to change the name of World Wide Photo "to some nice Germanic form." He also suggested the *Times* fire its manager because he was Jewish and had "a highly independent spirit" that angered the regime.

Birchall rejected both ideas believing they would offer no protection. By changing the company's name, he wrote "we should retain all the odium plus the additional stigma of being afraid." Firing the firm's Jewish manager was even more ill advised, he added. "Are we editorially and personally to speak for freedom and then, for the sake of a slight profit, to give the lie to all our protestations by yielding to the pressure of these miserable fanatics?" Birchall reported that he tried to persuade Enderis "with such emphasis as the good Lord would give to me"; unconvinced, Enderis insisted that his recommendations be passed on to top management. Both Adolph Ochs, who was still nominally in charge, and Sulzberger sided with Birchall. Sulzberger shot back: "I'm sorry if this is disturbing to Mr. Enderis, but what in the name of Heaven does he think a jaw is for except to set it firmly when the occasion demands."[26]

Enderis' chief job was to make sure the newspaper did not antagonize the government too much. Enderis performed this task well. In 1934, for example, the *Times* published what Enderis described as a "poisonous cartoon" that depicted Hitler along with the graves of Nazi leaders Ernst Rohm and Edmund Heines who had been killed in a party putsch in June. The caption read: "And the Fuehrer Said Only Death Can Us Part."[27] After complaints from the Secret State Police and Reich Ministry of the Interior, Enderis, with the help of the American consulate, was able to persuade them not to ban sale and distribution of the *Times*. The conversations were not particularly cordial, Enderis groused to his managing editor, insinuating that his editors in New York were as much to blame as the Nazis. Enderis pointedly reminded the managing editor "of the traditional custom which leaves the head of a 'friendly government' immune from lampooning of such a malicious variety." Whatever the *Times* editors believed, "the Fuehrer . . . in his triple capacity as Head of the State, Chief of the Government and Leader of his party . . . is the three-ply IT."[28]

James apparently appreciated such advice, or at least Enderis' efforts at placating the Nazis, believing he was the reason the *Times* bureau in Berlin was not closed in 1935. "This is a left-handed compliment from a news point of view but nevertheless there is something to it," James wrote to Sulzberger in passing along Enderis' request for a raise the following March. Sulzberger agreed to a $10 per week raise for Enderis, who was the highest paid member of the bureau.[29]

Enderis also tried to keep other *Times* reporters out of too much trouble. This was particularly helpful to Birchall, who came and went frequently, each time depending on the German government to sanction his return. "I have frequently been a sore trial to Guido and undoubtedly have been accountable for some of his loss of sleep," Birchall acknowledged.[30] In early 1936, after receiving "intimations" from Enderis that "for the present anyway my return there would not be welcomed," he devised a plan to stay away for a while. He would then return to write "some attractive nonpolitical piece that would be all up [the German government's] street." The result, Birchall hoped, would be that "I should be left in peace if not actually complimented and afterward any idea of throwing me out of Germany on my past record would be impossible."[31] The strategy worked well enough that Birchall was able to return and cover the Olympics in Berlin that summer. Reporters for other news organizations were not so lucky. Columnist Dorothy Thompson and the *Chicago Daily News*' Edgar Mowrer were among the American correspondents expelled from Germany.[32]

Enderis also ran interference for Tolischus with the Foreign Office's press department. In November 1937, the Nazi organ *Voelkische Beobachter* criticized one of Tolischus' articles. Other newspapers noted the "heavy attack" on Tolischus and suggested that he might be expelled. A nervous Tolischus approached the American consul in Berlin, who agreed to protest the denunciation and to find out whether it presaged expulsion. The consul, however, wanted the bureau chief's approval before he acted. Enderis would not give it. He feared the consulate's intervention might "prejudice" the *Times*' relations with the government, which made him particularly anxious because he had submitted the article that had provoked the attack. Assured by a press department representative that *Voelkische Beobachter* had acted on its own, and that "as far as the press department was concerned the incident was closed," Enderis insisted the American embassy stay out.[33] Tolsichus was allowed to remain, at least for a while.

Four months later, Enderis dealt with a more serious risk to Tolischus. In March 1938, the Germans threatened to expel Tolischus over a week in review piece that described the government's restrictions on the German press.[34] Enderis engaged in "extended consultations" with many government officials who agreed to overlook the offense. After fixing the problem, Enderis went out of his way to say he considered Tolischus' story "too one-sided." Had he seen the story ahead of time, he scolded, it might have been handled more objectively.[35]

Managing Editor James understood his Berlin bureau chief's sympathies. "It is entirely understandable that, living for so long in the midst of the Germans, he has absorbed a certain amount of the German point of view," he explained. "It would be remarkable were it otherwise. There is no ignorance in the office here concerning this circumstance; it is fully realized." Not all the New York editors were quite so sanguine about Enderis' tendencies. When James proposed that the editors give some leeway to *Times* reporters operating in nations with authoritarian press regimes if they could not always provide hard-hitting information, Sunday Editor Lester Markel agreed. The "fellows in censored countries" should be reassured that they would not "get the gate" if they declined to do something that the editors asked for fear of the repercussions, Markel wrote. But he insisted on one exception. "Why don't you so tell the boys with the exception of Enderis, who has so many alibis now without the donation of an additional one?"[36]

How Enderis' absorption of "a certain amount of the German point of view" affected the *Times* reporting of Jewish issues is hard to gauge. The impact seemed to be more in what Enderis did not do – and discouraged others from doing. From the earliest days of the Nazi regime, his editors seemed to have to prod him to do stories about Jewish persecution. After receiving a suggestion from a Harvard Medical School professor, Sulzberger, in May 1933, asked for a story about the fate of German Jewish scientists. Three months later, James was still cabling Birchall about the story that Enderis said he could not do.[37] Enderis seemed particularly reluctant to do stories about concentration camps, which were admittedly difficult to report. Although anti-Semitic legislation and Hitler's anti-Semitic rants were well publicized, details of concentration camps and other abuses were not. Even Birchall cited difficulty in obtaining information as the reason why he was unable to provide the story on concentration camps his editors in New York had requested during the 1936 Olympic Games. Reporting difficulties notwithstanding, Enderis tended to downplay abuses in the camps. He killed one story suggested by James after interviewing an inmate in the Oranienberg camp and concluding that the prisoner "makes normal impression," gave no indication of "maltreatment," and had told Enderis that since arriving several months ago he had gained 8 pounds.[38]

Enderis also seemed particularly perturbed at having to chase down news stories that originated with the Jewish Telegraphic Agency. The antipathy may have stemmed from an incident in August 1934. While Enderis was away, a new JTA correspondent stopped in at the *Times* Berlin bureau. Shortly thereafter, the Gestapo detained the JTA reporter and questioned him about remarks he had made during his *Times* visit. That led a JTA editor to inform the *Times* that the Gestapo may keep "spies in the Berlin office of The New York Times and probably in other American newspaper offices." Enderis took offense at that notion. After visiting Gestapo headquarters and being assured by a "most courteous official" that the Gestapo did not maintain "a stool-pigeon in our bureau" and did not intend to "shadow us," Enderis urged James to go slow. Enderis seemed to take as much offense at the JTA correspondent as he did at the idea that the *Times* might be harboring spies. Enderis passed along another reporter's observation that the correspondent, "full name is Israel Albert" Leviton, was an "inquisitive, highly Semitic looking person who didn't seem to care what or how he talked." Enderis concluded that the *Times* staff had been mistaken in accommodating Leviton, who "impressed me as being of the communistic-intellectual type." As an afterthought, Enderis mentioned that he wished that the bureau could disregard JTA stories entirely. "They reach us over the open wire, embarrass us and provoke official irritations whenever we try to run them down," he complained.[39,iii]

Enderis frequently discredited stories of Jewish persecution that came from the JTA – such as the story about Jewish girls being requisitioned as prostitutes in the Lodz ghetto in November 1939 – or from other sources. Earlier that year, he effectively discounted an AP story that suggested the Germans had ratcheted up their demands on the Jewish community. The *Times* ran the original story on page one, but then, at Enderis' prompting, carried the German Embassy's denial and assumed in subsequent stories that no such request had been made. "I was not surprised to hear that even Jewish leaders had assured the Times that my story was incorrect," the story's author, Louis Lochner, wrote a colleague in London. "I know too well how these things are done. After all, men who leave concentration camps also sign statements to the effect that they had a perfectly glorious time!" Lochner insisted he was right, however, and the *Times*' denial was wrong. This was not the only time Enderis was wrong. Asked to make

[iii] JTA dispatches were a tricky issue for the American press in general. JTA Managing Editor Jacob Landau explained why the Associated Press had dropped its service around 1939–40. "I have reason to believe that every time the AP carried a JTA report from Germany, their man in Berlin was called on the carpet by Goebbels' Department." 4/2/48, JTA Collection, Box 1, "Report to the board of directors" Folder, AJHS.

contingencies in case of war, the bureau chief insisted in May 1939 that he did not have to. "I do not believe that war is ever coming at all," Enderis explained. It came 3 months later.[40]

Enderis' attitude did not seem to change much once the war started. Ten days after the Germans invaded Poland, Birchall felt obliged to cable James to apply "screws" to Enderis who was "automatically expressing" the German position. If he can "only send propaganda they want printed, why pay transmission fee?" Birchall asked. When a UP U-boats story that the Germans "hotly resented" appeared in the *Herald Tribune* in November 1939, Enderis seemed perturbed that the *Tribune* reporter's "inexcusable blunder" would make his efforts to placate the authorities more difficult. Enderis also needed to be asked twice by James to write about the "Jewish reservation" in Poland that was to hold at least 1 million Jews. James' second query was prompted by a letter to the editor from a *Jewish Morning Journal* editor who accused the *Times* and other newspapers of covering up the conditions on the Lublin reservation, which was a "veritable inferno," an "insane asylum." James did not print the letter, but he did cable Enderis: "What's situation Lublin reservation? Many here worried about it." Enderis apparently did not reply, although a week later the *Times* ran a story from the Paris bureau that said Hitler had dropped plans "for a purely Jewish reservation near Lublin," and instead wanted a "bigger mixed Polish-Jewish reservation." Berlin's contribution was two paragraphs that said "it was reliably learned" that Jews from Germany and Austria would not be sent to Poland at the present time.[41]

On the story of Jews in the Reich, as on others, Tolischus and Birchall provided a counterweight to Enderis. Tolischus wrote detailed, disquieting stories about Nazi outrages against the Jews, particularly during Kristallnacht. After many threats, however, the Germans did indeed banish Tolischus. In March 1940, the government informed him that his permit to remain in the country would not be renewed, although he was later told that if he left for 6 weeks he would be readmitted. He then followed the invading Germans into Denmark and Norway. In Oslo, Tolischus penned a parting assessment of German intentions for his bosses in New York in a memo marked "Confidential." He prophesied the fate of European Jews. "The Poles, like the Jews, are marked for extermination – physical extermination for the Jews and for those Poles who cannot reconcile themselves to German rule, national extermination for the remaining Poles through later absorption in the same manner in which other West-Slavic peoples were absorbed in what is now known as the Prussians."[iv]

As he would do with Nussbaum's warning a few months later, Sulzberger, who saw a copy of the memo, considered the information important enough to send it to his friend at Treasury, Henry Morgenthau. Morgenthau in turn passed it on to FDR in Warm Springs with the note: "Arthur Sulzberger gave me, in strictest confidence, the inclosed [sic] letter from his correspondent in Berlin. I found it so interesting that I am sending it to you."[42] Soon thereafter, the *Times* sent Tolischus to Japan to cover the increasingly tense situation in the Pacific. After Pearl Harbor, he was arrested and spent much of the war in Japanese captivity.

Birchall, for his part, came to understand the suffering of Germany's Jews. He became friendly with the Ochs relatives whom the publisher had entrusted to his care, even developing an infatuation for Elizabeth Abt that continued through her residence in New York. Politically, he no longer believed Hitler was a "moderate" trying to rein in rabid anti-Semitic extremists. His 1940 book, *The Storm Breaks*, emphasized that the Jews were a "personal obsession of Adolf Hitler." By the time the book appeared, however, Birchall, like Tolischus, was long gone from Germany. As a citizen of Great Britain, his usefulness to the *Times* in Europe diminished once his country and Germany went to war. The *Times* moved Birchall to a more placid post in Ottawa. When Sulzberger wanted to put another displaced correspondent in Canada, he asked Birchall to join the editorial board, even though the publisher had once objected to an "Englishman being associated with the editorial page." Birchall declined and then retired. He spent the rest of the war volunteering for British War Relief.[43]

So in the spring of 1940, as the war and the persecution of the Jews intensified, the *Times* Berlin bureau consisted of Guido Enderis and two young, relatively inexperienced reporters. C. Brooks Peters had joined the bureau in June 1938 at the age of 24, after having studied at the University of Berlin. Percy Knauth, who was born in Queens but moved to Germany with his parents and graduated from a German gymnasium

[iv] Although the use of the term "extermination" in 1940 did not mean the murder of 6 million people, the contrast between "physical extermination" for Jews and recalcitrant Poles, and "national extermination" for the remaining Poles, does suggest that Tolischus knew the Germans had a different, more ominous fate in store for Jews.

in Leipzig, was just 25. He had joined the *Times* a year before, after a short stint at the *Chicago Tribune*, and was still a probationary employee. The *Times* Berlin bureau was at its weakest just as its responsibilities were greatest.

After months of what was referred to as a "phony war" – a period of relative quiet following the defeat of Poland – World War II began in earnest in the spring. The Germans rolled into Denmark and southern Norway in April, then stormed Holland, Belgium, and France in May. Italy joined the war in June, and the Battle of Britain began in July. By the fall, Germany had marched into Rumania, and Italy had invaded Greece. Germany then cobbled together the Axis, an alliance of Germany, Italy, and Japan, soon to be joined by Hungary, Slovakia, and Rumania. For the *Times* that meant having to follow the fierce fights in the British skies, the trampling of independence in Scandinavia, collaboration in France, repression and resistance in the Balkans, and an oppressive occupation in Poland.

The *Times* had always prided itself on the scope of its international coverage. James would boast that before the war his newspaper's "foreign service" was "far and away the most complete and extensive of any American newspaper."[44] The *Times* had multiple reporters in London, Paris, Berlin, and Rome, and it also stationed correspondents in less central locations, including Athens, Belgrade, Budapest, Bucharest, Istanbul, and Sofia.[45] Even so, the *Times* did not have enough manpower to cover a severalfront war in the methodical and comprehensive fashion it had pioneered. The *Times* began reassigning reporters to the various European capitals and beefing up its editorial staff in New York to handle what was sure to be an avalanche of copy from the far reaches of the continent.

At that time, *Times* management made several key decisions that would prove fateful to its coverage of European Jewry. For one thing, London would be the linchpin of its European operation and its most talented reporters would be located there. James Reston, who would become a legendary Washington bureau chief and columnist, began his *Times* career in the London bureau the day World War II started. Raymond Daniell, an outstanding *Times* reporter for over a decade, was reassigned from Mexico City to London to head the bureau. His editor considered him "among the best 'diggers' in the profession."[46] Once there, Daniell proceeded to hire what would prove to be the *Times*' future stars and top editors. Clifton Daniel, who would marry a president's daughter and manage the *Times* during the turbulent 1960s, started his *Times* career in wartime London, as did the *Times*' famed war correspondent and 1950s London bureau chief Drew Middleton.

At the beginning of the war, the London bureau consisted of Daniell and Reston, along with James D. MacDonald and David Anderson. "We were all without our families," Reston recalled, "though Daniell dealt with this deprivation by marrying Tania Long of the *Herald Tribune* and adding her to the staff." (The daughter of *Times'* Berlin financial correspondent, Robert Crozier Long, who died in 1938, Tania Daniell had been raised in Berlin.) The *Times* reporters lived a romantic albeit dangerous existence, with even the simple task of traveling back and forth to work proving risky once the bombs began to fall. Arthur Sulzberger took care of that. "[W]ith the enthusiastic approval of the publisher, who picked up the tab, we all moved into the Savoy Hotel with our office supplies and personal belongings," Reston wrote. It "was a sturdy building, with the deepest shelters and one of the best restaurants in town." Milton Bracker, who joined the bureau later in the war, had one big complaint: he had to pay a 15% service charge for the two waiters, maid, and valet that tended to him and brought breakfast to his room every day. He did not, however, complain about his hotel room, which had air conditioning, an ivory phone in the bathroom, and "a tub big enough to play water polo in."[47]

It made sense for the *Times* to concentrate its top talent in London as the war intensified. Britain was a decisive battleground as the skies over England filled with German airplanes determined to bomb the British into submission. Especially during the latter half of 1940 and the first half of 1941, the outcome of the war hung on Britain's ability to hold off the Germans single handedly. In addition, reporters in London were able to operate more or less freely. Although there was wartime censorship, it was, as Sulzberger would later describe it, "liberal," and Great Britain was still an open society. As long as they did not divulge military secrets, reporters for the most part were able to report and write what they wanted. London also received transmissions from the European continent, Africa, and the Middle East more easily than New York, making it a logical place to edit foreign copy. The additional editing and transmission burden contributed to Daniell's constant griping that the bureau was understaffed.[48]

A certain Anglophilia also crept into the *Times*' decision to make London its base for wartime coverage. Sulzberger was an unabashed

Anglophile; London was his favorite city, and he visited frequently. His solicitude for the British was probably best expressed in the *Times*' coverage of the evacuation of British children to the United States during the summer of 1940. More than 200,000 British families wanted to send their children to safety in the States, which required changes in American immigration law. In June and July, the *Times* published nine impassioned editorials with impatient headlines such as "No Time to Lose" and "They Must Be Saved," imploring Congress to make the necessary changes.[49] The *Times* also ran three front-page stories about the British children during those months, five photo spreads mostly of small, tow-headed children, and a magazine article accompanied by dozens of children's pictures.[50] (Contrast that with the single editorial the *Times* ran the previous summer advocating the admission to the United States of 10,000 mostly Jewish children or the eight editorials they would run about refugees during the entire war.)

Whatever the reasons, the result was that stories out of London often took precedence over those from the occupied countries. While the top talent went to London, the *Times* continued to rely on its preexisting network of foreign correspondents to handle events in German-allied nations. Before the war, the *Times,* like most American news organizations, tended not to stock its foreign bureaus with its top reporters who had paid their dues in more mundane stateside assignments to be rewarded with glamorous foreign posts. Instead, those hired for foreign bureaus tended to be natives of the countries they covered, or British journalists or freelancers who had long lived in those countries. Often they seemed to be hired more for their familiarity with the countries they covered than for their journalism skills. They were also hired because they came cheaply, at least compared with their American counterparts.[51] At the beginning of the war, events in Poland, France, or Rumania were seen as a secondary story to be covered by second-rate reporters. Nowhere was that more evident than in Berlin. Rather than strengthen the problematic bureau once the war began, *Times* management allowed it to languish.

For 7 years, Guido Enderis' appeasement strategy with the Nazi government had been the subject of grumbling within the *Times* and among the gossipy Berlin press corps. In his *Berlin Diary* (p. 41), William Shirer described Enderis as "minding the Nazis less than most." Although the complaints never moved beyond journalism circles, in the fall of 1940, they threatened to. Arthur Sulzberger received a letter from a former *New York Times* city desk reporter and part-time Geneva correspondent that began with a provocative question: "Don't you think it is about time that The New York Times did something about it's [sic] Nazi correspondent in Berlin?" Warren Irvin accused Enderis of engaging "in a loud-mouthed defense of Nazism" that he "publicly proclaims" in the Adlon Bar. Irvin ended with a threat: "I don't want to do anything to hurt my own paper; but I feel that my loyalty to my country comes first, and if some action is not taken I shall feel compelled to publish these facts."[52] Irvin later said he had been compelled to write Sulzberger when he noticed that Nazi radio, whose reports he monitored for the BBC, often quoted the *New York Times*. When he checked, he found the articles were by "our old friend Guido Enderis," Irvin later told Sigrid Schultz, a *Chicago Tribune* reporter who shared his opinion of Enderis.[53]

James, in trying to explain the situation to Sulzberger, chalked up Irvin's animosity to the fact that Irvin and Enderis had argued when Irvin was in Berlin. James pleaded ignorance of the "merits except that Irvin drinks more than Enderis, who drinks very little." Still, James acknowledged there was something to Irvin's overall complaint. "I realize that the inferences are all against Enderis," he wrote, "but I realize that if you fire him, or withdraw him from Berlin, that will close our Berlin Bureau." The best strategy James suggested was to make sure Enderis wrote very few stories – "the less we had from him, the better."[54] James also recommended that the publisher warn Irvin that his charges could be the basis of a libel suit by Enderis.[55]

Sulzberger followed that course, hinting at a possible libel suit and suggesting that if Irvin published "what you call 'facts'" the publisher would "controvert them publicly" and "give the reasons" why Enderis was "a useful and valued member of The Times staff."[56] In August 1939, after a visit to Germany, Sulzberger had indeed praised all his Berlin correspondents. "I have always known that Berlin must be a tough assignment," he wrote Editorial Page Editor Merz, "but I never guessed how tough it is, under this regime, until I saw these three able men of ours at work." If Sulzberger had since soured on Enderis, he did not let on.[57]

Irvin responded that "what I call facts *are* facts" and that "Enderis has made no secret of his pro-Nazi sympathies." He added: "I don't question the usefulness and value of Mr. Enderis to The New York Times. I *DO* question the right of the greatest American newspaper to maintain a pro-Nazi as its Chief Correspondent in Berlin in times like these." Yet, Irvin did not go public with his charges. Two years later, when Irvin returned to the States from London, he visited the publisher and returned to that sensitive subject, although American correspondents were no longer in Berlin. "Sulzberger informed me The Times 'Had to do business' in Germany," Irvin recalled, "and that, for this reason, Enderis was needed there."[58] (When Bureau Chief Raymond Daniell later suggested hiring Irvin in London, James nixed the idea.[59])

Enderis was needed there, but not to write stories. Before Irvin's letter, James had complained that Enderis was not writing enough, causing the bureau chief to plead that he was swamped with "administrative details" and "coaching junior staffers." After Irvin's letter, James was no longer complaining. In an inversion of the typical newspaper editor's bemoaning a reporter's lack of productivity, James practically crowed about Enderis' inactivity. In August, September, and October 1940, James boasted, Enderis produced only 224 words, 1,550 words, and 338 words, respectively. During that same period, the other two Berlin reporters each published more than 50,000 words.

One problem seemingly was solved: a known German sympathizer was "smoothing out difficulties in the collection of news and in transmission" but not writing many news articles.[60] That left another problem, however. As Germany conquered half the European continent and intensified its persecution of the Jews, the *Times* had just two reporters to cover these events from the German capital, and both were under 30 with a combined 3 years of professional experience in Germany. The *Times'* response was to rely heavily on the wire services, even though that ran counter to the newspaper's general practice. *Time* magazine, in a story about the *Times* overseas staff, pointed out that "an estimated four-fifths of all foreign news the *Times* prints (communiqués excepted) comes from its own men."[61] The *Times* London bureau did not even have news agency tickers. James Reston recalled that when he first began working there, he asked Frederick Birchall where the tickers were. Birchall replied: "We don't have any. We think they discourage the reporters from going out and getting the news on their own."[62]

In 1940 and 1941, *Times* Berlin reporters got much of the primary news on their own, and left the secondary news to the wire services. The secondary stories continued to be news about the Jews. During the first

2 full years of war, the *Times* used almost twice as many wire stories about the conditions of Jews as articles written by its own reporters. Of the 38 stories about the Jews that originated in Berlin and were published in 1940 and 1941, 13 came from the *Times* itself, 16 from the Associated Press, and 9 from United Press. Even if New York specifically asked for a story, the Berlin bureau might not provide it. In early 1941, for example, James asked Enderis to have the *Times*' Amsterdam correspondent send something on the establishment of a ghetto there. The bureau chief deferred. Enderis explained that he had just managed to get the Amsterdam correspondent released from German custody, and that given "his present position," the correspondent preferred not to send anything. Nothing was available about the Amsterdam ghetto in Berlin, he added, and an Amsterdam stringer assured him there was no foundation to the "Amsterdam ghetto rumor." The *Times* went ahead and ran an AP story on the Germans ordering non-Jews out of the "the old Jewish quarter of Amsterdam" in preparation for a possible ghetto there.[63]

The wire service reporters, particularly the senior correspondents – Lochner for the AP and Frederick Oeschsner for UP – may have also been more interested in the Jewish story than their *Times* counterparts. Lochner had arranged for Rabbi Nussbaum to meet with Arthur Sulzberger to inform him about the Madagascar plan as well as other concerns. Ruth Nussbaum considered Lochner "a great friend of ours," who would pass along information about the Germans' plans for the Jews and "was very helpful in many ways."[64] In his book, *What About Germany,* published in 1942, Lochner devoted several pages to the plight of the Jews, describing forced labor battalions, lower food rations, and deportations to Poland.[65] UP correspondent Oechsner included an entire chapter on "The Anti-Semite" in his 1942 book, *This Is the Enemy*, in which he too chronicled the 9 years of waves of Jewish persecution, "each exceeding the previous one in ferocity."[66]

In contrast, there was only one reference to Jews in *Times* reporter Percy Knauth's 233-page book, *Germany in Defeat*, published in 1946, after the camps were liberated and the full horrors of the Holocaust were well known. Knauth noted that two of several concentration camp inmates he met in Buchenwald were Jews. (When the book was published, Knauth had already left the *Times* and was working for *Time* magazine.) Even Tolischus did not address the Jewish situation as a question worthy of much attention in his 1940 book, *They Wanted War*, published after he had left Germany and was free to write whatever he liked. He briefly mentioned that Jews were banned from the press and from the arts, and were not allowed to receive marriage aid. He mentioned Jews in general references to Hitler's opponents, but he wrote nothing about the centrality of anti-Semitism in Nazi ideology.[67]

The fact that the *Times* tended to use wire service stories for its reporting on the condition of Jews in Germany made it less likely that the articles would receive prominent display. News organizations have a decided preference for their own staff-produced work. Yet the stories that were published, all inside the paper, left little doubt about how difficult the situation had become for Germany's remaining Jews. There was no doubt about their authenticity; official pronouncements or reporters' first-hand observations provided the basis for most of these stories. Comparing the wire service and *Times* stories about Jews also revealed an interesting pattern. The stories provided by the *Times* Berlin bureau included notes of optimism that punctuated the overall story of discrimination and deportation.

Times stories published in 1940 described an ever-tightening stranglehold on Jews in Germany. Jews could shop for food only between noon and 2 P.M. when little was left and what was available was second rate. Jews had to remain indoors after 8 P.M., although an article gamely reassured that "the hardship of this is less than it might appear" because they could not attend theater, concerts, or opera anyway, and would have put their non-Jewish friends at risk by visiting. (A new regulation allowed landlords to break the lease of a non-Jew who regularly received visits from Jews.) Jews had plenty to occupy them during the day, however. Of Berlin's remaining 96,000 Jews, almost one-third were forced to clean streets, shovel snow, build roads, and perform other manual labor. For the minuscule number of Jews still able to emigrate in the summer of 1940, new regulations specified precisely what they could take with them; an adult Jewish woman could carry two dresses, two aprons, one pullover, two pairs of street shoes, three personal towels, and three dish towels.[68]

Some of the new regulations were adaptations to the war, as the British began bombing German cities in 1941. Jewish laborers, unlike Aryans, were not paid for their time in air shelters, or entitled to recover for damage they suffered in air raids, the *Times* reported. Nor were Jewish hospitals allowed to paint red crosses on their roofs to alert British planes that life-saving institutions lay below. Soon Jews were also banned from public transportation if it would mean taking a seat that would otherwise go to an Aryan, and from sleeping and dining cars entirely. Jews could not use phones even for emergencies.[69]

As the war came home to Germany, conditions for American reporters there, which had long been difficult, grew worse. "By March 1941, like many in the American press colony, I had had enough," *Times* correspondent Knauth said, "enough of being bombed by British fliers to whom, in our hearts, we wished all luck as we took shelter from their bombs; enough of listening to Nazi propagandists telling us what we should write of Germany's greatness, enough of being checked on day and night by the Gestapo shadowers."[70] Knauth was so discouraged he left Berlin the following month for a job in the *Times*' Sunday Department in New York,[71] leaving just Peters and Enderis in Berlin. To AP correspondent Lochner, the turning point came later – after August 1941 – but he found the situation just as bleak. "The position of the American correspondents became increasingly difficult," Lochner wrote. "More and more we were excluded from press conferences staged in honor of pro-Axis statesmen. More and more we had to listen to vulgar diatribes against America and the American chief of state at the daily press pow-wows."[72]

During the second half of 1941, the Germans introduced new restrictions on Jews in the Reich. A *Times* story, by the Stockholm bureau's Bernard Valery, described stepped up action against Jews, including house searches and the appointment of "a high SS leader, Herr Eichmann." Eichmann, whose first name, Adolf, did not appear in the story, "has been invested with full powers regarding treatment of Jews, which tends to make him a virtual dictator over them," the story explained. Interestingly, the article's headline, written by editors in New York, told a different story. "Unrest in Reich Cited in Sweden; 'Opposition Circles' Appear and 'Pessimists' Are Being Arrested, Says Report." Deep in the story it made clear that "so-called 'opposition circles' . . . first of all, means those Jews still living in the country."[73]

The following month, those Jews encountered the ultimate form of social segregation – they were forced to wear a large yellow star bearing the black superscription, "Jude." The *Times* carried a UP story about the mandate that all Jews older than the age of 6 wear the star firmly sewn to the left breast of a piece of clothing. When the regulation went into effect on September 19, 1941, the *Times* reported that a "considerable number" of the stars "were seen on Jews standing in line before food shops" after

4 P.M., the new hour Jews were allowed to shop. The reporter noted that most Jews wore the stars on their topcoats because only one was issued per Jew at a cost of 10 pfennigs and the stars had to be permanently attached. The significance of the star was also apparent, although the story's placement on page nine might suggest that it had not been. "This represents the first time in history Jews have been required to wear signs of identification in Germany," the article stated flatly. Another article, also on page nine, explained the "35 provisions" issued by the German government on how to wear the star. It was not enough to wear the star on public streets. The star had to be worn, for example, every time a Jew stepped into his yard, or whenever he answered the doorbell to face a gentile. If he covered the star with a shopping bag or briefcase while walking on the street, he would be sent to a concentration camp. A later story suggested the law's impact on Germany's dwindling Jewish population: 200 Jews committed suicide in Berlin.[74]

That fall, Jews were also being evicted from their apartments and told not to look for new living quarters, the *Times* reported. Aryans were moved into each apartment after an auction of its contents. The October 23 issue of *Voelkischer Beobachter*, the Nazi Party organ the *Times* had been eager to advertise in 7 years earlier, contained 17 auction notices covering two score apartments in upscale neighborhoods, a *Times* story reported. "The sales are said to be well attended" as they offer linen and wearing apparel, carpets, typewriters, radios, silverware, and vacuum cleaners. Similar sales were scheduled in Frankfurt, Mannheim, and Breslau, the *Times* noted. A *Times* reporter apparently attended an auction in the "fashionable West End, which had attracted what Berliners disparagingly call an East End crowd, professionals and amateurs," the *Times* stated. "The atmosphere was that of a popular holiday with the auctioneer master of ceremonies and 'the life of the party.'"[75]

While furniture was being shipped from the West End to the East End of Berlin, the Jews who owned that furniture were being shipped to Poland, according to the many wire service accounts the *Times* carried in 1940 and 1941. Before he left Berlin in 1941, the *Times*' Knauth came upon a roundup of Jews near where he lived. Knauth said that when he asked a policeman what was happening, he was told, without qualification, "These are Jews. They are being sent away to be resettled."[76]

In February 1940, the *Times* reported in stunning detail about deportations from Stettin. According to the UP version in the *Times*, Nazi Party officials and policemen appeared at the doors of 800 Stettin Jews, told them to pack a single suitcase with clothes, a bundle of food, and cooking utensils, and be ready to leave within 8 hours. A week later, the *Times* Berlin bureau reported that only 20 Jews, the residents of an orphanage, were left in Stettin. Even the 80 inhabitants of two Jewish homes for the elderly, the oldest being 86, were expelled. "Those who could not walk were carried to the station on stretchers," the *Times* explained. The 1,100 Jews then left Stettin at 4 A.M. aboard "a long train of freight cars," it was reported. "Not all of these cars, in spite of the freezing cold, were closed nor had any provision been made to heat them. Before leaving, each person received 10 marks in cash and a small bag of cold food."[77]

The train's destination – German-controlled Poland. Two weeks later, the *Times* reported the conditions there. "The Stettin Jews . . . are said to have found the existing barracks so badly overcrowded and the food and sanitary arrangements so inadequate the local German officials refused to take responsibility for any further transports that might arrive," the *Times* Berlin bureau reported. As part of a pattern of making the best of a bad situation, the *Times* found a silver lining. For one thing, Berlin officials were not responsible for what happened to the Stettin Jews. Local Stettin officials issued the deportation order without consulting Berlin, the *Times* explained, and the order could not be rescinded. "[B]ut there is ironic justification in its fulfillment since it has probably saved other German Jews from a similar fate," the *Times* reported. The "highest authorities" had stepped in and stopped further deportations from old Reich territory.[78]

That did not do much for the 200 Stettin Jews who died within a month of their arrival in Poland, according to the *Times*.[79] Nor did it ultimately signal a change in German policy, which was apparent to other journalists as soon as the deportations were halted. Former *Nation* editor Oswald Garrison Villard wrote a letter to the *Times* editor warning that the halt "can only be a temporary interruption for the determination to 'wind up' the Jewish situation in this way was manifest when I was recently in Berlin." There was little doubt where this policy of dumping thousands of people into "the greatest concentration camp in history" would lead – "one vast charnel house," he predicted. "For sadistic cruelty – yes, for deliberate wholesale murder – I know of nothing in history to surpass this atrocity." Villard ended his letter with a plea: "It is my earnest hope that THE TIMES will continue to focus public attention upon the plight of the Jewish victims of Hitler bestiality."[80]

Within months, the deportations started again. "Before the present hostilities began Chancellor Hitler stated publicly that another war would mean the elimination of the Jews," an August 1940 AP story carried by the *Times* stated. "Now city after city is systematically being cleared of Jews." That the deportations were part of an overall German strategy was reaffirmed in two separate Nazi publications, *Schwarze Korps* and *Voelkischer Beobachter*, and picked up by the *Times*.[81]

The pace of deportations quickened in 1941 with Viennese Jews being targeted in February 1941. A *Times* story carrying Knauth's byline from Berlin confirmed "foreign reports of the mass deportation of Jews from Vienna to Poland," although it still tried to sound a positive note, adding "the forced migration does not seem to have reached the extent reported abroad."[82] The *Times* story is tellingly silent on the "foreign reports" to which it was referring. The reports were from the JTA.[83] James had conveyed news of the reports to Enderis in Berlin.[84]

A week later, another *Times* story – this one with a Vienna dateline meaning the reporter had traveled to the Austrian city – provided more details. "The large-scale transfer of Viennese Jews to Poland seems to be well under way," the *Times* story stated. "The first train left here Feb. 14 with 960 deportees and a second train five days later with nearly 1,100 bound for an unannounced destination, presumably the Lublin region of Poland.... By next Fall, if not earlier, it is planned to remove all of Vienna's 50,000 to 60,000 Jews, leaving this the first large city in the world without Jewish population. Ultimately, it is proposed to expel all Jews from the entire Reich." Those facts, however, did not appear until the sixth paragraph; the top of the story emphasized that Jews could avoid being shipped to Poland if they could come up with the money to transport themselves to America. The story sounded a hopeful note. "The majority, possibly all those deported, have found their new homes much more comfortable than they expected or even dared hope, according to telegrams received by relatives or friends remaining in Vienna under 'prepare for departure' order," the story said. "For the present and presumably the indefinite future their living quarters are new wooden barracks with electric lights and heat, the telegrams stated."[85]

By October 1941, Berlin's Jews were joining those from Vienna on the one-way trip to Poland. Relying on AP and UP accounts, the *Times* described the arrival in Berlin of 20,000 Jews from the Rhineland on their way to Poland. Berlin Jews were soon to follow. "The evacuation of

Jews – perhaps the greatest campaign against them since the 'window smashing' of Nov. 9, 1938 – has continued in full swing for several days, it was learned from usually reliable sources," the *Times* version of a UP story stated. "Special transports of 1,000 or more Jews leave nightly for Poland, and it is said that at least 20,000 will be sent to that country."[86]

Again, the stories, which were based on first-hand observation and official Nazi publications, made clear German intentions. "Complete elimination of Jews from European life now appears to be fixed German policy," an AP story in the *Times* stated. "Several times each week transports now start eastward with Jews from the Rhineland and Westphalia, Berlin, Prague or Vienna." The refugees, most of whom were on their way to Litzmannstadt, [the German name for Lodz] although some were being sent to Riga or Minsk, had to leave behind wedding rings, watches, fountain pens, and shaving outfits, according to Jewish sources quoted in the *Times*. Two days later, the *Times* carried an AP account that 48,000 Prague Jews had been sent east and all Jews were to be cleared out of Bohemia-Moravia cities "within a short time," according to *Dienst Aus Deutschland*, the Nazi commentary. Only 90,000 of the 200,000 Jews in the protectorate at the time of German occupation were left, the story stated.[87]

A United Press reporter went to a surburban Berlin freight yard to watch Jews getting on trains and leaving for "'somewhere in Poland.'" He noticed that the Jews, a score at a time, left canvas-covered trucks to board the freight cars. Jews with special passes were allowed in the yard, presumably to say goodbye to friends or relatives on their way to Poland. "Those Jews leaving the yard showed few signs of emotion," he wrote in the account published in the *Times*. "One was asked whether the train was made up of passenger or freight cars. Casting a quick glance over his shoulder, he said, 'Freight cars – but they are full of people.'"[88]

Since Knauth's departure in April, the *Times* Berlin bureau had been limping along with just Enderis and Peters. In August, Peters broke his wrist and decided he too had had enough. He left Berlin that fall. George Axelsson, an experienced 42-year-old, was to replace him. The Swedish-born Axelsson had become a *Times* staff member in 1936, after covering the Spanish Civil War as a freelance writer. A big, heavyset blond and horse-racing fan, he had first been based in Paris for the *Times* and had jumped from trouble spot to trouble spot. In 1940, he followed the German armies as they ringed British forces at Dunkirk. He then returned to German-occupied Paris as caretaker of the *Times* bureau there.[89] Transmission problems meant that Axelsson filed few stories from occupied France. After months of frustration, it was decided that he would close the Paris bureau. Axelsson joined the depleted Berlin bureau in October 1941.

The addition of Axelsson, however, did not alter the bureau's tendency to put the most positive spin on the increasingly desperate situation of Reich Jews. If anything, the stories during what would prove to be Axelsson's short reign became even more strained.[90] In perhaps the strangest story of them all – one of just three bylined stories from Berlin during the first 2 years of war, and the only story that appeared alone on the page and was relatively long (13 paragraphs) – Axelsson came up with a novel explanation for the intensification of attacks on German Jews. Anti-Semitism had increased because non-Jews' attitude toward Jews had softened, Axelsson explained, thus the government had to lay a "propaganda barrage." The main thrust of the story seemed to be to argue that "the rigorous official attitude toward Jews does not have the complete support of fair-minded Germans." In addition, the story suggested that deportations to Poland might in fact be a blessing. Jews deported to Poland "are proving themselves to be experienced technical workers," the story continued. "At Litzmannstadt [Lodz] they are paid one and a quarter marks a day and provided with board, lodging and medical care, the latter being extended by Jewish doctors and nurses sent from the Reich for that purpose."[91] (That was not how Frederick Oeschsner of the UP saw it. In his book he wrote that the Jews, after "a nightmare trip to the East," arrived in Poland to live in "squalid, unsanitary houses" in the ghettos or were sent to labor camps.[92]) Axelsson did not cite a single source for any of his observations.

Another strange story, again from the Berlin bureau but this time without a byline, described an interview with a "high ranking Storm Trooper manager" of 11 war plants. The story, based on the interview and visits to three factories, was a sympathetic profile of the beleaguered manager, who was trying to solve his labor problem "by mass recruiting of foreign workers and by organizing the board, lodging and leisure time questions somewhat in the manner of a captain of an immigrant steamer looking after his passengers." The reporter seemed impressed with "my manager guide, who combined in his forceful personality the top-flight energetic executive as represented in most movies and a Nazi evangelist."[93]

In mid-November 1941, Propaganda Minister Joseph Goebbels laid out a 10-point charter for the Nazi campaign against Jews, which the

Times reported on page 11 from a UP account. (In this case, James was not pleased to use a wire service story. "Upee twentyfour hours ahead you on Jewish story," he chided Enderis by wire.[94]) "In this historical showdown every Jew is our enemy, regardless of whether he is vegetating in a Polish ghetto or delays his parasitic existence in Berlin or Hamburg, or blows the war trumpets in New York and Washington," the story quoted Goebbels. "The current developments," Dr. Goebbels said, "are fulfilling Adolf Hitler's prophecy on Jan. 30, 1939, that the Jews in Europe would be exterminated if 'international finance succeeds in hurling the nations into a world war.'"[95]

The *New York Times* Berlin bureau would not be there to cover the fulfillment of Hitler's prophecy. After Germany declared war on the United States in the wake of Pearl Harbor, German authorities rounded up all American correspondents in Berlin – with one exception. Guido Enderis was the only American journalist who was not arrested and detained in Bad Nauheim. As he had during World War I, Enderis was allowed to remain in residence at the Adlon Hotel.[96] As a citizen of neutral Sweden, Axelsson was not detained either. The *Times* even had hoped he might be able to stay in Berlin as its correspondent "directly or indirectly." Enderis proceeded to methodically close the bureau, leasing the space to a German news bureau "for the duration of hostilities."[97] For this war, however, Enderis did not remain in Berlin. He joined the *Times*' enlarged Berne bureau, while Axelsson went to the *Times* Stockholm bureau. From their respective bureaus, the two former Berlin correspondents would continue to follow the escalating war on the Jews.

3

"Worthy of France"

The Vichy Government's Anti-Semitic Laws and Concentration Camps

EDITORS at the *New York Times* first learned that 7,000 Jews from Baden and other western provinces of Germany had been sent to France not from the *Times'* three reporters in Berlin. Nor did the news come from the *Times'* three reporters in France. It came from Arthur Sulzberger's cousin.

By the summer of 1940, Fritz Sulzberger, who had sought Arthur's help in immigrating to America, had settled in Southbridge, a small town in Massachusetts, and was again practicing medicine. His wife and two children were with him, but he had left his 68-year-old mother, Bertha, in Karlsruhe in the province of Baden. In October 1940, Fritz read in another newspaper that all the Jews in Baden had been deported to France. "As my mother is living in Baden you can imagine how worried I am," he wrote his cousin Arthur, whom he then asked to help obtain more information.[1] Arthur responded that he was not sure he could help. "Some time ago, when we asked our office to make inquiries, we got word back that the government frowned on our using our bureau for any reason other than for legitimate news purposes," he wrote Fritz. "However, I shall see what can be done. If we cannot reach your mother specifically it's possible that we can find out if the Baden story is true." He then forwarded Fritz's letter to his managing editor, Edwin James, with a note asking him to "see what you can do in connection with the attached."[2]

The Baden story was true. Four days later the *Times* reported that Jews from Baden, the Palatinate, and the Saar had been sent to France in late October.[3] Fifteen days after that, it was confirmed that Bertha Sulzberger was among those 7,000 and had been interned in Camp Gurs at the base of the Pyrenees. Over the next year, Arthur Sulzberger worked gallantly to free the older woman – whom he had never met and to whom he was related only distantly and then by marriage – from one of the worst of the several concentration camps for Jews and other "undesirables" in France. Yet, the publisher's private efforts were never buttressed by public gestures. His newspaper never condemned the French concentration camps in an editorial. In fact, the *Times*' only editorial comment was to support the State Department's decision to refuse a French offer to let interned Jewish refugees immigrate to the United States. Sulzberger, at the least, condoned the *Times* coverage of the treatment of Jews in France, even though *Times* correspondents wrote story after story rationalizing the French government's anti-Semitic legislation and excusing the deplorable conditions in the French camps.

When the Germans invaded France in May 1940, Percy J. Philip, a Scotsman, headed the five-reporter bureau in Paris. He had been hired at the end of the First World War by James, who was then Paris bureau chief. Philip, known for his "long experience in French affairs and redeeming love of France and the French," succeeded James as bureau chief in 1931.[4] Lansing Warren, a 46-year-old Californian, had also been hired by James during his Paris duty. After graduating from Stanford University, Warren had served as an ambulance driver in France during World War I and won the French Carte de Combattan and Croix de Guerre. Jobs at various California newspapers led him to the European staff of the *Chicago Tribune.* The *Times* lured him from the *Tribune* in 1926. Over the next decade and a half, Warren was based in Paris, although he traveled throughout Southern Europe for the *Times.* Gaston H. Archambault, a French native known as "Archie," had been working for American newspapers for 40 years, including stints at the *New York Herald*, *Chicago Daily News*, and *New York Sun*, before joining the *Times* in 1933. He was also a World War I veteran, having spent 41 months in the trenches and winning the Croix de Guerre. Daniel Brigham, a 31-year-old American, was a relative newcomer, having joined the bureau in 1936 after having been a freelance journalist. Newest of all was Jerzy Szapiro, the *Times*' former Warsaw bureau chief, who had fled Poland through Rumania to Paris shortly after the German invasion of his country.

The 200 German planes dropping 1,100 bombs on Paris in early June 1940 must have looked familiar to Szapiro as he and his *Times* colleagues sat in their office at 37 Rue Caumartin, churning out front-page stories.[5] On June 10, the *Times* reported that Nazi tanks were within 35 miles of Paris. The next day it said the government had fled the capital. The *Times* reporters, along with assorted relatives and staff people, were not far behind.

Eleven people crammed into three decrepit cars and headed south, away from the German invaders on highways jammed with people and vehicles. Four million French, Belgian, and others flooded the highways ahead of the Germans. "We left in that crawling, choking stream of vehicles," Lansing Warren later wrote. "All of Paris was on the go, in the midst of a fog of thick oily smoke which had rolled over the Seine Valley for two days."[6] A few days later, having spent the nights sleeping in the grass by the side of the road or under the verandah of an abandoned restaurant, they arrived at the Orleans home of the office secretary. "Archie and I left the party there, after a wash, for Tours to get and file news," Philip said.

There was plenty of news to file. As Philip and Archambault typed in Tours and tried to send their stories to New York, the Germans took Paris and broke through the famed Maginot Line. "If my despatches [sic] were lousy as I think they were you can set it down to all the anxiety and tiredness of these two days," Philip explained to James.[7] On June 23, the *Times* reported that the French had signed a truce with the Reich. The *Times* bureau reestablished itself in Vichy, the seat of the new French government. The bureau soon found some stability, unlike many of the "human avalanche" of French, Belgians, Luxembourgers, Dutch, Poles, and Jewish refugees from the Reich who rolled into unoccupied France in the summer of 1940. A million and a half young Frenchmen were herded in the opposite direction, taken to prisoner-of-war camps in Germany.[8]

The *Times* journalists' job in France was to make sense of the chaos, a task made more difficult by the departure of three of its five reporters. Szapiro followed the Polish government-in-exile to London, where he continued to work for the *Times* and the exile government's public relations operation. As a citizen of Britain with which France was now at war, Philip had to leave the country, even though he made a personal, ultimately unsuccessful appeal to Vice Prime Minister Pierre Laval to let him stay. The *Times* moved Philip to Ottawa, replacing his fellow Brit, Frederick Birchall. "Mr. Philip has been away four weeks to a day, during which time Mr. Warren, Mr. Brigham and myself have been holding the fort, not without difficulties both material and moral," Archambault wrote somewhat forlornly to James in July.[9] Before long, Brigham would be gone as well, dispatched to Berne, Switzerland, where he would be a persistent problem for his editors in New York.

The *Times* editors seemed to have faith in the two remaining reporters, Archambault and Warren.[10] They would cover the southern third of

France controlled by the newly installed government of Marshal Henri Philippe Petain and Vice Prime Minister Laval. George Axelsson, recently hired and back from covering the British forces' retreat to Dunkirk, would cover German-occupied France, the remaining two-thirds of the country that included Paris. He also would serve as caretaker of the *Times* bureau in that beleaguered city. Unlike in Berlin, where the *Times* would rely heavily and uncharacteristically on wire services for their news about the Jews, these three reporters wrote almost all the *Times* stories about the Jews in France in the year and a half before America's entry into the war.

One of the first stories to bear Axelsson's byline and a Paris dateline appeared in July 1940 and was about the 30,000 Jews, "mostly poor, small shopkeepers," who had decided to stay in Paris after the German invasion. Like much of his and his colleagues' reporting over the next year and a half, the story strove, one might even say strained, to strike a positive note about the fate of France's Jews. Bearing the fairly sanguine headline, "Paris Jews Await Their Fate Calmly," the story noted that Jews were besieging the U.S. Embassy for visas and pleading with the Soviet consulate to place them under its protection. Yet, the story concluded, most Jews were resigned to their fate, which they were convinced would not be too bad. During a tour of the city's ghetto in the Fourth Arrondissement, or ward, "where lived really Orthodox Jews," Axelsson interviewed an elderly man in the second-hand clothing business. "For seven years I have done nothing but get out of Hitler's way," the story quoted the old man. "First I left Berlin, then Vienna, then Prague, so this time I decided I'll stay. I have done enough wandering, and whatever happens now I don't care." Again sounding a theme that would repeat itself over the next year and a half, the story attributed the more positive outlook for French Jews to the fact that the French, not the Germans, would be in control. The Petain government "alone would decide what is going to happen to us," the article quoted a doctor. In the reporter's neutral voice, Axelsson also reassured that "[r]umors of a census of the Jewish population in Paris are pure invention."[11]

Two months later that "invention" was enacted into law. An ordinance adopted in late September 1940 required a census of Jews in the occupied zone, prohibited Jews in the free zone from returning to occupied France, and specified that Jewish shops in the occupied zone must bear a sign indicating its Jewish ownership, the *Times* reported. A follow-up story said that Jews would have to register within 18 days and have signs in their shop windows within 28 days. Imprisonment, heavy fines, confiscation of property, or all three, would be the punishment for failing to comply. The story, which had Axelsson's byline, estimated that the law would affect 50,000 Jews. The story also described how the Paris newspapers reported the news. *La France au Travail*, for example, printed the decree with the headline: "Fight against parasites takes shape."[12]

The ordinance seemed to have the desired effect; the *Times* reported 2 days later that Jews were registering in "great numbers" at police stations and "subprefectures" (a prefect was the local executive agent of the French state) throughout the occupied zone. By November, the Germans were appointing "French administrators" for "Jewish" concerns. The measure, a *Times* story stated, was designed to "suppress 'the real danger to French economic life represented by the solidarity of the Jews.'" Over the next few months, short items would appear from time to time updating the "Aryanization" of Jewish businesses, which in January 1941, for example, was "going forward rapidly."[13] Each item expanded the list of Jewish businesses sold to an "Aryan" purchaser through a German-appointed commissioner, including major operations such as the Galeries Lafayette department store and the investment fortunes of Lazard Freres and the Rothschilds.

When the French government in August 1940 seized the "wealth and private estates" of Baron Edouard de Rothschild and Louis Louis-Dreyfus, "who hold two of the five great fortunes of France," the *Times* reported the news on the front page but never mentioned that Rothschild and Louis-Dreyfus were Jews. The story suggested that their fortunes had been confiscated because they had fled to the United States; the Baron and Baroness de Rothschild, and their daughter, Bethsabeem, arrived in New York, the story noted, carrying a bag of jewels valued at $1 million. The story also mentioned others whose fortunes had been confiscated, most of whom were Jews, but none of whom were identified as such in the *Times* story. Only in a page eight story the next day did the *Times* mention that French radio had inaugurated "an anti-Jewish campaign" that accused the prominent citizens who fled France at the time of the military collapse, including the Rothschilds, of proving that they were "Jews before they were French."[14]

Once the anti-Semitic ordinance for the occupied zone made clear that the Germans, not the French, would dictate what would happen to the Jews in the northern part of the country, the *Times* reported the information in short, straightforward stories of no more than a couple of paragraphs. The articles resembled those that other *Times* reporters had written about similar legislation adopted in Austria and Czechoslovakia when the Germans took control there. They read like the stories still other *Times* reporters were writing in 1940 and 1941 about anti-Semitic legislation in Rumania, Slovakia, Yugoslavia, Hungary, Bulgaria, Belgium, Luxembourg, and the Netherlands as the Germans solidified their new Axis alliances. The *Times* presented the news with minimal analysis of the Germans' true intentions; presumably, their intentions, at least the most immediate ones, were apparent – to socially and economically isolate the Jews in any country over which they had influence. In southern France, however, the *Times* reporters had a different agenda. They almost never reported the news of the French government's mounting anti-Semitic decrees without interpreting the moves to cast the Vichy government in the most positive possible light.

The first Vichy legislation against the Jews came in August 1940, just 2 months after the fall of France. The *Times* reported that the French government had removed restrictions that muzzled press attacks on Jews, effectively freeing newspapers to engage in an anti-Semitic campaign. Still, the article sounded a note of caution, explaining that the Vichy government's attitude "has not been defined on the Jewish question." A month later, the government's attitude began to be defined. On October 2, Lansing Warren reported that the French government was about to issue a law establishing a "definite status for Jews in France." He predicted that the decree would ban Jews from public office and from positions in the press, and would set quotas for their participation in education, medicine, and other professions. Another story reassured, however, that the law would not be an extension of the notorious Nuremberg Laws to France. Besides, the government had announced that "no racial or religious discrimination is intended," Warren wrote.[15]

The story officially announcing the measure, again by Warren, confirmed that Jews would be excluded from the press, radio, and movies, and with rare exception from high public offices, from educational and judicial positions, and from becoming military officers. Still the second paragraph noted that "this measure is less drastic than the German laws" and is "somewhat more moderate" than those in the occupied zone. The law allowed Jews to retain their civil rights as French citizens and did not prohibit marriages between Jews and non-Jews. It also included a "more moderate" definition of who is a Jew than the German regulations. Only in the penultimate paragraph of a 14-paragraph story did it mention another law published that day that authorized the government to intern foreign Jews in concentration camps.[16,i] Not all reporters were quite so convinced of the law's liberality. *Time* magazine described Vichy's decrees as "so un-French, so very German in accent that the outside world found it hard to believe they came from the mouth of an old fighter for France . . . Petain."[17]

The conviction that Petain was a fighter for France may be what led the *Times* astray in its reporting on Vichy. Much as they had with Hitler and Goering in the early stages of the Nazi regime, *Times* reporters identified a split between the head of state, Henri Petain, and his second-in-command, Pierre Laval, over the Jewish question. Like Goering, Laval was portrayed as the hardliner pushing for the most severe anti-Jewish laws, whereas, like Hitler, Petain, was described as resisting more extreme measures.[ii] When Laval was ousted from his position as vice-prime minister at the end of 1940, the *Times* hailed it as a great victory for the anti-Nazi forces in Vichy.[iii] In an unusual move, former Paris Bureau Chief Philip, who had been sent to Ottawa in August, wrote a letter to the editor revealing the *Times* reporters' perspective. Petain was "actuated only by love of his country," Philip explained, whereas Laval was motivated by "hatred of England." The letter suggested that Philip's "former colleagues" in the Vichy bureau had all along been interpreting the situation in those terms but could not state it directly until Laval had been kicked out. Philip did not limit his support for Petain to an outsider's letter to the editor. The Sunday after his letter appeared he wrote a column for the News of the Week in Review section, hailing Petain as "France's savoir," who decided to "abandon the unequal struggle" against the Germans only because of "love and pity for his people." Philip was not the only *Times* reporter enamored with Petain. Vichy reporter Archambault wrote a January 1941

[i] Marrus and Paxton, *Vichy France and the Jews*, 12, assess the law differently, concluding that Vichy's Statut des juifs, particularly the authorizing of the internment of foreign Jews, "went farther than the German ordinance of the previous week."

[ii] *Ibid.*, 17–9, concluded that both Petain and Laval, although not rabid anti-Semites themselves, were basically indifferent, leaving the "field to zealots."

[iii] Historians have been more equivocal, suggesting a variety of reasons for Laval's ouster, but the consensus seems to be that his removal did not signal a desire to change basic Vichy policies. *Ibid.*, 83.

magazine piece about the "Frenchman of the Hour," Marshall Petain, whose "honesty and dignity give the key to his character."[18]

Identifying the *Times* reporters' preference for Petain and the Vichy government is easier than explaining how or why it came to be. One possibility is that support for Vichy tended to play into the U.S. war aims, which journalists by and large accepted. The government's goal was to portray the United States as defending the freedom-loving peoples of the world against Nazi tyranny. That the people might collaborate with the tyrants did not fit this world view. The government particularly sought to maintain this view of the French, as embodied in the Vichy government and in Petain himself. Laval should be attacked "constantly with the greatest violence, describing him as a traitor and German agent," the government's propaganda strategy for France advised. "Continue to avoid direct attacks on Petain," or the Vichy government generally, which should neither be blamed nor excused "for weakness in the face of German pressure."[19]

The reporters own sensibilities probably also had a role. As it did in Berlin and elsewhere, the *Times* in France tended to hire correspondents who were natives, such as Archambault, or had a particular affinity for the country and the culture, such as Philip and Warren. It is not surprising then that correspondents in France tended to sympathize with France and the French people. That identification might have extended to the subtle, French anti-Semitism that assumed Jews, even French-born ones, were somehow foreign. Other American correspondents in France seemed to have accepted that perspective. "Jews usually regard themselves as quite French, explaining the obvious differences as being due to greater intelligence or brilliance," P. W. Whitcomb, an AP correspondent in France wrote in 1942 explaining why Jews should not participate in any American propaganda efforts toward France. "But the French feel this innate difference keenly, and though a national tact prevents them from emphasizing it in peace time, war and defeat have produced a nerve-wracked resentment of non-French points of view."[20] This might have led some journalists to be less harsh toward Vichy's anti-Semitic legislation, which tended to be cast in nationalistic, rather than strictly racial, terms.

Petain, or the "Frenchman of the Hour" as Archaumbault described him, presided over dozens of concentration camps, the administration of which constituted "one of the darkest chapters in Vichy policy toward the Jews."[21] Even before the German invasion, France had established a system of internment camps for foreigners, including German Jewish refugees who had fled Nazi oppression, and Spaniards and international volunteers who had rushed across the border at the collapse of Republican resistance to the fascist Franco regime. Under Vichy, the number of camps grew to 31 and Jews, either those dumped there by the Germans or rounded up by the French, were their principal inhabitants.

The *Times*' first report that Jews were being imprisoned in camps in the unoccupied zone came in a roundabout way. Deep in a September 1940 article about the arrival of the Dixie Clipper airplane – the *Times* routinely covered the New York landing of ships or planes from overseas – was an interview with Dr. Joseph Stokes, Jr., of the American Friends Service Committee. Stokes had just toured unoccupied France for the Quaker relief organization. Nine paragraphs into the 12-paragraph story, Stokes described the existence of concentration camps in Saint-Cyprien and Gurs for Jews from the French provinces, Alsace and Lorraine, that had been incorporated into the Reich. Dr. Stokes would describe the conditions at Saint-Cyprien, which he visited, only as "not good." He also predicted that "many Jews" in both occupied and unoccupied France would "find their way to concentration camps." What Dr. Stokes observed were 3,000 Alsatian Jews who had been sent into the unoccupied zone in July and another 1,400 German Jews who had been pushed over the border in August.[22] Another 7,000 Jews, this time from Baden and other western German provinces joined them in October, including Bertha Sulzberger.

Fritz Sulzberger had been trying to get his mother out of Germany since January. When his father, Sigmund, who was Arthur Sulzberger's second cousin, died, so had his mother's hopes of emigrating with Sigmund's low visa number. After receiving an urgent letter from Fritz, Arthur wrote his brother David, who was with the National Refugee Service. Arthur hoped the service could help Bertha obtain a visa number to correspond with the number her husband had before he died. In the letter, Arthur told his brother that Bertha's current number from the American consulate in Stuttgart was "so high it would probably take two or three years to get around to it." As they waited for a reply, Arthur sent Fritz $50 as payment for his father's preparation of the Sulzberger family tree and asked that Fritz "use it in some way to be of assistance to your mother." The National Refugee Service, however, soon informed Arthur that it could not help advance Bertha's number, as did a "a friend in the State Department" whom Arthur contacted personally. So Bertha was still stuck in Karlsruhe with a high visa number on October 22, 1940, when, with a 20-minute notice and unable to take anything with her, she was rounded up and sent in a sealed cattle car across the border into unoccupied France.[23]

After Fritz provided the information, the *Times* story about the deportations ran on November 3, 1940. The page 21 story from the Berlin bureau focused primarily on the German government's keen interest in Vichy edicts against the Jews and the sense that "a decisive solution of the Jewish problem is gaining ground among European nations." The story noted only in passing that Jews from western German provinces had been sent to France. A more detailed story followed a week later apparently based on interviews with relief agency officials. The story gave some sense of the panic that must have seized the Jews forced out of their homes, with at most $2.50 and "very little beyond the clothes they wore." It also conveyed some of the trauma. "Much suffering resulted when families were forced to separate, the men going to one concentration camp and the women and children to another," the story explained. The men were sent mostly to Camp Saint-Cyprien, Le Vernet, or Les Milles, while the women and children, ranging in age from 6 months to 98, were sent to Gurs, the story stated. There, they "were forced to live in small wooden barracks with not enough water and practically without food supply," the *Times* reported. On a brighter note, friends and relatives could forward $50 a month for each individual in a concentration camp, the story quoted relief organizations.[24]

Whether based on the *Times* reporting or his own sources, Arthur Sulzberger knew that money and supplies could be gotten to Bertha. So soon after learning that she was in Gurs Ilot K-20, he asked Marie-Claire Raick, who, along with her family, was living in his White Plains estate, to help. Sulzberger knew Raick, a Belgian Catholic, from the summer he had boarded with her family in Brussels during a college vacation. When Germany invaded Belgium, Sulzberger had cabled Raick, urging her and her family to travel to Paris. From there, a *Times* correspondent had helped them get to the States. Sulzberger learned that Raick's sister, Jean Chabry, was living near Gurs. So Sulzberger had Raick cable her sister to see if Chabry could give Bertha $50 a month, provided by Arthur, and possibly arrange for her to live outside the camp. Raick's cable explained that Arthur's "distant cousin" had a "desperate need food clothing."[25]

A *Times* story that appeared a few days after Raick sent the cable to her sister indicated how desperate that need was. In the Gurs camp, which was "for Jews deported from German territory," conditions "have been admittedly inadequate, owing to the unexpected numbers of the internees," the story from the Vichy bureau stated. What is striking about this story, and similar ones that followed, was the emphasis on Vichy's lack of responsibility for the conditions and its gargantuan efforts to improve them. As soon as the story labeled conditions "inadequate," it immediately added that "funds have been appropriated by the government which will provide for considerable improvement." The additional francs would "provide sleeping accommodations, blankets and fuel, all of which are lacking" at Gurs. "The military commander has been doing his best to improve conditions as Winter sets in," the story stated.[26]

First-hand accounts from former internees who had arrived in the States provided a glimpse of how bad things were in the camps. Dr. Rene Hartogs told a *Times* reporter who interviewed him upon his arrival in New York that refugees transferred from one camp to another were locked in cattle cars without food, water, or sanitary equipment for as long as 4 days at a time. During his 3-day trip between camps, five prisoners committed suicide, he said. At Saint-Cyprien, nearly all 15,000 inmates were stricken with cholera and 500 died. "There were not shovels to dig graves with and no coffins to bury the bodies in," Hartogs, who had served as camp physician, told the *Times*. "We dug shallow graves with our hands and cremated those we could." A Vichy official later denied Hartogs' account of widespread cholera, declaring, in a *Times* story, that the report of a cholera epidemic was "a fable."[27]

The *Times* also printed letters from those still in Gurs. "This is the greatest tragedy the world has ever witnessed and it is hard not to get desperate," Helene Buchdahl wrote. Mela Picard recounted "the trip in the dark, cold railroad car, three nights and four days, shaken, thirsty and desperate." At the camp, she described "shivering from the cold," amidst a sea of mud, and being "separated by barbed wire" from "my boy," whom she saw but once a week. Picard wrote that there were 17 funerals yesterday and 24 today. "This alone is sufficient to lower your spirits," she wrote.[28] Estimates are that more than 1,000 people died of starvation, dysentery, and typhoid during those first few months, or more than 10% of the population.

Given these conditions, the 40,000 civilians interned in unoccupied France at the end of 1940 did everything they could to get out. Many had already obtained visas to the United States. Yet, the American consulate in Stuttgart, where many of the refugees, including Bertha, had received their visas, would not release their papers.[29] So those interned in Gurs had to apply anew to the consulate in Marseilles, meaning they would have to "go again through all the routine they had already accomplished," a *Times* story said.

Arthur Sulzberger probably knew the obstacles he would encounter in trying to get Bertha a visa. When Max Nussbaum visited him the previous summer, the rabbi's main mission was to inform the publisher of the American consulate in Berlin's reluctance to grant visas to Jews.[30] After years of trying, Nussbaum and his wife, Ruth, had finally received a visa outside the normal quota limits; Stephen Wise had found an Oklahoma congregation willing to attest to its need for a rabbi and its ability to support him financially. Before departing Berlin, the Nussbaums promised the Jewish community that as soon as they arrived in New York they would try to publicize the plight of the Jews left behind. According to Ruth Nussbaum, that is what her husband did in his two meetings with Sulzberger in September 1940.[31] But the *Times* never ran any stories about the visa problems, nor is there any record of the publisher asking his staff to look into it.

In early 1941, a rival publication, *PM*, published two stories about difficulties refugees had in being admitted to the United States. The second one charged Assistant Secretary of State Breckinridge Long of erecting unnecessary road blocks for Jews trying to immigrate. "If Mr. Long is to continue in his present position, most refugees in unoccupied France might as well give up hope of ever obtaining U.S. visas," Tabitha Patran and William Walton wrote. They concluded: "If he [Long] is not anti-Semitic himself, he has certainly countenanced anti-Semitism in the administration of a problem for which he is responsible."[32] In 1941, the *New Republic* and the *Nation* also ran stories about the difficulties the State Department and local consuls imposed on Jews hoping to immigrate.[33]

A few *Times* stories acknowledged the bureaucratic impediments, although they did so in a backhanded fashion. In a story about Viennese refugees cabling friends and relatives to send money so they could book passage to the United States and avoid deportation to Poland, the article mentioned that U.S. consuls would not issue visas unless the applicant could produce a ticket with a specific sailing date. The story also said that the German shipping line tended to overcharge refugees and impose fees for cancellations for any reason, including the unavailability of a boat. Later that month, a *Times* front-page headline read: "Last Sea Route From

Lisbon to U.S. Stops Ticket Sale to Refugees." The *Times* story explained that American Export Line ended the last remaining regular passenger service directly from Europe to the United States – the route by which thousands of Europeans had escaped. Typically, the front-page story about "refugees" never mentioned Jews.[34]

Still, the *Times* publisher persisted in trying to help his distant cousin escape. After having "received one or two rather desperate cables from the old lady," her son and his wife, Else, had decided it would be easier for Bertha to go first to Cuba and from there try to obtain a visa to the United States. So they figured out the process for obtaining a visa to Cuba. It would cost $3,510: $2,000 for an irrevocable line of credit at a Havana bank; $500 for a "land bond" to be deposited with the Cuban government; $135 for a return passage, if necessary; $350 for broker and attorney's fees; another $350 for steamship passage between Lisbon and Havana; plus assorted deposits and service fees.

The first trick was getting the visa. Having neither the funds nor the connections, Fritz and Else Sulzberger turned to their cousin. In late November 1940, Arthur Sulzberger had his assistant, Peter Brown, visit the Counsel General of Cuba in New York City. Sulzberger informed his bureau chief in Washington that Brown saw the consul "for a brief moment, but was not cordially received. Quite the contrary, the consul seemed anxious to wash his hands of anything in connection with visas." The publisher then asked Arthur Krock if he would "have someone apply to the Cuban representative in Washington to determine whether this is the best way to go about it, whether it is legal in every sense, whether this is the least expensive way, etc." Then he warned Krock to remember the *St. Louis* incident. "All of those refugees had visas but they were not permitted to land because they had been issued by the wrong authority. Incidentally, these had been secured with graft."

The Cuban ambassador in Washington proved more helpful than his counterpart in New York once he was assured Bertha Sulzberger would stay in Cuba only temporarily. The ambassador concluded that most of the expenses were "in conformity with Cuban law." The ambassador told Krock that the arrangement should be made through the consul in New York City, "but that, confidentially, they have had other complaints he is not very obliging." Instead, the ambassador suggested that the arrangements be made in Havana. Arthur Sulzberger then had his bank deposit $2,000 in a Havana account.[35]

In the meantime, Bertha Sulzberger's situation in Gurs worsened. She cabled her son: "send food, clothes, underwear and medicine." Jean Chabry had received from Bertha a list of things she needed, but could not get transportation to the camp. Fritz learned from his aunt, who was living in Portugal, that she "sends the required things continuously" to her sister, but apparently nothing got through.[36]

A *Times* story published in January made clear why Bertha was frantic for outside help. The American Friends Service Committee, which had investigators there, disclosed that 15 to 25 people per day were dying at Gurs. The report, which was picked up by a *Times* correspondent in Philadelphia, the relief organization's home base, described the camp's "unbreathable atmosphere of human hopelessness." A large number of those interned, which included 500 children and 1,200 people older than 70 years of age, were "in a state of critical undernourishment, the fatty bodies having completely disappeared," the page 24 story said. They were also under chronic threat of typhoid fever due to lice and of serious infection from the ever-present rats. In the barracks where the refugees lived, "one distinguishes confusedly rather than sees the sixty people lying on their mattresses, or standing, for there are not tables, nor chairs. The children cannot play and the women cannot work. During rain this desolate sight is accompanied with a confused noise of crying and sobs. Air space for each person is notoriously insufficient." It was also impossible to keep warm, the report noted. "The majority of the barracks are penetrable by rain and wind, and there was insufficient wood for heating the barracks or even for coffins."[37]

Yet, within 2 weeks, the headline, "Vichy to better life in internment camps," appeared atop a *Times* story from the Vichy bureau. It was the first of many *Times* stories that stressed not the suffering in the camps, but the efforts the government supposedly was making to ameliorate them. The article promised "a human solution" for the foreigners, whom the *Times* described as being interned for "reasons that range from being suspect to being destitute." Being Jewish was never mentioned. Ten days later, the *Times* Vichy bureau noted that "some improvement in conditions" had been reported for the 10,000 German Jews who were identified as inhabitants of the camp. "Most of them show appreciation," the director of the camp was quoted as saying of the "efforts that have been made 'to make conditions in the camp endurable.'" A United Press story a few days later also pointed to the steps the government was taking to improve the camps, mostly by preparing new centers to which the current inmates would be moved. The story was somewhat more careful than the *Times* had been to attribute claims of improvement to the government, quoting at length a spokesman who maintained that "the terrifying stories in the foreign press" about the camps were "absolute lies." The headline written by a *Times* editor, however, undid whatever care the UP reporter had exercised. "Refugees' Plight Is Eased by Vichy," the headline stated, without qualification. "36,000 Will Be Transferred by March 15 to Five New Camps 'Worthy' of France."[38]

At first, at least according to the *Times*, it seemed as if improvements would not be necessary for most of those languishing in French concentration camps because they would soon be allowed to leave. In December 1940, the *Times* reported that a refugee committee had received "an official Vichy government decree under which all interned refugees from Germany, Austria, Danzig and the Sudentenland part of Czecho-Slovakia who can prove that other countries are willing to admit them will be released immediately from concentration camps." The United States would be willing to go along, the *Times* suggested. A story out of Washington reported that 2,000 refugees would be able to leave the war zone after U.S. officials acted "favorably on nearly all applications." But shortly after that, a front-page story – one of the few that even touched on the plight of Jews in France – made clear that wholesale emigration of refugees was not to be. The *Times* Washington bureau reported that the U.S. government had rejected a "French plea to take exceptional measures toward facilitating the migration of thousands of refugees of many races and nationalities." The story was hazy on who those refugees might be, although the inside jump explained that the French ambassador had requested the United States and other Western Hemisphere countries provide refuge for those in France, "particularly Jews forced out of Luxembourg, Belgium and Germany."[39]

The U.S. government's rationale for rejecting the French offer became somewhat clearer the following day when the *Times* printed on page 11 the entire text of Secretary of State Cordell Hull's reply to the French ambassador. Hull indicated that the French government's concern was primarily with the German Jewish refugees dumped in France, and that the U.S. government's rejection of the request also was based on that fact. Hull indicated that under the "basic principles" of the Intergovernmental Committee on Refugees, which had been established in 1938 to try to solve the refugee crisis, "no distinctions shall be made between refugees on grounds of race, nationality or religion." Given the Vichy government's attempt to distinguish between Jewish refugees driven out of Germany and others in the camps, combined with the fact that U.S. immigration laws "do not permit of any further liberalization," the U.S. government said it would have to decline the French offer.[40]

The U.S. rejection of the French proposal for the transfer of refugees "leaves the problem here in a very acute stage," Lansing Warren wrote in a page seven story that appeared the following day. The refugees "are passing the Winter under conditions of great hardship in the insufficient shelter of hurriedly constructed camps," he wrote. Still, Warren was quick to point out the French government "has appropriated a considerable sum for the improvement of these camps," and that all inmates, whether Jewish, French, or Central Europeans, received "the same treatment."[41] In an editorial – the only one that addressed the plight of Jews in France although it never referred to Jews – the *Times* defended the State Department's position. The *Times* seemed to suggest obliquely that the State Department's real problem was that the Germans, not the French, were behind the effort to get rid of some refugees and keep others.[42] The U.S. government should "re-examine our immigration laws so far as they affect legitimate refugees," "eliminate red tape," and see that "our consuls do not abuse their discretion," the editorial stated. That, however, was as far as the government should go. "What we cannot do is to delegate to any foreign government the power to determine priorities among candidates for admission to this country," it said.[43]

Although his editorial page on principle rejected drawing distinctions among categories of refugees, Sulzberger in practice was doing everything he could for one refugee. In January 1941, Sulzberger put his Havana correspondent, Ruby Phillips, on the case. Phillips filed a petition for Bertha's entry to Cuba, attaching proof of the $2,000 Sulzberger had deposited in a Havana bank. She also signed a notarized document stating that she would personally assume financial responsibility for Bertha when she arrived in Cuba – guaranteed by her boss, of course. Phillips then put her newspaper connections to work. She had one of the *Times* stringers contact a friend, who was the director of immigration. "As you know, everything in Cuba is done through friendship," she wrote Sulzberger's assistant Peter Brown. In less than 2 months, Bertha Sulzberger's permission to immigrate to Cuba was granted "in really record time," Phillips noted, when the immigration director "took personal charge of the matter." Phillips knew to return the favor. She agreed to visit the Tiscornia Immigration Station along with a photographer to take pictures of "improvements" the director made, which "will please [him] very much."[44]

Mrs. Sulzberger's travails, however, were not yet over. Fritz Sulzberger quickly arranged with Thos. Cook & Son, a travel agent, to book first class passage from Lisbon to Havana. But Bertha's visa, which had been issued in Lisbon, had to be transferred to Marseilles, the closest port to Gurs. In the meantime, Fritz explored the possibility of moving his mother to a hotel at a cost of at least $650 for a 10-month stay. Unable to raise the money and unwilling to borrow more from Arthur, Fritz decided to let Bertha remain in Gurs. In a letter, Arthur reassured Fritz about his indebtedness, telling the doctor to send $50 or $100 whenever he could. He agreed, however, that Fritz should not spend another $700 or so to get his mother out of Gurs. So in March 1941, Bertha Sulzberger, along with over 10,000 other Jews, remained interned in the concentration camp.[45]

That month the *Times* and other American news organizations provided a first-hand account of life in five concentration camps in unoccupied France.[iv] In September, Lansing Warren had appealed to the Vichy government for permission to visit Gurs and other camps. For 6 months, the government refused his request, which had been joined by other American correspondents. Finally, in March 1941, the French government agreed to give reporters a tour. In his story announcing that American correspondents would soon be allowed to inspect some camps, Warren took credit for any improvement. "It is acknowledged in government circles that the reorganization and the improvement of conditions for interned foreigners has been to a large extent the result of the action of the American correspondents," Warren wrote. "Their continual questions and insistence upon visiting the camps have kept the whole question before the authorities."[46]

[iv] Jews in the occupied territories were also arrested and put in one of three camps, Beaune-la-Rolande and Pithiviers in Loiret and Drancy outside Paris. Marrus and Paxton, *Vichy France and the Jews*, 166. American correspondents never visited those camps, although they reported that Jews were sent there.

Over 5 days at the end of March, 19 reporters, photographers, and newsreel men, including the *Times*' Warren and a *Times* photographer, visited Récébédou, Noé, Le Vernet, Rivesaltes, and Argèles-sur-Mer. Warren did not visit Gurs, although he included descriptions of it based on accounts of inmates who had previously been imprisoned there. The three stories Warren wrote about his tour gave a general sense of camp conditions, yet poor writing and reporting made it almost impossible to figure out who was imprisoned in these camps and why. Long, roundabout sentences and vagueness created much of the confusion, but Warren's determination to vindicate Vichy also contributed to the articles' lack of clarity. It would have been one thing to have presented Vichy's "side" by attributing explanations for camp conditions to Vichy officials. But the defense came in the voice of the narrator, a far cry from the *Times*' customary objective tone.

The lead of Warren's first story made no secret of his perspective on Vichy's predicament. "Amid circumstances that are draining all her resources France is making an important effort to improve the lot of 30,000 foreigners who are still detained in camps in the free zone," read the first of 21 paragraphs on page two. The American correspondents who visited the camps were "distressed by many of the things they saw," the lead continued, but realized "that no criticism can be brought, both because of the endeavors now under way and because of the many prior claims on France's generosity that the nation is having to face." The story then contrasted the plight of "hundreds of thousands of foreign refugees" to whom the French government gave shelter in an "unexampled act of humanity," with the 1.5 million of "France's finest men" who were prisoners of war "under conditions that can hardly be as favorable for most of them as for the majority of foreigners guarded here." (André Jean-Faure, who became inspector general of camps and internment centers in April 1941, made a similar tour shortly after the correspondents and reached much harsher conclusions.[47])

Warren seemed determined to sort out those who deserved to be interned from those who did not. "There are undoubtedly certain dangerous individuals confined who merit detention," he wrote. Warren never mentioned that Jews were imprisoned for being Jews, even though they made up more than 60% of the camp population. Warren's conviction that "dangerous individuals" were imprisoned in the camps colored his approach to reporting and writing the story. The inmates he interviewed wanted to talk about "the lack of food, about the dreariness of life in the camp and even about mistreatment," he wrote with a tone of impatience. At the Rivesaltes camp, some women swarmed around him and "became hysterical." They were "thrusting notes and written pleas on the visitors at every opportunity." But Warren kept asking inmates, as he explained: "Why are you interned here and what can be done for you?" He did not, he noted, "receive many practical answers."[48]

Heinz Soffner, a former officer with the Federation of Austrian Emigrants in Paris, took issue with some of Warren's conclusions in a letter to the editor the *Times* published almost 2 weeks later. For most internees, "there was no original reason at all" for their internment, he wrote. Nor would Soffner, who had fled to New York, let the French government off the hook, blaming problems in the camps on a "stubborn, malevolent, xenophobe [sic], and even – at least for an important part – pro-fascistic and pro-Nazi French administration." His sentiment was echoed in another letter to the editor from the executive secretary of the American Committee to Save Refugees who condemned the "unintelligent – and we might add callous – handling of the refugee problem by the Vichy government."[49]

Warren wrote another, equally long story that described what he found in each camp. The story, which appeared on page 25, concentrated on the camp at Argèles-sur-Mer for Spanish militiamen. Warren labeled it the worst of all the French camps, with "crude wooden sheds without floors" where 12,000 inmates slept on vermin-filled sand and ate "extremely small portions." The good news, however, was that the number of Argèles inmates had dropped from a high of 70,000 persons, many of whom had been allowed to return to Spain. The authorities promised that the camp would soon be closed entirely. The conditions in the other camps he visited were much better, Warren wrote. Rivesaltes, for example, had concrete buildings with tiled roofs and floors that "could easily be kept clean." (Except, as Vichy's inspector general for the camps later noted, there was so little water that "basic conditions of cleanliness" were not possible.[50]) Rivesaltes held mostly Jewish women and children, although Warren did not mention that, referring to it as the family camp. Conditions in Noé and Récébédou – a large percentage of whose internees also were Jews who had spent the winter at Gurs – were better still, according to Warren. The inmates described Gurs as "hell," Warren wrote, but they insisted they were "100 per cent better off here."[51]

In the final story based on his camp tour, Warren returned to the question of who was in the camps and why, but it evinced the same confusion as his first story. Again, he seemed preoccupied with who should be allowed to emigrate on the merits and who should continue to be locked up, concluding only that each case "requires investigation." The French government's aim, Warren wrote, "has been to retain in camps only those persons who are destitute, physically unfit or unwilling to accept conditions of the working formations." (Vichy organized labor battalions for able-bodied male foreigners, about one-third of whom were Jews and two-thirds were Spaniards.) But the French government lacked the "large organization" necessary to decide in each case whether the person should be allowed to leave the camps.[52]

At the end of April, the *Times* ran two photos from the family camp at Rivesaltes, one of the barracks's interior with women crowded inside and another of a grim group of men, women, and children identified only as "some of the refugees." The following Sunday, the *Times* published those photos again in its weekly photography section, along with two others of a child eating from a bowl and group of adults crowding around the American correspondents as they toured the camps. With the headline, "Scenes of War," the caption explained that 30,000 foreigners "representing more than a score of nationalities" were held in "detention camps." The caption continued: "France is seeking to improve conditions but the problem is a tremendous one."[53]

Warren wrote a story in early May declaring that since the correspondents' visit to the internment camps "much progress has been made in the improvement of conditions for the inmates." He noted Vichy's decision to open emigration offices and distribute milk in several camps, organize instruction for children in Rivesaltes, and create a convalescent center in the two camps for elderly persons.[54] Whatever improvements took place, however, were never more than cosmetic. Historians have concluded that conditions in the French camps "were really not much different from those in Nazi concentration camps."[55]

As the last of these stories was published, Bertha Sulzberger began to make progress toward leaving France. Having received a visa from Cuba, she was transferred in April from Gurs to Les Milles, which was meant to be a jumping off place for refugees who had obtained permission to emigrate. Shortly before she arrived there, a *Times* reporter and photographer visited the camp. (The story does not have a byline.) Like the other camp stories that were soon to appear, this one presented a relatively optimistic view of conditions. Bearing the headline, "France Improving Foreigners' Camp," the *Times* reported that a visit "gives evidence of the active efforts that are being made to improve the situation of the foreigners interned in France." The camp, in a former brick factory, has "been put in passably comfortable condition," it said, with cots and straw mattresses, wood stoves heating each room, and daily medical attention.[56] The next day, the *Times* ran two photographs: one of detainees who "while away the long hours," and the other of the outside of the camp.[57] Michael Marrus and Robert Paxton have a different take on Les Milles: "Many Jews waited there for weeks or months under appalling conditions, however, as they became entangled in one bureaucratic snarl or another."[58]

Bertha Sulzberger was more fortunate than most. (In fact, another Sulzberger relative who apparently never sought Arthur's help, Paula Priester Sulzberger, died in Gurs, while her husband, Max Sulzberger, perished in Auschwitz.[59]) In May, she was moved to the Hotel Terminus Desports in Marseilles in anticipation of her voyage to Cuba. Because a condition of Bertha's visa was that her stay in Cuba be temporary, Arthur also signed an affidavit that month attesting to his willingness to provide financial support for her when she eventually immigrated to the United States. In July, Bertha received all her emigration papers to Cuba and was scheduled to depart on August 10. But *Times* Havana correspondent Phillips then raised a red flag. In June, the State Department had instructed its diplomatic and consular offices to deny visas to anyone who had parents, children, a spouse, or siblings living in territories controlled by Germany, Italy, or Russia. The *Times* reported this change in policy on its front page, purportedly the result of the "Nazi practice of forcing such immigrants to become espionage agents through threats of actual torture of their close relatives." State Department officials regarded the change as "absolutely essential," the story said, "in view of the great amount of evidence that the Nazis actually have employed such terroristic measures to their advantage in more than isolated cases."[60]

As it had with the State Department's rejection of the Vichy offer to allow foreign Jews to emigrate, the *Times* defended the U.S. government position. In an editorial, headlined, "No Ban on Refugees," the *Times* stated that the policy had been "widely misunderstood." The policy would "protect the country against those who might be induced to act as spies," the editorial said, but it would not reduce the number of immigrants admitted. "In short, the doors are not being closed," the *Times* opined. "They are being more closely watched."[61] Many other newspapers also accepted the State Department's policy as "readily understandable," as the *New York Herald Tribune* put it. Some did not. The *Philadelphia Record* focused on the policy's "severe blow" to refugees.[62] Among Jewish publications and liberal periodicals, such as the *Nation* and the *New Republic*, the denunciations were intense.[63] Prominent journalists including Max Lerner, William Allen White, and Dorothy Thompson signed a statement calling the policy "a serious and unnecessary departure from cherished American traditions."[64] Even a former *Times* editorial writer, James G. McDonald, who had subsequently become a member of the Advisory Committee on Political Refugees, objected to the policy and pushed the *Times* to change its position. He wrote the publisher to request that he and another committee member discuss the issue with "you and your colleagues."[65] The *Times* never published another editorial on the topic.

Historians have concluded that the new policy did in fact "close the doors" to more immigrants. "Many fugitives from Nazism, almost on the point of escaping Europe, were turned back by the shift in policy," David Wyman concludes in his study of U.S. immigration policy through 1941. "The *Entre Americain de Secours* in Marseilles related that only a few of about 100 people who had previously been promised visas were finally able to obtain them."[66] Bertha Sulzberger was among them. As her son explained to Arthur's assistant, Bertha had "no more relatives in Europe," so she would be allowed to enter Cuba relatively confident that she would soon make her way to the United States. On September 7, 1941, almost a year after she was shoved into a cattle car, Bertha Sulzberger sailed on the *S. S. Nyassa*, second class, from Lisbon to Havana.[67]

Arthur Sulzberger's personal involvement with the immigration issue was not yet over. He had signed affidavits for two other German-Jewish refugees who became ensnarled in the U.S. immigration bureaucracy. Shortly after Iphigene Sulzberger's cousin, Thea Midas, arrived in the States, her husband, Erich, asked the publisher's wife to sign affidavits for his parents, Joseph, 65, and Emilie, 59, who were still in Furth. Erich could not sign the affidavits because "my earnings and 'fortune' are too small." He pleaded with his cousin by marriage to "help me to do what my mother asked me, in a secret message: 'Save us. Here is the hell.'"[68] Although his family in the States did not know it at the time, a month after the younger

Midases left, Joseph and his brother, Lothar, had been severely beaten. In November 1938, during Kristallnacht, Nazi thugs attacked the two men, both in their sixties, and forced them to sign a document relinquishing ownership of the successful plate glass company that had been in the family for generations.[69]

Within 4 days of receiving Erich's request for help, Arthur Sulzberger signed the affidavits for the Midases who reached London 1 week before the war started. Iphigene's aunt sponsored Lothar and his wife. By spring 1941, the Midases wanted to join their son and his family in the United States, but their affidavits were too old. In April 1941, Erich Midas asked Sulzberger to sign new ones, which he did promptly.[70] The visa bureaucracy was not so swift. No action had been taken on the visa applications when the policy making immigration more difficult for those with close relatives still under Nazi control went into effect. The policy changes also transferred visa-issuing authority from consuls in individual countries to the State Department in Washington. Although a *Times* editorial had promised that under the new procedures "action on visas will be expedited," that was not to be. Processing applications proceeded slowly, leaving 4,500 applications backed up by mid-September.[71] The Midases' applications, which had been resubmitted to the State Department, were caught in that logjam.

By November 1941, the situation had not improved. Even an anticipated liberalization of the "close relatives" policy was not realized in practice. When the State Department issued formal federal regulations in November, they were indeed more liberal on paper, due in part to lobbying from refugee agencies, including McDonald's advisory committee.[72] The regulations specified that the continued presence of a close relative in Europe could supplement other reasons for denying a visa, but the regulations suggested that relatives alone could not be the basis for a denial. As applied, however, the "close relatives" policy still threatened to exclude refugees,[73] as Arthur Sulzberger soon learned.

Citing the November regulations, the chief of the visa division informed Erich Midas in March 1942 that his parents' case "has not resulted in a favorable recommendation to the American consular officer concerned." Presumably, the State Department was concerned that Joseph Midas' younger brother, Hugo, was still in Germany. (Hugo Midas and his wife, Lilly, eventually were deported from Furth to their deaths.) Erich Midas forwarded the State Department letter to Sulzberger who wrote the department asking for an explanation. "It has been the privilege of Mrs. Sulzberger and myself to help several refugees come to this country," he wrote. "I know of none who has more rapidly adjusted himself to American life than Erich Midas, the son of these parents whose entry it is now questioned." Sulzberger then volunteered to give "direct information" or answer questions when he was next in Washington. Sulzberger received a perfunctory reply that "the information in this, as in other cases, is confidential and may not be divulged." The publisher was not satisfied, wanting to know "if I cannot be treated on a little different basis" in being given the information.

Sulzberger then turned, as he often did, to his Washington bureau. He wanted the bureau to find out if the State Department "really has anything against" the Midases. If it did, "I do not wish to commit myself," he explained, but "if it hasn't I am willing to go to the limit for them." The bureau suggested that Sulzberger tell Erich Midas to request a formal review of his parents' case. In June 1942, the family made the request, and in August, the hearing took place in Washington. Sulzberger did not attend, but he was willing to call on his highest-placed contact, sending Secretary of State Hull a letter explaining the family's predicament and attesting to their virtues. It might not have been high-level intervention that eventually led the Midases' visas to be approved, however. Their daughter, Lisl Midas Loose, who testified at the hearing, attributed her success to something else: "I cried."[74] Joseph and Emilie Midas immigrated to the States within the year.[75]

After a brief stay in Cuba, Bertha Sulzberger was also able to immigrate to the United States. In October 1941, the U.S. State Department granted her a visa. Arthur received what remained of the $2,000 he had had deposited for Bertha in the Havana bank, and Fritz paid the publisher back for all his expenses. He had one more request of his cousin – to publish his letter to the editor complaining about a new U.S. government policy. "All of the Jewish refugees who came to this country during the last five years and who have the misfortune to have been born in Germany have been declared 'enemy aliens,'" Fritz Sulzberger wrote. "But who are these enemy aliens? Were they not the first victims of Hitlerism? Did they not lose home, profession, friends and everything which makes life worth living through the brutality of Hitler Germany.... In Hitler Germany they were declared 'enemies of the state'. Now they are 'enemy aliens'. Will they never find rest?" Arthur, however, believed it would not be wise to publish such a letter from "a man who is not yet a citizen."[76] The letter did not appear.

As Jews locked in French concentration camps struggled to emigrate or just to survive in 1941, those outside faced a worsening situation, even from the *Times*' perspective. For one thing, as the *Times* reported on its front page at the beginning of February, the Germans had forced Vichy to restore Laval.[v] In a story on newly announced compensation for Jewish civil servants ousted from the government, the Vichy bureau hinted at what Laval's return might mean for the Jews. Since Laval's "eclipse[,] anti-Semitism has been quiescent," the story said, but his return meant the government might no longer be so "liberal." A month later, the announcement that the Vichy cabinet would soon appoint a "general commissariat to deal with 'the Jewish question'" seemed to confirm those fears. Such an appointment "can be considered as a preliminary to the tightening of the enforcement of the status of Jews in the unoccupied zone," the Vichy bureau reported.[77]

But soon the *Times* reporters returned to their previous practice of glossing over Vichy's anti-Semitism. When Xavier Vallat was named the commissariat 3 weeks later, the *Times* Vichy bureau described him as a "lawyer and extreme right wing member of the Old Parliament," yet the story offered some reassurance. Although Vallat was "no friend of the Jews," his "present task is limited to applying existing laws," it said. Two days later, however, the *Times* reported that Vallat would "draft all legislation relating to Jews" and "fix the date for liquidation of all their property." Still, the *Times* did not drop its optimistic tone, noting that "it has been stressed that there is no intention to despoil them, nor is there evidenced now any widespread feeling against Jews in general." The *Times* continued to suggest that the real culprit was not Vallat or Vichy, but the Germans. In reporting in April 1941 that "steps are being taken" to take a census of all Jews in cities in unoccupied France, the *Times* emphasized that the impetus came from Germany. "In the unoccupied zone the desire is to be as liberal as possible, but the fact remains that pressure may be brought to bear in more than one way," the story concluded.[78]

[v] The *Times* judgment that Laval had been restored to his position turned out to be premature. He did not rejoin the Vichy cabinet until more than a year later.

Impatient to establish clear procedures in both the occupied and unoccupied zone, the Germans did pressure Vichy in early 1941. Commissariat Vallat set about drafting a new Statut des juifs that would replace Vichy's earlier law and would also apply to the occupied zone. In May, the *Times* reported that a "uniform" statute was in the works that was designed to remove Jews from "every job where they have a hand on the lever of any French activity – banks, industry, commerce, press, radio, cinema, publishing and the theatre, as well as public administration." In June, the government announced its new Jewish law. Gaston Archambault, writing in the *Times*, stated that that law would replace an October 1940 statute that was "marked by a measure of liberalism"; still, the new law would be "more lenient than the 'Nuremberg ghetto laws.'" The law banned Jews from any work except agricultural and manual labor, and defined Jews by race as well as religion, Archambault wrote. As an afterthought, the story also mentioned that 12,000 French Jews had been arrested by the police and placed in concentration camps.[79]

The next day, the *Times* Vichy bureau reported that the government was requiring that Jews register themselves and their possessions with a penalty of 1 month to 1 year imprisonment, a fine from 100 to 10,000 francs, and the possibility of being interned in a special camp. Jews had to register by July 2, another story declared. The Vichy government then restricted the proportion of Jews studying to be lawyers, doctors, and other "higher faculties" to 3%. Jews were also ordered to leave the city of Vichy in 1 week.[80] The *New York Herald Tribune* described the new law as a "final drastic decree," and other newspapers expressed shock.[81] There is no sense of shock in the *Times* reports. *Times* editors did not consider any of these stories terribly important, placing them on pages 5, 11, 14, 7, and 4. While other newspapers editorially condemned France's collaboration, the *Times* editorial page was silent.

After a few extensions, duly noted in the *Times*, the Vichy government closed jobs to Jews on September 15, 1941. But the *Times* did not announce the next phase of Vallat's legislative agenda, what Marrus and Paxton describe as "the gravest step yet taken" – the extension of "aryanization" of Jewish property to the unoccupied zone. The law, which applied to French as well as foreign Jews, authorized the state to confiscate all Jewish property. Non-Jewish trustees were appointed and charged with either liquidating the property or selling it to a non-Jew. Although the *Times* reported extensively on the progress of "Aryanization" in the north, it did not trumpet the launch in late July 1941 of a similar program in the south. The only mention was a five-paragraph item headlined, "Vichy order sales of Jews' businesses."[82] The Germans invaded the Soviet Union on June 22, a critical event in the war, but not one likely to have affected reporting in France. The *Times* consistently placed stories about Jews in France inside the paper, so it is unlikely the front-page news out of Russia would have displaced them. The more likely possibility is that Warren, Archambault, and Axelsson were preoccupied by French news that clearly took precedence over the fate of the Jews – the growing popular discontent with German administration of the occupied zone.

In August 1941, Communist resistance groups began direct attacks on the occupation forces, causing the Germans to strike back. At the same time, the Germans cracked down on Jews in the occupied zone, seizing their radios and bicycles and arresting them by the thousands. The *Times* went to great lengths to push the first story line – surging resistance among the French and retaliation by the Germans – as it downplayed the new wave of Jewish persecution. From the end of August to mid-September, the *Times* published eight front-page stories about French resistance to the Nazis, including five consecutive page one stories beginning August 22.[83] (The *Times* also continued to push the theme that the Vichy government was the last, best holdout against the Nazis. Another front-page story that month was headlined, "Vichy Reported Defying Berlin; Public Indignation and Threat by Marshal to Quit Said to Have Checked Pressure." Archambault's story a few days later supported that assessment, reporting that French crowds cheered Petain for his rumored firmness in responding to Nazi demands.[84])

Only once, when the two stories seemingly intersected, were the Jews mentioned on the front page. The August 22 story, by Lansing Warren from Vichy, centered on actions taken by French authorities to try to quell "outbreaks of disorders and sabotage" in Paris. As part of that story, it also mentioned that "6,000 persons identified as Jews" were arrested in the Eleventh Arrondissement. Still, the disquiet in Paris, rather than the roundup of Jews, was what propelled the story to the front. In fact, the story cast doubt on whether those arrested were actually Jews – as the headline couched it, "All Taken Are Termed Jews." An AP item, tacked onto the bottom of the story, referred to "alleged Jews," suggesting that both the *Times* and AP reporters considered the claim that Jews were arrested to be camouflage for the taking of subversives.[85]

That perspective was expressed more directly in a *Times* editorial and opinion column the next day. The editorial stressed that the events in Paris demonstrated the inevitability of "revolt" of those enslaved by the New Order "wherever there is even a glimmer of hope that revolt can be successful." Jews were not arrested, at least not for being Jews, the editorial explained; the German and French Nazis were merely using the familiar "trick" of calling "all opponents of the regime Jews." In fact, the editorial pointed out, few Jews lived in the ward where the arrests occurred. *Times* foreign policy columnist Anne O'Hare McCormick shared that view, writing that "unrest in France has reached a pitch" and that the Germans have rounded up "thousands of people in a working-class district" and called them Jews. "The subversive force" is "so active it can no longer be concealed and is labeled 'Jewish' to hide its real character," she wrote.[86] McCormick's column seemed a deliberate attempt to bolster the U.S. government policy of fostering resistance in Nazi-occupied countries. Six days earlier, McCormick – who wrote gushing letters to her "great friend," President Roosevelt, and visited the White House for private meetings nine times during the war[87] – had built a column around the president's comments at a press conference. "The main implication" of the President's words, she wrote, "is that the subjugated peoples must be encouraged and fortified to expect liberation before the influences now at work disarm them economically and morally as well as physically."[88] She and the *Times*' other editorial editors seemed determined to encourage and fortify the resistance, not only in France and not only in 1941, as will be seen.

Despite the certainty expressed on the editorial page, reporters seemed to change their minds about who exactly had been arrested. The next day the *Times* carried a UP account that referred to the arrest of 7,000 "Communist Jews," although later in the story it described the comparative ease with which Jews could be segregated and thus arrested because of identification papers stamped with a large "J." By September, *Times* reporters seemed to have concluded that Jews indeed had been arrested. In describing the subsequent arrest of "some hundred leading Jews, mostly belonging to the liberal professions" in a September 9 story, the *Times* matter of factly mentioned the previous arrest of 6,000 Jews who "were rounded up in the Eleventh Arrondissement and sent to concentration camps." Later stories referred to previous "mass round-ups of Jews that have been staged in different districts."[89] Those stories were not on the front page, nor did the *Times* revisit the issue on the editorial page. In fact, 4,000 Jews altogether were arrested in Paris in August 1941, with many of those arrests occurring in the Eleventh Arrondissement.[90]

As well as denying that Jews were the target of mass arrests, the *Times* also ignored Jews' involvement in targeted arrests. Three of the front-page resistance stories in August and September 1941 recounted the taking and execution of hostages in retaliation for attacks on Germans, as did another three in October.[91] Although the Germans at first targeted Communists and anarchists, the proportion of Jews among the hostages was always high. As Marrus and Paxton explain, the Vichy authorities eagerly sought "those responsible" for the attacks; but "for Vichy, 'those responsible,' always included the Jews."[92] Yet, the *Times* rarely, and never on the front page, mentioned Jews among the hostages. The one time it did was in a page six story that claimed the Petain government had persuaded the Nazis not to execute Jewish hostages in retaliation for anti-Nazi terrorism.[93] If the roundup of thousands of Jews did not merit the front page, neither did the destruction of Paris synagogues. In October 1941, explosions destroyed six of Paris' dozen synagogues. Archambault's story, which appeared on the third page, stated that "there is no clew [sic] yet to these perpetrators."[94] Two days later, the *Times* featured a photograph passed by German censors of one of the bombed synagogues.[95]

To Marrus and Paxton, the August arrests and hostage episode "provided a dress rehearsal for the massive roundups, internments and deportations soon to follow."[96] By December, the *Times* intimated what the future held for France's Jews. It reported that the Vichy government had modified its Jewish statute to conform with the one in the occupied territory and extended its application to the 360,000 Jews in North Africa. It noted that all Jews who had entered France since January 1936 in both the occupied and unoccupied zone had to be "incorporated into work formations or confined in concentration camps."[97]

If the tenor of the *Times* coverage of the Jews in France had not changed by the end of 1941, the course of the war certainly had with repercussions for the *Times* reporters there. As soon as Germany declared war on the United States after the attack on Pearl Harbor, French native Archambault left for Berne, where he remained until the liberation of Paris. George Axelsson had already left France in October for a short stay in Berlin. Lansing Warren remained in France until the Americans landed in North Africa in November 1942, when he and his wife were arrested, along with other American correspondents, consular officers, and Red Cross workers. They spent the next 2 months imprisoned by the French in Lourdes and were then shipped to Baden, Germany, the province from where 7,000 Jews, including Bertha Sulzberger, had been expelled in October 1940.

For the next 13 months, Warren and his fellow Americans would live under guard in a hotel in Baden, with regular excursions to church, the cinema, and for the women, the hairdresser.[98] He would be freed in February 1944, write about his experiences and be stationed in Washington before returning to the *Times*' resurrected Paris bureau in October 1945. Most of the expelled Jews, however, would never return to Baden. In September 1942, the *Times* reported that the "8,000 Jews from Baden who, during the Autumn of 1940, were deported to unoccupied France, are now reported to have been sent to Poland. . . . Recent inquiries about persons known to have been in Warsaw or Lublin elicited the reply that those concerned had either 'moved elsewhere' or had died."[99]

4

"A New Life in Nazi-Built Ghettos"

German Domination of Poland, Rumania, and the Baltic States

In 1941, Eliahu Elath was in Ankara on a mission for the Political Department of the Jewish Agency, the quasiofficial body representing the Jews living in British-held Palestine. Elath, who had learned much about the perilous position of Jews in occupied Europe, wanted to relay the news to the American Jewish Congress in New York, but feared he could not rely on the usual channels. Strict British military and political censorship might block its transmission, and the Turkish censor could strike such information in mail from Ankara to the United States. Elath decided to turn to the *New York Times* for help.

Knowing that each evening the *Times* transmitted the daily news over state radio to the *Times* offices in New York, Elath believed he could devise a code that would enable him to relay information embedded in the regular broadcast. He would need the help of a *Times* reporter. He had two choices: Ray Brock, the *Times* regular Ankara correspondent and a non-Jew whom Elath barely knew, or Cyrus Sulzberger, the *Times* roving foreign correspondent, nephew of the publisher, and a Jew whom he knew fairly well. Elath chose Brock rather than ask for help "from an assimilated and anti-Zionist Jew, who was a member of the paper's establishment as well." Brock agreed to use Elath's code during his broadcasts. "All this was done without [Brock's] superiors in New York knowing about the arrangement between us," Elath recalled years later. "He realized the importance of the matter for our cause and decided to chance all the risks involved."[1]

Elath probably made the right choice in entrusting his code to Brock rather than Sulzberger. (Sulzberger did end up using a code in dispatches he sent over Ankara radio – to send love notes to his girlfriend in Athens.[2]) Brock proved a reliable supporter of the Jews in Palestine, so much so that he would eventually run into problems with his editors at the *Times* – although they apparently never learned of his role in the secret transmissions. By contrast, Cy Sulzberger did not evidence much interest in the fate of the Jews in the countries he covered, even though he was stationed in some of the most critical regions at the most critical times: Austria in 1938 as Germany annexed the country; the Balkans in 1940 and the first half of 1941 as savage pogroms broke out in Rumania; the Soviet Union in the second half of 1941 and the beginning of 1942 as mobile killing squads roamed through eastern Poland and the Baltic states; and eventually in the Middle East in 1943 and 1944 as Palestine became the last place of refuge for Europe's surviving Jews.

In the 2 years before America's entry into the war, the *Times*' reporting from Rumania and the other Balkan states, led by Sulzberger, mirrored its coverage in France and Germany. *Times* reporters witnessed the persecution of the Jews, but treated it as a minor footnote to a far more important story: Germany's efforts to forge and sustain the Axis alliance. Poland, which was mostly closed to western reporters, and the Soviet Union, which was governed by strict censorship, presented a more formidable challenge. Still, Sulzberger did not pursue reports of mass murders of civilians in the Soviet territories, and the *Times* treated the well-substantiated news of the establishment of disease- and starvation-ridden ghettos in Poland as routine, back-page fodder.

In the spring of 1939, during a dinner in London, Arthur Sulzberger and his chief foreign correspondent Frederick Birchall persuaded a 27-year-old freelancer to become a *Times*man should the world go to war.[3] When Germany marched into Poland several months later, Cyrus Sulzberger, Arthur's nephew, signed on. Cyrus Leo Sulzberger shared his uncle's assimilationist orientation, if not its Classical Reform underpinnings. His father, Leo, was Arthur's eldest brother. According to a story Leo's and Arthur's mother told, she and Cyrus Sr. had decided not to give their children any religious instruction, until the young Leo complained that his cousin could recite prayers and he could not. Rachel Sulzberger proceeded to rear the children as Jews. When he was 16, Leo again confronted his mother; this time, he complained that she had made a mistake in raising him as a Jew, that she should have left him alone to decide for himself. She agreed that he should be free to "choose no religion, or his own, or Buddhism, or any of the Christian faiths."[4] It is not surprising then that

Leo's son, Cyrus, would later write that he grew up learning "little about religion," and was largely ignorant of Jewish customs and history. Only a divinity school course on the history of the Jews he took as a Harvard undergraduate made him aware of "the persistence of anti-Semitism throughout time."[5]

Leo worked in the family textile business and his son grew up comfortable, if not wealthy. When Cyrus was 14, his father died suddenly of pneumonia. Cyrus then forged a surrogate father–son relationship with his Uncle Arthur. Still, when he graduated from Harvard as an aspiring journalist, Cyrus was reluctant to call on his family connections. For his part, Arthur, who had not yet been given the official title of publisher, was hesitant to bring another Sulzberger into the *Times* until his succession was secure.

So Cyrus Sulzberger began his journalism career as a general assignment reporter for the *Pittsburgh Press*. He subsequently went to work for the United Press in Washington and then as a freelance correspondent in Europe for several London newspapers. One of his assignments brought him to Austria immediately after the Anchluss in 1938, when Germany added that country to the Reich. As Sulzberger recollects this period in his voluminous memoirs, two things stand out, which would mark his wartime coverage for the *Times* as well: his insistence upon having the best possible time amidst the horrors of war and his discomfort with reporting on the fate of the Jews in the countries he covered. As he described in a paragraph or two that included the expropriation of Jewish-owned businesses in Austria, the Jewish corpses that filled the Danube, and the 12,000 terrified Jews who showed up daily at the soup kitchen run by the "Israelite community," he noted that he somehow managed to have a good time. "I still had gay moments for a reason of singular cruelty: Vienna contained many attractive women who knew they were ultimately doomed," he wrote. "Some of these poor creatures attached themselves to any American and often proposed marriage. They suffered the sad illusion that a wedding certificate automatically entailed a United States passport. Others, wiser or deprived of hope, merely wished to be carefree while awaiting the Brown Death."

Cyrus Sulzberger was not oblivious to the plight of Austrian Jews, who experienced in a few months the terror and economic privation that German Jews had experienced gradually over 5 years. At one point, Sulzberger managed to sneak into the Jewish section of the city morgue to examine the records. By comparing the ledgers with the actual bodies, he found that at least two of the five corpses listed as suicides had been beaten to death. "I have never known a man to kill himself by punching out his own eyes," Sulzberger later commented. He said that he planned to "write a sensational series of articles," but ultimately could not bring himself to publish a single word. "This was neither courageous nor helpful to those I wished to aid by describing the Nazi brutishness," he recalled. "However, I shed it, all of it, and rode off to Carlsbad with a Czech major, focusing my attention on the lovely grain and hop fields of Sudetenland and the new troubles they obscured."[6]

Even before Cyrus Sulzberger joined the *Times*, there were misgivings about the wisdom of the arrangement. Birchall, who in the spring of 1939 had tried to persuade Cyrus to come aboard, had grown cold to the idea by late summer. He suggested that the *Times* pay Sulzberger $100 a week, rather than the somewhat presumptuous $120 he had requested. Cyrus then bragged to Birchall that he had arranged with a military attache to use the attache's diplomatic pouch in exchange for a report that Cyrus had done freelance for the *Times*. Birchall was not impressed. "Without any such wish on my part, and indeed to my intense dislike, I seem to find myself constantly in the situation of having to spank you for things that your enthusiasm prompts you to do without clear thinking," Birchall wrote Cyrus in August. The *Times* report was not his to give away, Birchall lectured, certainly not in a deal with the government. "This is a little matter of ethics – academic perhaps, but then I am particular about ethics – that you overlooked. And it ought to be damn good for you to be called down for it, as hereby I now do call you down."

Birchall then tried to head off the impending hire. "I begin to fear that taking on that young man would involve the handling of a stick of dynamite that might very inconveniently go off on us," he wrote James the same day he upbraided Cyrus. James did not acknowledge Birchall's complaint; he just wired him to pay Cyrus $120 a week. Birchall tried again a few days later, cabling James: "Am frankly fearful of overimpetuousity committing in a delicate situation." Cyrus, for his part, apparently did not respond to Birchall: he decided to work around him. He cabled New York that he was having trouble reaching Birchall and that he did not necessarily need to because he assumed he was "working directly under James." Indeed he was. Like many *Times*men who would succeed him, James apparently realized there was no premium in alienating the publisher's nephew. Cyrus was hired and Birchall was asked to return to New York.[7]

Cy Sulzberger became a roving foreign correspondent, who hopscotched between Albania, Bulgaria, Greece, Hungary, Rumania, Turkey, and Yugoslavia. A tall, thin man whose glasses hid grayish eyes and who wore the foreign correspondent's requisite worn trench coat, Cyrus understood the advantages of working for the *Times*. "In Budapest I lived (with Felix) [his wirehaired terrier] in the Dunapalota Hotel, a sign of my lofty *New York Times* status which had whipped me from the beer and sausage of a free-lance to the champagne and *foie gras* congruent with big-paper prestige," he wrote. He relished his new, high-living status. "Curiously enough, despite the swirling gloom, I had a most enjoyable time. I was carefree, fear-free; my newspaper paid me enough to live quite merrily and I was surrounded by excellent journalistic stories."[8]

By most accounts, Cyrus Sulzberger was a talented reporter. By most accounts, he received attention from the publisher out of proportion to his talents. The family connection always loomed large. Early in Cyrus' career, Arthur told James that his nephew wanted his byline to read C. L. Sulzberger rather than Cyrus. C. L. it was, which, a couple years later, put James in something of a predicament. Cy's mother called the managing editor, asking that the byline be changed to Cyrus L. It was. Then Cyrus called, demanding it be switched back. "You have got to help me," James wrote the publisher. "Shall I go ahead and disregard mother's request in favor of son? Should I tell him where the request came from for the change? Or, do you want to settle it?" Arthur settled it. A talk with his sister-in-law elicited her permission for Cyrus to have whatever byline he wanted.[9]

That was not the last time Arthur Sulzberger would show special solicitude for his nephew, who referred to Arthur as "uncle A" in office correspondence. When Cyrus sought help to obtain a visa for Marina Ladas, a Greek woman he had become infatuated with, and her mother, Arthur called Breckinridge Long, head of the State Department's visa section. When Long could not help because American consuls had been ordered out of Greece, Arthur then turned to Undersecretary of State Sumner Welles who "promised to intervene personally." The effort was aborted when Marina's mother decided to stay in Greece, and Cyrus and Marina decided to marry, resulting in a change in her visa status. Later, Cyrus again asked for help in obtaining a visa for Marina.[10]

After their marriage in Jerusalem in January 1942, at the home of a pastor of an interdenominational church who performed the ceremony,

Cyrus and Marina decided to return to the United States. Cyrus wanted space for three (Felix the dog included) on the Pan American clipper from Cairo, and for the *Times* to pay his wife's $1,300 ticket as well as his own. He asked James to make the request of his uncle. Arthur agreed to cover the costs and the War Department agreed to let the Sulzbergers have priority on the Clipper, after the publisher intervened. "I'm told it will cover Mrs. Sulzberger as well but the dog better be a lap dog or it won't get on the plane," wrote Luther Huston of the Washington bureau.[11]

Still later, when the Italians sentenced Marina's brother, Alexi Ladas, to death as a spy in August 1943, Arthur Sulzberger appealed to both Sumner Welles and Secretary of State Cordell Hull for help. Cy had suggested that his uncle even "enlist aid" of Roosevelt.[12] Hull contacted the Vatican and the War Department who had forces in the area that might be able to protect Ladas. In addition, the State Department contacted the Italian military authorities and the Allied military authorities in the Middle East. By October, Alexi Ladas had been freed.[13] Perhaps most useful of all to Cyrus, Arthur helped his nephew receive a draft deferment so he could continue to cover the war rather than have to fight in it.[14]

If Arthur was willing to call on the secretary of state to help his nephew's brother-in-law, it is not surprising that journalists in his own organization understood the importance of that familial tie. Daniel Schwarz, who started in the Sunday section in 1929 and eventually rose to become its editor, said Cyrus was not much liked at the *Times* because "he visibly traded on this relationship" with the publisher. "He would say 'Uncle Arthur' at lunch when everyone else still referred to him as Mr. Sulzberger," Schwarz recalled.[15] That editors treated Cyrus gingerly is evident in one exchange. Given the cost of transmission and a shortage of space in the newspaper, the *Times* at one point late in the war had limited its foreign correspondents to 600 words per story. "Cyrus sent well over 1500 words last night," the cable editor informed James. "Has the moment come yet to send him a message." James sent Cyrus a carefully worded cable: "Nothing would give us greater pleasure personally than to run your long stories in toto. However we cant do it and eye earnestly recommend six hundred word limit which others observe." Cyrus' response: "Will limit dispatches six hundred wherever possible," but that would "occasionally [be] impossible."[16]

The editors had reason to be concerned about Cyrus' clout. "Cy resented any suggestions that he took advantage . . . but . . . it was hard for our editors to ignore his special status with the publisher's family," Turner Catledge, who was assistant managing editor at the end of the war and would later become executive editor, said. Catledge recalled an incident involving a six-part series Sulzberger wrote based on an interview with General Douglas MacArthur. Catledge and other editors believed the series was "awfully thin," and should be boiled down to one article. When Cy became "furious," Arthur "backed his nephew all the way," Catledge explained. The publisher "decreed not only that all six articles should run, but that the first was to be carried on the front page."[17]

The family connection meant that even at the beginning of his *Times'* career Cyrus received a plum assignment. Having taken control of much of Eastern and Western Europe by the summer of 1940, the Germans turned to southern Europe. They sought to expand the Axis not by conquest but by forging alliances with Balkan nations, particularly Rumania. Rumania had a homegrown fascist movement, the Iron Guard, which played an increasingly important role in the government after King Carol II's regime acquiesced in the summer of 1940 to Soviet demands that it cede the provinces of Bukovina and Bessarabia. The Rumanian government then tightened its ties to the Third Reich, and began to enact anti-Semitic legislation. The Guard, which probably did not need any German encouragement, began a series of vicious pogroms. As Rumanian soldiers withdrew from the provinces that bordered the Soviet Union, they turned their anger against the Jews, who supposedly were pro-Soviet.

Cy Sulzberger tackled the primary story – the Axis' expansion. His lack of interest in the secondary story – what was happening to the Jews – is evident in his memoirs. Although there is much about wine, women, and song, the only reference to the persecution of Jews during those years is one sentence about his time in Bucharest in July 1940: "All over the country the murder of Jews began."[18] It was left to the wire services and Eugen Kovacs, the *Times* regular Bucharest correspondent, to handle the lesser story – the fate of 800,000 Rumanian Jews.

A pattern of news coverage was set that would be followed in other conquered countries and for many years – the Jews' fate would be an inside story. In a July 3, 1940 front page story about Rumanians mourning the loss of Bukovina and Bessarabia, Jews were mentioned only after the story had jumped inside: "Legislators are understood to be preparing a Jewish law similar to that of Italy." An AP story on the same inside page,

page 4, revealed that wealthy Jews, fleeing the cities for refuge in the country, were said to have been dragged from trains and beaten. "There were reports that some were hurled beneath the wheels of moving trains or shot in their seats in the darkness as the trains sped through tunnels," the *Times* reported.

Similarly, the following day, Sulzberger's page one story dealt with the changes in the Bucharest regime and only on page five, where the front page story continued, did it mention the possibility of anti-Semitic legislation and the stirring up of sentiment against the Jews. Sulzberger did write an inside story (July 6, 1940, p. 4), headlined "Anti-Jewish Acts Mount in Rumania." Even so, the anti-Semitic acts were not mentioned until the fifth paragraph: the first 4 paragraphs being devoted to the relative "tranquility" in Rumania and the likelihood that the Soviets might be backing off. The anti-Semitic acts described in the story were rioting against Jews who showed "great joy" at the Russian occupation of some territories. The cold-blooded murder of Jews was also treated as inside news. On July 9, the *Times* ran a story on page 12 that focused on Rumania's new cabinet, but also described "the deaths of a large number of Jews" in the regions of Rumania bordering the ceded Bukovina district. In Dorohoi, the *Times* reported, Drl Axner, president of the Jewish community, had been shot along with his wife and children. During the funeral for the Axner family, soldiers with machine guns arrived at the cemetery and shot the mourners.[19]

Many of these inside stories were written by Eugen Kovacs. Kovacs had been raised in Budapest; studied at the French Institute in Riom, France; and earned doctorates in law and political and economic science from Budapest's University of Technology and the Oriental Academy. He served as an officer in the Imperial Army during World War I. In 1926, at the age of 31, he joined the *Times* and was assigned to Bucharest, where he remained for 14 years. In 1940 Rumania, however, Kovacs had a problem: he was a Jew. As he wrote straightforward dispassionate accounts of anti-Semitic measures, he knew he might be subject to them. On August 10, 1940, Kovacs wrote a detailed, page five story on recently enacted anti-Semitic legislation, which, among other things, barred Jews from working as professionals. A day earlier, the *Times* carried a UP account reporting that the Rumanian government had rounded up Jewish journalists and sent them to concentration camps.[20]

In September, King Carol II was forced to abdicate and Ion Antonescu took control of the government, with the Iron Guard's Horia Simia as second in command. The change in government led to even more anti-Semitic measures. As Kovacs wrote a story explaining that the government was closing all but the largest Jewish schools, as well as synagogues and Jewish hospitals, his own children's school was closed. His daughters went instead to regular Rumanian schools where they were harassed. The police searched his home. Rumania then barred Jews from working for foreign news organizations. "The government has ordered all Rumanian Jews employed by foreign newspapers and news agencies to cease working for these organizations immediately," a *Times* story said. "Thus Eugen Kovacs, who has been correspondent for *The New York Times* in Rumania for fourteen years, has been forced to end his duties."[21]

Kovacs appealed directly to Arthur Sulzberger. "The files of the *New York Times* bare [sic] witness to the manner in which I have accomplished my task here and I think you will agree with me that I have been a loyal and thorough worker," he wrote. "I never considered myself merely the correspondent of a newspaper but a member of the *New York Times* family the members of which are proud to serve their paper without regard to their own interests." He asked for Sulzberger's help in obtaining a visitor's visa to the United States – the regular immigration quota was filled. "I know the *New York Times* has no obligation towards me but I know that you will feel for me and understand my situation. . . . The sooner I leave here the better from all points of view."[22]

The *Times* Washington bureau had the State Department cable the consul in Bucharest to find out what was holding up the visa. Delbert Clark of the Washington bureau told James that Kovacs was probably having a hard time persuading the consul that he would have some place to go once his visitor visa expired.[23] On October 11, Kovacs' position became even worse as German troops marched into Bucharest. The *Times* reported the presence of the German troops in a front page story in which Jews were mentioned only in the twelfth and last paragraph: "The Iron Guard is reported checking the whereabouts of all Jews. No reason is given."[24] After Kovacs stepped up his pleas to James and Guido Enderis in Berlin, the German Embassy told an editor in the *Times* Washington bureau that it would intervene on behalf of Kovacs if the *Times* would promise he would not engage in anti-German propaganda once in the

States. James was reluctant to make such a promise because he did not expect Kovacs to be working for the *Times* should he make his way to America. Sulzberger prodded him: "Ask Mr. Kovacs for such assurance and he can have our statement on his."

In November, however, Kovacs' request for a visa was rejected. He cabled James that he, his wife, and two daughters had "left Bucharest because personal safety was endangered." He went to Budapest, and James then suggested he proceed to Sofia, where the managing editor cabled him $100 to buy winter clothes and other things. Kovacs and his family arrived in the United States in late 1941, although it is not clear under what auspices, where he wrote occasional pieces for the *Times*. He soon earned James' ire, however, by "mixing in Balkan politics." After several warnings, James decided to let him go, despite Kovacs' plea that "my job on the *Times*, the only means of existence of [sic] me and my family, is more important for me than the future of the whole world." Kovacs died shortly after that of a heart attack at the age of 48. The *Times* sent his widow $1,000, including $600 in insurance money.[25]

With Kovacs gone, the plight of Rumanian Jews receded further into the back pages of the *Times*, even as their situation worsened in 1941. Economic and social legislation barred Jews from owning ships and urban real estate. It required them to register all property, engage in forced labor, remain in their homes at night, and even turn over part of their wardrobes to the government – all of which the *Times* reported inside in a paragraph or two.[26]

The Iron Guard rebelled against the Antonescu government in January, plunging the country into chaos. The Guard blamed the Jews for their conflict with the regime, inciting more pogroms. The *Times* described the outbreak of violence against the Jews, but always as a secondary element of a front page story about general unrest in Rumania or in a perfunctory inside story. In the seventh paragraph of a January 25 front page story about the rebellion, it stated that "scores of Jews were reported slain in basement executions in their homes." Only in a page five story were the basement executions explained. Using street fighting as cover, "more extreme elements of the insurgent Iron Guard in Bucharest" murdered "an estimated 300 Jews they had herded into cellars and then turned machine guns on them," the *Times* reported. "In one block of apartments in the Jewish quarter eighty-nine men, women and children were reported slain."[27] At least 600 Jews were slaughtered in Rumania during this period.[28]

Reporters who had been in Rumania had no doubts about what had happened to the Jews.[29] Once he had left the country, correspondent Leigh White of the Overseas News Agency described what he had seen in Bucharest. As would many journalists over the next five and one-half years of war, White alluded to World War I atrocity stories. But he did so specifically to acknowledge that, although an earlier generation of reporters may have been duped into reporting propaganda, he had not. In fact, what he had witnessed happening to Bucharest's Jews far exceeded anything he could have imagined, he explained, including Jews being doused with gasoline and set on fire or burned in their homes, shops, and synagogues. He also reported reliable information that Jewish women had had their breasts cut off and Jewish men had been butchered using "kosher" slaughtering techniques.[30]

The Germans, who wanted a stable Rumania as they prepared for the invasion of Russia, sided with Antonescu, who put down the rebellion. The next 5 months marked a period of relative calm for Rumania's Jews that was broken decisively and irrevocably by the German incursion into the Soviet territories.

Similar anti-Semitic restrictions – although not accompanied by widespread pogroms – were imposed in other south central European countries in 1940 and 1941 – and dutifully reported in the *Times*. Even before Slovakia and Hungary, along with Rumania, joined the Axis in November 1940, they enacted anti-Semitic legislation. Slovakia barred Jews from restaurants and required them to clean the streets. Jews were blocked from living on certain avenues, and from shopping and appearing outdoors at certain hours. In Hungary, an anti-Jewish bill forbid Jews to "drive automobiles, become midwives, hoist the Hungarian flag, buy anything from a peasant or sign any legal document." Bulgaria too enacted anti-Semitic legislation before it formally allied with Germany in March 1941. Jews could not use Bulgarian endings for their names, hold government jobs, marry Bulgarians or employ them as domestic servants. The *Times* recorded all these restrictions in short, inside stories.[31]

Anti-Semitic legislation also followed in the wake of Germany's occupation of Yugoslavia, although the response depended on the state. Croatia moved quickly to strip Jews of their citizenship, confiscate their property, and restrict their practice of medicine and law. The Serbs, however, resisted the Germans. The only mention of the fate of the Jews on the *Times* front page during this period chronicled that resistance. With the headline,

"Nazis Held Ready to Crush Serb Guerrillas and Jews," the *Times*' Ray Brock reported that a German order to clear out the foreign diplomatic corps from Belgrade was a "first step" to "exterminate Serb guerrillas" and "unleash a ruthless anti-Jewish pogrom." Jews had been segregated and forced to wear yellow armbands. Jewish men were organized into labor gangs to clear bomb wreckage and excavate bodies. Jewish shops were looted and sealed. "'But this,' say the Germans, is just the beginning,'" the *Times* reported.[32]

The end was in Poland. But Poland, during the first 2 years of war, proved more difficult for journalists to cover than any other part of the continent. With a few exceptions, Poland was closed to Western correspondents. When the Germans invaded Poland in September 1939, the *Times* correspondent there was 43-year-old Jerzy Szapiro, whom his editors believed had done "a wonderful job."[33] Szapiro, who had been the *Times*' Warsaw correspondent for 12 years, had the advantage of being a Polish native with an excellent command of English; he had the disadvantage of being a Jew. A decade earlier, Szapiro had showed Arthur and Iphigene Sulzberger around Warsaw, including a stop in the Jewish section. Iphigene Sulzberger, who described Szapiro as "a handsome young Pole," recalled his words in her memoirs. "As we toured the city he spoke of what a miracle it was that Poland was now free of Russian tyranny and that the country's Jews no longer had to live in terror."[34] Ten years later, Szapiro was as terrified as the nation's 3 million other Jews. He fled eastward as the Germans moved into Poland, eventually escaping to France through Rumania.[35] The *Times* dispatched Otto Tolischus from Berlin to tour Poland, but as the Germans clamped down he too left. Germany annexed the western part of what had been Poland to the Reich. As part of the Nazi–Soviet pact, the Soviet Union got the eastern part of the former Poland. Germany administered the section between, which included Warsaw and Lublin and became known as the Gouvernement General.

Reporting from all three sectors was difficult. Without correspondents there, Western news organizations, including the *Times*, had to rely on second-hand sources. The Polish government in exile based in London regularly received short, radio messages from secret transmitters in Poland or longer, detailed reports on microfilm brought by secret couriers.[36] Its Polish Information and Interior Ministries thus issued several releases that fairly accurately and comprehensively described the Nazis' actions against Polish Jews. During the first 2 years of the war, however, the

Polish government's overriding concern was that publicity about the persecution of Jews not interfere with "the cultivation of public sympathy with the tribulations of the Poles." As a result, information that the Polish authorities conveyed to the West about the Jews, although plentiful, "was for the most part deeply embedded in general Polish propaganda literature."[37] At this stage, the *Times* had some misgivings about the usefulness of exile government information. In August 1940, London Bureau Chief Raymond Daniell doubted whether former Warsaw correspondent Szapiro should remain on the *Times* payroll because of his relationship with the exile government.[38] "The little news that originates in the refugee governments – and untainted with propaganda – can be and is, I think, adequately covered by the present staff," Daniell wrote James.[39]

Jewish organizations, such as the American Joint Jewish Distribution Committee, which had operatives in Poland in 1940 and 1941, also funneled some information to Western news organizations. At the end of January 1940, for example, the *Times* reported the Joint Distribution Committee's finding that 250,000 Jews had died since September of "military operations, disease and starvation," and that 80% of the remaining Jews "'had been reduced to beggary.'"[40]

Much of what was reported in the *Times* came from official German decrees published in official German organs. In fact, official German sources often quickly confirmed information originally attributed to Jewish organizations. So, shortly after Jewish organizations announced the implementation of forced labor, the Berlin bureau reported that "high German Storm Trooper and police leaders" in the German government in Poland had issued a series of decrees, including one requiring forced labor. Two hundred to 300 Jews were already clearing snow in Cracow, the story said.[41] Significantly, the *Times* did not seem to give greater credence to the stories with official confirmation than those attributed to Jewish groups. All appeared inside the newspaper, and none contained qualification of the facts included.

The *Times* did not use one important source of information about the Jews in Poland – the Jewish Telegraphic Agency. "Very little news is filtering through from Poland in the services of other American news agencies which consider Nazi-held Poland as completely cut off from the rest of the world," a JTA report stated. "The J.T.A., however, through various efforts is bringing out the news about Jewish life in the ghettos of Poland." The JTA covered Poland primarily through correspondents in

Switzerland, Sweden, and Hungary.[42] The *Times*, however, had canceled its subscription 3 years earlier and had not resubscribed.

Whether from the JTA, the exile government, Jewish organizations, or the German government, information reaching the West provided an unequivocal picture of what was happening to the Jews in Poland – they were being herded into sealed ghettos to which Jews from other parts of the Reich were also being shipped.[i] On January 6, 1940 (p. 2), the *Times* reported that in addition to the reservation near Lublin, the Germans were establishing ghettos in Warsaw, Radom, Minsk, and Mazowiech. The story also indicated that 45,000 Jews, mostly from Prague and Vienna, had already been sent to Lublin. Two months later, the *Times* Berlin bureau reported that 80,000 Jews in Cracow "are gradually being pushed back to the ghetto," according to "the picture furnished by the official Gouvernement General organ, *Warschauer Zeitung*."[43]

The largest ghetto, the one in Warsaw, supplied the most information. In October 1940, a reporter even visited Warsaw and saw at least the outside of the ghetto. AP Berlin correspondent Alvin J. Steinkopf was the only non-German correspondent allowed to tour the "General Gouvernement" accompanied by two German public health officials. After his 1-week visit, Steinkopf wrote a story that appeared on page 38 of the *Times*. The first 10 paragraphs of his story described the devastation apparent even 1 year after the German conquest. Warsaw "still looks like an untidy backyard," he wrote. He then noted the Jews on the streets wearing blue and white armbands and the new concrete wall around the ghetto. "The wall is eight feet high and so tight a cat couldn't get through it," Steinkopf wrote. It surrounded 100 or more city blocks "into which the population is crowded with astonishing density, and closes off 200 streets and even street car lines – it is built right over the rails." The ghetto had 18 entry points, the story continued "but at a moment's notice the authorities . . . can close off the entire district." A half-million Poles and Jews lived inside the walled area, where Steinkopf apparently was not allowed. "'It is not a wall against the Jews,' I was told by Dr. Jost Wallbaum," director of health in German-occupied Poland, Steinkopf wrote. "'It is a wall against typhus.'"[44]

[i] The Rumanians were also establishing ghettos. At the end of October, the *Times* carried an AP account of an official Rumania news agency report that ghettos had been created in the neighborhood of the Bug River in Russian Ukraine, to which Jews living in Bessarabia and Bukovina were being sent. 10/27/41, 4.

By the time the ghetto was officially sealed 1 month later, the pretext that the wall was erected to halt the spread of typhus was mostly dropped. (Typhus did rage in the ghetto where, the *Times* reported in January 1942, 300 people a day were dying from the disease.) The seven-paragraph story from the AP in Berlin bore the unambiguous headline, "Wall Will Enclose Warsaw Jews Today; 500,000 Begin 'New Life' in Nazi-Built Ghetto." That new life, the story indicated, would include severe overcrowding with "as many as seven persons living in one room." The story reported that "effective tomorrow," the date the story appeared, those wanting to leave or enter the district must have a special pass. Within 9 month, the *Times* Berlin bureau noted that "the task of confining all Jewish residents of Warsaw within a ghetto . . . now is reported to have been wholly completed." A later story gave estimates of the number of Jews living in "the ghettos of the main centers" in Poland: 530,000 in Warsaw; 150,000 in Lodz; 120,000 in Lwov; 80,000 in Bialystok; 60,000 in Wilno [Vilna]; 50,000 in Cracow; and 40,000 in Lublin.[45]

What life was like in those ghettos was revealed in September 1941,[ii] when Henry Szoszkes, who had been on the Warsaw Jewish Council and who had served as a source for the earlier story about Jewish women being forced to become prostitutes, released detailed information to news organizations. Former President Herbert Hoover, who was then leading food relief drives in Poland and elsewhere, thought highly enough of Szoszkes, who was also well regarded by American Jewish groups,[46] to write to Arthur Sulzberger personally to alert him to the story. "He has kept in intimate touch with his people since he got out of Poland," Hoover wrote of Szoszkes. The former president urged the *Times* to publish an article based on Szoszkes' information "as to the treatment which these people are receiving, and the desperate plight in which they are now living."[47]

The article was published after Sulzberger passed along the information to James.[48] "The appalling conditions under which some 3,000,000 Polish Jews must struggle to live in 300 ghettos throughout Nazi-dominated Poland are revealed by authoritative statistics received in the United States and made public yesterday by Dr. Henry Szoszkes," the article's lead stated. The article reported that, in the Warsaw ghetto, deaths rose from

[ii] A reporter for the *Saturday Evening Post* actually went inside the Warsaw Ghetto several months earlier but, guided by a high-ranking Nazi leader, he received a rather sanitized version of life inside the walls. The *Saturday Evening Post*, 4/5/41.

80 per day in May to 240 per day by July – 15 times the death rate in the ghetto in July 1939, before the outbreak of war. "'Many families living in the Warsaw ghetto who are unable to provide for themselves, let alone bury their dead, have adopted the practice of leaving corpses in the streets and courtyards,'" Dr. Szoszkes is quoted as saying. Children between 1 and 5 years of age, no longer allowed a daily ration of milk, made up a large proportion of the deaths.

The article explained why starvation "stalks throughout the ghettos." The daily bread ration was only 3 ounces with occasional "handouts" of a few potatoes and some saccharine. Prices on the "free market" were 90 zlotys per kilo for butter (about $8 per pound), 30 zlotys per kilo for bread, and 50 zlotys per kilo for sugar. Yet "for the great mass of Jews in Polish ghettos," there was only one source of earning: compulsory labor that paid 18 zlotys or about $3.50 per week. It would take a week and one-half to earn enough to buy a kilo of bread. The problem was not just in Warsaw. "'In the city of Radom, where the ghetto now houses about 7,000 Jews, practically all of them are destitute and starving,'" the *Times* reported.[49]

Despite the specificity of the information and the credibility of the source, the *Times* considered this story no more important than the others it had run about Jews in Poland. The story appeared on page 31 and the *Times* never followed up with additional reporting or a single editorial. Six months later, on March 1, 1942, Szoszkes provided an update, predicting that if the rate of "10,000 dying monthly now of starvation and sickness" continued, "there will be no more Jews in Poland in five or six years." The *Times* ran the story on page 28.

Whether from Jewish organizations or German officials, whether based on second-hand information such as that received by Szoszkes or eyewitness accounts such as the one from the AP's Steinkopf, the stories all appeared inside the *New York Times*. The problem was not the quality or quantity of the information available. In December 1941, a U.S. government intelligence report attested to its accuracy, noting that "there is nothing that my informants have to say [about conditions among the Jews in Poland] that it is not generally known from the daily press. . . ."[50] Still, from the perspective of the *Times*' editors, what was happening to the Jews in Poland was not important enough to warrant the front page.

While Jews were being amassed in ghettos in Poland, the Final Solution had already begun in the Soviet Union. On June 22, 1941, Germany turned on its ally and invaded the Soviet Union. As the Germans blitzed through parts of Soviet-held Poland, Lithuania, the Ukraine, and the Baltic States on their way to Moscow, they also began murdering Jews by the hundreds of thousands. Special mobile killing squads, known as the Einsatzgruppen, often assisted by local Poles, Ukrainians, Lithuanians, and Balts, went village by village, town by town, slaughtering Jews. The German invasion also enabled Rumania to reclaim the provinces it had handed over to the Soviets a year earlier. Pogroms erupted during the renewed chaos, with huge massacres in the border city of Iasi and in Bukovina and Bessarabia. The Einsatzgruppen occasionally assisted Rumanian soldiers and policeman. All told, an estimated 1.5 million Jews were murdered in the Soviet territories between June 1941 and the end of 1942.[51] Only 17 stories appeared in the *Times* soon after the massacres occurred, and just five of those specifically mentioned Jews as being among the victims.[52] For most mainstream newspapers and particularly for the *Times*, the Einsatzgruppen's killing spree was the least reported event of the Holocaust.[iii] Not so for American newspapers and magazines that served the Jewish community. From the beginning of the German invasion "the Jewish press provided fairly exact accounts of the atrocities committed against the Jews," Alex Grobman concludes. The news also received wide coverage and sparked many editorials.[53]

There are a number of reasons why the *Times* overlooked this story. For one thing, it was a very difficult story to get. Unlike much of the anti-Semitic campaign up to this point, which was divulged in official publications and edicts, the Nazis were extremely secretive about the start of the Final Solution. In addition, the killings often occurred in isolated areas near to the front lines that "were virtually cut off from the outside world."[54] Richard Lichtheim, the Jewish Agency's representative in Geneva, who was among the first Westerners to learn of many of the atrocities committed against Jews, complained in 1942 of the year-earlier events: "It was extremely difficult to obtain reliable reports or confirmation by eye witnesses of what happened in the Baltic States. There is very little traffic and no correspondence at all between these States and neutral countries."[55]

[iii] Phillip Knightly, in his study of war correspondents, *The First Casualty*, 244, reaches the same conclusion about the coverage of the military campaign in the Soviet territories. "[T]he Eastern Front remained throughout the most poorly reported part of the Second World War," he observes.

To make matters worse, the Soviet government kept the American reporters closest to the action on a short leash. If reporting from Berlin was difficult, reporting from Moscow was nearly impossible. "[T]he boys say that the censorship in Berlin is child's play alongside the Russian censorship, and so the life of a newspaper man is about as restricted as it is possible to imagine," an American official whose office the *Times* relied on to pass uncensored letters to the States wrote Arthur Sulzberger from the Russian capital in October 1941.[56] That had long been the case.[57] While the Germans relied on postpublication intimidation and harassment, the Soviet Union employed more restrictive, prepublication censorship.

The *Times*' Moscow problems intensified once the war began. The newspaper had sent its longtime Central European correspondent, G. E. R. Geyde, to Moscow after the Germans had arrested him and forced him out of first Vienna and then Prague. Geyde had little familiarity with Russia and less with the Russian language. The *Times* sent him there at least partially because of his leftist sympathies, which James had complained of in a letter to Arthur Sulzberger.[58] Sulzberger shared James' impression that Geyde "had some good strong left leaning." Sending Geyde to Moscow was apparently a last ditch effort to cure him of his supposed political bias. "[F]rankly, one reason why I had him put there was because I thought he would find out that all was not gold that glittered," Sulzberger wrote, "and that being thus presented with the other side of the picture his views might be tempered."

Whether Geyde's views were tempered by his Moscow assignment was not readily apparent from the articles he wrote. The Soviet censor made it extremely difficult to get out any news. "The censor has been particularly ruthless about what he censored, and little news of any importance comes through even late," Sulzberger wrote to Laurence A. Steinhardt, the U.S. ambassador to Moscow and a Columbia classmate. Sulzberger entertained the possibility that the Soviets, not Geyde, were the primary problem. "We noted with considerable interest that when [longtime *Times* Moscow correspondent Walter] Duranty was in Moscow during Geyde's vacation he was able to send through very little indeed. If an old hand like him has his wings clipped it would seem to indicate that the trouble lies deeper than the man."[59]

Still, Sulzberger suspected that Geyde might be aggravating the problem. "Undoubtedly he [Geyde] was much harassed prior to his going to Russia and very much mentally disturbed since his arrival in Moscow,"

Sulzberger wrote. Sulzberger wanted Steinhardt's advice on whether to keep Geyde, or any correspondent, in Moscow. "There seems to be little question that by continuing to keep a correspondent in Moscow we run the risk of giving greater credence to these Tass [Soviet-run news agency] stories," he wrote.[60] Five months later, in September 1940, the *Times* printed three long articles by Geyde recounting his difficulties with the Soviet censors.[61] It then closed its Moscow bureau, and Geyde left the paper.[iv] After war broke out between Germany and the Soviet Union in June 1941, the *Times* hurried to reopen its Moscow bureau and sent one of its star reporters to staff it.

Cy Sulzberger, fresh from covering the German incursions into Rumania, Yugoslavia, and Greece, arrived in Moscow in July 1941. There, he encountered the same difficulties as previous *Times* reporters. "About a dozen of my stories . . . have been completely killed," Cyrus wrote to his uncle. "Others have been terribly massacred. Please don't think I'm the sucker that some of my dispatches would seem to indicate." Cyrus even asked to leave. "It is perhaps hard for you to realize why a reporter would be willing to give up the lead story of the day, but I haven't had a day off in two years and the last year has been plenty of strain physically and mentally. My nerves are now shot and my resistance lowered."[62] Cy hung in on his first tour for the rest of 1941 and a few months into 1942, traveling to the Caucasus and Central Russia, and twice to the front and to the Volga Valley region. In his memoirs, he acknowledged that the restrictions severely limited what he was able to report. "When we asked to go to the front we were taken to collective farms and factories. We were not permitted to send anything that had not originated in an official press conference or a Soviet publication. As a result the news we dispatched concerning military operations was invariably late, incomplete and overoptimistic."[63] As future *Times* columnist James Reston, who accompanied the publisher to Moscow as his assistant in 1943, wrote: "You don't gather news in Moscow, you go where you're invited and collect clues or impressions."[64]

Clues to the horrendous happenings in the Soviet territories could be found in a few *Times* articles out of Moscow. A three-paragraph

[iv] Geyde eventually worked for British intelligence in the Middle East and was "an early advocate" of sending Palestinian Jews into Nazi-occupied Europe to organize resistance. Gilbert, *Auschwitz and the Allies*, 182.

January 1942 item based on "authentic information from Stockholm" said that the Germans were killing civilians with typhus in Eastern Poland and Soviet White Russia. Another, from Kuibyshev, included this sentence: "To the little that is known about German conduct in occupied Soviet territory – except for atrocities reported by the Russians – may be added scanty details from the Ukraine." Given the difficulties Moscow journalists had in gathering and reporting what might be considered routine news, it is not surprising that they learned little more than scanty details about the massacres just behind the front lines. It is also not surprising that Cyrus Sulzberger did not aggressively pursue the information. In some cases, Sulzberger was willing to track down information from those who fled the territories. He wrote a 13-paragraph story based on "the opinion of persons who have just managed to escape from the occupied area," who told him of the obstacles the Germans faced in organizing a "puppet, theoretically independent government" in the Ukraine.[65] Yet, as he had demonstrated in Vienna and the Balkans, he was not inclined to follow the travails of the Jewish population.

Because Cyrus Sulzberger did not write much about Jews, either in *Times* stories or in his memoirs, discerning his motive is difficult. His assimilationist orientation probably contributed to his lack of interest, yet so did his journalistic orientation. Sulzberger did not consider the problems of a powerless minority part of the natural province of a foreign correspondent. Indeed, Cy Sulzberger would come to epitomize the high-flying foreign correspondent who viewed his job as becoming intimate with powerful foreign leaders and using news columns to convey their ideas. "When I was new at The Times, a clerk on the Foreign Desk assured me, straight-faced, that C. L. Sulzberger . . . never spoke to anyone below the rank of prime minister unless it was to tell them where to put his luggage," former *Times* reporter Richard Shepard wrote. "That was probably a gross exaggeration, but it indicated a state of mind."[66] Sulzberger himself confirmed that he preferred the upper echelons. "Rule A for a newspaperman is that 'leaks' are the food of the trade," he wrote in his memoirs, "and over the years I have found that, as with the best drinks, the leak always fizzes from the top. The desire for indiscretion at the upper levels seems compelling."[67]

Contrary to Sulzberger's rule, high-ranking officials were being discreet about murdering Jews in 1941, while low-level soldiers were not. Berlin reporters heard German soldiers back from the front boasting about atrocities. "All during the campaigns in the East, all one had to do was go to one of the waiting rooms of the railroad stations in eastern Berlin and listen to the Black Guards arriving from or leaving for the front," *Chicago Tribune* correspondent Sigrid Schultz wrote. "They seemed to enjoy describing how they had locked Poles and Jews into cellars and then thrown hand grenades through windows left open for the purpose."[68]

In October 1941, the Germans even took 28 foreign correspondents from Berlin on a tour to show how they were handling conquered Polish and Ukrainian territories. For those alert to the plight of the Jews, the controlled expedition was illuminating. One of the stops was the "walled city" in Cracow in which Jews were required to live. Hans Frank, who administered the Gouvernement General, told the reporters that all Poland's 2.1 million Jews "must go into these 'Jewish living quarters,'" the *Herald Tribune* reported.[69] United Press Berlin correspondent Frederick Oeschsner learned even more. He discovered that "a mass slaughter of the Jews by the Nazis on a scale unparalleled in modern times" was taking place in Poland and occupied Russia, as he wrote in his book published the following year.[70] Scattered reports managed to find their way into newspapers, although not the *Times*. With Percy Knauth and Brooks Peters gone, and George Axelsson not yet settled in, Enderis was alone in the Berlin bureau in October 1941. No one from the *Times* went on the Germans' tour of the Soviet territories.

Perhaps the primary reason that the *Times* had fewer stories on the massacres in the Soviet territories was that the newspaper had cut itself off from the one source that most consistently and accurately reported them – the JTA. The JTA "is the principal source of information about the Jewish communities isolated from the rest of the world by the Nazi regime," the news agency boasted, fairly accurately.[71] The *Times*, however, received none of this information directly. It had cancelled its subscription to the news agency in 1937, and therefore, was not getting the service in 1941 and 1942, unlike its New York competitors, the *Post* and the *Herald Tribune*.[72] So while *Post and Tribune* editors combed through JTA releases in the newsroom, deciding what to include and what to discard, no *Times*man routinely came across JTA stories, even though the newspaper likely learned of some of them through other channels.

The JTA relied on a variety of sources for news of the massacres, including the press in occupied countries. In October 1941, its Zurich correspondent read in a Ukrainian newspaper that Jews throughout the

Ukraine were being expelled from their homes and taken to an unknown destination. In one town, Zhitomir, only 6,000 of 50,000 Jews remained, the Ukrainian newspaper reported. The JTA correspondent relayed the information to the agency in New York, which included it in that week's bulletin.[73] Along with reading the foreign press, JTA correspondents in Switzerland and Sweden also interviewed people who had escaped from those areas. The correspondents were able to cable their reports to New York with "no restrictions."[74]

The JTA also depended on the Polish government-in-exile, particularly for information on events in the eastern parts of Poland. Members of the Polish underground would learn of the shooting of Jews in a town near where they operated and then transmit that information to headquarters in Warsaw. If considered reliable, the information would then be sent to the government in London. If it was successfully received and deciphered, it would then be disclosed.[75] The JTA's London office was "in constant touch" with the exile government, particularly the Jewish members of the Polish National Council, who maintained contact with Jewish underground groups in Poland.[76] The first exile government report on mass killings of Jews was dated August 30, 1941, but did not arrive in London until mid-October. It described the execution of 6,000 Jews in Czyzew near Lomsa on August 27, 1941, what is now known to be 1 of 60 locations in eastern Poland where executions occurred that summer. The government released the report to the press at the end of the month. The JTA published it in its October 29, 1941 bulletin.[77]

The *Times* seemed to have learned indirectly of a JTA story about the Germans' and Ukrainians' murder in August 1941 of thousands of Galician Jews and thousands more Hungarian Jews deported to Galicia. The JTA carried the news on October 23,[78] and the *Times* ran a strikingly similar story 3 days later without a byline or a dateline, which suggests it received it in an unorthodox fashion. The *Times* story, which ran on page six, was based on eyewitness accounts of Hungarian soldiers and letters reaching Hungary. It estimated the deaths at 15,000. "Reports tell of the victims being machine-gunned as they prayed in their synagogues and of being shot as they fled from their assailants," the *Times* story said. "The deaths are reported to have been so numerous that bodies floated down the Dniester with little attempt to retrieve and bury them."[79] The story was basically accurate, although it underestimated the number murdered, which was closer to 14,000 to 16,000 Hungarian Jews and another

10,000 Ukrainian Jews from nearby towns and villages.[80,v] (Five months later, S. B. Jacobson, an official with the American Jewish Joint Distribution Committee (JDC) who had just left Hungary after 2 years in the Balkans, corroborated the murder of Hungarian Jews in Galicia, and the deportation of tens of thousands of Slovakian and Rumanian Jews to Poland during a press conference, which the *Times* covered.[81])

The *Times* missed entirely what Walter Laqueur describes as "a sensational and remarkably accurate" JTA report dated November 25, 1941, which told of the execution of 52,000 men, women, and children in Kiev.[82] The executions, which have come to be known as the Babi Yar massacre, occurred over several days in September 1941. The JTA report made it clear that the Jews were not killed in a riotous pogrom, but were "systematically and methodically put to death." Later disptaches indicated that the numbers were an estimate of those killed, but there was no doubt the murders had been the result of "systematic, merciless execution carried out in accordance with the cold blooded Nazi policy of Jewish extermination."[83]

The *New York Journal American* published an article on page two on the 52,000 Jews killed in Kiev. The *Times*, however, carried not a word about it until more than a month later when Soviet Foreign Minister Vyacheslaff Molotoff broadcast the news over Radio Moscow. According to the *Times*, Molotoff charged that German authorities had "perpetrated massacres, villainy and bestial outrages in Soviet territories they had occupied." The Germans had killed thousands of noncombatants, including "52,000 men and women, particularly old men and children." Although Molotoff first referred to the victims as "Russians, Ukrainians, Jews and any one loyal to the Soviet," he then said that at Kiev's Jewish cemetery "a large number of Jews were lined up, ordered to lie down, then shot with automatics." Molotoff continued: "Then they were covered with earth . . . and another batch brought up, treated similarly and buried immediately above them." Molotoff also charged that 8,000 had been shot in Kamenetz and Podolsk, 3,000 in Mariupol, several thousand in Kerch, and "'tens of thousands'" in Rostov. The *Herald Tribune* relied on the same UP account, but ran the story in a prominent position on the front page.[84]

[v] In August, the *Times* reported estimates of 8,600 Jews dead as part of the Rumanians retaking of Soviet territory. 8/4/41, 3, 8/28/41, 7. The number of dead in the Rumanian pogroms are still only estimates, with between 3,200 and 13,000 believed to have been killed in Iasi, and another 10,000 murdered in the provinces in July. Ionanid, *The Holocaust in Romania*, 108.

The next day, the *Times* printed a longer story on page eight that described Molotoff's charges as "one of the most terrible indictments in modern warfare." It said the reports of massacres came from troops who had retaken villages and towns. "The German manner of war," Molotoff said, is not "the mere excess of isolated and undisciplined military units or individual German officers and soldiers." The story repeated the numbers murdered in individual towns adding the toll in Lwow, Odessa, and Dniepropetrovsk. It never mentioned Jews.[85]

Nor did the *Times* editorial, "Nazi Fury in Russia," that appeared the following day. The *Times*, however, did not doubt the reliability of the information, even though Molotoff was the source. Although the number of dead "is not likely to be accurate to the last digit," the editorial noted, "the Nazis themselves have prepared us to believe the charges." It specifically distinguished these accusations from those made during the previous world war against the German government, "which had sufficient respect for civilization to try most anxiously to refute atrocity charges." In contrast, "the Hitler regime is the result of a deliberate, long-continued program of atrocities," and its leader "would not hesitate to exterminate the whole Russian nation if he could," the editorial said.[86]

A third story about Babi Yar appeared more than 2 months later in March 1942. *Times* Moscow correspondent Ralph Parker, who had just replaced Cyrus Sulzberger, reported on page eight that "no fewer than 50,000 Russians and Ukrainians have been murdered by the German occupation forces in Kiev, according to information in possession of a newspaper office here and considered reliable." Although Jews were not mentioned among the 50,000 murdered, the story added obliquely that "pogroms against the Jews . . . have been worse than anything known before in the old Ukrainian capital."[87]

The ambiguity about the victims' Jewish identity may have been the result of a deliberate Soviet strategy. Although the Soviets were eager to highlight the "bestial outrages" of the German occupiers, they were not so intent on establishing that most of the victims were killed for being Jewish, not for being "loyal to the Soviet." Nor did the exile governments go out of their way to emphasize Jewish victims if it meant minimizing the suffering of non-Jews. In November 1941, when the governments in exile released a statement on civilian deaths, neither the report nor the *Times* story about it mentioned Jews. The exile governments' Inter-Allied Information Committee charged that "more than 100,000 persons had been executed to enforce Axis domination in the occupied countries of Europe," the *Times* story said.[88]

Reporters made similar choices, even when they were not simply relating what an exile government had said. For example, after his release from a German prison, having been exchanged for Axis nationals, Glen M. Stadler of the United Press wrote a 13-paragraph story that was picked up by the *Times* and run on page four. The lead described the "nearly 400,000 Europeans" killed by "Adolf Hitler's firing squads" and the $36 million in cash and goods looted. Yet, the seventh and eighth paragraphs – the only ones that refer to Jews – made clear that almost all those killed were Jews and much of the looted property had been owned by Jews. "In Latvia, Estonia and Lithuania the killing of Jews amounted to an open hunt, reliable sources have established," Stadler wrote. "Upward of 100,000 met death in these Baltic States alone, and more than double that many have been executed in Western Russia." So, according to Stadler's own estimates, at least three-fourths of "the 400,000 Europeans" were Jews, yet he never made that clear at the top of the story. Similarly, only the eighth paragraph indicated that: "Appropriation of Jewish property, carried out systematically by the Gestapo, has contributed a large part of the $36,000,000 of German plunder in the occupied countries."[89] The following Sunday, the *Times* News of the Week in Review, in summarizing the top news stories and referencing the Stadler story, noted a "conservative guess" that occupation forces had executed 250,000 to 500,000 people, but never suggested that most of them were Jews.[90]

American newspapers picked up stories the *Times* did not. The AP described a massacre of hundreds of Lvov citizens, and the *New York Post* noted more than 70,000 civilian executions in August 1941. The *New York Journal American* in November published a page one story on the massacre of 25,000 Jews in Odessa. At the beginning of June, New York newspapers, the *World Telegram, Journal American*, and *Herald Tribune*, picked up another UP story, this one by Joseph Grigg. Grigg reported "one of the biggest known mass slaughters" in Latvia where S.S. troops and Latvian irregulars shot 56,000 men, women, and children. "There is even an official German newsreel of squads shooting Jews in the streets of Riga,"[vi] wrote Grigg, who had "made a particular study of the Jewish problem" during his previous 3 years in Germany.[91] "In Lithuania about

[vi] The film was shown during the Nuremberg war crimes trial.

30,000 Jews, according to most reliable estimates, were killed by special 'cleanup' squads brought from Poland with the knowledge and approval of German civil administration. The entire Jewish population of many towns and villages was driven into the country, forced to dig graves and then machine gunned. In one city alone, more than 8,000 were killed." Grigg explained that the murders were part of Hitler's vow that war would mean the destruction of the Jews and that "those of us who lived in Germany know that he and his agents have done everything possible to make the prophecy come true."[92]

PART II

1942–1945

5

"To Awaken the Conscience of Christendom"

Pressure to Publicize the First News of the Extermination Campaign

HITLER'S prophecy for the destruction of the Jews moved closer to realization with a new Nazi plan devised in January 1942. Almost as soon as the Einsatzgruppen had gone into operation in the Soviet territories in June 1941, it became apparent that the mobile killing squads were too unwieldy to accomplish Hitler's goal of a Jew-free Europe. So on January 20, 1942, senior German officials met at Wannsee in suburban Berlin to establish the administrative procedures that would expand the murder machine. The Germans' solution to the Jewish problem would escalate beyond killing hundreds of thousands of Jews through mass starvation, sporadic pogroms, widespread disease, and back-breaking labor; they were poised to murder millions in specially designed, efficiently operating extermination centers.

Camps for mass gassings had already been set up in Chelmno, north of Lodz, and at Birkenau, part of the Auschwitz facility in Silesia. In the first half of 1942, the major extermination centers, Belzec, Sobibor, Birkenau, Maidanek, and Treblinka, began operation. The mobile killing squads were not finished yet either. They made a second sweep through the Crimean, adding another half-million Jews to their tally.

As industrialized mass murder got underway, the World Jewish Congress, an umbrella organization for dispersed Jewish communities and groups, received in its New York headquarters "a constant stream" of information about the plan from its officials in Geneva, Lisbon, Stockholm, and London.[1] For the first half of 1942, the Congress tried to confirm that the worst was true; during the second half, the organization struggled to get the world to believe it.

The fact that American journalists could no longer cover occupied Europe from inside made both tasks more difficult. After the attack on Pearl Harbor and the declaration of war, *Times* correspondents were either imprisoned or forced to leave German-controlled territory. (Only Lansing Warren remained in Vichy until November 1942.) Instead, Stockholm and Berne, the capitals of neutral Sweden and Switzerland, would serve as listening posts for news from Germany and its satellites. So George Axelsson, a Swedish native who had been in Berlin, returned to Stockholm to join *Times* reporter, Bernard Valery. The other *Times* Berlin correspondent, Guido Enderis, moved to Berne, along with former Vichy correspondent Gaston Archambault, and an unsavory stringer, Jules Sauerwein. Daniel Brigham was already in Berne, having been sent there from Vichy a year and a half earlier. Reporting the fate of Jews behind enemy lines thus fell primarily on reporters particularly ill suited to the task.

During the first months of 1942, only a few hints of the existence of death camps appeared in the *Times*.[2] The stories were spotty because at that point so was the information. As Richard Litchheim, who was stationed in Geneva for the Jewish Agency, wrote a colleague in mid-May 1942 about 20,000 Slovakian Jews who had been sent to Poland: "What is happening in Poland when the transports are arriving there is not yet known."[3] Litcheim would soon find out.

On May 29, Ignacy Schwarzbart, a Jewish member of the Polish National Council in exile in London, received a short report stating that "in the conquered East, the process of extermination of the Jews is being completed." The report mentioned that only 8,000 Jews were alive in Vilna, the others having been killed and, that in the Ukraine "the Jewish element ceased to exist." A longer version of the report from the Bund, a Jewish Socialist organization in Poland, reached London shortly thereafter.[4] The first sentence read: "From the day the Russo-German war broke out, the Germans embarked on the physical extermination of the Jewish population on Polish soil." The Bund report described the Germans' tactics of driving Jews into a town square, a cemetery, or nearby woods, having them dig their own graves, and then shooting them with machine guns or killing them with hand grenades. It listed the numbers killed at specific locations: 30,000 in Lwow, 15,000 in Stanslawow, and 5,000 in Tarnopol. One thousand Jews a day were being gassed in Chelmno, the report said. "The details given in the Bund Report were precise, and, as we now know, accurate," concludes historian Martin Gilbert.[5]

The Polish government-in-exile, which had received the report, disclosed its content to the British Broadcasting Corp. The BBC broadcast the information on June 2, 1942. Four days later, the Polish cabinet sent a note to the Allied governments stating that the "extermination of the Jewish population is reaching an unbelievable scale, with the Nazis slaughtering tens of thousands of Jews in towns throughout Poland." The next day the exile government's prime minister, Wladislaw Sikorski, repeated this statement in a speech broadcast to Poland.[6] On June 10, Schwarzbart, who was a Zionist, and Szmul Zygielbojm of the Bund, the only Jewish members of Polish National Council, brought the issue before the council. On June 13, the *Times* published Goebbel's pledge to "carry out a mass extermination" of Jews in reprisal for Allied bombings of German cities.[7] It had not yet, however, written about the Bund report.

Within the *Times*, a single Jewish massacre was causing controversy. On June 15, Bernard Valery, a *Times* correspondent in Stockholm, wired a story about the murder of 60,000 Vilna Jews to New York via the *Times* bureau in Berne. Daniel Brigham phoned Managing Editor James to say that he was "relaying Valery's story as received here tonight." But Brigham had his doubts. "We have checked a bit with usually well-informed sources, who are skeptical that such a mass elimination could have been carried out without Geneva being aware," Brigham told James. "Questioned as to his 'Polish eye-witness,' Valery suggested we insert 'confirmation lacking.' He added that 'naturally the local press would not touch the story but the local representative of the Polish Telegraphic Agency sent it to London.' "[8]

The story ran in the next day's *Times* on page six, with the qualification that Valery had suggested. "Sixty thousand Jews of Vilna were put to death between May 7 and May 20 by the German-controlled Lithuanian police, according to reports brought here by a Pole, who said he was in Vilna until May 24," the story stated. "The Polish refugee's story of the Vilna massacre of which he said he was an eye-witness, is impossible to confirm now." (That qualification marked one of only three times during the war that a *Times* story about the extermination of the Jews explicitly stated that information could not be confirmed.) The story, which was true, included some of the horrible details of the end of Vilna Jewry. "The Jews, men, women and children, were taken from sundown to dawn in trucks to the suburb of Ponary, where they were mowed down by machine-gun fire," Valery wrote in the *Times* describing the weeks-old massacre. "The executions continued every night until May 30, the Pole related, and during the day members of the Lithuanian police collected and sold the clothing of their victims."

To get the account into the next day's paper, Valery was willing to insert a qualification, but he continued to insist on the story's accuracy. When James sent Valery a cable the day the story appeared saying "lots skepticism here re your Vilna story," Valery wired back: "Feel certain bonafide my informant whose name and name ship on which he arrived here am sending you via different channel probably next week will also send his affidavited deposition." Nor would Valery let the matter drop. The following day he sent James another cable.

> Understand criticism provoked staggering figures Vilna story. I had previously several stories to the same effect and similar figures which I never used because I did not consider the source reliable. Please refer to the United Press Stockholm dispatch of March 16 giving the directmeasures [sic] which the Germans adopt in Eastern Europe. '86,000 Jews executed Minsk with machine-pistols' and giving further details which I have reason to believe the UP correspondents obtained from reliable eye-witnesses. Also refer to Frederick Oeschsner's from Lisbon on May 18. For your information it is now rumored in Baltic circles here that out of 25,000 Riga Jews only 300 are left and the others are presumed murdered.[9]

Valery's editors in New York apparently never asked him to confirm the Vilna story, follow up on the Minsk executions, or track down the "rumor" about the Riga Jews. In fact, Valery wrote few other stories for the *Times* about what was happening to the Jews. In a few months, he would not even be working for the *Times*.

For it turned out the person most skeptical about Valery's Vilna story was not Brigham in Berne or James in New York; the most skeptical *Times*man was in Stockholm making life difficult for Valery. Although technically a neutral, George Axelsson had been kicked out of Germany soon after the country had declared war on the United States for working for a newspaper of an enemy power. At the beginning of 1942, the *Times* sent him to Stockholm, where he had been raised, but where he had not lived for 26 years. Safely ensconced in the new capital, Axelsson wrote a seven-part series on conditions in Germany – five news stories, including three that appeared on the *Times* front page, and two articles for the magazine. The stories focused on the German home front, describing deprivations of food and materials, and propaganda efforts to explain military setbacks on the Eastern front. Axelsson even wrote a travel log for the magazine based on a "tour of hotels, restaurants and shops" in Berlin, in which he griped about the scarcity of taxis, movies that "are not entertaining," and food that "is not brilliant," including "watery ice cream" and vegetables "that taste of chemicals." Not one of these seven lengthy stories mentioned what was happening to the Jews in Germany.[10]

When the Ponary story appeared on June 16, Axelsson was particularly dismissive, describing it in a cable to James as "Valery's plugged nickel on Vilna."[11] He would take a still more skeptical stance on the even more horrific news to emerge from Eastern Europe at the end of June and into July. Within the year, Valery, who would prove to be right about the massacres, would be gone. Axelsson, who would prove to be wrong, would remain at the *Times* for another 13 years.

The *Times* finally carried an account of the Bund report at the end of June, although only the most careful of readers would have known it. On page five of the June 27 issue, the *Times*, as it often did, stacked similarly themed, short stories one on top of another. The top story announced the Germans were offering 10,000,000 Czech crowns for information leading to the arrest of Czech partisans who had assassinated S.S. leader Reinhard Heydrich. The middle stories reported that a total of 800 people had been shot in Nazi reprisals since Heydrich's killing and that five people had been shot in Poland for striking back at Germans who had hit them. The bottom story carried this news: "700,000 Jews were slain by the Nazis in Poland." The *Times* attributed the information to "an announcement of the Polish Government in London." The story continued: "'To accomplish this, probably the greatest mass slaughter in history, every death-dealing method was employed – machine-gun bullets, hand grenades, gas chambers, concentration camps, whipping, torture instruments and starvation,' the Polish announcement said." CBS in New York had re-aired the BBC broadcast on the Bund report, apparently prompting the *Times*' story.

Three days later, Schwarzbart, the Jewish Polish Council member, held a press conference in London under the auspices of the World Jewish Congress. The *Times* ran a UP story based on the press conference, which meant it had not sent a reporter. "'The Germans have massacred more than 1,000,000 Jews since the war began in carrying out Adolph Hitler's proclaimed policy of exterminating the Jewish people,' spokesmen for the World Jewish Congress charged today," the *Times* reported on June 30. "They said the Nazis had established a 'vast slaughterhouse for Jews'" in Eastern Europe. The *Times* recited the death figures, which included more of Europe than the initial Bund numbers: 700,000 murdered in Lithuania and Poland, 125,000 in Rumania, 200,000 in Nazi-occupied parts of Russia, and 100,000 in the rest of Europe. "Thus about one-sixth of the pre-war Jewish population in Europe, estimated at 6,000,000 to 7,000,000 persons, had been wiped out in less than three years," the *Times* stated. The story also said that Jews deported from Germany, Austria, and Czechoslovakia were being shot by firing squads at the rate of 1,000 daily. The story appeared on page seven. In contrast, the *Herald Tribune* ran a much longer front-page story the same day, bearing the byline of its London correspondent, William W. White.

A more detailed story from the *Times* London bureau fared little better. The July 2, page six story described the Polish exile government's call for the Allies to retaliate against Germans as "the only way to save millions of Jews from certain destruction." The story quoted Zygielbojm, who received the Bund report, as saying its "sources were absolutely reliable, although the story seemed too terrible and the atrocities too inhuman to be true." The *Times* story also specified the path of the murderous campaign, which began in East Galicia the previous summer; spread to the Vilna, Kovno, and the Slonim districts by the fall; encompassed "special gas chamber on wheels" in Western Poland by winter; and extended to Central Poland, including Tarnow, Radom, and Lublin by February. " 'This shows,' the report concludes, 'that the criminal German Government is fulfilling Hitler's threat that, whoever wins, all Jews will be murdered.' " The *Times* story stated, however, that the 700,000 figure mentioned in the Bund report "probably includes many who died of maltreatment in concentration camps, starvation in ghettos or forced labor."

The *Times*' treatment was similar to that of many other American newspapers that tended to put stories about the Bund report and the Polish government's follow-up on inside pages. The *Herald Tribune* and the *New York Journal American* were exceptions.[12] The *Times* alone, however, ran a story that seemed deliberately designed to quash reports of wholesale slaughter. The July 4, page four story from Stockholm did not have a byline, but was almost certainly written by Axelsson. "No figures are available here on Jewish massacres in Nazi-occupied areas except those furnished by refugees and occasional newspaper correspondence from Germany," the story's lead stated. "They permit any conclusion one wants to make from 100,000 to 1,500,000." At first glance, the story seemed to be a direct refutation of the Bund report, except the sources for that report were neither "refugees" nor "newspaper correspondence." What is more likely is that Axelsson was responding to Valery's memo to James a few days earlier laying out the massacres in the former Soviet territories.

Although he equivocated on the number of victims, Axelsson seemed certain about who was victimized and why. "As a rule the Germans treat the Jews according to whether they are productive or nonproductive and whether Reich Jews or Jews in Polish and Russian territory," he wrote. "Usually the productive ones are placed in the war industry, but undoubtedly the others are subjected to great hardships and sufferings. Among the latter the mortality due to starvation and ill treatment is bound to be enormously high." In other words, the Germans were not deliberately executing Jews; the Jews were dying of starvation and ill treatment. Axelsson then took on the reports of massacres directly. "In the Ukraine last October Berlin correspondents of United States and Swedish newspapers reported they had seen mass graves at Zhitomir where 40,000 Jews were said to have been massacred after the entry of the Germans," he wrote. (Axelsson, who had just arrived in Berlin, did not make the trip, nor did anyone else from the *Times*.) "But these estimates appear to have been based on hearsay. The correspondents also stated they saw no Jews anywhere in Poland or the Ukraine, but the official German explanation of this was that 'the Jews fled with the Bolsheviki.'"

Besides being wrong – at least a million Jews had been slaughtered, including many who were "productive" and from the Reich – the story is strange on several accounts. All the other stories on the extermination campaign had been prompted by a news event – a report being released, a press conference being held, or an interview being conducted. But this story was not pegged to any event. The reporter and/or his editor decided that the paper needed a response to the reports of Jewish massacres and so provided one. In addition, the information in the story was not attributed to any sources, it was merely asserted. The lack of attribution was unusual for a newspaper that prided itself on adherence to objectivity, and thus the attribution of all information a reporter could not verify independently. Valery, for example, had carefully attributed all the information about the Ponary massacre to his Polish source.

Why Axelsson wrote such a story is difficult to determine. Having been in Berlin just 6 months earlier, he had witnessed firsthand the Nazis' maniacal persecution of the Jews. Just 3 days after he dismissed the possibility of mass executions, in fact, he wrote about Germany's "latest anti-Jewish measures," which made it "an offense for Jews to stroll along the streets at a leisurely pace" and reduced "the rights of Jews to zero."[13] Still, his odd approach to some stories and his failure to mention Jews once in seven stories about the German home front suggest that their fate was not one of his overriding preoccupations.

Or, Axelsson's skepticism might have had less to do with his attitude toward the Jews and more to do with his attitude toward a colleague. The Jews may simply have gotten caught in the crossfire of an escalating war between Axelsson and Valery. Axelsson considered Valery insolent; he would later cable James that he could not understand why he should "accept from him what [Paris Bureau Chief] Philip and [Berlin Bureau Chief] Enderis wouldn't have taken from me." Once Valery had staked out his position that the Jews were being massacred, Axelsson might have felt obligated to prove him wrong. Although James recognized that Valery had been in Stockholm first, there was no doubt whose side the managing editor was on. He referred to his former Berlin correspondent as "the excellent Axelsson," and cabled Valery: "Axelsson in charge now. If you can work with him that's one thing. If you can't that's another." Three months later Valery decided he could not – "work under Axelsson impossible," he cabled – and quit.[14] Although the problem seemed to be a struggle over power rather than over content, it did mean that a reporter who believed the multiplying reports of the destruction of the Jews was gone, and one who expressed doubts remained.

It is not clear what impact the squabble in Stockholm had on the *Times*' overall treatment of the first reports of the extermination campaign, which continued to appear inside throughout the summer. Deborah Lipstadt concludes that in July and August 1942 most major American dailies allotted just a few lines to the extermination campaign and stuck the stories somewhere between pages 3 and 10.[15] The *Times* July 22 front page did have a story about a rally in Madison Square Garden, which described the "mass demonstration against Hitler atrocities," and featured President Roosevelt's statement that the "American people will hold the Nazis to 'strict accountability' for their crimes of oppression." But it was not possible to tell from the *Times* coverage – or from the president's statement for that matter – exactly what those crimes were or against whom they were directed.

The day the rally story appeared, widespread deportations from the Warsaw ghetto began. The JTA transmitted the news 5 days later, and a

Times story appeared 2 days after that. Like the original story on the Bund report, this one was the last in a stack of other war-related stories. "Nazi authorities in Poland are planning to 'exterminate' the entire Warsaw ghetto whose population is estimated at 600,000 Jews, a Polish spokesman asserted tonight on the basis of reliable reports from the Continent," the *Times* reported on July 29 (p. 7). Over the next 2 months, 270,000 Jews would be sent from Warsaw to the gas chambers of Treblinka, which had just begun operation.

Two major events occurred that summer that accelerated the West's knowledge of the Nazis' ultimate intentions toward the Jews. Within view of the American press, thousands of Jews from France were shipped to Poland. Simultaneously, German sources in Switzerland revealed that the Nazi government had a plan to kill all Europe's Jews in one horrifying blow. The *Times* Berne bureau was well positioned to cover both stories, but ill equipped to do so. Former Berlin bureau chief Guido Enderis had brought to Berne his sympathies for the Germans, as Vichy reporter and French native Gaston Archambault had his for the French. Later in the war, their Berne colleague, Daniel Brigham, who had his own limitations as a reporter, complained to his managing editor that on news stories he had "to pander to easily wounded susceptibility – Guido on German subjects and Archie on French." Enderis also continued his habit of writing very little, although without the compensating connections to the government.[16]

If Archambault and Enderis sympathized with the French and Germans, respectively, one member of the Berne bureau went beyond sympathy to what was most likely active collaboration. Jules Sauerwein, a French native, wrote for two newspapers, the collaborationist French paper, *Paris Soir*, and the *New York Times*. James, who knew Sauerwein from his days as the *Times'* Paris bureau chief, was fond of him. Herbert Matthews, who had been a *Times* reporter in Paris when James was there, recalled that Sauerwein fed James "much of the material" that appeared in James' front-page stories on French politics. According to Matthews, James was "not a good foreign correspondent or war correspondent," whereas Sauerwein was "remarkably knowledgeable" and well connected. So if James needed information, Sauerwein would get it, easily reaching whatever high-ranking French official he wanted. (Matthews confessed to relying on Sauerwein himself.) James also palled around with the fat and witty Frenchman, both of them loving food, wine, and women.[17]

Throughout the Second World War, James went out of his way to keep Sauerwein on the *Times* payroll, at first at $300 a month, even though he had a reputation as a Nazi sympathizer. In July 1940, soon after the French defeat, Sauerwein wrote to James applauding Vichy's role in Germany's new Europe. That letter was followed in 1941 by one James later acknowledged Sauerwein "should not have written about Germany being sure to win the war and the only thing for France was to take her place in the new Europe alongside of Germany." James sent a translated summary of Sauerwein's letter to Arthur Sulzberger that encapsulated the Frenchman's view that France would collaborate with Germany to "create a dignified state in Europe." James suspected the British obtained the letters as they went through airmail in Bermuda and sent copies to "the folks in Washington." The *Times* then stopped using Sauerwein's articles "because of some very emphatic things said to us from Washington sources." The *Times*, however, continued to pay him $300 a month even after the ease with which he traveled between Paris and Berne led to the conclusion that "he would not do that unless he was in pretty good with the Germans."[18]

Sauerwein's connections did not sit well with other *Times*men in Berne. In fact, Brigham called Sauerwein a German agent in front of office staff and others, and Sauerwein threatened to sue him for libel in Swiss court. Sauerwein eventually abandoned the idea of a lawsuit, but then refused to come to the office because of Brigham's hostility. At least one other member of the Berne bureau believed Brigham was not too far off the mark. Archambault said his own "attitude is – and will remain until further orders – that J.S. is a member of our organization and should receive at least the minimum courtesies." But he did not think much of Sauerwein's reporting, describing his "daily gleanings" as "propaganda rather than news and that propaganda is all one-sided." Archambault concluded: "J.S., in short, is a confirmed 'new European' who is keeping in reserve certain connections, including ours, should things go awry." At the end of 1942, the *Times* cut Sauerwein's salary to $150 a month, but continued to pay it for another 2 years even though the paper did not use him as a correspondent. He occasionally provided the paper with tips for others to track down. One thing finally severed the connection. On the Friday before American troops liberated Paris in 1944, Sauerwein fled the French capital and arrived in Portugal in a German plane. Still, the *Times* paid him $1,000 more in 1945 to "get out of the arrangement."[19]

Brigham too had his problems, although they had less to do with politics and more to do with accuracy. In October 1942, Cyrus Sulzberger complained that Brigham's story about the appointment of the Soviet defense commissar "was a complete phony." Nor, according to Cyrus Sulzberger, was that an isolated incident. Brigham "is obviously inclined towards sensationalism and lack of caution (I think his record speaks for itself) and instead of coppering up reports as unconfirmed goes out all the way on a limb."[20] James told the publisher that he believed Cyrus was right about Brigham – a sentiment apparently prevalent at the *Times* and in the journalistic community. London Bureau Chief Raymond Daniell cabled James about a Brigham story that he described as "up to his usual standard" – "twas plain fake."[21] *Time* magazine, in an April 12, 1943 article, even singled Brigham out for criticism. After praising *Times* foreign correspondents as "certainly the best in the U.S., perhaps in the world," *Time* added: "*Times*men are by no means perfect. Daniel Brigham, in Switzerland, has often been fooled by German propaganda and has repeatedly missed accuracy, spurred by phony tips and his own imagination."

The final member of the Berne bureau, Gaston Archambault, was not known as inaccurate or a collaborator. In fact, his two sons had fled to London in 1942 and were fighting for the Free French. But it seems likely that his sympathies as a Frenchman blinded him to the faults of the Petain regime in 1940 and 1941. By January 1942, Archambault had started to sour on Petain, describing his New Year's Day appeal as "pathetic" and acknowledging his difficulty in acting as "Chief of State" because of the "German occupation of three-fifths of France." Yet, he soon wrote an opinion column from Berne that assured "collaboration" between France and Germany was "dead as a doornail," and might even have been "stillborn."[22] Throughout 1942, Archambault viewed the intensifying persecution of the Jews and their ultimate deportation as a minor story, whose consequence lay in what it meant for the French regime and the French people. (Interestingly, Archaumbault wrote most of these stories from Berne, even though the *Times'* other Paris bureau stalwart, Lansing Warren, was still in France until November.)

If collaboration ever was "dead," it was resurrected in April 1942, when Pierre Laval was restored to his position in the Vichy government, an event that the *Times* chronicled on the front page and in six separate stories – none of which mentioned what it would mean for the Jews in France. While Petain remained Chief of State, Laval took over key positions in the French cabinet that led him to become in effect the head of the Vichy government. *Times* editorial board member Anne O'Hare McCormick used Laval's return as an opportunity to praise Petain, whom she described as having "done a magnificent job of stalling." Because of Petain's effective "delaying action," and France's unwillingness to cooperate, Hitler had to turn to Laval, "the most unpopular man in France," she wrote. "Laval is the symbol of [Hitler's] defeat, the sign not of cooperation but of French refusal to cooperate."[23]

With Laval in place, the Germans did indeed step up their demands for cooperation in two key areas. They insisted that hundreds of thousands of French workers be shipped to Germany to toil in its factories and that Jews in France be deported to Poland. The *Times* treated the first story as significant news, chronicled in five front-page stories, and two editorials that appeared in the autumn of 1942. The second story, the deportation of tens of thousands of Jews under what the *Times* described as "brutal" conditions, was not a front-page story, except on a few occasions when it overlapped with what the newspaper considered more important news. The *Times*, particularly in stories by Archambault, also tended to view the deportations in terms of what it meant for the Vichy government, rather than for the Jews.

On July 18, the *Times* reported on page six the arrest of more than 12,000 Jews in Paris, although the headline incorrectly described the Nazis as conducting the 2-day operation; 9,000 French police actually made the arrests. The article did accurately note that the "'aliens'" were "to be sent to the east." Eight days later, the *Times* explained that the "alien refugees" arrested, now a total of 15,000 to 20,000, were to be sent to concentration camps in Poland (as were 60,000 Jews from Amsterdam, the story noted in an aside). "Reports reaching London told of scenes of terror and despair as the families were carted off to concentration centers," the last paragraph of the page 16 story said. "A Jewish woman with her three children in her arms was said to have jumped from a fifth-floor apartment. All were killed." The story also suggested that French leaders were not responsible; Petain and Laval were reported to have "refused to cooperate in such a ruthless purge," the story said.[i] A later story provided more horrifying details of the Paris roundup. Jews were dragged from their homes and

[i] According to Marrus and Paxton in *Vichy France and the Jews*, 228–34, Laval readily agreed to the deportations of foreign Jews and Petain, at the least, went along.

ejected from hospitals, including a cancer patient who had been operated on 12 hours before and a "woman beside whose bed the police stood while she was being delivered," the page 14 story said.[24]

Although the confirmed arrests of thousands of Jews did not merit a front-page story, one source's suggestion that the Pope might intervene did. "Pope Is Said to Plead for Jews Listed for Removal From France," the front-page headline on August 6 declared. The unnamed Berne reporter who sent the story claimed that he had "learned from a usually reliable source in Vichy" that Pope Pius XII had protested to Petain against " 'the inhuman arrests and deportations' " of Jews to Silesia and occupied parts of Russia. The source turned out to be not so reliable; the Pope remained silent, although other Catholic clergy did stage vigorous protests, as the *Times* would later chronicle.[25] The rest of the story, however, was accurate. "Late reports from the occupied zone last night received here via Stockholm announced that the first trains carrying Jews to concentration camps in Poland and Russia left Paris early yesterday," it said. A two-paragraph UP item from London tagged onto the end of the story said Laval had agreed to surrender all Jews of foreign origin in the occupied zone and 10,000 Jews from the unoccupied area. When 7,000 Jews were rounded up in the unoccupied zone in late August, the news appeared in short items on pages three and five.[26]

Yet, in September, another story about the Pope's supposed involvement based on unconfirmed reports, made the front page. The September 20 story by the notoriously unreliable Brigham speculated that the meeting between the Pope and Myron C. Taylor, President Roosevelt's personal representative to the Vatican, meant that "some important action in favor of an oppressed religious minority" would be "carried out under Vatican auspices."[27] No such action took place.[28] Two days earlier, the arrest of a member of the Archbishop of Lyons' staff, who had preached tolerance toward the Jews, also appeared on the front page.

As the deportations continued, French citizens in both the occupied and unoccupied zones witnessed the heartrending scenes of Jewish families being torn apart. At first, only adults were deported east. The *Times* reported on August 27 (p. 3) that "3,500 Jewish children ranging in age from a few days to 10 years" had been "left behind during the recent gigantic roundup of 25,000 Jews in occupied France." The unattended children became such a dicey political issue that the Germans began pushing children across the border into the unoccupied zone so they would become Vichy's headache.

Vichy then changed its policy. "No one and nothing can turn us from the policy of purging France of undesirable Jewish expatriates," an "authorized source" told the UP in a story printed in the September 12 *Times* (p. 2). The government therefore had decided to deport children along with their parents. The "authorized source" was almost certainly Laval, who said virtually the same thing at a press conference reported on Paris Radio.[29]

This new policy meant children began to fill the trains leaving France for the east. Laval then faced pressure from relief organizations and the U.S. State Department to allow several thousand Jewish children to emigrate. On October 15, the *Times* reported on page 11 that the United States, Canada, and the Dominican Republic had agreed to accept 5,000, 1,000, and 500 Jewish children from France, respectively. Laval, angered by the publicity, then cut the number of exit visas Vichy would issue to 150. He also insisted that those emigrating be bona fide orphans, meaning only those whose parents were known to be dead, not just deported east and presumed dead. Before final arrangements could be made in November, however, the Allies had landed in North Africa and relations between Vichy and the United States were severed.

By the fall, the clerical and other protests over Vichy's Jewish problem had dissipated. Another problem preoccupied the clergy, the nation, and the *New York Times*. After Laval's plan to exchange French POWs for volunteers to work in German factories fizzled, the Germans insisted on obligatory labor service for young men. To most French people that was "the *real* deportation," as Marrus and Paxton put it.[30] So, apparently, was it for the *New York Times*. In mid-September 1942, the *Times* ran two front-page stories, two editorials, and a week in review item on Vichy's willingness to supply forced labor to the Germans.[31] (No *Times* editorial or week in review item ever referred to the deportations of Jews, even in passing.) The *Herald Tribune*, in contrast, ran one editorial, "The Jews in France," that attacked the actions of Vichy's "puppet government," and another, "Laval and the Jews," that denounced Vichy's leader.[32]

One *Times* front-page story did refer to Jews; but, as was the case with the Catholic protests and the resistance arrests the year before, the reference was linked to a more important story, forced labor. The September 16 story described Secretary of State Cordell Hull's press conference in which he warned Vichy that the conscription of French labor would be viewed as providing aid to a U.S. enemy and deplored Vichy's anti-Jewish measures. Hull's statement, as quoted in the *Times*, suggested that the secretary was aware of the Nazis' grander plans. Vichy's willingness to deport Jews meant delivering them "to enemies who have announced and in considerable measure executed their intention to enslave, maltreat and eventually exterminate them under conditions of the most extreme cruelty," Hull said. "The details of the measures taken are so fiendish in their nature that they defy adequate description." When Vichy went ahead the next month and conscripted men for German factories, the action made the front page, as did two more stories on forced French labor later that October.[33] An October 31 story reporting Hull's condemnation of just the Jews' plight, however, appeared on page five.

In the meantime, tens of thousands of Jews in France had been packed into sealed cattle cars. Until that point, the *Times* stories simply stated that the Jews were being sent to the east, or to perform forced labor in the east, or to Polish concentration camps, or to "an unknown destination." Within a month, events in Geneva, London, New York and Washington, DC, would reveal their destination.

In early August 1942, Gerhart Riegner, the World Jewish Congress' representative in Geneva, learned that German sources had confirmed that the Germans intended to annihilate the Jews. A German industrialist had told Swiss businessmen of a plan being considered in Hitler's headquarters to kill nearly 4 million Jews in the fall using prussic acid. "[I]t was the first report from a well-placed German source of the intent and plan to destroy the Jewish people entirely," Richard Breitman concludes.[34] Once the Germans' ultimate intent was established, the fragmentary news about deportations and death began to fit together – the Germans were shipping Jews from all over Europe to Poland to kill them.

The *New York Times* reporters assigned to follow events in occupied Europe would not be the ones to disclose this information. Riven by distrust of each other's abilities and motives, hobbled by their own limitations as journalists, members of the *Times* Stockholm and Berne bureaus did not pursue the story of what was happening to Europe's Jews, nor did they receive directions from New York to do so. If a release or a report passed their way, they would shuffle it into the next day's paper. But none of the reporters had the inclination, the fortitude, or the stature to make the extermination campaign an important story for the *New York Times*.

That left it to Jewish groups, particularly the World Jewish Congress, to try to get the word out.

As he had since fleeing Berlin and establishing himself in Geneva, Riegner tried to inform his World Jewish Congress colleagues of the latest, devastating news. The congress had originally been headquartered in Paris, but had moved to Geneva at the outbreak of war. A year later, the headquarters moved again, this time to the even greater safety of New York. Rabbi Stephen S. Wise, who headed the American affiliate, assumed leadership of the international group as well. Unlike most of the congress' leadership, Wise was thoroughly American. Although born in Budapest, the grandson of the chief rabbi of Hungary, he had been brought to America as a baby. He graduated from Columbia University and was ordained a rabbi in the early 1920s. He turned down an offer to become rabbi at Manhattan's Emanu-El, the tony East Side synagogue Arthur Sulzberger attended, when the influential trustees Louis Marshall and Jacob Schiff would not promise him sufficient autonomy. He then founded his own "Free Synagogue" on the West Side, becoming an important figure in both the Jewish community and Democratic politics. By the 1940s, Wise, in his 60s and ill, was slowing down but remained a commanding figure and gifted orator.

So it was to Wise that Riegner tried to send a telegram on August 8, 1942. The telegram described the "alarming report" that a plan was "under consideration" for all Jews being sent to the east from German-occupied or -controlled countries to be "at one blow exterminated to resolve once and for all Jewish question." The telegram contained some inaccuracies: by the summer of 1942, the plan was not "under consideration" but well under way; it was being implemented not in "one blow" but by thousands of lethal blows. The message also contained a qualification: the information was being transmitted, it said, with "all necessary reservation as exactitude cannot be confirmed," although it added the informant had "close connection with highest german authorities and his reports generally reliable."

Riegner planned to send the telegram using the U.S. State Department's cable facilities. He went first to the American consul in Geneva and then to the British consul, having also decided to send a telegram to the World Jewish Congress' London headquarters. American officials took down the message but ultimately refused to send it, informing Riegner 2 weeks later that they were "disinclined to deliver the message in question in view of the unsubstantiated character of the information which forms its main theme." The British, too, had reservations about transmitting Riegner's cable but went ahead, mostly because it was addressed to Sidney Silverman, head of the congress' British section who also happened to be a member of Parliament. When Silverman received the telegram he followed Riegner's cabled instructions to "inform and consult New York."

Riegner's telegram and the news that it brought intensified a debate within the World Jewish Congress on how best to publicize the ongoing war on the Jews. Riegner and his Geneva colleague Lichtheim of the Jewish Agency had long pushed for more publicity "in the British and American press and over the radio, but sofar [sic] very little has been done in this respect." They wanted "cases like the persecutions and murders going on in Slovakia, Croatia, Romania etc." to be mentioned "more frequently and more vigorously in the press and by speakers of the democracies," Lichtheim wrote.[35] Others, mindful of how editors might react to "Jewish propaganda," argued that the congress needed to provide as specific information as possible. "The entire section on the situation of the Jews in the occupied Baltic and Soviet territory is particularly lacking in concrete details," wrote Louis Shub, an American Jewish Committee staff member, in a July 1942 internal memo critiquing a press release. "It is quite impossible to impress editors with such statements as this: 'From one case to the next the massacres became more gruesome and horrible.'"[36]

Still others argued for publicity, but not the kind that played up Jewish suffering. Max Beer, a well-known socialist, wrote a memo advocating that Jewish suffering should be mentioned only in the context of atrocities against other people. When asked by an American magazine to write about Nazi atrocities, Beer "built up" his story "around the theory that Hitler's regime was cruel in general." He cited instances in the Netherlands, Poland, and Norway, rather than "utilize all the stories about persecution of Jews." To do otherwise, Beer argued, would be to "ask Americans to fight for the Jews," rather than for themselves, and to play into Nazi propaganda that "this is a Jewish war." He concluded: "Nothing would be more disastrous from the Jewish point of view than to assume that there is a duty to stress always Jewish sufferings and Jewish problems because they are Jewish."[37]

This was a common but by no means uncontested view, which World Jewish Congress leaders debated throughout the year. One of the most outspoken proponents of publicity about "Jewish problems" was A. Leon

Kubowitzki, a 46-year-old lawyer who headed the congress' European Affairs Section. Born in Lithuania and educated in Belgium, Kubowitzki moved to New York in late 1940, where he seemed to comb the *Times* for stories about the fate of the Jews. His reading led him to a conclusion. Although the congress had been instrumental in drawing attention to the Bund report in July, the message was not getting through to the American public. In August, before World Jewish Congress leaders in New York had learned of the Riegner telegram, Kubowitzki pushed for a concerted publicity drive. "I can only repeat that our people in Europe are being exterminated in cold blood and that we must do something about it, even if we are not sure that we will meet with success," he wrote in a memo to Wise and other congress leaders. In words that would prove prescient, he wrote: "It is my impression that nothing similar to what has been done in this way for the Zionist cause has been tried with regard to the galuth and the plight of Jews in Europe, which is now the most urgent of our problems." He pushed the congress to stage a conference of "prominent non-Jewish personages" and to call a press conference of the news weeklies to "tell them candidly of the conspiracy of silence which surrounds the massacres of Jews." He wanted the congress to publish a special biweekly bulletin on the massacres and deportations. "The non-Jews and the Jews who don't read Yiddish are not aware of the situation," he wrote. "If it were known, public opinion would revolt." He added a disgusted postscript, apparently upon learning of President Roosevelt's most recent statement on atrocities. The president's statement "won't help us," he concluded. "There is not a word about the Jews, nor a word about the deportations."[38]

Indeed, when the *Times* reported the president's statement on its front page the following day, the August 22 story never mentioned Jews. The article by W. H. Lawrence from Washington was headlined: "President Warns Atrocities of Axis Will be Avenged." The story quoted the president saying "the barbaric and unrelenting character of the occupational regime will become more marked and may even lead to the extermination of certain populations." In explaining what the president meant, Lawrence, wrote only: "This was a reference to such Nazi terroristic acts such as the destruction of Lidice, Czechoslovakia, in punishment for the assassination of Reinhard Heydrich, Germany Gestapo leader."[39]

Kubowitzki continued his complaint a week or so later, still unaware of the Riegner telegram that Wise had just received and still insisting that ignorance was a central problem. "In all our recent discussion on the present Jewish situation in Europe and the lack of reaction on the part of the Jewish public as well as of American public opinion," he wrote, "the same argument was heard again and again: the non-Jews and the English reading Jews are not informed of what is going on."[40]

The Riegner telegram further complicated the debate on publicity. Undersecretary of State Sumner Welles, whom a distraught Wise had contacted, told the rabbi not to disclose the news to the press until State had been able to confirm it. Wise generally encouraged press attention to Jewish persecution, but when confronted with the enormity of a plan to eradicate all Jews, and faced with Welles' reticence, Wise agreed to keep quiet.[41]

There are differences of opinion on Wise's decision to withhold the news pending State Department confirmation. Some praise his wisdom in not hurrying to disclose information that could too easily be dismissed as propaganda, while others contend that the aged and ailing rabbi was cowed by his reverence for Franklin Roosevelt. Regardless, little appeared in the press in September and October 1942 about what was happening to the Jews in Europe. On September 3, the *Times* reported on page five that 50,000 Jews from Germany and Czechoslovakia "have been thrown into the fortress at Terezin," better known by the German, Theresienstadt. "'All hope for them has been abandoned,' the [Czech government] spokesman said." The *Times* also published one of its infrequent editorials on the Jewish problem on September 12 (p. 12). Entitled "The Sound of the Shofar" to coincide with Rosh Hashanah, the beginning of the Jewish year 5703, the editorial noted that the Nazis had "given the day a non-sectarian significance," by "making war on [the Jews] Hitler really began the war against an unnumbered multitude" of nations. "The Jewish people stood in the front of the firing line," the *Times* opined. "They were the first to fall." A front-page story 10 days later, however, did not count them among the fallen. In reporting on the release of an Inter-Allied Information Committee survey, the *Times* noted that 207,373 people had been executed by the Nazis in Europe. The survey did not mention the number of Jews who had died, nor did the *Times*.

Even as they awaited word from the State Department, World Jewish Congress leaders called a meeting of major Jewish organizations to plot their next move; arousing public opinion was a key element in all their strategies. In early September, Agudas Israel, an Orthodox group, cabled the congress about the decimation of the Warsaw ghetto and urged its leaders to "do your best to arouse such American intervention appealing to statemen [sic] and public opinion." Soon thereafter, the congress' London office suggested to Wise "urgent action" that included calling a press conference, and convincing "leading political religious other authorities" to issue declarations. The importance with which the congress viewed public opinion can be seen in a congress official's efforts to try to get the United States and other friendly countries to issue visas for Jewish children caught in occupied Europe. The first step – the "idea must be widely publicized," the congress' Arieh Tartakower insisted. "Press conferences have to be called and a series of articles published in leading newspapers and magazines."[42] (The effort may have backfired, however, when Prime Minister Laval reacted negatively to publicity and refused to grant promised visas to Jewish children in France.)

After 3 years of intense persecution and 3 months of extermination reports, Jewish leaders knew they still were not getting through. "There has been no real awakening of the public conscience here on the whole issue," Arthur Lourie of the Emergency Committee for Zionist Affairs wrote Lichtheim on September 25. Among Jews, "certainly there is some knowledge and a sense of horror and ineffectiveness in the face of calamity, but as far as the general American public is concerned – while from time to time there are news stories dealing with the deportations and massacres – the whole thing remains remote, and interest centers, perhaps inevitably, on affairs near home."[43]

But Wise and other Jewish leaders were still holding back what was likely to be the most explosive news yet – the Germans' annihilation plan. Kubowitzki, for one, was growing restless. "I believe that our prolonged silence risks becoming complicity," he wrote the World Jewish Congress leaders at the end of September. At the end of October, Kubowitzki and 78 congress officials and 22 expert guests met to discuss the European situation. Nahum Goldmann, head of the congress' administrative committee, chaired the meeting and stressed the importance of prominent press coverage. "Our only weapon is public opinion," Goldmann said, according to the meeting's minutes. "We plan to have the President or Cordell Hull receive a delegation of Jewish representatives in connection with the most recent Nazi barbarities; a statement would then be issued, and a press conference held. Coming from such high authorities, the story would get front page publicity, and this is the best way to reach the public." The other officials who spoke agreed on the need for publicity, although some did not think it was necessary to involve the State Department, assuming the congress could get enough press attention on its own.[44]

From Switzerland, Lichtheim and Riegner also continued to press for disclosure.[45] By October, Riegner had spent 3 hours listening to Gabriel Zinvian, a Baltic Jew who was in a hospital ward in Switzerland, provide an eyewitness account of the end of Latvian Jewry, including almost all of Riga's Jews.[46] (*Times*' Stockholm reporter Valery had learned of the massacre 4 months earlier, but the newspaper had not followed up on the information.) Lichtheim and Riegner presented what they knew to Leland Harrison, the U.S. minister in Berne, who decided they were telling the truth and forwarded their information and his own conclusions to Welles in Washington.

In the meantime, the news was seeping out in other ways. On November 16, 78 Jews from occupied Europe had arrived in Palestine, having been exchanged for German civilians. On November 24, the *Times* ran a three-paragraph story on page 10, noting the Hebrew press' black bordered "reports of mass murders of Jews in Poland" based on the eyewitness testimony of recent Palestine arrivals. Kubowitzki used the *Times* story to chide his colleagues at the Labor Zionist organization, Poale Zion. Quoting the *Times*, Kubowitzki asked what Poale Zion had done to carry out a resolution adopted at the last convention promising that Jewish groups would "explore every means for arousing responsible quarters to the necessity for action."[47]

That same day, Welles finally told Wise, who along with his son, James, traveled to Washington to see him, that their worst fears were realized. The Germans were set on a course to exterminate all Jews. Wise could now tell the press, as long as all the newspapers received the information at the same time and the names appearing in the documents from Switzerland were not disclosed.[48] The Wises quickly called a press conference attended by half a dozen reporters, but no one from the *New York Times*. Alvin Rosenfeld, a reporter for the International News Service fresh out of Columbia Journalism School, recalled the briefing. "Did I write a story about it? Yes. Did it make one of the wires? Yes. Did papers pick it up? Yes. Did anybody believe it? I doubt it. Did I believe it? Yes, perhaps halfway I believed it. I believed a little bit of it. I didn't believe all of it. It was beyond the comprehension of everybody in this country."[49]

When the news that the State Department had confirmed a German plan to kill all the Jews finally appeared in the *New York Times* on November 25, it was tacked to the bottom of two related stories. First came a story by the London bureau's James MacDonald who reported on the latest Polish government-in-exile report. As an indication of how rapidly "the Jewish population had been cut down," the story quoted Polish officials who said "only 40,000 October ration cards had been printed for the Jews in the Warsaw ghetto, where the population last March was 433,000." The story also reported that Jews were being loaded into freight cars so crowded that they died of suffocation or from starvation and thirst. " 'Wherever the trains arrive half the people are dead,' " the *Times* said. "Those surviving are sent to special camps at Treblinka, Belzec and Sobibor [in Southeastern Poland]. Once there the so-called settlers are mass-murdered."

Beneath that story was one relayed by a *Times* reporter in Jerusalem that, for the first time in the *Times*, mentioned Auschwitz as an extermination center. "Information received here of methods by which the Germans in Poland are carrying out the slaughter of Jews includes accounts of trainloads of adults and children taken to great crematoriums at Oswiecim, near Cracow," the lead read, using the Polish term for Auschwitz. "Polish Christian workers have confirmed reports that concrete buildings on the former Russian frontier are used by the Germans as chambers in which thousands of Jews have been put to death." The orders, which came from Nazi Gestapo chief Heinrich Himmler, "have been authenticated by non-Jewish neutral persons who have visited Nazi-occupied Eastern Europe," the story said.

Finally, came an AP story from Washington: Rabbi Wise "learned through sources confirmed by the State Department that about half the estimated 4,000,000 Jews in Nazi-occupied Europe had been slain in an 'extermination' campaign,'" the *Times* reported. The newspaper quoted Wise as saying he had awaited confirmation since Labor Day. " 'The State Department finally made available today the documents which have confirmed the stories and rumors of Jewish extermination in all Hitler-ruled Europe,' Dr. Wise said." All three stories appeared on page 10.

The *New York Herald Tribune* ran the State Department's confirmation on page one, but most newspapers placed it on inside pages and attributed the information to Wise rather than the State Department. That might have been because the State Department had in off-the-record conversations sought to distance itself from Wise. November 1942 was also a critical month in the course of the war, with the British defeating Axis forces at El Alamein in Egypt, the Americans landing in North Africa, and the Russians holding Stalingrad. *PM* was one of the only newspapers to run a series of stories based on the extermination news and to call for an activist rescue policy.[50]

Following the Wise press conference, the story picked up momentum. Stories appeared in rapid succession in the *Times*, although all inside the newspaper. A *Times* London reporter interviewed Polish council member Schwarzbart, who told him that 1 million persons, nearly one-third of Poland's Jewish population, had perished. The November 26, page 16 story, which described Poland "as a mass grave," correctly noted that hundreds of thousands of Jews had been sent from the West, including France, to Poland, although it incorrectly mentioned that mass electrocutions were taking place at Belzec. Two days later, the Saturday *Times* reported on page seven that the Polish National Council had voted a resolution protesting the German crimes against the Jewish population in Poland. The story quoted Jewish council member Schwarzbart murmuring that in his horror he "could not find words to express my feelings; I cannot speak." According to the story, his fellow Jewish colleague Zygielbojm added in a broken voice: "There is nothing I can say except to hope the Germans will be defeated before they kill all my people." The *Times* chose not to editorialize about the extermination campaign that week, nor did an item appear on Sunday, November 29, in the News of the Week in Review section.

Like hundreds of other American newspapers, the *Times* published an editorial on Wednesday, December 2, to coincide with a day of mourning called by Jewish organizations. The lengthy, lead editorial – one of only two lead editorials on Jews throughout the war – stated that "it is believed that 2,000,000 European Jews have perished and that 5,000,000 are in danger of extermination." Still, the headline, "The First to Suffer," highlighted the *Times* editors' continuing conviction that Nazi crimes against the Jews were on par with those against other peoples and were the result, not of murderous anti-Semitism, but of Nazism's "need of a scapegoat." The *Times* opined: "The attack upon the Jew was the first employment of the Nazi strategy – of bringing overwhelming power against the weakest of its chosen enemies. . . . The Jew was the first number on a list which has since included people of other faiths and of many races – Czechs, Poles,

Norwegians, Netherlanders, Belgians, French – and which, should Hitler win, would take in our own 'mongrel' nation."[51,ii]

Along with the editorial, the *Times* reported on the various activities leading up to and occurring on the day of mourning, as well as the Palestine assembly's appeal to the Allies to rescue European Jews.[52] On December 4, the *Times* ran a story from its London bureau with the headline: "Two-thirds of Jews in Poland Held Slain," based on another report from the Bund in Poland. In addition to recounting the overall numbers, the page 11 story described the Warsaw ghetto, where only 30,000 Jews remained, "as in a state of nervous tension approximating mass insanity." The report concluded "with an ardent appeal to save 500,000 survivors from 'inevitable death.' It is useless to pass resolutions or to punish the Germans after the war, says the appeal. The need for action is immediate."

The story prompted Kubowitzki's most emotional written outburst so far, in which he quoted the *Times* lead. "I read today in the 'New York Times': 'Only 1,250,000 Jews are still alive in Poland of the 3,500,000 before the German occupation, according to a report received in London from secret Jewish Labor groups,'" he wrote Wise. "May I take the liberty of asking you, Dr. Wise: what are you going to do about it? Since July 27 I am desperately beseeching you and Dr. Goldmann with proposals on how to stop the murderers of our people. . . . If this heavy burden is too heavy, why don't you allow us to share it with you?" Kubowitzki warned: "Why do you expose our memories to be spat upon by future generations because we acquiesced in the crime of inaction in such a time and did not try everything, I say everything in the world?"[53]

It has been argued that Wise's reticence stemmed from his conviction that his friend, President Roosevelt, would come to the Jews' rescue. Indeed, Wise and representatives from four other Jewish groups met with Roosevelt on December 8. Roosevelt told the Jewish leaders that the government knew the facts about the extermination campaign but that it was hard to know what action to take.[54] The president did not say a word about the extermination campaign at the press conference he held that week or

[ii] The *Times* was not the only newspaper that did not grasp the depth of German anti-Semitism. As Lipstadt, *Beyond Belief*, 176–80, explains, American newspapers offered a range of explanations for the Germans' deportations of Jews to Poland from the need for a scapegoat to the use of Jews as slave labor.

at any of the press conferences he held about twice a week over the next 15 months – nor was he asked.[55] Nor did the Jewish delegation's meeting with the president generate the kind of publicity World Jewish Congress officials had assumed it would when they met a month and a half earlier. Instead of page one, the *Times* reported on page 20 Roosevelt's pledge to the delegation that he would consider naming a commission to investigate the crimes. Even many journalists did not know that Jewish leaders had met with the president. When columnist Dorothy Thompson gathered a group of newspaper people a week or so later to try to drum up support for a response, she found they "had never heard about the Jewish delegation which had been received by the President." She also found little support among the group for reprisals or even establishing havens.[56]

World Jewish Congress officials recognized that more needed to be done to awaken the public. One congress leader suggested "the Jewish masses demonstrate in procession of hundreds of thousands," so "the Christian population and public opinion in general may be aroused and Government circles will be moved to come out with official declarations and warnings."[57] Others in the congress worried about how the non-Jewish community would perceive processions. The congress appointed a committee to look into the matter.[58]

No disagreement surfaced over overall objectives, however, or the need to enlist the press in accomplishing them. At a December 14 meeting in the congress' New York offices, the officials agreed that they would advocate: "stern warning by the United Nations; havens for those that can be saved; establishment of the Commission to investigate the crimes against civilian populations," and a drive to inform "the Axis people" that there would be "strict accountability" for those crimes. They also called for "a regular program to acquaint the American people with the meaning of this new horror against civilian populations." To do this, the officials suggested calling a conference of top editors at leading newspapers and syndicates, enlisting non-Jewish groups and individuals to take out advertisements, and persuading radio war programs to mention the mass murders. The meeting resolved at least one issue. After months of debate about whether to universalize the tragedy, the group decided the "emphasis should be placed on the Jewish aspect."[59]

In the short run, the World Jewish Congress focused on a declaration to be issued by the United Nations, the joint name for the Allied governments, on Thursday, December 17. After much prodding by the congress and other Jewish leaders, Great Britain drafted a declaration condemning the extermination campaign. The United States and the Soviet Union accepted the draft with some alterations. World Jewish Congress leaders in New York then sought to ensure that upon release the declaration would receive the maximum amount of publicity. The British Foreign Office assumed it would. In rejecting the Poles' idea of a conference in conjunction with the declaration, Under Secretary Richard K. Law explained to the congress' London office that it was unnecessary because "there was already such great public interest in this question that there should be no difficulty about securing adequate publicity."[60]

On December 17, British Foreign Secretary Anthony Eden introduced the declaration into the House of Commons. After a few comments, the members stood silent for 2 minutes. The next day the *New York Times* finally broke its front-page silence on the war against the Jews. (Not all newspapers considered this announcement as important as the *Times*; the *Herald Tribune*, for example, ran the story on page 17.) The editors did not make the declaration the lead story, assigning it just one column in the middle of the page. In fact, the editors believed it was less important than another, more prominently displayed story: "City in Confusion in Test of Double Air Raid Signals." Still, the *Times*' story bore the headline, "11 Allies Condemn Nazi War on Jews," and it stated that the United Nations had decried Germany's "cold-blooded extermination" of the Jews. Interestingly, when the *Times* moved beyond reprinting the declaration (the bulk of the story) to assessing it, the extermination campaign's targets were broadened to include "other innocent civilians who have been the victims of reprisals and persecutions."

That same day (p. 26), a *Times* editorial acknowledged that the declaration would shock civilized people. Although "Hitler's Terror" was not the lead as the editorial earlier in the month had been, this time the *Times* offered no qualifying "it is believed" to its recitation of the horrors. "For this statement is not an outcry of the victims themselves to which many thought it possible to close their ears on the ground that it might be a special plea, subject to doubt," the *Times* opined. "It is the official statements of their own Governments, based on officially established facts. . . . The most tragic aspect of the situation is the world's helplessness to stop the horror while the war is going on."

Not all publications agreed. The *New York Post* editorialized that the Allies needed a "serious plan" to rescue European Jews, as did the liberal weeklies, the *Nation* and the *New Republic*. In an essay entitled "Out of the Depths," a World Jewish Congress leader, most likely Kubowitzki, reacted to the *Times* suggestion that the world was helpless until the war was over. "Pure twadde," he wrote of the *Times*' "editorial pep-talks." "As far as it relates to the Jewish people in Nazi Europe, victory becomes every day a more hollow word and will be a bitter derision if physical salvation doesn't come *before* the war is over."[61]

The World Jewish Congress took pride in the press attention it had helped generate and that most major U.S. publications had condemned the Nazis' extermination plan in editorials. A few congress members worried about too aggressive a publicity strategy. Yet, Stephen Wise rejected the tactics of what he and his colleagues called the "sha-sha Jews" for "whom silence is the only method of dealing with the Jewish problem" – "sha" being the Yiddish word for "quiet." Wise endorsed the congress' approach. "I am not sure that we have succeeded in averting the worst of calamities for our people but at least we have tried, and there is no question but that it is our duty to awaken and to challenge the conscience of Christendom."[62]

Having accomplished their first goal, a "stern warning by the United Nations," the leaders moved to finding havens for Jews and establishing the culpability of Germans and collaborators. The officials knew they needed American public opinion on their side, which they believed could be obtained through editorials in the mainstream press.[63] Congress officials began carrying out some of the publicity strategies they had outlined earlier in the month. They apparently never called a conference of top editors, but they did scurry to solicit proclamations from various non-Jews and to secure corporate advertisements condemning the atrocities.[64]

After a late December meeting, Kubowitzki wrote in his diary that the congress had "developed an impressive program of what would be done in the field of publicity."[65] There were already signs, however, that the congress' strategy to secure "the editorial support of the press in a continuous series" was not working. The day after the United Nations' declaration, its information office released "Persecution of Jews," a 12-page, country-by-country account. The *Times* carried the story, but on page 23. The following Sunday, the *Times* published its annual "Highlights of the Year in Review," a month-by-month listing of what it considered the year's most important events. The plight of the Jews was not mentioned until December and then only once, as the last of three items for December 17.

The other items: a plan to use universities for military training and the federal price administrator's resignation.[66]

By the next month, attention to the singular fate of the Jews had faded even further. On January 18, Cyrus Sulzberger wrote a front-page story from London, headlined: "End of Some Peoples Feared in 1943." There was only one reference to the Jews in the lengthy story: "At the close of last year the Jewish section of the Servtian Gestapo closed down – there were no more living Jews within its operating sphere." The editorial page followed Sulzberger's story with an editorial, "War of Extermination," which also ignored the Jews. "Hundreds of thousands of many nationalities have already been deliberately slaughtered by the Gestapo . . . and the remnants of some smaller nations are now being deported, transplanted, brutalized by slavery or terrorism," the *Times* opined. An appeal from three Anglican Archbishops to the British government to find havens for European Jews appeared on page 26, even though *Times'* London bureau reporter, Milton Bracker, described it as "perhaps the most important appeal on behalf of Jewish and other refugees."[67]

Kubowitzki fretted about the lack of attention in his diary. "I called [Palestinian artist and writer Nahum Gutman's] attention to the fact that the cable about the conference of the English members of Parliament with Eden had been printed only on page nine of the New York Times and without comments whatsoever," he wrote on January 29, referring to a four-paragraph story from London about a meeting to push for speedier help for the Jews. "I suggested that he organize the sending of letters to the Editors of the Times."[68] No such letters appeared in the *Times*, and a similar story that told of Parliament members planning to offer refuge for those threatened by extermination appeared 6 days later, this time on page 10.[69]

Still, there was hope that the press would pay attention to Riegner's and Lichtheim's latest report, which was dated January 19. (The State Department did. A few days after the report was received, State instructed its ambassador in Berne not to allow private organizations, such as the congress, to use its cable facilities any longer.) The report had additional information about the fate of Jews throughout Europe: an accelerating pace of murders in Poland; a growing number of deportations from Berlin and the near completion of deportations from Vienna; the "indescribable" living conditions of the 130,000 Rumanian Jews in Transnistria; and the difficulties of the "self-governing" community in Theresienstadt.

The report also included detailed eyewitness affidavits from three people (their names were withheld) who had recently arrived in Palestine from Poland. A man from Pietrokow described the October deportation of 18,000 persons, including his children, from the ghetto there. A woman recounted the roundups in Random in July where "machine-guns were set up and old people, children, pregnant women, and [hospital] patients . . . were mowed down in the street." More than 35,000 people were packed 150-to-a-freight car and "left for parts unknown," she said. In Bendin, another woman recalled, all the Jews, "even the newly born," were herded in August into two football fields, where they remained without food or drink in the pouring rain for 36 hours, until 5,000 of them were carted away. "It has been said that they were sent to Oswiencim[sic], where there are two large crematories and where it is thought all these people were consigned to the fire," the Bendin woman said.[70]

The congress' New York office received the cable with the report's highlights on February 9, 1943. Extensive newspaper coverage, congress leaders hoped, would keep pressure on the Allied governments to try to save at least some of Europe's Jews. So they prepared a press release, attaching the eyewitness affidavits, and sent it to dozens of newspapers, including the *Times*.[71] The *Times* ran a story on February 14, quoting almost word for word from the congress release. "Mass execution of Jews in Poland on an accelerated tempo was reported by European representatives of the World Jewish Congress in a communication made public by Stephen Wise," the *Times* lead said. "In one place in Poland, 6000 Jews are killed daily, according to the report dated Jan. 19." The five-paragraph story did not include any of the eyewitness testimony. It ran on page 37.

6

"Amidst the Advertisements on Page 19"

Placement Decisions and the Role of the News Editors

THROUGHOUT 1943, the *New York Times* continued to run stories about the extermination of the Jews inside the paper. Stories about the end of individual ghettos appeared on pages 10 and 5. Stories about the end of entire Jewish communities appeared on pages 2 and 6. Stories that tallied the mounting death toll appeared on pages 9 and 7. Stories that told of the extension of the murderous campaign to Italy and Bulgaria appeared on pages 8, 35, 4, and 6. A story on the precise methods used at the Treblinka extermination camp appeared on page 11. Stories that contained eyewitness testimony from the just-liberated areas of the Soviet Union appeared on pages 3, 10, and 19.[1] Even the stirring accounts of the Warsaw ghetto uprising and the rescue of Danish Jews were told almost exclusively inside the newspaper. The breakthrough that World Jewish Congress leaders assumed had occurred when the United Nations confirmed Germany's extermination campaign had not happened. The plight of the Jews still was not considered important enough for the front page.

Although one man, the assistant night managing editor, essentially made the day-to-day decisions that kept the extermination campaign off the *New York Times*' front page, his actions were the product of the newspaper's tangled corporate culture. They came about because of who was *not* making those day-to-day decisions, who *was* making the decisions, and most important, whom everyone in the organization looked to for guidance on the story. The decisions were not being made by the reporters charged with covering occupied Europe. Only one of them had the kind of clout that would lead editors to alter a story's placement because of his authorship, and Cyrus Sulzberger was not particularly interested in the story of the destruction of the Jews. Nor was the managing editor, Edwin James, making the decisions. Instead, the placement decisions lay with the night editors, known collectively as the bullpen, and particularly the assistant night managing editor, Neil MacNeil. Looming behind the editors was the publisher, who was not issuing orders but who was nonetheless calling the shots.

At most newspapers, the person holding the top editorial position would be responsible for which stories would receive the most play. The *Times* managing editor in the 1930s and 1940s did not embrace that role. Edwin L. "Jimmy" James, a Virginian by birth, became managing editor in 1932, replacing acting editor, Frederick Birchall. James had just spent 13 years in Europe for the *Times*, having first been assigned to the continent to follow the American Army during World War I. At the end of the war, he stayed on as the *Times* Paris correspondent and then as its chief European correspondent and Paris bureau chief. James was famous for his brightly colored, fashionably tailored suits. Damon Runyon, the popular writer and film producer, described "dressy James," as he was then known, as a "smallish chap as fresh as paint."[2] In France, James developed a close relationship with the *Times* publisher; Adolph Ochs enjoyed visiting Paris and having his bureau chief squire him to fine restaurants and clubs. That helped James secure the position of managing editor a few years later and hold it until his death on December 3, 1951.

Back in New York, James' "dressy" way apparently played worse on Times Square than on the Champs Elysees. James Reston, the *Times* London correspondent and future executive editor, described James as "a dumpy little Virginian who dressed like a racetrack gambler and carried a walking stick." Reston was no more enthusiastic about James' approach to running the paper. He did not like James' prickliness in responding to criticism. When serving as the publisher's assistant in 1943, Reston would send notes commenting on news coverage to Sulzberger who would, if he agreed with them, pass them along to James and other top editors. "James was particularly hostile to these little notes, since his skin was a lot thinner than his skull," Reston commented. Nor did Reston like the fact that James departed for dinner each evening at 6 P.M., leaving the bullpen in control of the newsroom.[3]

The bullpen referred to the three or four desks in the southeast corner of the *Times* newsroom where the night editors sat. Raymond McCaw, a

Nebraska native in his mid-50s who had started as a copy editor at the *Times* two decades earlier, was the night managing editor. Neil MacNeil, also in his 50s and another *Times* veteran of more than 20 years, was assistant night managing editor. They ruled the bullpen, and at night the bullpen ruled the *Times*. "Technically the bullpen editors were under the managing editor, but during Edwin James's era their judgment went unquestioned," *Times* chronicler Gay Talese explains. MacNeil "worked the night shift, arriving in the newsroom at 6 P.M. just as Edwin James was leaving, and James, anxious to get out, was pleased that he had such experienced subordinates as MacNeil to hold the fort through the night."[4]

To some, James' willingness to hand off responsibility made him an effective manager; he exercised his influence through the staff. Along with the publisher, he decided who would be hired or fired, who would receive raises and appealing assignments, or who would languish in a news backwater.[5] Foreign correspondent Herbert Matthews found James to be "loyal to his men," perhaps too loyal because Matthews also concluded that the *Times* "had some of the worst correspondents in the game through unknowingly hiring incompetents or misfits and then being too loyal to fire them."[6] For the top editors, James would basically back off, allowing them to run their own show. "In all the years I have spent on newspapers I have not encountered James's superior as a managing editor or worked under a supervision more harmonious and intelligent," wrote Washington Bureau Chief Arthur Krock. The reason: "James was ever the protector of my belief that the Washington staff was better qualified than distant editors and executives, including himself, to decide on the evaluation and presentation of the run of the news within its purview."[7]

To others, particularly Reston and Turner Catledge, each of whom would hold the top editorial position at the *Times*, James' willingness to abdicate authority was unpardonable.[i] "The night editors' autonomy

[i] Arthur Sulzberger came to share Reston's and Catledge's assessment, although he did not do much about it until 1951. That year the publisher named Turner Catledge executive managing editor to assist James and specified that Catledge's responsibilities would extend over a 24-hour period. Knowing that MacNeil would never go along with such an arrangement, James refused to stick the notice of the change on the newsroom's bulletin board. Sulzberger did it himself. When MacNeil saw the notice, he did not bother to take off his overcoat. He said he would start his vacation immediately and wanted to be retired when it was over. Sulzberger ultimately persuaded MacNeil to stay until McCaw, who was then hospitalized, returned to work. But MacNeil never got over what he considered a betrayal. "He made a terrible mistake. He fell in love with the newspaper," said

existed because Jimmy James didn't want a fight, didn't want any trouble, only wanted to enjoy the prerogatives of the managing editor's job and to be out of the office by early evening," writes Catledge, who in the mid-1940s was a Washington correspondent being groomed for *Times* management. "Each of the decisions involved may be small in itself, and not seem worth a fight, but the sum of the decisions, night after night will determine the character of the newspaper."[8]

The front-page decisions were most important in shaping the paper's character.[ii] Most newspapers have night editors who make the final decisions about what will appear in the next day's paper and where. But those editors answer to the managing editor and make important decisions in close consultation with him or her. At the *Times*, in the 1940s, they did not – a fact even James acknowledged. In dismissing the notion that "Mr. Sulzberger, with a majority of the stockholders of the paper on hand," decided whether a story got on page one, James identified the real decision maker. "Our Night Managing Editor is free and untrammeled," James said in a speech near the war's end. "He plays no favorites. He does what he thinks best; that is why he has his job."[9]

The *Times* night editors did what they thought best, regardless of what the daytime editors wanted. James did not even run an afternoon meeting, a staple of most newsrooms, to discuss the next day's paper among the editors, and to give them guidance on how to play various stories. Catledge recalled that James and the night editors would go for weeks without talking. "James always left a batch of memos for the night editors, and many evenings I'd see one of them glance at them, then throw them in the wastebasket," he said. McCaw, in turn, sent James notes that read like missives from an irritated boss to his barely competent secretary. "I should be greatly pleased to return from my vacation and find a dictionary in the

his son, Neil MacNeil, Jr. "Corporations don't have souls." Neil MacNeil, Jr., 10/25/01 letter to author. See also, MacNeil to Sulzberger, Sulzberger to MacNeil, 1/12/51, AHS File, NM Folder, NYTCA; Sulzberger to MacNeil 1/26/51, ELJ File, NM Folder, NYTCA.

ii Reporters viewed it that way as well. When he was stationed in Algiers and covering major battles, *Times* reporter Milton Bracker described his reaction upon seeing a cable listing all his front-page stories. "I realize I'm being fed on dangerously luxurious food – annoyed when my name is only second or third for the day, rather than in col. 8 [the lead position]. When you've had several streamers, and oodles of 3, 4 and 5 column leads, you're unlikely to be satisfied with anonymous inside stories ever again." M. Bracker to V. Bracker, 10/12/43, M95–133, Milton Bracker and Virginia Lee Warren Papers, Box 1/13, WSHS.

bull-pen for the exclusive use of the bull-pen," McCaw wrote James at one point. At another, he told James exactly what he planned to do with a running story about events at a political convention. "My opinion is that it is an utter waste of space, and during this coming convention on any night that we find ourselves very tight I shall throw it out of the paper."[10]

Deciding the stories that would appear in the *Times* was always a demanding job, even more so during wartime when the *Times* received 1 million words per day. Of those words, the bullpen editors had to select about 125,000 to appear in the next day's newspaper. "All this volume of news has to be read and appraised and edited – it is the equivalent of seven average-length novels – in a few hours, for our first edition is timed for 10:45 p.m.," MacNeil wrote in *Without Fear or Favor*, a book about metropolitan newspapers. Each story, whether written by a *Times* correspondent or picked up from a wire service (AP alone delivered 175,000 words in 24 hours), would be assigned to one of six desks. Each desk, had a head, an assistant, and as many as 14 other copy editors (known then as copyreaders) who would assess a story's importance, edit it for style and substance, and write a headline. Throughout the war, Theodore Bernstein headed the cable desk, which handled news from abroad, as well as news about foreign affairs that originated in the United States. That made him the frontline person for all war news and news about the persecution of the Jews. Bernstein, a native New Yorker, had become, at the age of 35, the youngest man ever appointed cable editor. That was in 1939, 6 months before the war started, and he held that position for the next decade. In addition to supervising the cable desk's copyreaders, Bernstein took charge of the production of as many as six maps a night depicting the ebb and flow of the war and wrote many of the big war headlines. Often working from 3 P.M. to 3 A.M., he was also the last person to scrutinize the front page before it went to press.[11]

Deciding what would go on that front page was the night editors' most important task. Desk heads, such as Bernstein, would prepare a daily "budget," listing their most important stories, essentially recommendations to the night editors on how to play the news. As Bernstein and his copyreaders read the stories assigned to their desk, the night editors appraised "the whole news picture of the day," MacNeil explained. Even before the stories were fully copyedited, they would decide the "most significant, or most interesting" stories that would fill the eight columns on page one. Usually, MacNeil would have the paper laid out by the time McCaw arrived, somewhere between 9 and 10 at night. McCaw, who was technically MacNeil's boss, could have changed the lineup, but he almost never did. On MacNeil's days off, his assistant, Clarence Howell, took over. (McCaw and MacNeil did not have a particularly close relationship. On MacNeil's last night at the *Times*, he mentioned to McCaw that he would not return. All McCaw said was, "Yes, I know." They had been together in the bullpen for 20 years.)[12]

So night after night, MacNeil, with some input from Bernstein and even less from McCaw, decided the 12 to 15 stories that would appear on the *Times*' front page. Leading newspapers averaged about 200 columns of news per day, meaning only 4% of the news could appear on the front. By the end of the war, with newsprint rationed, the amount of space in the *Times* had dropped to roughly 150 columns per night. MacNeil understood that his job could be controversial. Editors "are subject to constant criticism over burying stories on inside pages," MacNeil wrote. "Much of it comes from pressure groups. When their angle in the news gets prominent display it is taken for granted as being their due; when it is not, the managing editor is roundly condemned." Although MacNeil believed journalists could resist pressure groups, he knew they could not avoid subjective judgments altogether. "It is almost impossible to touch a news story without giving it some editorial interpretation," he wrote. "The space assigned to it; the headlines it will carry; the page, and the position on the page it will finally occupy; the way it is written; all involve editorial judgment. . . . With complete objectivity on the part of every reporter and editor, each story nonetheless represents editorial appraisal. It is one thing to display a story prominently on page one; another to place that story in some obscure column among the advertisements on page 19."[13, iii]

On the day after Christmas, 1943, amidst ads for Lane Bryant's $2.95 rayon blouses and Saks Fifth Avenue's winter clearance sale, the night editors

[iii] Lester Markel, the *Times* Sunday editor, shared MacNeil's view of the importance of placement. The reader "does not generally realize that, from the propaganda viewpoint, the way a story is written is no more important than the way it is 'played' – by which is meant the way it is placed in the newspaper, on page 3 or on page 19," Markel wrote in 1945. "The judgment as to what stories shall go on the first page of a newspaper is as editorial decision as there is." "In the Newspapers," draft chapter, 9/20/45, Lester Markel Collection, Box 16, WSHS.

placed on page nineteen a story about the last days of Kharkov's 15,000 Jews. The massacre had occurred exactly 2 years earlier, but eyewitness testimony had just become available as the Soviets slowly liberated territory once held by the Germans. Sara Sokola, a 40-year-old library clerk whose account was judged "accurate" by the Soviet commissioners who had investigated it, told her tale to the *Times*' Ralph Parker. Parker, who had previously been in Prague and Belgrade for the *Times*, had replaced Cyrus Sulzberger in Moscow in early 1942. One of the few Moscow correspondents to speak Russian, Parker did many interviews with eyewitnesses to German atrocities during the war.

Sokola explained that she was among 15,000 Jews who were ordered on December 15, 1941 to walk seven miles to an abandoned tractor plant outside Kharkov. "'Old people, little children and sick people lay dying beside the road,'" she was quoted saying. "'And we who walked were corpses, too.'" Their destination – a cluster of wood huts with open doors, no windows, and no furniture. "The imprisoned Jews died of neglect and exposure for that winter was exceptionally severe," Parker wrote. The accommodations were only meant to be temporary anyway; every so often trucks would pull up to a hut, load its occupants, and drive to a location outside of town. There, all the passengers would be shot. An inhabitant of Sokola's hut bribed the Germans to keep them at bay for awhile.

Soon Sokola was moved to another hut, whose next-to-last survivor had been taken away. "'It was a horrible sight,'" she told Parker as it was recorded in the paper. "Fouled bedding and stale food lay in a horrible mess. On a trestle in one corner was a dead man, in another a baby was still alive, sucking the finger of its dead mother. That night we were ordered to get ready to leave the next day. And that night a woman in birth pangs was brought into our hut. She knew that the child she was bringing into the world was already condemned to death and in her agony she prayed that it might be born dead. That child's birth decided me to risk everything to escape." Which Sokola did, although Parker decided "her escape is another story," and did not describe it.

It is easy to second guess news judgment and difficult to discover all the factors that went into it. The bullpen editors likely had many reasons to tuck that story deep inside the paper. The events described occurred two years earlier and were already generally known as the story itself indicated, although Parker sought to give it a timely angle by concluding that "nothing so awesome in horror had happened in the war in Russia as the birth in the prison hut of that child at Christmas time." Or Parker, who also worked for the *Times* of London, may have been the problem. The British Parker was highly regarded when he served as the *Times* correspondent in Prague in 1939, but he seemed to have lost his way when his wife was killed during his next assignment in Belgrade in 1940. He subsequently fell in love with his Russian secretary, who apparently swayed him to a strong pro-Soviet perspective. Although he would work for the *New York Times* for another 6 months after the Kharkov story was published, when he filed it he was already in the doghouse with his editors and the publisher for his Marxist sympathies.[14] The editors may also have been dubious about any story written by Parker and verified by Soviet commissioners. These are all plausible explanations, except that the decision to run the Kharkov story in "some obscure column among the advertisements on page 19" was not an isolated judgment. Night after night, story after story, no matter the course of the war, the bullpen decided throughout 1943 that news about what was happening to the Jews should go inside the paper.

It did not matter whether the stories were straightforward recitations of facts. The news that the Germans had erased the Krakow ghetto in "a three-day massacre that started March 13, and also eliminated the ghetto in Lodz," appeared in an April 12, page five story. The news that "all Jews in Amsterdam have been deported by the Germans to Poland, thus completing the removal of the entire Jewish population of the Netherlands," appeared in a June 23, page six story. The news that 3 million Jews had "been destroyed by planned starvation, forced labor, deportations, pogroms and methodical murders in German-run extermination centers," appeared in an August 27, page seven story.

It did not matter whether the stories offered a glimmer of the Jews' unparalleled suffering. After stating matter of factly that the "Germans have almost wiped out Austria's 200,000 Jews by extermination or deportation," a November 8 story portrayed the few left behind: "Occasionally a Jew may be seen in a Vienna street, thin, underfed, with ragged clothing and split shoes, always wearing sewn to the left breast pocket a big, yellow Star of David inscribed 'Jude.'" That story appeared on page six. When the Germans began killing Jews in Italy, the *Times* reported on October 10: "The Germans started by plundering the villas of wealthy Jews along the Italian lakes in the north. Ten members of one family, including servants and chauffeurs, who resisted the Germans at their home near Lake Maggiore, were reported to have been killed and their bodies thrown into a near-by lake." That story appeared on page thirty-five. As hundreds of thousands of Jews were herded into the Treblinka extermination center, the *Times* on August 8 explained what happened to them: "'Children with women go first, urged on by the whips of the Germans. Faster and faster they are driven and thicker and thicker fall the blows on heads paralyzed with terror and pain. The silence of the woods is shattered by the screams of women and the oaths of Germans. The victims now realize their doom is near." The story continued: the cells were sealed, steam was forced through, the suffocation began. It was over in 15 minutes. "Cold water is sprayed on them with a hose after which the grave-diggers pile the corpses on a platform like the carcasses of slaughtered animals. . . . The execution of men is carried out in the same way." That story appeared on page eleven.

It did not matter whether the news seemed solid or was subject to doubt. In fact, the single story in 1943 that expressed uncertainty about the information it relayed received the *Times*' most prominent news display short of the front page. William Lawrence's November 29 account of the slaughter of 50,000 Kiev Jews, which he wrote after he and other newspaper correspondents toured the recently retaken site, appeared on page three with this disclaimer: "On the basis of what we saw it is impossible for this correspondent to judge the truth or falsity of the story told to us."[iv] Still Lawrence recounted in great detail the story related by three Soviet prisoners who claimed to have unearthed the bodies from the 2-year-old massacre and then burned them in September 1943 in anticipation of the Russians' return to Kiev. Rows of 100 bodies per layer were stacked in a pyre and then set aflame. "Each pyre took two nights and one day to burn," one of the prisoners, Efim Vilkis, 33, "an Odessa-born Jew," was quoted saying. The conflagration lasted forty days. Vilkis and the two other prisoners said they escaped, using keys found in the clothes of the disinterred Jews, once they realized they too were about to be killed.

[iv] Lawrence later wrote that he had doubted that "50,000 Jewish people had been murdered here," and got into "furious arguments" about how to report the story with CBS's Bill Downs, "who believed it all." Bill Lawrence, *Six Presidents, Too Many Wars*, New York: Saturday Review Press (1972), 92. Lawrence was at the height of his frustration with the Moscow assignment. He had been begging his editors to transfer him for months. Just before he went to Babi Yar, he noted other Moscow correspondents' willingness to print unverified assertions and then to retract the claim in a subsequent story. "But, meanwhile, the damage of false reporting had been done," he wrote to James. 11/17/43, ELJ File, MB Folder, NYTCA.

Nor did it matter if the stories described heroism in the midst of unmitigated horror. Consider the *Times* coverage of two events now considered emblematic of the Holocaust. On April 22, 1943, a tiny, three-paragraph item appeared at the top of the *Times* front page, with the enigmatic headline: "Secret Polish Radio Asks Aid, Cut Off." The transmission, as received in Stockholm the night before and related in the next-day story's second paragraph, came from inside the Warsaw ghetto.[v] "'The last 35,000 Jews in the ghetto at Warsaw have been condemned to execution," the broadcast said. "Warsaw again is echoing to musketry volleys. The people are murdered. Women and children defend themselves with their naked arms. Save us. . . .'" Then, the story said, the station went dead. The *Times* story also sputtered to an end. The next and final paragraph explained that listeners in Stockholm believed the message spoke of the last 35 Jews, whereas those in London thought it said 35,000 Jews.

By the next day, the *Times* had resolved that indeed 35,000 Jews were resisting "the armored cars and tanks" that had moved into the ghetto. But by then the story had also moved inside the newspaper, never to reemerge. "The battle was still raging when the Polish exile government in London received its latest news last night," the *Times* London bureau reported on page nine. The first stirrings of resistance had also appeared inside the paper. A month earlier, another message had been received from Warsaw asking that German prisoners of war be held hostage in return for the safety of the city's Jews, as the Germans prepared to liquidate the ghetto. The March 19, page eight story reported that the message from Warsaw closed with the words: "You must rouse the whole world to action."

Two months later, the world was still not roused. After the stories on April 22 and 23, the *Times* did not mention the uprising again until two weeks later, this time on page seven. "A battle has been raging for seventeen days in Warsaw's ghetto," according to the *Times*. "The Jews, fighting against annihilation by the Nazis, were reported using bedspreads as bunkers and fighting with arms smuggled into the ghetto." The end of the battle received similar treatment in the *Times*. "All Warsaw

[v] The U.S. Government's Bureau of Overseas Intelligence credited this report in the *New York Times* as providing the first known account of the uprising. Office of War Information, Bureau of Overseas Intelligence, Central Files, Box 304, NA.

Jews held 'liquidated'" and "all buildings in the ghetto were still burning," the newspaper reported 1 week later on page six.[15] On May 22, the headline on a page four story read: "Jews' Last Stand Felled 1,000 Nazis."

The lack of media coverage also doomed one Jew in London. In mid-May, as the ghetto battle was winding down, Szmuel Zygielbojm, the Jewish representative on the Polish National Council who had been instrumental in drawing attention to the Bund report 1 year earlier, committed suicide. "My comrades in the Warsaw ghetto perished with weapons in their hands in their last heroic impulse," he wrote in a suicide note. He saw his death as one last attempt to seize the world's attention. "Perhaps by my death I shall contribute to destroying the indifference of those who are able and should act in order to save now, maybe at the last moment, this handful of Polish Jews who are still alive from certain annihilation." In early June, the *Times* ran a story about Zygielbojm's suicide and the entire text of his note – on page seven.[16]

In the fall, as more details emerged about the Jews' valiant last stand, the *Times* still ran the stories inside. A September, page six story based on "detailed reports published in Polish underground papers," explained what had prompted the rebellion.[17] Another story the following month added more information, describing in detail the lopsided battle. The wire article, picked up from the North American Newspaper Alliance, established the story's credibility. "The sources of the following account are unchallengeable," it stated. "[T]hey include reports to the Polish Government in Exile from its agents within Poland, from the underground press, from records of the Jewish Socialist Workers' party and personal eyewitness accounts from persons who are constantly reaching neutral and friendly countries. Dates, names, localities and figures are factual. They are definitely for the record." The record indicated that after 3 days of continuous fighting, the Germans switched tactics, bombarding the ghetto from outside its wall and from the skies. The struggle continued for 5 weeks, the story said, then it was over. "The ghetto, which once contained more than 100,000 rooms, 2,000 commercial establishments and 3,000 stores and factories, lay in ruins," the story concluded. "The remaining 20,000 persons crept out of the debris and were herded like cattle to their slaughter house." By June 30, not a single Jew remained in the ghetto, said the story, which appeared on page eight.[18]

The heroism of the Danes received no more attention than the martyrdom of the ghetto fighters.[vi] On September 30, 1943, during Rosh Hashanah services, German police and Gestapo agents began rounding up the 7,000 Jews in Denmark. Just 3 days later, the *Times*' George Axelsson reported the arrests and the prisoners' likely future. "It is believed here that the Danish Jews are facing the same fate as those in other countries under the German heel," he wrote from Stockholm. "In other words, they will be shipped to Poland, German-occupied Russia and never will be heard from again." But the page twenty-nine story also included a hopeful note: boats harboring Jews and piloted by Danes were "running a gauntlet of German patrol boats" to reach Sweden, which had offered asylum. (Axelsson still could not quite abandon his tendency to describe the Germans as acting out of rational impulses rather than unbridled race hatred. "The Germans have a crying need for foreign exchange at present and observers here think the action against the Danish Jews may be largely a financial operation," he explained in the story's concluding paragraph.)

The next day, a Monday, the *Times* ran a story that said more than 1,000 Jews had reached Sweden, most of them on Saturday night. "Braving the icy Oeresund, Jewish refugees of all ages and conditions arrived on the Swedish coast," the page seven story from Stockholm said. "Some even swam the strait – two miles wide at its narrowest point." From then until October 8, and again on October 13, the *Times* ran stories about the Jews' escape, the Danes' assistance, and the Germans' retaliation. They appeared on pages 6, 9, 2, 5, and 10.

That the night editors determined the Jews' annihilation was not a front-page story is clear. Why they decided that is not. The bullpen editors wrote nothing about the newsworthiness of the persecution of the Jews at the time and died before growing Holocaust awareness might have prompted their reflection. Raymond McCaw died in 1959, Neil MacNeil in 1969, and Theodore Bernstein in 1979. Nor did they write memoirs that might at least have hinted at their thinking. Unlike *Times* foreign correspondents, political reporters, and executive editors who have produced numerous, often voluminous memoirs, the bullpen editors were

[vi] The Bulgarians' resistance to deporting their Jews received even less attention, a single story on May 27, 1943, p. 3.

not moved to record their exciting exploits on the copy desk. MacNeil did write a memoir, along with two journalism texts, *Without Fear or Favor* and *How To Be a Newspaperman*, and a 1944 policy analysis of the postwar world. But, his memoir, *The Highland Heart in Nova Scotia*, concerns MacNeil's Scottish heritage and early years at his grandparents' home in the isolated province, not his newspaper career. Bernstein, who became known as the *Times* grammarian and style expert, wrote six books, all on language usage. McCaw did not write a book. The nighttime editors did not even explicate their policy decisions in memos to the staff. In fact, they probably never thought of their decision to relegate stories about the Jews to the inside as a policy at all. Having a "policy," or a set approach to a news event, was for lesser newspapers, those with a political or sensationalist tinge. Instead, the *Times* editors each day would make an "objective" determination of the newsworthiness of a particular story compared with other news stories on that day.

The closest any of them came to discussing the extermination of the Jews in print was a few references in MacNeil's 1944 book. In *An American Peace*, MacNeil made clear that he understood the Germans had "deliberately set out to exterminate the Jews of Europe," that "their savagery in the Ghetto of Warsaw will foul the pages of history for a thousand years," and that the Jews' "situation is the most desperate of all, their sufferings the greatest of all." Yet, he also tended to conceive of the "inhumanity" of the Nazis as of a piece, afflicting "Jews, Poles, Czechs, Greeks, Norwegians, Netherlanders, Belgians and Russians," all of whom "have suffered unspeakable torture and hardship, millions of them dying miserably." In this, and in his opposition to a Jewish homeland in Palestine, MacNeil's perspective resembled that of his boss, Arthur Sulzberger.[19]

Although the bullpen editors did not make their news judgments explicit, their implicit priorities are apparent in the written record they did leave – more than 2,000 wartime editions of the *New York Times*. It is possible to observe not only the stories about the Jews that went inside the paper, but also the stories the editors considered more important and ran outside. Some of those decisions are incontrovertible and therefore not particularly illuminating. Throughout the war, the war was what dominated the *Times* front page. From the invasion of Poland and the bombing of Britain, through the blitz of the Lowlands and the attack on Pearl Harbor, through the taking of the Philippines and the turnabout at Midway, to the siege of Stalingrad and the landing at Normandy, the *Times* devoted much of its front page to recording the back and forth of a thousand battles. With the fate of Western civilization hanging in the balance, the war itself was and should have been the *Times*' top priority.[vii]

The wartime *Times* is a remarkable achievement. Every night, the nighttime editors shepherded into the next day's paper detailed and ever-changing maps, military communiqués of both friends and enemies, full texts of reports and declarations, and voluminous reporting on victories, defeats, and stalemates. But the *Times* ran 12 to 15 stories on its front page every day and, even leaving aside domestic stories, many of them were about events other than major military engagements. The *Times* coverage of two such episodes offers clues to the bullpen editors' priorities. Both involve German "outrages" against civilian populations and thus are similar to stories about the persecution of the Jews. Yet, these story lines – German reprisals against resistance movements in occupied countries and Nazi persecution of Christians – made the front page 57 times during the first 3 years of war.

Consider the Christian story first. In 1940, August Cardinal Hlond, the Polish primate to the Pope, issued a report on attacks on priests and other Catholics in Poland in the wake of the German occupation.[20] The *Times* first ran a front-page story previewing the report and then ran front-page stories 2 days in a row on the report when it was released, including two stories on the second day. All three stories were the offleads, meaning they occupied the second most important position in the paper. (The *Times* never ran back-to-back front-page stories about any Holocaust-related event, including the United Nations declaration in December 1942 or the liberation of the camps in 1945, nor did any such stories appear in the lead or offlead position.) When weeks later the Vatican added data on the persecution of Jews, including the execution of 53 people in retaliation for the murder of a policeman, the story ran on page six. On May 9, 1942, another story about Nazi attacks on Christians appeared on the front page, even when more important news might have been expected to intervene. The *Times* three-deck, banner headline bellowed, "Japanese Repulsed in Great Pacific Battle," about the events leading to the decisive Battle of Midway. Even so, the newspaper still found space "above the fold"

[vii] At least one *Times* reporter, however, believed his newspaper overdid the reporting of incremental changes in individual battles from military theater headquarters, considering it "as every newspaper person knows – basically rewrite" of War Department releases. M. Bracker to V. Bracker, 8/24/43, 9/18/43, M95-133/1/13, WSHS.

(the top half of the paper) for a prominent, two-column story headlined: "German Cardinal Indicts Nazi 'War on Christianity.'" The story by Daniel Brigham reported that a leader of religious opposition in the Reich informed the Vatican that Nazis were blackmailing believers and using spies to pressure the clergy. Probably the most unsettling such story appeared at the end of 1942, as the news about the mass extermination of the Jews was confirmed. In the midst of stories about the extermination campaign that ran on pages 10, 11, or 12 came a front-page story with the headline: "Nazi Morality on Animals' Level, German Catholic Bishops Warn." The December 5 story on a "new pastoral letter" condemned not mass murder, but "the encouragement of loose sexual relations for raising the birth rate." It attacked the Nazis for doing away with "essential segregation of sexes during youth meetings by day and night . . . promiscuous comradeship that exposes young girls to the gravest moral dangers."[21]

In fact, for Jews to be mentioned at all on the front page, it helped if the story had a prominent Catholic angle. In January 1940, for example, the *Times* ran a front-page story about how the Pope helped a Boston tailor find his sister and her children in German-occupied Poland. During 1941, the *Times* ran dozens of stories about what was happening to the Jews in Germany, but only one appeared on the front-page – it told of the arrest of the dean of a Catholic cathedral for praying for Jews. The arrest of thousands of Jews in France in the summer of 1942 did not warrant the front page, while the arrest of a member of the archbishop's staff for helping them did. Even rumors of the Pope's possible intervention to stop the deportations were considered more newsworthy than the deportations themselves. The trend continued in 1943, with front-page stories on a report on Reich churches' assistance to Jews and a failed attempt by the Pope to ransom Rome's Jews.[22]

Given the night editors' silence, it is possible only to speculate on why they considered stories about Nazi attacks on Christians to be more important than the far more devastating assault on the Jews. They may have been catering to the newspaper's Catholic audience. A prewar incident illustrates this concern. In 1937, then chief European correspondent Birchall asked James for advice on how much coverage to give to the ongoing trials of priests in Germany accused of homosexual offenses. "The interest here in the Catholic trials is very keen and, as you know, we have many Catholic readers and some way or another, most of them think the Pope is going to do something with Hitler," James replied.

"Therefore, I think we should continue to have very ample coverage." James even defended the copydesk's decision to delete from an earlier story several paragraphs that suggested the priests' guilt. "I feel that if you were here in close touch with the resentment of the Catholics, you would understand the deletion of two paragraphs which said in effect that the priests were guilty. That seemed to us a bad thing to say about thousands of them now facing trial."[23]

The *Times*' solicitude for Catholic readers became even more important in the wake of the Spanish Civil War. *Times* reporter Herbert Matthews' reporting from the Republican side angered American Catholics, who strongly supported Franco and accused Matthews of being a communist. That the *Times* carefully balanced Matthews' dispatches from the Republican side with pro-Franco dispatches from another *Times* correspondent did not appease them. The Roman Catholic Archdiocese of Brooklyn helped organize a campaign against Matthews and the *Times*, and the Catholic Press Association officially protested to Sulzberger. *Times* editors acknowledged a drop off in Catholic readership. After complaints about an Ash Wednesday story, McCaw wrote James in 1939: "The Tribune, as you know, has been slopping over on Catholic stuff lately apparently trying to pick up some of our rabid Catholic friends who have quit the Times because of the Matthews stuff." A few months later, McCaw complained to James about the failure to cover a Catholic event. "I think this was a rather unfortunate oversight in view of the fact that we are trying to win back some of our former friends among the Catholics," McCaw wrote.[24]

The *Times* may also have been reacting to U.S. government propaganda – or at least making a similar calculation of the news value of Christian persecutions. In early 1942, the government's propaganda agency issued a number of press releases highlighting the plight of Christians in occupied Europe. As a note on one such release stated: "One of our constant objectives is to use all evidence of Nazi persecution of Christian churches and church people." Or another note: "Part of the continuing campaign to show that the Axis and its satellites are the enemies of Christianity." And still another: "Again plugging the theme that Nazi ideology and Christian ideals are irreconcilable."[25]

The church's hierarchical nature also might have helped propel stories about Catholics to page one. Journalists evaluate stories at least partly based on the perceived importance of the source. If the Vatican issued a report, or a council of bishops made a statement, journalists could easily determine how important the source, and thus the story, was. Indeed, the Vatican was considered a news source to top all news sources. Matthews, perhaps seeking to make amends for his Spain reporting, wrote of the 1940 report about persecution of Catholics in Poland: "The world knows the truth and believes it, and the belief comes precisely because it was the Vatican that said so." He later termed the Vatican the only "neutral source in the whole world that was completely above suspicion."[26] (That the Vatican could be accused of engaging in biased, "special pleading" on behalf of its clergy in Poland did not seem to lessen the report's news value.) In contrast, Judaism had no encompassing organized hierarchy, no clear line of authority that would enable reporters to identify who spoke for the Jews. Plus, the Jewish community was notoriously unorganized with a proliferation of groups and individuals all prone to issue reports and statements. Roosevelt in fact complained that the Jews would be easier to deal with if they had a Pope.[27]

The most important factor in the prominence of stories about Catholic persecution was the background of the *Times* editors. It is often said of the mid-century *Times* that it was a paper "owned by Jews and edited by Catholics for Protestants." The bullpen in particular was known both inside and outside the office as having a Catholic orientation. "The night desk has enjoyed a reputation for some time as direct descendants of the Catholic hierarchy," Ira Hirschmann, a Bloomingsdale executive wrote in 1944 to Laurence Steinhardt, U.S. Ambassador to Turkey. Both men were friends of Arthur Sulzberger. "This is predicated on: (a) Their Catholic tinge. (b) Their sweeping decisions with regard to news and personalities which they employ ruthlessly." Gay Talese writes that "though no one could prove it, Neil MacNeil, Raymond H. McCaw . . . and others were said to reflect a Catholic viewpoint when appraising the news, with the results ranging from the playing down of stories about birth control to the playing up of stories expressing alarm over communism."[28]

The idea of a *Times* "edited by Catholics" may have been overblown – James was a Methodist; McCaw, a Presbyterian; and Bernstein, a Jew[29] – but the importance of the Catholic influence was not. MacNeil, who configured the *Times* front page almost single handedly, was a devout Catholic and unabashed about expressing his faith. MacNeil was what his son described as "a prominent Catholic layman," active in his Queens parish.[30] Born in 1891 in Dorchester, Massachusetts, MacNeil spent much of his childhood at his grandfather's farm in Washabuckt, Nova Scotia, which he described as living in "rural, Catholic isolation." He graduated from the University of St. Francis Xavier in Nova Scotia. He started as a copyreader at the *Times* in 1918 and steadily worked his way up through the copy desk to the post of assistant night managing editor, a job he got in 1930 and held for the next 21 years. During those years, MacNeil did not shy away from professing his beliefs publicly. MacNeil made speeches denouncing the decline of religious values and criticizing public schools for not promoting speech in "defense of God." He also inveighed against communism; in those days such attacks often went hand in hand with devout Catholicism. His books too were peppered with advocacy of religion and assaults on communism and the Soviet Union. In 1949, MacNeil received the Catholic Institute of the Press award. His intense devotion to his religion was so well known that it was mentioned in the fifth paragraph of his *New York Times* obituary. Only one other night editor could match MacNeil's intensity of belief. His assistant, Clarence Howell, who took over on MacNeil's nights off, was a Catholic convert "who was almost fanatically religious."[31]

Given his commitment to objectivity in journalism, MacNeil would not have deliberately used the *Times* to expound his religion. Yet, even he acknowledged that personal beliefs colored journalistic judgments. The journalist's "own political, economic, racial, religious, and social background is there with him at all times, no matter how he strives to forget it," MacNeil wrote in his book about journalism. "It will inevitably intrude, probably without his knowing it, when he wants to be most fair and accurate." MacNeil's solution – an objective editor who compensates for a reporter's inherent prejudices – did not address the problem of how to check a biased editor. Correspondent Herbert Matthews said it was "beyond question" that the bullpen "allowed their sincere and natural partisanship to influence the way they handled my copy" during the Spanish Civil War – a view that was confirmed by comparing cables Matthews sent to the bullpen with what was published.[32, viii] MacNeil's Catholic sympathies also likely affected the *Times* coverage of Christian persecution during World War II. MacNeil was interested

[viii] Apparently neither the editing, nor the presence of a pro-Franco, Catholic reporter covering the other side, placated American Catholics.

in what was happening to his coreligionists in occupied Europe, and respected, even revered, the sources that provided information about their plight.

Stories about the suffering of Jews and of Catholics did not necessarily compete for public attention. Some traditional Catholics, however, tended to see it that way. Father Charles Coughlin, a Detroit priest known for his virulent anti-Semitism, complained in his hugely popular radio broadcasts that the American press and American government were more concerned about the fate of Jews in Germany than about Catholics in Mexico and Spain. The *Tablet*, the Brooklyn Archdiocese's weekly newspaper, which supported Coughlin, consistently editorialized that the mainstream media overplayed the persecution of Jews at the expense of the "far worse persecution of Christians."[ix] (Liberal Catholic publications, such as *America* and *Commonweal*, were more sympathetic to the plight of the Jews.)[33] Although MacNeil had been a friend of Father Coughlin's and his Forrest Hills home was in the Brooklyn Archdiocese, MacNeil's son described his father as being a "militant" opponent of anti-Semitism, who was "appalled" by Coughlin's statements and broke with him over it. But the Catholic Church's concern for the disparate treatment of their followers probably at least entered the equation of what stories MacNeil decided to put on the front page.

In June 1942, as the first news reports about the extermination of the Jews reached the West, another "atrocity" captured the interest of the editors of the *New York Times*. After partisans assassinated Reinhard Heydrich, the top S.S. man in Czechoslovakia, the Germans retaliated against one tiny Czech town. On June 10, the Germans marched into Lidice, shot all the men, sent all the women to concentration camps, placed the children in "educational institutions," and leveled the village. To the *Times* editors, the murder of 480 people was big news, worthy of two front-page stories, four editorials, and an item in the week in review section.[34] There were also three front-page stories leading up to the destruction of Lidice and one more in its aftermath.[35] The interest in Lidice was so intense that it even carried a story about the killing of 258 Jewish men in the Berlin suburbs to the front page. The men were killed and their

[ix] Andrew Sharf in *The British Press and Jews Under Nazi Rule*, London: Oxford University Press (1964), 91, 94, found that the two Catholics newspapers he studied were among the publications most skeptical of Jewish atrocity claims.

families deported for allegedly planting five bombs at an anti-Soviet exhibit "the day Heydrich was killed," the June 14 story by George Axelsson explained. "Observers are inclined to see a link between the Berlin executions and the massacre at Lidice in Czechslovakia after the assassination of Reinhard Heydrich," the story stated, although it never explained the supposed link.[36] Two weeks later, the Bund report describing the deaths of nearly 3,000 times as many Jews appeared on page five, below two items describing further retaliations for the Heydrich assassination.

Lidice was one of many reprisal stories featured prominently on the *Times* front page. In the first 3 years of war, 41 such stories appeared, involving the murder of as many as 250 civilians,[37] and as few as 1.[38] Many of the front-page stories involved the deaths of fewer than 100 people.[39] Most resistance and reprisal stories came out of France,[40] but there were also stories out of the Netherlands, Norway, and even Germany and Poland.[41] When Gestapo agents raided a Warsaw building housing an underground press, flung hand grenades into its windows, and shot 83 people in a nearby house, the story warranted the *Times* front page. *Glos Polski*, the underground newspaper, reappeared after a short break, the story said.[42,x] The raid occurred just 2 weeks before the Warsaw ghetto uprising that led the Germans to destroy hundreds of buildings and thousands of lives, yet received no more front page attention.

Contrasts between the prominence of reprisal stories and those involving Jews also can be seen within the same day's paper. On January 27, 1943, the front page proclaimed, "250 Slain Resisting Nazis in Marseille," while page 10 noted, "Liquidation Set for France's Jews." Even unconfirmed stories about resistance deaths were front-page fodder, while verified ones about Jews were not. "Completely unconfirmed reports reaching here tonight said 800 persons were killed in Grenoble and Lyon in Armistice Day rioting in France," read the lead of a November 12, 1943 front-page story from Berne. (Two days later, a page twelve story reported that all had been quiet on Armistice Day and no deaths had been confirmed.) That same day the lead of a page four story stated that the "Germans have been using badly needed soldiers to hunt down Jews in Rome," and "troops have

[x] The Polish Information Center, the Polish government's propaganda arm in New York, often issued releases on raids and resistance at underground newspaper offices in Poland. See, for example, Polish Information Center Papers, Box 2.3, Cables from London, 9/42, and Box 2.9, Cables from London, 3/8/43, HIA. Why that particular raid warranted a front-page story bearing James Reston's byline is not clear.

been loading men, women and children into trucks and transporting them to unknown destinations." Similar contrasts can even be found within the same story. "2 Die in Marseille in Bastille Parade," read the July 15, 1942 headline, a theme that was developed at the top of the page one story. Five paragraphs down, the story noted the day was "marked by the severest of measures against Jews," who could no longer set foot in public establishments. The list of banned places was "so comprehensive that Jews have nothing left but to remain at home or walk aimlessly in the street," the story said. If they chose to walk aimlessly in the street, they faced one additional requirement; Jews in France had to wear a Star of David, the story announced.

As with the stories of the persecution of Christians, the *Times* night editors had sound editorial reasons for considering reprisal deaths to be important news. Resistance in occupied countries might help to derail the German war machine, as the severe retaliatory measures seemed to corroborate. Thus, these attacks and counterattacks could be considered war news. Even more important, they could be considered good war news, something that was in short supply, especially in 1942, as the United States suffered defeats in the Pacific and Africa. If journalists could not figure this out for themselves, the U.S. government was happy to point it out. Rebellion in "Fortress Europe" became a popular propaganda line on the theory that it both served to bolster sagging morale and helped fuel fears of Nazi barbarism. In February and March 1942, as the Office of War Information (OWI) was getting off the ground, it identified resistance and reprisal as worthy of a "campaign," or a concerted effort on the agency's part to drum up interest in the story among the press. As a note on a March 1942 press release said: "A story on one of our continuing lines – to report all information concerning sabotage and resistance to Nazi pressure in occupied Europe." That month the agency issued a series of press releases on resistance in the Balkans, Belgium, Norway, Yugoslavia, and the Netherlands. In June, OWI officials decided to make the massacre at Lidice "the one cap-stone incident of the Axis terror and barbarism, which will fire the United Nations to smash the Nazi beasts." In the last 2 weeks of June, OWI issued four press releases on Lidice and sent a kit with background material to journalists. The campaign paid off with both newspapers and radio covering Lidice extensively and newspapers printing heated editorials. The War Writers Board even launched a drive to rename a town in Illinois, Lidice.[43]

The *New York Times* got on board, running editorials proclaiming, "Lidice the Immortal," and arguing in favor of a "Lidice, Illinois." The *Times* featured the renaming of the Illinois town on its front page and again on the editorial page. A testament to OWI's success in making Lidice "the cap-stone incident of Axis terror" came in August, when the *Times* sought to explain President Roosevelt's statement that the German occupation "may even lead to the extermination of certain populations." Although the president's comment came after the *Times* had published several stories about the mass slaughter of Jews in Poland – and the World Jewish Congress' Leon Kubowitzki was waiting for the president's statement to mention Jewish suffering – the *Times'* William Lawrence identified only one relevant atrocity: "the destruction of Lidice, Czechoslovakia." A year later, on the first anniversary of the town's destruction, the *Times* ran an editorial on Lidice's lasting symbolic value. On the second anniversary, yet another *Times* editorial affirmed that Lidice recalled "to all the world 'the most arch act of piteous massacre' that Hitlerian war has bred."[44]

The Jews who died in the Kharkov massacre did not have the same chance to become immortal. There were no OWI press releases about the murder of the 15,000 men, women, and children there. There was no campaign to rename an American town, Kharkov, Illinois. That is partly because the U.S. government did not choose to make those victims or millions more like them, propaganda symbols, for reasons that are discussed in Chapter 8. But neither did the *Times* editors highlight their deaths, even though a story 2 weeks after the Lidice massacre stated: "Nazi atrocities even worse than those committed in Czechoslovakia were reported yesterday from Poland. . . . "

The incongruity of putting stories about the murder of 480 civilians on the front and the murder of millions inside was apparent to some at the time. In a December 1942 speech, Senator Edwin C. Johnson of Colorado noted that he had seen on page seventeen of a "particularly well known, widely read newspaper," a story about 2 million Jews having been "mowed down by machine gun fire, choked to death in poison gas chambers and buried alive." The story had been "substantiated" by the State Department. "Think of it! Two million human beings created in the image of the Father deliberately destroyed by beasts in men's clothing, *and it barely made Page 17* [emphasis in original]," Johnson said. "Is it because these two million human beings happened to be Jews that the story is so well hidden? I challenge the American press for a reply – and the radio news commentators – and the leaders of Democracy and of the United Nations. Why should we not hear at least the same strong words of condemnation heaped upon the perpetrators of these indescribable horrors as was heard immediately after the Lidice tragedy, when an entire Czech village was wiped out by the Nazi barbarians. THE JEWS HAVE SUFFERED A THOUSAND LIDICES [emphasis in original]."[45]

The American press never rose to Johnson's challenge of explaining why one Lidice was more important than a thousand Kharkovs, or why the resistance in the Warsaw ghetto was not as uplifting as the reappearance of a Polish newspaper, or why the Danes' defiance was less impressive than the French's demonstrations. The *New York Times* editors' very silence suggests a partial answer. At least during the first 3 years of the war, the night editors were not so much suppressing information, as not recognizing its importance. The plight of the Jews was just one circumstance among a constant flow of news events that had to be "appraised" for the next day's paper. "Wide knowledge and quick decisions are necessary on a hundred different news items," MacNeil said of the judgments he made every night in the early 1940s. Among those hundred items requiring quick decisions, the increasingly horrific reports on the Jews' fate did not stand out. Each time such a story was "appraised," the editors determined it to be not as important as the 12 or 15 stories that appeared on the front page. Germany stokes its war machine, primary story. Deportation of Jews, secondary story. Troops march into Rumania, primary story. Pogroms eradicate Rumanian Jews, secondary story. Vichy government consolidates power, primary story. Consequences for French Jews, secondary story. Germany invades Russia, primary story. A thousand Lidices follow, secondary story. The editors did not necessarily perceive the link among the speeches of Nazi officials in Berlin, pogroms in Rumania, Aryanization of businesses in France, bulging ghettos in Poland, and the eerie absence of Jews from the Soviet territories. They did not grasp that the resources and effort the Germans were putting into their war against the Jews, not to mention the depth and breadth of human suffering, made that fight almost as important as the worldwide one.

Stories about other civilian casualties emerged from the news flow because they managed to capture an editor's attention. Guided by his personal beliefs, and those supposedly of the *Times* readers, MacNeil plucked stories about the persecution of Catholics from the news stream. Those stories were then appraised as page one material and routinely slotted for the front. Reprisal stories too emerged from the rush of news. OWI helped identify such stories for editors, who fished them out and packaged them for the front. Occasionally, stories about the Jews rose to the surface, if attached to another news event destined for the front page, such as a statement by the Pope, the president, or the United Nations. Other stories sank, such as the resistance of the ghetto fighters or the reprisals against the Danes, when the drag of the Jewish story outweighed the other themes.[xi]

The Jews did not have a powerful external advocate, such as the U.S. government or the Pope, to draw the editors' attention to their plight. Nor did the Jews have an internal advocate at the *Times*. *Times* correspondents reporting the story abroad were not in a good position to call their editors' attention to the extermination of the Jews. Different reporters in different countries covered the story at different moments. The reporters regularly assigned to the story tended to be ones with the least credibility among their editors. At home, the top editors who were themselves Jewish might have been looked to, fairly or not, to take the lead on pushing the story of the Jews' persecution, much as MacNeil did with Catholics. Washington Bureau Chief Arthur Krock tried to hide his background, as is discussed in Chapter 8. Lester Markel, the Sunday editor, was the most comfortable with his origins and most willing to challenge the *Times*' orthodoxy on Zionism, yet, the sections he edited – the *New York Times Magazine*, the week in review, and other Sunday supplements – were not noticeably different in their treatment of the Jews than the rest of the paper.[xii]

Theodore Bernstein, who as cable editor would have been responsible for editing all the stories about the Jews' persecution and would have made the initial recommendations about their placement, did not conceal being Jewish. Bernstein was raised on Manhattan's Upper West Side in an enclave of elegant brownstones owned by second- and third-generation German Jews. His father, Saul Bernstein, was a successful lawyer who

[xi] That the reprisal stories swamped the first news of the extermination of the Jews can be seen in the Press Intelligence Bulletin, a government-compiled index of news stories and editorials in 425 newspapers. During June and July 1942, extermination and reprisal stories both appeared under the "Axis occupied territory" heading. So Bernard Valery's story about the Vilna massacre, for example, appeared along with 17 other news stories and 27 editorials about Lidice. Press Intelligence Bulletins, FDRL.

[xii] The magazine, for example, ran only two articles during the entire war exclusively about the Jews, both by outside novelists: Sholem Asch's "In the Valley of Death," (2/7/43) and Arthur Koestler's "The Nightmare That Is a Reality," (1/9/1944).

counted financier Bernard Baruch among his friends. Ted was bar-mitzvahed at Temple Emanu-El, where the Sulzbergers later belonged. But the Bernsteins were not religious, and as an adult, Bernstein never attended synagogue and considered his Jewish origins a burden he unfairly had to bear. As a student at Columbia University and editor of its school newspaper, he was denied the top journalism prize, a traveling fellowship, because he was Jewish. The professor who selected someone else felt so guilty that he personally intervened to get Bernstein a copyreader position at the *Times* upon graduation. Bernstein joined the *Times*, working there for another 47 years, and rising to the position of assistant managing editor. Still, Bernstein felt that being Jewish kept him from getting as far as his talent and dedication would have dictated. Gay Talese claims the rejection led Bernstein to retreat into the craft of editing, becoming the *Times* "technical genius, its supreme authority on grammar and rules."[46]

Bernstein never complained or criticized the *Times*. "Did he murmur a word against the *New York Times*? Never," said his niece and literary executor, Marylea Meyersohn. "It was his home, his refuge, his family." He accepted what Meyersohn referred to as the *Times*' "genteel anti-Semitism." Bernstein did not object when the *Times* refused to hire Daniel Schorr as a foreign correspondent in the 1950s, apparently because the newspaper had enough Jews on the news staff.[47] During World War II, Bernstein would have been even more hesitant to assert himself. Named cable editor the year the war started, he was new to the position and was considered relatively young to hold it. In addition, a personal tragedy had solidified his ties to the *Times*. In 1938, Bernstein's 3-year-old son, Eric, was stricken with spinal meningitis, which resulted in severe brain damage. "My aunt, it killed her," Meyersohn said of Bernstein's wife, Beatrice, who refused to have other children. "But Teddy had the *Times*. . . . He gave himself over to the *Times*."

If the persecution of the Jews could float beneath the editors' level of consciousness at the beginning of the war, by 1943 it would seem that it no longer could. The persistence of reports of mass murder on an unprecedented scale, the credibility of the sources supplying the information, the horrific nature of the methods employed, and the sheer number of people involved would all seem to point to a breakthrough. The *Times* editors surely should have recognized both what was happening and its importance, and they may have. MacNeil's statement that the Germans "deliberately set out to exterminate the Jews of Europe" appeared in a book published in October 1944, 6 months before the camps were liberated. But by then, several years into the war, the haphazardly adopted and only dimly understood practice of consigning stories about the Jews to the inside had ossified into something akin to a policy. For the harried night editors, it was easier to continue operating on automatic pilot, rather than consciously change a practice, something they were not inclined to do by temperament or training. *Times* chronicler Talese describes the bullpen editors as "men who, through the years, had slowly and patiently worked their way up through what was probably the most tedious and unheralded craft in the newsroom. Copyreading." MacNeil, McCaw, and Bernstein spent their entire *Times*' careers on the copydesk for a combined 111 years. They were a "special breed of journalists," Talese writes of copyreaders, "indoor creatures, retainers of rules, anonymous men."[48] As careful men favoring measured words and precise routines, the bullpen editors did not easily change their practices, nor did they perceive it as their job to change policies. That was for the managing editor. But Edwin James, who never mentioned the plight of the Jews in the regular Sunday opinion column he wrote throughout the war, apparently did not try to change the policy of putting stories about the extermination of the Jews inside the paper – and he was unlikely to have been listened to had he tried.

That left one person who could set the tone for the *Times*' coverage of the persecution of the Jews. MacNeil Jr. suspects that Arthur Sulzberger established an explicit policy that stories about the extermination campaign should be downplayed, although he acknowledges "my father never talked to me about this in any way; he never talked about any painful things if he could help it." MacNeil Jr., who became a distinguished journalist in his own right as *Time* magazine's congressional correspondent, said the consistent placement of these stories inside the paper "could not have happened by itself, but was obviously a policy that could only have come directly from the publisher." MacNeil Jr. does recall that his father "never trusted Sulzberger, whom he regarded as a businessman out of place, without journalistic experience or instincts." MacNeil Sr. grew so nervous about the publisher, in fact, that he had his stockbroker hunt down one of the few available shares of the family-owned company so, as his son explained, "if worst came to worst he would have ready access to the annual stockholders' meeting where he would raise [holy hell] at whatever outrage he might suffer." MacNeil never raised a ruckus at an annual meeting, but his son assumed he acquired that share in the mid 1940s to protect himself. "I suspect he had to be embarrassed about the Holocaust coverage by The Times and his role in it. The policy had to come from Sulzberger and I suspect that's why my father wanted a share of Times's stock. He had reason to question Sulzberger's judgment."[49]

No record of such a policy could be found in the *Times* archives. That does not mean it did not exist. Such a memo might not have been included in the *Times*' less-than-comprehensive files, or the policy may have been communicated verbally, and thus no record ever existed. But the more likely explanation is that no record exists because there was no need for an explicit policy. "There is a tendency, even on the best newspapers, for the economic, political, and social views of the owners to seep down through the entire organization," Neil MacNeil wrote in 1940 about a publisher's influence in general, although he had to have had his boss, Arthur Sulzberger, in mind. "Reporters viewing the event and editors passing judgment on it are inclined, be it ever so slightly, to see it from the publisher's angle. They doubtless want the approval of their superiors, for interesting assignments, promotion, and higher salaries usually await such approval. Few will bite the hand that feeds them. Almost without knowing it the news favors the owner's viewpoint. The story in which the publisher is interested becomes a 'good story,' and vice versa."[50]

The *Times* publisher was able to effectively communicate his views to the staff. "Sulzberger did not want to be an aggressive, dominating publisher, hurling thunderbolts at an awed staff," Catledge writes. "His style was more reserved, more subtle, and I think more effective. He sought executives who shared his general outlook, and he tried, by word and deed, to set a tone for the paper." Even outsiders understood this. In assessing 30 American newspapers and wire services in February 1943, the Polish exile government's propaganda arm in New York noted for the *Times*: "A. H. Sulzberger exclusive responsible." It made no similar comment about any other publisher.[51]

"Sulzberger made his likes and dislikes known via memoranda which we called the 'blue notes' because they were written on blue paper," writes Catledge. "Hundreds of these blue notes rained down on me over the years, on great matters and small."[52] During the war, Sulzberger instructed his editors on everything from using undated leads, to printing military communiques in agate [tiny type], or putting a box around selected convention events. The bullpen editors may have ignored the managing editor, but they listened to the publisher. "Since James passed on the publisher's instructions, as well as his own, a code had been worked out to denote Sulzberger's requests," Catledge explains. "If James said in a memo, 'It is desired that . . . ,' the bullpen editors understood the particular instruction came from Sulzberger, and was not to be ignored."[53]

Everyone in the organization understood where Sulzberger stood on issues involving Jews, without his having to write it down. "The *Times* had a policy of not going heavily into Jewish matters, any kind of Jewish matters," said MacNeil Jr., who worked as a general assignment reporter for the *Times* from 1943 until he entered Harvard in 1945. "It was just kind of a sense of things, a sensitivity by the publisher. He was Jewish and therefore shouldn't emphasize it." The editors, Jewish or not, understood the publisher's sensitivity. "James was not Jewish. People like that felt it, it didn't have to be told in so many words," said Daniel Schwarz, a *Times* editor beginning in 1929. "They knew what the policy of the publisher was."

Arthur Sulzberger's long-standing position that the Jews should not be singled out, whether for persecution or for salvation, hardened throughout 1942 and 1943, as he became embroiled in a nasty, partisan, and public fight with some of America's top Jewish leaders.

7

"All Jews Are Not Brothers"

The Publisher's Fight with Zionists

DURING 1942, as the *Times* published accounts of the millions already dead in Eastern Europe and the millions more in imminent danger, Arthur Sulzberger issued a written order to his staff about how to handle the unfolding events. A five-paragraph story on a speech by William Green, American Federation of Labor president, condemning "the slaughter of hundreds of thousands of Jews in Europe by the Nazi butchers," caught Sulzberger's attention. But it was not the condemnation or who was issuing it that interested Sulzberger. "I have been trying to instruct the people around here on the subject of the word 'Jews', i.e., that they are neither a race nor a people, etc.," Sulzberger wrote to his Washington Bureau Chief Arthur Krock at the end of December. The person who wrote the story's main headline ("A.F.L. Head Condemns Nazi Killing of Jews") "had learned his lesson," Sulzberger wrote. So had Green, who referred to "Jews." "But the fellow in the Washington Bureau who wrote the lead turned what Green said into 'the Jewish people.' Will you caution him?" Krock did, asking his deputy to "please issue the necessary instructions."[1]

For Sulzberger, the drive against Jewish nationalism – against conceiving of Jews as a people, against a Jewish homeland in Palestine, against the leaders who advocated those stances – overshadowed every other issue, even Hitler's plan to make Jewish nationalism an irrelevancy.

The fight between Sulzberger and the Zionists had been brewing for a long time. As a Classical Reform Jew like his famous grandfather-in-law, Sulzberger had watched with dismay as the Reform movement, led by two dominating rabbis, Stephen Wise and Abba Hillel Silver, drifted away from its anti-Zionist foundation. At first Sulzberger was willing to accept the compromise reached in the mid-1930s between younger Reform rabbis who wanted to declare their support for Zionism and the older rabbis of the Isaac M. Wise school who continued to oppose Jewish nationalism. To prevent open warfare within Reform ranks, the Zionists and the non-Zionists, as they preferred to be called, agreed that Reform organizations could support charitable and educational projects for the Jews living in Palestine. They could participate in the "upbuilding" of Palestine, as long as they did not further its political objectives.[2]

Sulzberger tried to hew to that line, occasionally praising the Palestinian Jews' economic success while eschewing their politics. Yet, in 1940, when President Roosevelt was looking for a liaison with the American Jewish community to replace Cyrus Adler, Sulzberger's cousin who had recently died, Sulzberger made sure the post did not go to "some Zionist or active Jewish Nationalist," particularly not Stephen Wise. When Roosevelt appointed Louis Finkelstein, Adler's replacement as head of the Jewish Theological Seminary, to the post, Treasury Secretary Morgenthau congratulated Sulzberger: "You certainly are a fast worker."[3]

By the early 1940s, Sulzberger concluded that the groups supporting the Jews in Palestine had not been upholding their end of the bargain in steering clear of nationalism. He had already stopped giving to the United Jewish Appeal and the American Jewish Joint Distribution Committee; he then also cut his gift to the UJA's New York campaign. In rebuffing a request that the *Times* write an editorial encouraging donations to the United Palestine Appeal, a UJA offshoot, Sulzberger suggested that the Zionists had broken the cease-fire by requesting funds for progress in a "Jewish National Home." Any *New York Times* editorial on Palestine, he assured the United Palestine Appeal, "would not be to your liking."[4]

A year later the *Times* published such an editorial, and it was not to any Zionist's liking. At the beginning of the war, a group of right-wing Jews from Palestine had come to the United States to lobby for the formation of all-Jewish fighting units to combat the Nazi menace. By early 1942, the idea was picking up momentum. American Zionist groups, as part of a coalition known as the American Emergency Committee for Zionist Affairs (AECZA), endorsed the idea despite their enmity for its original advocates, the Palestinian Jews led by Peter Bergson. A resolution had been introduced in the U.S. House of Representatives asking the State Department to request that Great Britain allow the formation of all-Jewish military units. So when the *New York Times* published an editorial on January 22 (p. 16) opposing the Jewish Army and Zionism in general – one of just two lead editorials on a Jewish issue that appeared during the entire war – it caused a stir.

The editorial concluded that such an army might "provoke an Arab uprising" while the British were holding off the Germans in the Mediterranean, and thus should be opposed on practical grounds. Even more important, the *Times* explained, were the philosophical objections. The real goal of a "separate Zionist army" was to make establishment of a Zionist state one of the Allies' "official war aims." That effort, the editorial implied, would raise the specter of American Jews having dual loyalties. It would lead to "much misunderstanding" among "people of other faiths," the editorial warned, who would believe that Jews wanted something different from what other Americans wanted.

The editorial, particularly its charge of dual loyalties, pushed AECZA to wage an "energetic propaganda campaign" in favor of the Jewish Army, including a rally at Carnegie Hall, and an effort to obtain support from other New York newspapers. Emanuel Neumann, who steered the committee's public relations, wrote a memorandum for *PM*, which served as the basis for an editorial on January 23.[5] The committee also enlisted various authors to write columns to appear in the *New York Post* and *Mirror*, among other papers. On January 26, the *Times* ran two letters, "representative" of the many it had received: one, from AEZCA's head, Stephen Wise, who criticized the editorial; the other, from City College philosophy professor Morris Raphael Cohen, who supported it. For his part, Sulzberger reacted strongly to the overall criticism, noting that "many of the Jewish nationalists think, just as Hitler does, that there should be room for only one opinion, theirs."[6]

Rabbi Abba Hillel Silver, an ardent Zionist, wrote to his lieutenant Neumann that the *Times*' editorial and Cohen's response, as well as a *Saturday Evening Post* article by prominent New York lawyer Jerome Frank, were the first volleys in what would prove to be a long battle among Jews. "The forces of assimilation . . . are hoping to make . . . all Zionists in America patriotic suspects," Silver wrote. "This is dangerous business." Sulzberger understood equally well that his message – that American Jews were not united behind Zionism – had to reach the right people. So he sent copies of the "Zionist Army" editorial and the responding letters to Secretary of State Cordell Hull and to Undersecretary of State Sumner Welles. Welles, whom Zionists at the time considered an ally but who in retrospect may have been cultivating both sides, replied that he read the *Times* commentaries with "a great deal of interest" and that "they have been helpful to me." Welles also indicated that he "particularly enjoyed" his recent conversation with Sulzberger and "should like to have another chance of talking further." Praise came from another official quarter as well. "All of us out here were much struck by your leader about the Jewish Army," Kenneth Buss of the British Office of the Minister of State in Cairo wrote to the *Times* publisher. "To me it recalled so vividly your reactions after your tour of Palestine. . . ."[7]

The Jewish press, which even before the editorial had attacked the *Times* as "hostile and unsympathetic toward Zionism" and as "defensive" on Jewish issues generally,[8] turned up the heat. In the February 1942 *New Frontier*, William Cohen wrote that the *Times*, which was "the most complete, respected and reliable daily newspaper in the world," possessed "feet of clay" when it came to "news of general Jewish interest and of Zionism." He placed the blame squarely on the publisher "who suffers from the Jewish maladies of self-hate and self-effacement," and thus, "has not the desire to inform his readers about barbaric atrocities committed on Jews in Russia or Poland." Cohen found the "Zionist Army" editorial particularly reprehensible. The *Times* "chose this unpropitious moment to plunge the dagger of betrayal in the back of the helpless millions of Jews who look anxiously to Palestine for a haven after the war."

One group of Rumanian Jews hoped not to have to wait until the war's end. In early 1942, they had boarded a rickety cattle boat, called the *Sturma*, to make the voyage to Palestine. The boat reached Istanbul, where it waited off shore, planning to repair a damaged engine. But the Jews could not land in Turkey without British assurances they were on their way to Palestine, which the British would not give. Turkish authorities then cut the *Sturma* loose, assuming it would find its way back to Rumania. It did not. On February 24, the boat, carrying 768 refugees, sank in the waters off Turkey, killing all but 1 person aboard.[9]

Enraged American Zionists made a concerted effort to draw public attention to the tragedy, without success. "Unfortunately the incident of the Sturma was reported very, very briefly in a few lines, and most people knew nothing about it," Emanuel Neumann noted. On February 28, the *Times* reported in four paragraphs on page two the sinking of a "Black Sea ship." According to Neumann, there were two exceptions to this minimal coverage: "*PM* which reacted almost immediately" and the *Washington Post*, "which carried a very strong editorial."[10]

To drum up more attention, AECZA ran an advertisement in the *Times* on March 11 calling for "a change of policy on the part of the Palestine

Administration" to prevent "this most recent of horrible and avertible tragedies." The ad announced a public meeting the next day at the Cosmopolitan Opera House. After the meeting, Neumann complained that the press, including the *Times*, did not report the event, even though journalists had attended. "We have had it confirmed that this was no accident due to pressure of war news, but to the deliberate policy apparently inspired from above," he wrote. "We understand that the British have made presentations to American officials and they apparently have passed the word that it would not be wise to allow what seemed like anti-British propaganda."[11]

Although nothing in the *Times'* records corroborates Neumann's information, Sulzberger certainly would have been sympathetic to a pro-British appeal. In fact, a year and a half earlier, the *Times* had run a story on the front page about the sinking of another refugee ship, the *Patria*, whose demise the British had an interest in publicizing. The *Patria* sank after Jews in Palestine, who had planted a bomb to cripple the ship so it could not be forced to leave Haifa with 1,771 refugees aboard, miscalculated the amount of explosives. The ship capsized, killing about 200 people. Thus, the *Patria* story, which was embarrassing for the Jews in Palestine, appeared on the *Times* front page, whereas the *Sturma* story, which was embarrassing to the British, did not.

From the press response to the *Sturma* tragedy, Neumann concluded that Zionists needed to do more. "I think all of us have a certain feeling of frustration that not sufficient [sic] is happening in this country in light of the tragedies we are suffering, in the light of the terrific burdens we have to bear, and the problem we have of mobilizing American opinion," he wrote in March.[12] Within 3 months, Jewish leaders would learn that the "tragedies" were in fact a catastrophe as the Bund report reached the West. The difficulty of changing public opinion would be aggravated by some prominent American Jews forming the first organization avowedly dedicated to undermining Zionism.[13]

Arthur Sulzberger was deeply involved in the founding of the American Council for Judaism. A year earlier, Sulzberger had been contacted by Morris Lazaron, a Baltimore rabbi who was thinking of forming a new organization dedicated to Reform's original principles as expressed by Isaac M. Wise. "Before making any move, however, I should like your confidential judgment," he wrote Sulzberger. "Would you support such a move?" Sulzberger responded that he was "deeply sympathetic."[14] Sulzberger's initial role seemed to be to egg Lazaron on. In November 1941, Reform's Central Conference of American Rabbis complained to Lazaron about his recent visit to England, during which Lazaron explained to British Foreign Minister Anthony Eden and U.S. Ambassador John Winant that American Jews were not behind Zionism. Lazaron asked Sulzberger how he should respond to his fellow rabbis' complaint. "I see no reason for not answering quite frankly and starting the fight," Sulzberger told him. In a letter the following month, Sulzberger mulled over his role. "The more I think it over the more I feel that the best service I can render is to be as complete a maverick as my inclination suggests. My job is to show all and sundry that I do not subscribe to the thesis that 'all Jews are brothers,' and that rather than attempt to avoid differences people like you and me should seek to create them." That December, Sulzberger invited 13 people to his home, including Laurence Steinhardt, his Columbia classmate and ambassador to Moscow, and Samuel Rosenman, FDR's speechwriter and close advisor, to convince them to sign an anti-Zionist declaration.[15]

Two months later, in February 1942, the Central Conference of American Rabbis moved from enforcing neutrality on Zionism within Reform ranks to taking a stand – in favor of a Jewish Army.[16] With so many rabbis in the Reform movement aligning themselves with the Zionist cause, others, such as Lazaron and Louis Wolsey of Philadepia, decided to convene their own meeting to combat Zionism. So while 500 Zionists, including Reform Rabbis Wise and Silver, met at the Biltmore in New York City in May, non-Zionists rabbis gathered in Atlantic City in June. Sulzberger alerted his "people to look out for" a speech Lazaron was to make at the Atlantic City meeting. A *Times* story describing Lazaron's attack on the patriotism of American Zionists prompted Lazaron to write Sulzberger that he felt confident that "you and I and The New York Times can work together."[17]

Lazaron was proven right later that month when Sulzberger helped write an advertisement the group was to place in the *Times*. Sulzberger continued to push Lazaron to more confrontational positions. "I don't believe that anything is to be accomplished by unity with the Zionists," Sulzberger wrote Lazaron at the end of June.[18] In August, Lazaron asked him to print in the next Sunday's edition of the *Times* a full statement of principles and a list of supporters. The newspaper obliged, using the precise language Lazaron had suggested for the preceding and concluding paragraphs. Sulzberger wrote Lazaron to offer "congratulations on the excellent statement." So did David Philipson, a pillar of Classical Reform Judaism, who considered the Sunday publication "quite a coup." He added, "I am glad to know that it was your letter to Arthur Hays Sulzberger that brought this about."[19]

As Sulzberger's involvement with Lazaron's group grew, so did his interest in Ichud, an organization that promoted a plan for a binational state of Arabs and Jews in Palestine. Judah Magnes, who had been the rabbi at Temple Emanu-El before immigrating to Palestine to head Hebrew University, proposed a confederation of Middle Eastern states that would allow for greater Jewish immigration while ensuring Jews did not become a majority. Sulzberger was enthusiastic from the start and used the *Times* to push the idea, publishing a long letter from Magnes and an even longer interview with him.[20] "You'll be happy know our ideas being actively promoted," Sulzberger cabled Magnes, offering to pay for him to come "here talk Ichud."[21] When he visited England in August and September 1942, ostensibly on a trip for the American Red Cross, of which he was a board member, Sulzberger dined with Anthony Eden and Lord Cranborne, the colonial secretary. He lobbied them for a state that could "stand a large immigration of Jews without upsetting the balance of power held by the Arabs." Sulzberger said he "found them both extremely sympathetic." Sulzberger also met with Prime Minister Winston Churchill for a 3-hour lunch at Chequers. Although their conversation covered many subjects, they never touched upon Palestine, according to Sulzberger's account. Years later, Sulzberger recalled that Churchill once "brushed me aside when I tried to talk Palestine to him, saying 'I know you are not a Zionist, but I am.'"[22]

Nothing Sulzberger did generated as much consternation, however, as a speech he delivered on November 5, 1942 at Lazaron's Baltimore synagogue. Sulzberger devoted most of it to his first-hand observations of Great Britain's stiff upper lip in the face of Nazi bombardment, and his plea that Americans stifle their criticism of the British. Near the end, he discussed the Jewish issues that had been preoccupying him throughout the year: his opposition to a Jewish Army and his advocacy of a binational state in Palestine. He grounded both positions in Classical Reform principles. "It is unfortunate indeed that those of us who believe that Jews are a religious body only – those of us who are unwilling to accept the Nazi connotation that we are a racial group apart – it is unfortunate that we should find it so difficult to put our views before the world," he told the congregation of seemingly like-minded Jews.

The Associated Press covered the speech, leading with Sulzberger's call for Jews and non-Jews to drop their support for a Jewish army. The *Times* printed the AP version of the speech the day after it was delivered. AECZA immediately called for rabbis and various Congressmen to issue statements in response, which they did; the *Times* ran the rabbis' rebuttal on November 16. "These two statements would serve in some measure to counter the impression made by Mr. Sulzberger," the minutes of an AECZA meeting stated.[23]

Sulzberger seemed both delighted and disturbed by the reaction to his speech. When lawyer Jerome Frank wrote to express his approval and to ask for a copy of the speech, Sulzberger replied: "I stirred a hornet's nest and they are buzzing angrily I'm glad to say." Yet, he also told Lazaron that "I don't want to make myself the spearhead of the attack on the Zionists and that isn't because I don't like a scrap but rather because I cannot disassociate myself from The New York Times. If I were to become too much involved people would think The Times was prejudiced in its reporting." But soon he was practically crowing to Lazaron: "My mail from that speech in Baltimore has been terrific. You have undoubtedly seen all the publications which tear me limb from limb. Fortunately I'm a centipede!"[24]

In the wake of the speech, Sulzberger and Samuel Margoshes, editor of a Yiddish language newspaper, exchanged letters that highlighted the *Times'* critical role in shaping American opinion on issues related to Jews. A previous *Congress Weekly* editorial had described the *Times* as a Jewish newspaper, provoking Sulzberger's retort that nothing "would be more useful or more truly save our American system" than to have "that fallacious idea eradicated." Margoshes replied that Jews "in the know" understood the *Times* was not a Jewish newspaper, but "the American public is still laboring under the misapprehension that both the Times and its publisher speak for most, if not all Jews." That made it doubly difficult "to explain to strangers that the New York Times is not the Jewish Big Brother who is speaking for us when we are in trouble and need help from others," Margoshes wrote. "For example, you can imagine our difficulties in convincing members of Congress, chiefs of government bureaus, clergymen, editors and other molders of American public opinion that Jews generally are not against the Jewish army, but for it."[25]

Margoshes' concern about the *Times*' influence among "molders of American public opinion" was well founded. As he had with the Jewish Army editorial, Sulzberger sent a copy of his Baltimore remarks to Undersecretary of State Sumner Welles, along with a Judah Magnes memo describing "the slogan Jewish State" as a "declaration of war by the Jews on the Arabs." Welles replied that he "welcomed the opportunity of talking" to Sulzberger about "the questions raised in the memorandum." He added: "I think you know how greatly I value your judgment."[26] In December 1942, Sulzberger wrote Secretary of State Hull that he wanted to come to Washington "to chat with you about certain Jewish questions which conditions in the world have made important not only to Jews but to everybody." He enclosed a *Times* advertisement that endorsed a Jewish Army. "It is scarcely necessary for me to advise you that this idea of a Jewish army is certainly not in line with the thinking of most of my friends who happen to be Jews," he wrote. Hull wrote him later that month: "As I look back over the past years I can scarcely think of any one whose friendship I prize more highly than yours. You perhaps may not realize what a fine public service you have rendered through your broad and statesman-like approach to public questions."[27]

While the fight over Zionism remained in the foreground, the news of the systematic annihilation of the Jews began to occupy both Sulzberger and his opponents. For 6 months, the *Times* had been reporting that Germany had a grand plan to kill all the Jews. But Sulzberger remained resolute that Jews as Jews should not, and probably could not, do anything special to save their fellow Jews. Philosophically, he reiterated that Jews were not a race or a people; therefore, it would be wrong to treat them as such. He wrote in December 1942, after the UN declaration confirming the extermination campaign had appeared on the *Times* front page, "I know that when I served in the Field Artillery during the last war my aim was not to destroy German Catholics or Protestants and avoid hitting German Jews. Being a Jew didn't matter so long as the question was not religious."[28]

Practically, he insisted that any Jewish effort to save Jews would fail. The day after the *Times* carried the State Department's confirmation of the extermination campaign, Sulzberger wrote to Joseph Willen of the Jewish Federation of New York City:

> As an American I am overwhelmed by the inhumanity of the treatment [the Jews of Europe] have received. That feeling is sharpened by my religious convictions which are Jewish, just as Christianity helps to shape the view of many of my friends, who deplore, as I do, what has been done to these greatly-to-be-pitied human beings. As a Jew I am concerned with what has happened to them because it has happened to them as Jews, and I resent that bitterly and fiercely.
>
> I do not believe, however, that I, as a Jew, am concerned because of any fear that it may happen to me if not checked. I know full well that that is true, but I also know that if that happens, America and democracy will be destroyed, which is much more serious than the destruction of a Jew or of all Jews both because America is a greater faith and because Americans as such can save Jews. But Jews as such cannot save either Americans or even themselves.[29]

The *Times* therefore continued to hammer the theme that however awful the Jews' fate it was similar to that of other oppressed peoples under the Nazi yoke. In mid-November, the *Times* editorialized on "religion under the Nazis," concluding that Jews as "the weakest and least numerous of the German religious minorities," could be "most safely persecuted." As "Nazism grew stronger," however, it could turn its fury on its true target: "the Protestant and Catholic communions in Germany," and "priests, ministers and congregations in conquered lands." The editorial went on to equate the unrelenting persecution of Jews in Belgium and the Netherlands, with attacks on "Christian organizations, schools, newspapers and social service agencies."[30]

Even the *Times* editorial that acknowledged that 2 million Jews were dead and another 5 million were endangered emphasized that Nazi crimes against the Jews were just "the first number on a list which has since included people of other faiths and of many races." The argument that the Jews were not being singled out for persecution also led to an important policy proscription; no steps should be taken separately to save them. "All I want as an American is that nothing be done now which will hinder or delay the winning of the War," Sulzberger wrote at the end of December.[31]

Because he believed agitation for a Jewish state would do just that, Sulzberger did not back away from a non-Zionist stance. In mid-November 1942, he met with other prominent New Yorkers to lay the groundwork for the American Council for Judaism. The council's official launch date was 6 days later on November 26, 2 days after the State Department confirmed the news of the extermination campaign. Lazaron noted the confluence of events and warned his fellow founder Wolsey not to hold a meeting scheduled for December 7. "We must be awfully careful about these things and not give those whom we oppose grounds to attack us," he wrote Wolsey. Wolsey, however, would not change the date. "Rommel is making his way to Egypt, or Rommel is getting into Palestine, or a holocaust is taking place in Poland, there is always a reason why we shouldn't do anything," Wolsey replied.[32]

Lazaron's admonition turned out to be prescient. "Objectively speaking, the Council had chosen an inauspicious moment for recruiting anti-Zionist sentiment," concludes David Shpiro. "American Jewry was awakening to the magnitude of the holocaust in Europe, and the Zionists realized that time had come to crush their Jewish adversaries." *Congress Weekly* condemned the council in its December 25, 1942 issue for frustrating and betraying Jewish hopes "while Hitler was employed in the systematic destruction of the Jews in Europe." *New Palestine* decried the council as "internal enemies of the Jewish people." Rabbis began to denounce the council and Sulzberger from the pulpit. Maurice Hexter of the Jewish Federation informed Sulzberger of "a most unfortunate incident" at a bar mitzvah his daughter attended. The rabbi "launched into a bitter attack upon you and upon me, and called upon you to resign from the Times and me to resign from Federation," Hexter wrote.[33]

Their response to the news of the extermination campaign further marginalized the anti-Zionists. "With the physical destruction of European Jews proceeding at an unprecedented rate, only the most fanatic of anti-Zionists could afford the luxury of besmirching the Zionist endeavor specifically designed to rescue the threatened communities," Samuel Halperin writes. "Reform Jews might still have reservations about the validity or wisdom of Zionist ideology, but few would risk being labeled an 'enemy of Israel' by an open hostility to Zionism."[34] Arthur Sulzberger was willing to take the risk.

In the wake of the United Nations' confirmation of the extermination campaign, Jewish groups began to clamor for rescue. Many saw unity as the first step. In January, representatives of thirty-five national Jewish groups met to plan a conference to "establish a common program of action" that would be held during the summer. Both the group and the meeting would be known as the American Jewish Conference. Sulzberger, however, was in no mood for unity. If anything, the reaction to his Baltimore speech hardened his position. "I am glad I spoke as I did in Baltimore if for no other reason than that it unmasked the viciousness of Zionist propaganda," he wrote to Judge Louis Levinthal, sending him a copy of the essay he wrote after his 1937 visit to Palestine. Sulzberger rejected the idea that at a time like this Jews needed to present a united front. "We need no other union than Shema Yisrael [Judaism's most important prayer]," he wrote. Nor would he accept that Jews needed special help. "Not that many do not need a place of refuge, but so do countless others who are not Jews." Levinthal sent a copy of the letter to Felix Frankfurter with the comment: "Isn't it a pity that a man occupying so influential a position is so limited in his understanding of the Jewish problem?" Frankfurter then shipped the letter to Treasury Secretary Morgenthau along with a sarcastic note: "Since you have come back refreshed and exhilarated you may be able to enjoy this from our Mr. Sulzberger."[35]

Sulzberger not only opposed a false show of unity, he actually advocated disunity. "I quite agree with you that a split is necessary in what is called Jewish opinion in this county," he wrote Lazaron in January. "The only thing that is important is that our fellow Americans, who are not Jews, realize that all Jews do not think alike on subjects other than those concerning religion."[36]

Jews did indeed differ over how to help their European brethren. Some pushed for the Allies to threaten to bomb German cities, execute German prisoners, or at least exchange German prisoners for Jews. Others argued for easing immigration restrictions and establishing safe havens. Still others insisted that winning the war quickly remained the only hope for Europe's Jews. American Jews also differed over tactics. The group led by Peter Bergson, who in the wake of the extermination revelations had taken up the rescue cause, became the most ardent advocates of a visible public campaign. Although it did not abandon its call for a Jewish Army, the group concentrated on rescue, officially changing its name to the Emergency Committee to Save the Jewish People of Europe. (Unofficially, it was the Bergson Group.) In emotional, full-page advertisements in the *New York Times*, it persistently and single-mindedly demanded immediate rescue.[37] At the other extreme was the American Jewish Committee, whose membership of well-to-do Jews of German origin preferred backroom diplomacy to bellicose demonstrations. Stephen Wise's American Jewish Congress found itself somewhere between, protesting both publicly and privately.

As Palestine, with its proximity to Eastern Europe and its established Jewish community of 600,000 loomed larger as a refuge, American Jews differed over how to make that happen. The *Times* may have been instrumental in putting a kibosh on at least one such rescue scheme. In mid-February 1943, the *Times* ran a story on Rumanian Jews in a typically inconspicuous location on page five that nonetheless caused a commotion within Jewish organizations.[38] The lead read: The Rumania government told UN officials "it is prepared to cooperate in transferring 70,000 Rumanian Jews from Trans-Dniestria to any refuge selected by the Allies. . . . The Rumanian Government has intimated that shipment to Palestine would be most convenient."[39]

Although the genuineness of the Rumanians' intentions has never been clear, several things were. The Allies, who objected to the rescue scheme, leaked the information to the press and thus undermined its chances for success.[40] The author of the exclusive story that sabotaged the Rumanians' release – Cyrus Sulzberger. In the story, Sulzberger made clear his views on the likelihood of rescuing Jews. Admitting large numbers of refugees to Palestine would be "dangerous" because of "the ease with which spies could mix with émigrés," he wrote, and "risky" because it would lead to discord with "repercussions in the entire Moslem world." Any haven more distant than Palestine would involve "numerous great difficulties" in transferring the refugees, he stated.

Jewish organizations were not so pessimistic in the spring of 1943. They believed that if they could mute their differences over Palestine it might be possible to hammer out a unified position on rescue. So major Jewish organizations worked to that end with two important exceptions: the Bergson Group, with whom established organizations refused to ally, and the American Council for Judaism, which opposed unity in principle. On March 1, the American Jewish Congress sponsored a "Stop Hitler Now!" rally that drew tens of thousands of people to Madison Square Garden. "Save Doomed Jews, Huge Rally Pleads," read the headline on the *Times*' front-page article the next day. The article stated that the 21,000 people inside the Garden – another 75,000 people were reportedly turned away – approved an immediate plan "to save as many as possible of the five million Jews threatened with extermination by Adolf Hitler and to halt the liquidation of European Jews by the Nazis."

The day after the story appeared the *Times* editorialized on the rally. "Sanctuary for Europe's Jews," the seventh of seven editorials, stuck to the line that "all who love freedom are now in the same predicament" as the

Jews. Still, the editorial recognized that the Jews remain "the particular object of Hitler's venomous hatred, condemned to death where others are sometimes let off with slavery." It endorsed, if tepidly, resolutions that called for the United Nations to negotiate with German and German-controlled states to rescue Jews and "for the United States to set a good example" by "revising in the interests of humanity the chilly formalism of its immigration regulations." Anne O'Hare McCormick went further in her "Abroad" column. "There is not the slightest question that the persecution of the Jews has reached its awful climax in a campaign to wipe them out of Europe," she wrote. "Nor is there any question that if we let Hitler commit this last atrocity, if the Christian community does not support to the utmost the belated proposal worked out to rescue the Jews remaining in Europe from the fate prepared for them, we have accepted the Hitlerian thesis and forever compromised the principles for which we are pouring out blood and wealth and toil."[41] Stephen Wise considered the *Times*' support so important that, in asking other newspaper editors to editorialize in favor of the rescue measures adopted at the rally, he referred to McCormick's "noble utterances" and quoted from the editorial.[42]

Whatever momentum for rescue the rally and unity moves had generated, however, soon petered out. Other rallies were held that month, including the Bergson-produced pageant, "We Will Never Die," that starred Edward G. Robinson and drew 40,000 to Madison Square Garden on 2 successive nights. But they never made the *Times*' front page, nor did pleas by scholars and scientists, rabbis, or the Archbishop of Canterbury.[43] Most press and public attention focused on a conference to be held by the British and Americans in April. Since the December United Nations declaration, the two governments had been under intense pressure to do something about the Jews' plight. After much diplomatic maneuvering, the State Department and Foreign Office finally agreed to convene a conference on the island of Bermuda.

Even before the conference began, all involved, including the press, understood the talks were likely to be a failure. Neither the press nor representatives of Jewish groups were invited to attend, and the conference's isolated location ensured their input from outside the proceedings would be limited as well. The British sent a high-ranking delegation, the Americans did not, and both delegations announced ahead of time that the talks were strictly exploratory. Jewish groups were so convinced that the conference was a sham that, before it began, the World Jewish Congress solicited critical editorials and succeeded with the *Herald Tribune*, the *New*

York Post, *PM*, and the *World Telegram*. Even the *New York Times*, in probably its strongest editorial of the war, predicted that whatever proposals came out of the conference "may well prove to be 'too little too late.'" The *Times* no longer considered the war an excuse for the Allies' inaction. "[I]t would seem that even within the war effort, and perhaps even in aid of it, measures can be devised that go beyond palliatives which appeared to be designed to assuage the conscience of the reluctant rescuers rather than to aid the victims," the editorial stated. The *Times* maintained its timidity about referring to Jews, however, using "refugees" throughout the editorial.[44]

The stories that appeared during the conference confirmed the grim prognosis. "The limits of achievement that may be possible as the result of the Anglo-American talks on the international refugee problem – already hinted at by both delegations in press conferences – became more clearly defined at the formal opening of the parley this morning," read the lead of the *Times* front-page story announcing the start of the conference. Subsequent *Times* stories made clear that the large-scale movement of refugees to safe havens was not possible, that Palestine could not serve as a place of refuge, and that the Allies were not willing to negotiate with the Axis for the release of Jews or to ameliorate their suffering. The conference was so ineffective that "visiting correspondents have dubbed it 'the no news conference,'" the *Times* reported.[45]

If, as many suspected, the conference's real purpose was "not so much to save the Jews from death as themselves from public censure," the Bermuda parlay could be considered a success. In its wake, press coverage of rescue demands seemed even more subdued. No criticism of the conference appeared on the *Times* front page, nor did the *Times* editorialize on the lack of results. "A Day of Compassion for the Jews," planned by the Federal Council of the Churches of Christ in America, received scant attention, even though the American Jewish Committee had hoped it would be "promoted in the press as widely as possible." The *Times* story ran on page 48.[46]

By the summer of 1943, despair was growing in the American Jewish community and along with it a conviction – Palestine offered the only hope for Jewish survival, and Arthur Sulzberger and his powerful newspaper were among those standing in the way.

Until 1943, the *Times*' coverage of events within Palestine – as opposed to immigration to Palestine – had not caused much consternation among Jewish groups. For the previous 15 years, the *Times*' primary Middle

Eastern correspondent had been Joseph M. Levy. Levy had been born in New Brunswick, New Jersey, in 1901, but had moved to Jerusalem as an infant. Levy was Jewish, but he was also familiar with Arab culture, having attended the University of Beirut and lived with a Bedouin tribe in the Transjordan desert for 7 months. He spoke eight languages, including Hebrew and Arabic. The *Times* hired him as a correspondent in 1928, stationing him first in Jerusalem, where his mother still lived, and then moving him to Cairo in 1935.[47]

The British, however, were not pleased with his presence there. "I found some of our people very disturbed as to the activities of your correspondent Levy in Cairo," J. W. Wheeler-Bennett, a British member of the Inter-Allied Information Center, wrote Arthur Sulzberger in 1940. "He has apparently sent a rather sensational report regarding the likelihood of an immediate German Putsch in Afghanistan which is wholly unjustified by the facts and at the same time somewhat detrimental to our interests." The British, who accredited all correspondents operating in the Middle Eastern theater, made it clear to the publisher that they could take away Levy's press credentials. Sulzberger suspected that the real problem was not Levy's accuracy but the British ambassador in Cairo's "pique" based on an incident during Sulzberger's visit to the region a few years earlier. Levy had managed to have the Cairo Museum opened so the publisher could see the Tutankhamen relics after the ambassador had nixed the idea. "That's the way history is made, you know," Sulzberger said. Still, the publisher instructed James to send Levy a cable: "Reports again received you confusing political with reportorial work. Suggest careful scrutiny since you will be unuseful elsewhere."[48] The issue soon became moot when Levy developed anemia and had to return to the States in November 1940. Levy returned to Cairo the following year, but the British again objected to his presence. Levy resettled in Jerusalem but had to return to the States in 1942 after again falling ill.

The British were not the only ones with doubts about Levy. *Times* editors considered Levy, who was in his early forties, a relentless complainer and suspected that his illnesses, variously described as anemia, heart disease, headaches, or sciatica, were "psychoneurotic." The publisher quipped of another reporter – he "knows more ways of making himself a pain in the neck than anybody I know (if Joe Levy will forgive me)." There were also political concerns. "He had a reputation of being so pro-Zionist that you had to be careful trying to appraise what he wrote," recalled Daniel Schwarz, a Sunday section editor who joined the paper in 1929, adding "personally he was a fine fellow."[49] The *Times* had similar concerns about another Jewish correspondent in Jerusalem, Julian Meltzer, who had been hired as a stringer in 1940, but whom Cyrus Sulzberger never trusted.[50]

The *Times* did not make a fuss when Foreign Secretary Lord Halifax warned in 1943 that returning Levy to Cairo "would be a great mistake." The British authorities' "wish is that the *New York Times* should be represented there by someone to whom they can extend every facility and their full trust," the publisher was informed.[51] The *Times* sent Cyrus Sulzberger, even though he may not have had the full trust of the British authorities. In November 1942, he too had an accreditation problem because of an unspecified "row I got into with the British in the Balkans." But he did have the full trust of his uncle. When the British threatened to deny Cyrus the necessary credentials, he wrote James: "Uncle Arthur had better talk to Lord Halifax in person" and appeal to "any powerful pals he has including perhaps [Lord] Beaverbrook, even Churchill." It did not take Churchill. Arthur cabled Minister of Information Brendan Bracken, and Cyrus received his accreditation.[52]

The British need not have worried. Cyrus Sulzberger soon published stories that dovetailed nicely with Great Britain's aims for the Middle East. The British line was that Jewish agitation for greater immigration would drive the Arabs into the Axis and endanger the war effort.[i] Arthur Sulzberger subscribed to this view, having said so the previous year in the "Zionist Army" editorial and his Baltimore speech. Cyrus Sulzberger apparently did, too. From May through August 1943, he wrote nearly a dozen stories suggesting the region was on the verge of violence due to the Jews' growing militancy over immigration. Almost as soon as the articles began appearing, Jewish groups protested. The articles were preparing "the public mind for a sell-out on Zionism on the spurious grounds that an attempt to fulfill the pledge of the Balfour Declaration would endanger the war effort," the *Jewish Frontier* maintained in its June 1943 issue.

A less extreme "sell-out" was in fact in the works. The U.S. State Department was pushing for a joint Anglo-American declaration to delay

[i] Joseph W. Bendersky, *The "Jewish Threat": Anti-Semitic Politics of the U.S. Army*, New York: Basic Books (2000), 319, concludes that the British deliberately exaggerated this threat.

discussion of Jewish immigration and statehood until after the war. Arthur Sulzberger favored such a declaration, working privately through Undersecretary of State Welles and Hebrew University President Magnes and, Zionists charged, publicly through his nephew's articles.[53] Cyrus' stories were just the beginning. In August, the *Times* began closely following the Jerusalem trials of two British soldiers and two Jews charged with smuggling guns into Palestine. The *Times* had the admittedly pro-British Alexander C. Sedgwick, who also happened to be Cyrus' uncle by marriage, cover the gun-running trial. The *Times* had hired Sedgwick, an American who had spent most of his childhood in Europe, as its Athens correspondent 2 years before the war started. The Groton- and Harvard-educated Sedgwick spent the early war years covering the British troops, an "association" he found to be "a happy one." In the summer of 1943, the 42-year-old Sedgwick was fresh from an assignment covering the British forces fighting in North Africa. "Frankly I didn't find the British such scoundrels as from time to time it is the fashion to believe," he later wrote describing his attitude that summer. "Besides I don't see why one shouldn't be pro-British if one is reasonable about it."[54]

To Zionists, in both Palestine and the United States, Sedgwick was not reasonable in his pro-British portrayal of the gun-running trials. The *Times* stories, which ran in August and September, made the threat of a Jewish Agency-led insurrection sound menacing and imminent. "Vast Ring with Huge Resources Linked with Jewish Agency at Smugglers' Trial," one headline read. "Two Men Alleged to Have Been Part of 'Treacherous' Group that Bought Arms," read another. Zionists also wondered why the *Times* would devote nine stories to run-of-the-mill criminal charges in far-off Palestine.[55]

Neither the *Times*' interest in, nor its depiction of, the trial was accidental, Zionists concluded. After the first three articles had been published, Carl J. Friedrich of Harvard's Graduate School of Public Administration wrote Zionist activist Emanuel Neumann to ensure "adequate corrections of the various factual misrepresentations will be offered." Neumann agreed that the "Sedgwick articles in the *Times* were horrible," but he was not sure that "correcting the misrepresentations" would be enough. "Actually, as I see it, this is only one manifestation of a well laid plot to discredit Zionism," Neumann wrote. "Involved in the plot are not only Arabs and certain British and American officials but also – I say it to my shame as a Jew – Arthur Hays Sulzberger, with a few other

Jewish renegades." Isaiah Berlin, then a young political attache working for the British Embassy in Washington, shared that assessment, if not the harsh language. On August 28, he sent a dispatch to London, noting Zionists' concerns over the trial, and the *Times*' coverage of it. "There seems no doubt that Sulzberger, so far as lies in his timorous nature, has generally decided to expose what he regards as a dangerously chauvinist movement."[56]

Jews in Palestine also worried. To Moshe Shertok, leader of the Jews there, the coverage of the gun-running trials was "in the centre of our problems" because it was designed "to create the impression that Palestine (and because of Palestine the whole Middle East) stands on the verge of an abyss of rioting and civil war, due, of course, to *our* violence in midst of a world war."[57] The *Times*, to its credit, reported on the Jewish Agency's concerns about the trial, if not its own coverage. After the two Jewish defendants were found guilty and sentenced to 7 and 10 years in prison, the *Times* built a story around a statement by the Jewish Agency's David Ben-Gurion that the trial had been a British plot designed to bolster its case for restricting Jewish immigration to Palestine.[58,ii]

Arthur Sulzberger denied that he influenced the *Times*' coverage. When a New York rabbi complained in September 1943, Sulzberger apparently told him "so far as the correspondents were concerned" he had "given them no instructions; if they reported adversely to Zionism it was because of their judgment of the facts." Sulzberger said something similar a few months later in responding to renewed criticism of the Palestine coverage.[59]

Sulzberger later received two lengthy letters from Sedgwick defending the fairness of the trials and denouncing the Jewish Agency. "There was no injustice committed either in the way the accused were tried or in the sentence that was meted out to them," Sedgwick wrote the publisher once the trial was completed. As for the Jewish Agency, Sedgwick believed its leaders cared "only for power in Palestine," and wanted a state "based

[ii] In a letter to Arthur Sulzberger 2 months later, Sedgwick wrote that he believed Ben-Gurion's statement "struck an almost hysterical note." He recalled Ben-Gurion's attitude toward the *Times*. "I remember that as Mr. Ben-Gurion handed me his statement . . . that I had the impression that he doubted if The New York Times would care to print their contents due to some prejudice he fancied the paper entertained against the Zionist cause." Sedgwick to A. Sulzberger, 12/21/43, ELJ File, ACS Folder, NYTCA.

upon a philosophy not unlike that of the Nazis." In fact, in a second letter, Sedgwick wrote that among Jews in Palestine "almost a Nazi system exists and is followed in many quarters," leading to children being "imbued with nationalistic ideas[,] race consciousness and obedience to the State as supreme power."[60,iii]

At least one *Times* reporter, however, believed the press in general, and the *Times* in particular, was allowing the British to dominate "our policy, militarily and politically" in the Middle East. Ray Brock, who had helped the Jewish Agency transmit messages to Stephen Wise from Turkey in 1941, had been considered "a damned good reporter" for the *Times*, according to Cyrus Sulzberger. But in 1943, the Middle East Theatre Command had asked the War Department not to accredit Brock and to get him to leave the Middle East, which it did. The *Times* did not object, at least partly because Sedgwick disliked Brock intensely and their editors did not want them in the same military theater. The *Times* then refused Brock's request to be sent to Yugoslavia because he "would not get the cooperation of the British." Brock returned home and began making speeches attacking British policy, as well as "the objectivity and truthfulness of The New York Times." Brock considered the gun-running trial a prime example. "News stories told of large quantities of ammunition and guns being seized by police in Jewish homes (in Palestine)," he was quoted in the *Indianapolis News*. "But the Arabs are the greatest gun-runners in the Middle East." Brock's remarks did not sit well with the *New York Times*. James wrote him soon after the Indiana speech: "I would like to have a letter stating whether or not you are going to keep this up, or are you going to stop it." Brock cabled back "eye shall continue say exactly what eye damn please."[61,iv]

The British and American governments had hoped to convince American Jewish groups to postpone the American Jewish Conference scheduled to

[iii] Sedgwick's characterizations of the Zionist movement, as well as Cyrus Sulzberger's, bear a striking resemblance to the reports of American and British intelligence officers stationed in the Middle East, including references to Zionism's "totalitarian, militaristic and National Socialist outlook." Bendersky, *The "Jewish Threat,"* 321–2.

[iv] Amazingly, by 1945, Brock was back working for the *Times* covering the first United Nations conference in San Francisco. He was also back helping Eliahu Elath who had used him as a messenger in Turkey in 1941. Brock provided the Jewish Agency with information on Middle Eastern delegations to the conference. Elath, *Zionism at the UN*, 43.

take place in New York at the end of August 1943. The State Department had even suggested that it would drop its push for a joint declaration curbing discussion of Palestine if the groups agreed to delay the conference. The British apparently assumed the negative publicity surrounding the arms trial would make American Jews reluctant to stage a large public meeting. The strategy backfired. The sense that Jews in Palestine were under siege only strengthened the resolve of American Zionists who were driving the conference. The Zionists even managed to quash the declaration in early August without agreeing to the quid pro quo. Thus, 500 delegates elected by 8,000 local organizations were set to meet in the ballroom of the Waldorf Astoria on August 29.[62]

Arthur Sulzberger was opposed to the very idea of an American Jewish Conference. When he learned that the Union of American Hebrew Congregations had agreed to join the conference, Sulzberger threatened to resign from the union's executive committee because of the departure "from its strictly religious function." He previously had hoped that the union of Reform congregations Isaac Wise had founded five decades earlier would be "the starting point for an affirmative religious Jewish policy so worded that it would obviously be a crack at the Zionist point of view." The Reform union's affiliation with the conference – which to Sulzberger meant it had "agreed to send delegates to a strictly Jewish meeting gathered together for other than religious purposes" – doomed that possibility. "I have felt the deepest ties and strongest associations with the religious concept of the Union," he wrote its president, Adolph Rosenberg. "[A]s a son-in-law of Mr. and Mrs. Ochs I was happy to lend what support I could to the splendid philosophy of Dr. Wise. I was hopeful that a rebirth of the Union's religious life might take place, and that the 'Nationalists' within its ranks might respect its religious position. That apparently is not to be and I regret it far more than you can imagine."[63]

That left the American Council for Judaism as the last bulwark of Classical Reform. In the spring of 1943, Sulzberger had helped persuade Lessing Rosenwald, a member of the family that founded Sears Roebuck, to take over the council's lay leadership. The Rosenwalds were prominent Reform Jews who donated heavily to Jewish charities, although Lessing was probably best known in the Jewish community as a member of America First, Charles Lindbergh's isolationist organization. In April 1943, Sulzberger, who had agreed to be a lay vice president of the council, also helped Rosenwald and others draft the group's statement of principles, inserting his preferred "Americans of Jewish faith" for "American Jews" throughout the document. He advised Rosenwald to run advertisements heralding the council's principles in "representative" newspapers. "After all, if we are going to stir up the animals, let's make them good and mad!" Sulzberger said. The next day, however, he thought better of it, cabling Rosenwald that the council should wait until it had "broad national backing."[64]

That was just the first of Sulzberger's second thoughts. He then decided that the council should not only forgo a national advertising campaign, but should avoid publicity of any kind until it had more support. The council's leadership disagreed. The leaders wanted to get as much attention as possible for the council's platform by releasing it to coincide with the American Jewish Conference. Sulzberger objected. Over the years, he gave somewhat different grounds for his disagreement: the statement's timing, its failure to be "affirmative" enough, and finally that it had not yet obtained "grass roots backing."[65]

As Jewish organizations prepared for the conference that summer, the need to do something for European Jews became even more apparent. Jan Karski, a Polish courier who had been inside the Warsaw ghetto and just outside the Belzec extermination camp, arrived in the United States and began making the rounds of government officials, Jewish organizations, labor leaders, and journalists. Among the journalists he met with were Walter Lippmann, George Creel of the *American Mercury*, Eugene Lyons of *Colliers*, and Anne O'Hare McCormick of the *New York Times*. Creel and Lyons would both write lengthy articles for the October issues of their magazines. McCormick, whom Karksi described as a "Ukrainian expert for the very important *New York Times*" and interested mostly in postwar Poland, wrote nothing about Karski or his revelations.[66]

At the end of July, the Bergson Group held a conference in New York to push rescue plans, which the *Times* reported in four inside stories. A few days later, the Polish government-in-exile announced that 1.8 million Jews were dead in Poland, which the *Times* also reported inside. A 19-page special issue of the *New Republic* devoted entirely to the plight of the Jews appeared in mid-August. Then, at the end of the month, just 3 days before the American Jewish Conference was to begin, the World Jewish Congress released a survey that found that 3 million Jews had already died as a result of "planned starvation, forced labor, deportations, pogroms and methodical murders in German-run extermination centers in Eastern Europe."[67] That news, displayed on page seven in the

Times, prompted the editorial page to take note of conference's opening and to advise the American government to "do everything it can to rescue innocent and persecuted people in Europe." The editorial added: "But we hope that this will be done with a realization that it is not any man's religion or any man's race that matters, but rather the fact that he is suffering for freedom's sake." The *Herald Tribune*'s editorial, "Out of the Holocaust," made no attempt to universalize the tragedy, and praised the congress' survey as "300 pages of carefully authenticated, factual reporting."[68] The *Herald Tribune* also ran a page one news story on the survey.

On the eve of the conference, it seemed as if the rescue agenda would receive considerable attention and that the divisive statehood issue would be put on the backburner. Delegates would unite to demand greater legal immigration to Palestine but not necessarily a state. Indeed, the *Times*' first news story about the conference emphasized the "impressive memorial service for the Jews who have died as a result of Adolf Hitler's persecution," and listed the Zionist Organization of America's five-point "program to help suffering Jews of Europe immediately." The points included "settlement in Palestine of large numbers of Jews as can be rescued," but said nothing about a Jewish homeland. The next evening, however, Rabbi Silver brought the issue to the forefront with an impassioned plea for Jewish statehood on the convention floor. When he finished, the crowd rose and burst into "Hatikva," the Zionist anthem. (Sulzberger would later needle Joseph Proskauer of the American Jewish Committee about how he "liked being led in the singing of the 'Jewish National Anthem.'"[69])

If Silver's rousing oratory dimmed the possibility of postponing the statehood issue and uniting on immediate rescue plans, the next day's *New York Times* doomed it. At the bottom of the August 31 front page, a headline read: "Rescue at Once of Europe's Jews Demanded at Conference Here." When the front-page story jumped inside, however, another news story announced, "New Jewish Group Appeals to Allies." Beside it was the full text of the group's "statement of principles" and a list of "the more than one hundred Jewish leaders from all over the country" that subscribed to them. Despite his reservations, Arthur Sulzberger had ensured the American Council for Judaism's statement occupied a half page inside his newspaper as the American Jewish Conference was under way. The council considered Sulzberger responsible for the favorable coverage. Or as Lazaron told Sulzberger, "profound appreciation was expressed to you [at a council meeting the next month] for the way in which our statement was publicized."[70]

No such appreciation was expressed at the American Jewish Conference. The day the statement appeared in the *Times*, delegates could talk of nothing else. The conference approved a resolution accusing the American Council for Judaism of "an attempt to sabotage the collective Jewish will to achieve a unified program" to solve "the tragic problems confronting world Jewry." The statement's "timing" was "reprehensibly impertinent," the resolution read, and "calculated to confuse American public opinion and disrupt the American Jewish community." The council was not the delegates' only target. "We blame also The New York Times for its ignorance and impudence," Rabbi Joseph Shubow of Boston said on the conference floor.[71] The rabbi followed up with a letter to the editor explaining the "thunderous applause" that greeted his comments. "In the face of the present titanic cataclysm and volcanic catastrophe which have almost wholly engulfed the Jewish people in Hitlerized Europe, the Jews are seeking to find refuge in their faith, in their history, and in the prophetic promise of national restoration," he wrote. "How can one, therefore, explain your complete lack of sympathy in this regard?" The newspaper *PM* considered the fracas serious enough to publish an article on September 2 headlined, "Jews Say Sulzberger Misuses the 'Times,'" and indicated that "resentment against Sulzberger overflowed."

The publisher did not defend himself then. Years later, he insisted that he did not have a "personal bias" in favor of the council, and that even if he had "it would not have affected the treatment of these questions in the news columns of The New York Times." Still later, however, he conceded the *Times* should not have run the statement. "While I agreed with the Council and not with the Zionists," the latter had a "greater claim to news space," he wrote.[72]

Silver's speech and the hullabaloo over the *Times*' publication seemed to unleash the Zionists. An overwhelming majority of the delegates approved a resolution calling for Palestine to become a Jewish Commonwealth over Proskauer's threat to withdraw the American Jewish Committee from the conference and Hebrew Union College President Robert Goldman's warning that such a demand would only hinder rescue efforts. The resolution was "hailed with delight by the Zionist elements of the conference as placing American Judaism on record for the first time in support of their aspirations, and received with dejection by the non-Zionists present," the *Times* reported.[73]

Sulzberger still managed to get the last word – at least in his newspaper. That week's News of the Week in Review identified the "core problem" the American Jewish Conference faced, a problem "common to all refugee peoples but sharply etched in the case of the Jews." After the Nazi regime ended, should refugees "seek new lives in new havens" or should they return to their native lands? The American Jewish Conference gave one answer, a Jewish Commonwealth, the week in review explained, but fortunately the American Council for Judaism provided "another answer," opposing a Jewish National state as "defeatism."[74]

The Zionists may have focused on Sulzberger's public actions, but they most feared his private ones – behind-the-scenes efforts to influence American policy. Within 1 week of the conference's tumultuous conclusion, Sulzberger was prodding the Roosevelt Administration not to alter its position on Palestine. When a story appeared in the *Times* including Secretary of State Cordell Hull's message to a Zionist Organization of America convention, Sulzberger sent Washington Bureau Chief Krock a copy of the article along with a command: "Would you be good enough to see if you can learn from Mr. Hull whether or not the fifth paragraph of the attached means that he is committed to the Palestine project." The fifth paragraph quoted Hull saying: "'The interest in which American citizens continue to manifest in the work of establishing a national home for the Jewish people in Palestine affords assurance that, as in the past, they will continue to contribute favorable assistance to the project.'"[75] A story in the next day's *Times* on President Roosevelt's message to the same convention only aggravated Sulzberger's anxiety.[76] Both Roosevelt's and Hull's statements "seem to me to be equivocal," he fretted to Krock. "I would appreciate learning whether or not I am correct in this respect and whether they have decided to play a lone hand or are acting with British approval. Smells awfully political to me with the weight on the side I don't like." Krock wired back: "Secretary Hull says the paragraph involves no change from the position you know. The message was sent as a courtesy and phrased politely; that's all."

Sulzberger would not let it drop: "What do they mean when they say 'no change'? Have they ever committed themselves to Zionism as such – involving national statehood – or are they merely in favor of the development of Palestine as a refuge where Zionists will be a minority of the population?" Krock replied: "The Secretary preferred to put his answer to your query in this form: 'In so far as we are aware neither the President nor the Secretary has ever committed himself with respect to Zionism as involving national statehood. Their public expressions relating to Palestine have been within the framework of the Balfour declaration.'"[77,v]

In October, the executive committee of the American Jewish Committee voted to withdraw from the American Jewish Conference, which "forever foiled the possibility of a unified coherent community emerging during the crisis." Each side blamed the other for the disunity and the inevitable result – an American Jewish community paralyzed to help their European brethren. In withdrawing from the conference, the American Jewish Committee's executive committee said its action was based on the conference's "subordination of other issues to the political structure of Palestine." In turn, three Zionist members of the American Jewish Committee withdrew from the committee because its action threatened '"to disrupt American Jewry at a time when unity is vital in our efforts to save the remnant of Jewry in Europe."[78]

In the meantime, the attacks on the *Times* mounted. Rabbi Milton Steinberg of New York's Park Avenue Synagogue met with Sulzberger to air a long list of grievances, beginning with the coverage of Palestine, and ending with the reporting of the just completed conference.[79] Rabbi Silver lashed out at Sulzberger, publisher of "the only American newspaper that has set for its mission a fight on Zionism," during a speech at a Hadassah Convention in late October. Silver had received ammunition for his speech a few days earlier. Louis Levinthal, one of the Zionists who had just resigned from the American Jewish Committee, sent him a copy of the essay Sulzberger had written on his 1937 trip to Palestine. The essay is "so revealing of the author's mental state that I thought you ought to read it, for Sulzberger, mentally sound or unsound, is a force to be reckoned with," Levinthal wrote. Silver returned Sulzberger's Palestine

[v] Five months later Sulzberger was still at it, although it is not clear whether something else triggered his concern. Krock wrote him: "You are determined to find out if the President and the State Department have a clear position in this matter [a Jewish state in Palestine]. They are determined not to have one, or, if they have one, not to tell you what it is. I checked once again today and [Undersecretary of State Edward] Stettinius repeated that neither the President nor Hull is taking a position, 'in that the Jews are themselves divided.'" Krock to Sulzberger, 2/3/44, AHS File, PZ Folder, NYTCA.

essay with the comment: "It is certainly revealing of the mental torment and confusion so characteristic of this type of Jew."[80]

Soon after the Hadassah speech, Sulzberger responded in a letter to Silver that he sent to several other people. He wrote that the "Zionist barrage of misrepresentation directed against me" had changed him from a non-Zionist to an anti-Zionist. "I believed it would be fundamentally bad judgment to entrust the responsibility of statehood to any group which so willfully perverts and distorts facts – a group which seeks to destroy the character of individuals who differ with it," he wrote on November 2. "I am opposed to Goebbels' tactics whether or not they are confined to Nazi Germany." He concluded: "I suppose you find it difficult to comprehend that I am concerned with equity for Zionists as well as for others, or that The Times values its warranted reputation for objective reporting too much to stoop to your methods. But then I'm not a religious leader – merely a working newspaper man who takes pride in his own and his journal's integrity."

Because Sulzberger had "broadcast" his "intemperate letter," Silver said he felt compelled to write back and take on the question of the *Times*' integrity. In a November 9 letter, Silver charged that the *Times* "has not reported Zionist news impartially and objectively as befits a responsible newspaper." Silver cited Cyrus Sulzberger's articles earlier that year; the "amazing amount of space" the *Times* devoted to the gun-running trials in Palestine and the "large and provocative display" given to the American Council for Judaism's statement "which no other paper in New York city, or in the country, found it necessary to do on the basis of objective reporting."[vi] The rabbi instructed Sulzberger to send his letter to everyone to whom the publisher had sent his letter.[81]

As these letters circulated among Zionists and anti-Zionists, Sulzberger grew increasingly concerned that his affiliation with the American Council for Judaism would hurt the *Times*. In September, he had agreed to read "carefully and critically" Morris Lazaron's manuscript, "Open Letter to Jewish Americans," as long as Lazaron changed the title. "I only recognize Americans of Jewish faith," Sulzberger chided. By November,

[vi] Silver had a basis for believing that the *Times* was uniquely hostile. Zionists usually found receptive audiences at American newspapers and magazines. Draft, Outline of Enlarged Program for Public Relations and Political Work (no date, in 1942 file), AS Papers, Series II, Folder 6, YU; Bierbrier, "The American Zionist Emergency Council," 96; Halperin, *The Political World of American Zionism*, 258.

however, the publisher thought better of the offer, declining to look at the manuscript so as to "preserve an objective approach to any news subject although I admit I find that pretty hard to do at times."[82] That month, Sulzberger also learned of several requests to change deliveries from the *Times* to the *Herald Tribune*. When his son-in-law Orville Dryfoos, a *Times* executive who would one day succeed Sulzberger, checked it out, he found that a news dealer on 86th and Broadway had "heard complaints about handling of Jewish news." Dryfoos promised to keep an eye on the situation. Sulzberger's anxiety also led him to ask for a survey of *Times* editorial comment on "minorities" from January 1, 1931 through November 30, 1943. The results were: 67 editorials that specifically mentioned Jews, 51 about Jews in Germany or German-occupied countries, most appearing before the war.[83,vii]

Sulzberger also decided that he had better improve his image with American Jews. The day after Sulzberger wrote his letter to Silver, the publisher informed his staff that he had hired Bernard Richards to "act in an advisory capacity to me in connection with certain matters, primarily concerned with Zionism." For the next 20 years, the *Times* would pay Richards of the Jewish Information Bureau, a retainer, initially $100 a month.[84] Richards' role turned out to be more than advisory. He also wrote letters to various Jewish organizations and publications defending Sulzberger and the *Times*. When the *American Jewish Outlook*, for example, criticized Sulzberger's donation of a synagogue lamp and candelabra to a church, Richards wrote a public letter in his defense. Attacking the *Times* publisher had "become too much of regular habit in Jewish journalism," he wrote, especially because Sulzberger "does not shrink [sic] his obligations as a Jew." Richards never disclosed in this letter, or any of the others that he wrote over the years, that he was on the *Times*' payroll. Years later, Richards would take credit for having been able to "conciliate the opposition" and "soften the attitude of A.H.S. and associates in the paper."[85]

The opposition was not much conciliated at the end of 1943. "In view of the fact that the New York Times occupies such an important place

[vii] The highest number of editorials mentioning Jews, 11, appeared in 1938, many of those related to Kristallnacht. The second highest number appeared in 1933 (8), followed by 6 in 1934 and 1935. During the war, 5 appeared in 1939, 1 in 1940, and 3 in each year of 1941, 1942, and 1943.

in the eyes of official Washington as of many other influential citizens and inasmuch as the Times' columns are being filled every day with all kinds of stories which are designed to undermine the Zionist movement, it is essential to begin attacking The New York Times itself," Henry Montor, executive director of the American Zionist Emergency Council (AECZA's successor), told Silver. He continued to press the issue, arguing in a subsequent letter that unless they criticized the paper it would "be regarded as a neutral organ, and as a paper which must obviously be fair to Jewish things because it is owned by a Jew."[86]

In early December, Zionists gleefully noted that Sulzberger had not yet responded to Silver. The rabbi's letter was a "complete refutation of his charges and such an adequate expose of his totally incongruous and indefensible position, that the exchange of correspondence will not be continued," Henry Monsky of B'Nai B'rith predicted. Sulzberger was indeed stewing over what to do next. A month after the first exchange, Sulzberger's son-in-law, his wife, and Richards got together to go over Silver's letter. They decided that Sulzberger should respond so "it cannot be said that it was not answered," Dryfoos informed his father-in-law after the three had met. The response should dispute the "more obvious" errors but emphasize that "The Times gives space to all points of view," they advised.[87]

Sulzberger never did respond to Silver directly. He drafted a letter but apparently never sent it. In it, he wrote rather mournfully:

> Whether I am a non-Zionist or a Zionist, I know I have, according to my own best lights, tried to fulfill my duties as an American Jew, giving also in the time of crisis considerable thought and effort to the tragic plight of our brethren who have been caught by the holocaust of the present war. My role as an individual is of course not identical with my duties as a publisher but I venture to think that I have on the whole struck a fairly good balance and not violated any of the rules of proper restraint.[88]

To many American Jews, restraint was not what was needed in the face of their brethren's "tragic plight." They took exception to one particular manifestation of the publisher's reserve. Six months after the Warsaw ghetto uprising, the *Times* published an editorial about the event. (No such editorial appeared while the ghetto burned.) What was striking was not the editorial's timing, but its characterization of the ghetto fighters. Nowhere in the October 1943 editorial did it mention that they were Jews.

"500,000 persons... were herded into less than 7 per cent of Warsaw's buildings," the editorial said, and "400,000 persons were deported" to their deaths at Treblinka.[89] In a December 31 editorial that also appeared in nine other publications, the *Jewish Times* of Philadelphia took the *Times* to task for featuring "the news in a way as if no Jews were involved in the tragic fray." The *Jewish Times* lamented: "Is it not a tragedy, a moral tragedy, another instance of Jewish self-hate, when a great paper like the Times, founded and published by Jews, tried to extirpate from its columns everything Jewish, even the things in which Jews must justly take pride?"

Richards advised Sulzberger to respond, but Sulzberger refused because he did not have "a very high regard" for the publisher. Sulzberger did explain himself when his friend, Jacob Billikopf, asked about the *Times* editorial. "It is perfectly true that in our editorial we chose to think of Jews as human beings instead of a particular religious group, and apparently Zionists don't like that. Jews must never be anything but Zionists – not human beings, not anti-Zionists – just Zionists!" His letter to Billikopf also indicated how deeply his battle with Jewish leaders had affected him. "'Times baiting' has become a very popular sport," he wrote. "I think I have pretty well disciplined myself to becoming indifferent to their attacks; but that is unfortunate because some time they might be right and I may not be able to recognize it when that millennium arrives because the skin they are developing on me will be too thick!"[90]

In a more reflective moment, Sulzberger explained his rationale for not identifying Jews as the primary target of the Germans' extermination campaign. "It has always seemed to me that whereas the Jewish community was correct, of course, in protesting the fiendish acts directed against Jews by the Hitler regime, they missed their great opportunity of merging their cause with that of other assailed peoples when Hitler finally declared war," Sulzberger wrote Horace Kallen of the New School of Social Research who had also noted the absence of any reference to Jews in the ghetto uprising editorial. "A minority, it seems to me, cannot save itself through its minority status but can only be successful if it can, with integrity, merge its cause with a larger movement.... That was the reason I deliberately referred to these persons of Jewish faith who battled so gallantly in Warsaw as unfortunate citizens of Poland." Still later he wrote Kallen, denying that he was repudiating his origins. "Jews should be able to stand up as Jews without in any way suppressing or denying their identity," Sulzberger wrote. "I merely think they should stand up as members of the Jewish faith, and that if they cease to be that they cease to be Jews whether or not the world permits them to make that decision."[91]

At the dawning of another year of war and extermination, Sulzberger continued to insist on his vision of Judaism as solely a religion. Given the Union of American Hebrew Congregations' refusal to withdraw from the American Jewish Conference after its Zionist declaration, Sulzberger insisted in January 1944 that the union accept the resignation he tried to tender the previous June. "I hesitate to break the physical bond with the Union that I inherited from Isaac M. Wise, but I comfort myself with the thought that possibly by my action I am strengthening the spiritual one," he wrote its president.[92] He continued to insist that American Jews should not unite on a rescue program. "Of course, something must be done for the poor fellows who are Jews," he wrote to a woman who had asked his position, "but it seems to me that you and I should work for that as Americans and humanitarians and not as Jews."[93]

By 1944, however, other Americans had persuaded the U.S. government that it had to do something to help the Jews in particular.

Fig. 1. *New York Times* Publisher Adolph S. Ochs, front row third from left, visited the *Times* Berlin Bureau in May 1930. To Ochs' immediate right is Berlin Bureau Chief Guido Enderis. Also in the front row, two seats from the right, is Edwin L. James, chief European correspondent who in 2 years would become the *Times* managing editor. (Source: New York Times Company Archives)

Fig. 2. The Nazi flag flew on the Berlin building that housed the *New York Times*' office. The *Times* leased space in the building, whose owners put up the flag. (Source: New York Times Company Archives)

Fig. 3. Publisher Arthur Hays Sulzberger who, from the time Hitler came into power in 1933, was in charge of the *New York Times*. (Source: Library of Congress)

Fig. 4. Frederick Birchall served as the *Times*' chief European correspondent from 1932 until 1939. He spent much of his time reporting from Germany, as well as assisting the publisher with business and family matters in that country. (Source: Library of Congress)

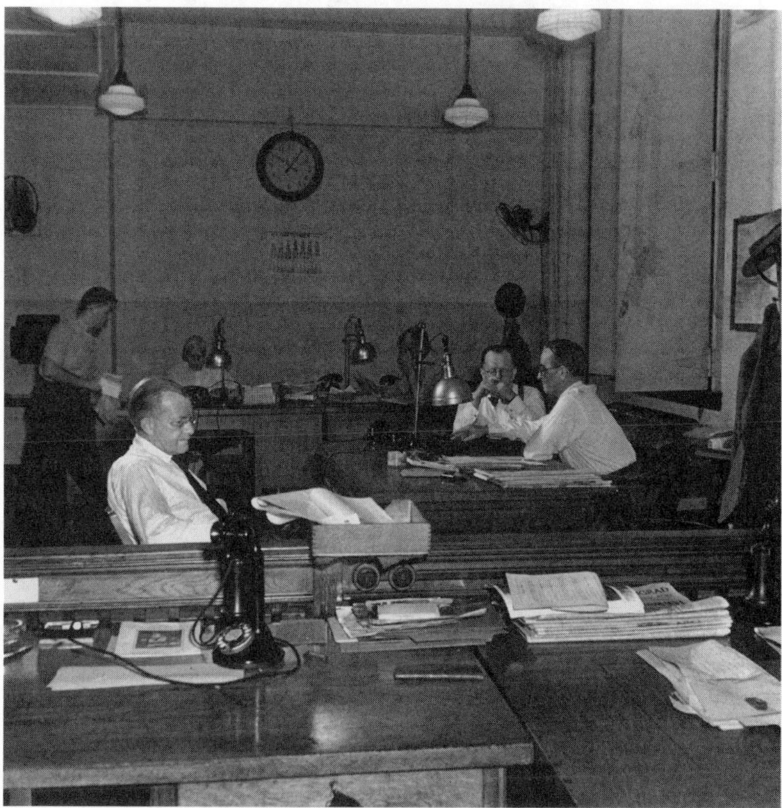

Fig. 5. Night Managing Editor Raymond McCaw, right, and Managing Editor Edwin L. James conferred in the "bullpen" in September 1942. The bullpen referred to the three or four desks in the southeast corner of the *Times* newsroom where the night editors sat. (Source: Library of Congress)

Fig. 6. Cyrus L. Sulzberger, the publisher's nephew, was a *Times* roving correspondent, reporting from the Balkans, the Soviet Union, and the Middle East during World War II. (Source: Library of Congress)

Fig. 7. Arthur Krock, the *Times* Washington bureau chief and columnist, allied himself with the forces in the U.S. State Department opposing rescue efforts on behalf of Jews trapped in occupied Europe. (Source: Library of Congress)

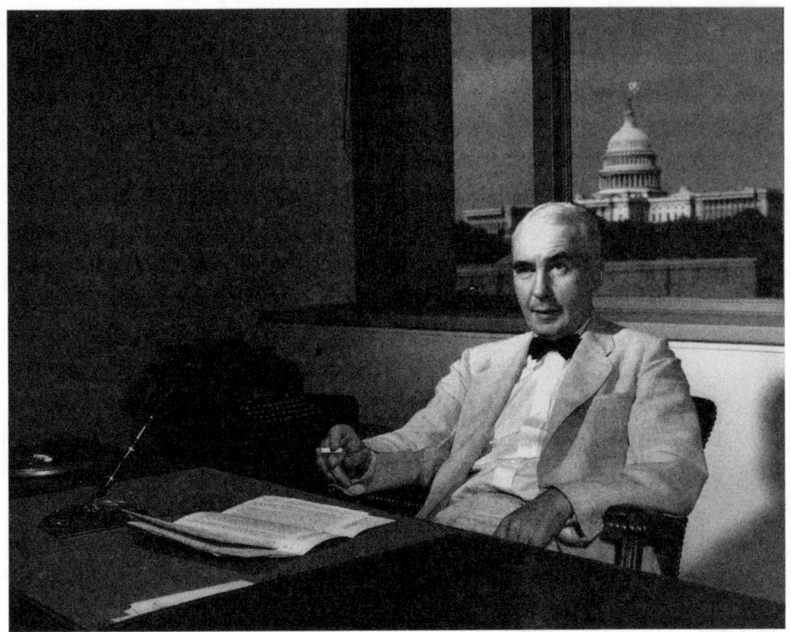

Fig. 8. Elmer Davis, director of the Office of War Information, was reluctant to emphasize Germany's campaign to exterminate the Jews in U.S. government propaganda. (Source: Library of Congress)

Fig. 9. *Times* Vice President Julius Ochs Adler, facing the camera with dark hat, was among a group of editors and publishers who toured German concentration camps in April and May 1945. Adler is shown here near the crematorium at Buchenwald. (Source: United States Holocaust Memorial Museum)

Fig. 10. As a reporter in Stockholm, a neutral listening post for occupied Europe, George Axelsson discounted reports of the murder of 60,000 Jews in Vilna. (Source: New York Times Company Archives)

Fig. 11. Rabbi Abba Hillel Silver, an outspoken Zionist leader, engaged in a public fight with the *Times* publisher over the newspaper's coverage of Palestine and other Jewish issues. (Source: United States Holocaust Memorial Museum)

Fig. 12. Rabbi Stephen S. Wise, leader of the World Jewish Congress, quarreled with the *Times* throughout the war over what he considered to be its attitude that nothing was news "which originates from and through Jews." (Source: Library of Congress)

Fig. 13. *Times* Publisher Arthur Hays Sulzberger, center, outside Hitler's air raid shelter in Berlin in June 1946. He also visited Germany, including a trip to a displaced persons camp, in August 1945. (Source: AP World Wide Photots)

8

"The Semitic Question Should Be Avoided"

German Atrocities and U.S. Government Propaganda

During the decade that Henry Morgenthau, Jr., had been Secretary of the Treasury and Arthur Sulzberger had been publisher of the *New York Times*, they had used their friendship in their professional roles only in the rarest circumstances.[i] For Morgenthau, January 1944 was one of those times. After intense public pressure, and sustained private lobbying from the secretary and his staff, the president on January 22 had signed an executive order creating the War Refugee Board, a government agency charged with saving as many Jews as possible during what would turn out to be the war's last year and a half. The day after, the *Times* ran a story about the new agency on page 11. The newspaper's ho-hum response disappointed Morgenthau, who had waged bureaucratic warfare and risked political capital to see the refugee board established. On the morning of January 29, he made one of his infrequent phone calls to the *Times* publisher to complain.

"Well, you carried it on – on the back page, about 18 or 20; the *Tribune* carried it on the front page," Morgenthau said in a phone conversation he recorded. (The secretary was mistaken about the page.) "A number of people have commented – they said, how funny that the *Tribune* should carry it on the front page, and the *Times* somewhere in the back."

[i] Sulzberger's conflicted feelings about his relationship with Morgenthau are evident in a letter he wrote Washington Bureau Chief Arthur Krock complaining about a column that criticized the treasury secretary: "The fact that Morgenthau is my friend embarrasses me. Friendship is difficult to preserve or cultivate in our profession. But why did you take that crack at him this morning?" Sulzberger to Krock, 5/24/40, AK Collection, Box 56, 1927–33, 1935–49 Folder, PU.

"Well, it was inside," Sulzberger replied. "I don't remember where it was."

"This is breaking new ground," Morgenthau insisted. "It's the most encouraging thing that's happened on this front.... And, the only reason that I've kept so quiet is that I don't want them in any way to appear critical of anybody, you see?... But it's really important, Arthur."

"Right. I've been talking about it, and I don't understand, for that reason, and I'll have to check it," Sulzberger said, promising to get back to the secretary.[1]

Morgenthau was right; the creation of the War Refugee Board broke new ground. During the previous 4 years of war, the U.S. government had deemphasized the unique suffering of the Jews in Europe in both its policies and its publicity. As a matter of policy, the government had only one objective – winning the war as quickly as possible – and it would not let any other goals deter it. As a matter of publicity, government officials believed the Germans' campaign to annihilate the Jews made for poor propaganda, and thus sought every opportunity to universalize the tragedy.

Given the government's approach, some have speculated that officials must have instructed the *Times* and other newspapers to keep the story of the Final Solution off their front pages. No document has been found to support this assertion, although such a preference could have been communicated verbally rather than in writing. The more likely scenario, however, is that the government did not have to give publishers' and editors' specific instructions. The government influenced the coverage by directing the flow of information, issuing statements about certain subjects, keeping quiet about others, playing up parts of the war, and downplaying others. A press corps that tended to define news as government actions would have gone along. The government's message that nothing special should be done to save the Jews also found a receptive journalistic audience. Most American newspapers, with very few Jews among their readers, were not much interested to begin with. The *Times*, which had a substantial Jewish audience, had more affinity for the topic, but the publisher's practical and philosophical beliefs meant that it too accepted that the Jews' suffering should not be singled out. The second most influential *Times*man on political issues went a step further; Washington Bureau Chief and columnist Arthur Krock allied himself with the forces in the State Department working hardest to stifle any rescue efforts. Until January 1944, the dominant forces in the government and those at the nation's most important newspaper were in sync.

The *Times*, like most mainstream newspapers, was obliging but not obeisant in the face of government attempts to control information during the war. The *Times* adopted that stance despite the newspaper's regular criticism of the Roosevelt Administration and Arthur Sulzberger's disdain for the president. The *Times* endorsed Roosevelt in 1936, but then lashed out at many of his second-term initiatives, publishing more than 50 editorials on the court-packing scheme alone. Krock, a political conservative who had never liked the New Deal, was among the president's most vociferous critics. The political animosity took a personal turn when Sulzberger learned the president had referred to a tax scheme the family had used to maintain ownership of the paper after Ochs' death as "a dirty Jewish trick."[2] The *Times* did not support the president's campaign for an unprecedented third term in 1940, and Sulzberger prepared his staff for even worse relations with the administration. Shortly after his victory, Roosevelt had denied a *Times* story on contemplated Cabinet changes. To the publisher, "the method" of the president's denial "suggests a continuance on his part of an effort to destroy the standing of the newspaper in the public mind."[3]

Sulzberger's patriotism, concern for the newspaper's standing, and commitment to defeating Nazism kept his antipathy for the administration in check. He wrote Roosevelt occasionally during the war and met with the president six times.[4] Nor did his dislike of the administration prevent him from doing what he perceived as his duty during, and even before, the United States' official involvement in the war. In May 1940, after Roosevelt wrote Sulzberger to complain about a front-page story on Mussolini's rejection of a supposed U.S. peace offer, the publisher replied: "None of us here on The New York Times would willingly do anything to complicate the many problems that present themselves to you daily in the foreign field."[5] Much later in the war, Sulzberger had the editorial section removed from the *Times*' newly introduced Overseas Weekly, which was sent to servicemen among others, because the paper might not endorse Roosevelt for a fourth term. "I did not wish to have this periodical fail to support the Commander in Chief among his troops," he wrote.[6,ii]

[ii] The *Times* ended up supporting Roosevelt on the theory that it was too risky to change administrations while still in the midst of a world war, even though Sulzberger termed

The *Times* also often bowed to demands from others in the administration. When the *Times* published an article that upset the president of Colombia because it mentioned pro-Axis sympathizers in that country, Undersecretary of State Sumner Welles complained to Sulzberger, who defended the article, yet then published an editorial praising the Colombian president's actions against Axis activities in his country. When the Bolivian government wanted two Bolivian journalists invited to the United States, the State Department asked the *Times* to issue the invitation. After Welles contacted Sulzberger, the *Times* agreed to go along, even though one of the journalists worked for a newspaper with a "dubious reputation." "It is my understanding that the New York *Times* is willing to do anything that we request them to do," Welles told another State official.[7]

The *Times* was most obliging when it came to national security matters. Even before the United States had declared war, the *Times* was sensitive to military considerations. When a United Press dispatch in February 1941 reported that airplanes had been "'secretly'" delivered to Hawaii, Sulzberger called Roosevelt personally. When he failed to reach him, the publisher had his staff contact the Navy Department. "The Navy requested that we not use the story, and it did not appear in The New York Times," Sulzberger later informed Roosevelt.[8]

Yet, there were limits to the *Times*' willingness to further the government's interests, even in military matters. The *Times* recognized that the military's dedication to secrecy at times served to cover up incompetence. Sunday Editor Lester Markel described the dilemma editors faced: the newspaper needed to "respect to the utmost the limits laid down for military security," but it also needed to be vigilant that the war "proceed without blunders and without favoritism." Executing that policy, however, "is a task for a Solomon, a Diogenes and an Atlas all rolled into one," Markel explained. "For it is ever difficult to decide where military security ends and a smoke screen for mistakes begins; or where public interest ceases and selfish newspaper enterprise takes over."[9]

The *Times* laid out its approach, and that of "every reputable newspaperman," in an editorial shortly before Pearl Harbor. The *Times* acknowledged the importance of secrecy in war, but pleaded that "news that cannot possibly aid the enemy be not arbitrarily suppressed." If there was

the president's decision to seek another term "as grave a disservice as was ever done this country." Sulzberger to Billikopf, 9/11/44, MSS 13/29/2, AJA.

a conflict, however, the editorial made clear the side it would take: "Where there is a choice that might affect the safety of our crews there can be no doubt that it is better to publish too little than too much."[10]

The *Times*' philosophy was tested within days of the attack on Pearl Harbor. Secretary of the Navy Frank Knox called Sulzberger to request that the *Times* not print details of the attack that the newspaper had learned independently. Over his Washington bureau chief's objections, the publisher agreed not to include the information. "I hope you will continue to stand on your hind legs and paw whenever I feel I am obliged to act as I did last night," Sulzberger wrote Krock on December 9.

> On the other hand, I hope you realize that I no less than you have the interests of The New York Times at heart and want to see us cover the news. . . . [B]ut very frankly if a request is presented to me in the name of the Navy, that sections of a story we are about to use is not in the best interests of the country, I do not feel that I have any other choice than to comply with that request. I admit there are limits to this. A time may come when this newspaper will have to throw all such self-restraint to the winds and take the consequences, but I do not think that time has come yet.[11]

Ten days later, the president issued an executive order establishing the Office of Censorship under Byron Price, the Associated Press' executive news editor who was on leave from the wire service. The office censored communications between the United States and foreign countries, including the mail, and asked the domestic press to voluntarily censor itself. (To receive accreditation in military theaters, which was required to enter those areas, war correspondents had to agree to submit their copy to military censors.) It issued a code listing the type of information that should not be published, such as "facts regarding munitions, production, troops, ships, airplanes, fortifications, weather and the like," unless it came through official channels. The *Times* editorial page soon praised the "sensible censorship" in the form of prohibitions that were as "clear and specific as it is possible to make them," without any "loosely-worded warning against publication of material calculated to lower morale."[12]

Throughout the war, the *Times* was willing to accede to the government when it believed information was concealed for genuine security reasons and to challenge censorship when it did not. The *Times* and other newspapers, for example, did not print anything having to do with atom smashing, atomic energy, or the use of radium or radioactive materials. The *Times* put an article on U-235, the atomic energy element with explosive force, "in the cooler" when the censorship board asked the paper not to run it. A few times, the *Times* even withheld more than the Office of Censorship might have. In the fall of 1943, the newspaper confirmed a widely circulated rumor that General George Patton had slapped two hospitalized soldiers, but concluded the story was so likely to be censored that it did not even try to get it approved. Columnist Drew Pearson had no such qualms, submitting the item and having its disclosure sanctioned. The *Times* even tolerated deliberate government misinformation. The *Times* and other newspapers learned that all the airplanes involved in Jimmy Doolittle's daring raid on Tokyo had crashed in China, where many pilots were helped by the Chinese underground. Yet, they did not contradict the official communique that said all the planes "'reached their destination.'"[13]

If the newspaper inadvertently made a mistake, it regretted it. In November 1943, the Office of Censorship objected to a published story about the president's scheduled meeting with Churchill and Stalin that described "comings and going around the White House." A censorship official wrote James: "Don't you think that publication of such factual information by a paper having the position and prestige of The New York Times encourages others to nibble at the request in the Press Code against revealing information concerning the President's movements?" Sulzberger agreed that "the story went too far."[14] The publisher believed so fervently in abiding by the code that he even informed the Office of Censorship when columnist Pearson supposedly violated it during an April 1942 speech attended by a *Times* reporter.[15] Sulzberger's attitude led to some grumbling among the staff. "Our readers must think we are asleep a great part of the time," Night Managing Editor Raymond McCaw complained to James after the paper would not print "very obvious stories" because of "all these silly censorship warnings." McCaw had earlier griped that "the publisher is very scrupulous about observing all the rules, even those fixed by a crackpot Secretary of the Navy."[16]

Yet, if the *Times* believed, as Markel put it, that security concerns were a "smoke screen for mistakes," it would challenge the withholding of information. Within weeks of the attack on Pearl Harbor, an editorial complained that the administration was concealing too much.[17] The following month, the *Times* learned of the damage that had been done to each American ship at Pearl Harbor, but, as Sulzberger had written to Krock, the time still had not yet come to throw "self-restraint to the winds." By the fall of 1942, the *Times*' was close to that point. Military correspondent Hanson Baldwin, who had just completed a trip to the Pacific, concluded that the government's failure to release information about Pearl Harbor, which the newspaper had held for 8 months, and its reluctance to disclose a spate of recent ship-sinkings was designed to protect incompetent Navy commanders. Baldwin, at Sulzberger's urging, met with the Office of Censorship's Price, and threatened to break the voluntary code. Soon thereafter, the Navy disclosed that three cruisers had been sunk and eventually released more details about Pearl Harbor, which the *Times* and other newspapers published at the end of 1942 in a series of front-page stories on the Navy's mishaps.[18]

The press threatened to break the voluntary code on another important story. Since Pearl Harbor, the U.S. government had a "strict taboo against using Japanese atrocities stories especially the atrocities against both civilian and military Allied prisoners." The government assumed press reports about the Japanese's harsh treatment would make prisoner exchanges more difficult and confinement conditions much worse.[19] Then a colonel, who had been on Bataan, sold his story to the *Chicago Tribune*. The newspaper did not publish it right away because the officer was still under military orders. When the colonel died in a plane wreck, however, his estate was no longer bound. The *Tribune* again threatened to publish the article. The government decided to lift the ban and release material on Japanese treatment of prisoners.

To the *Times*, and most other newspapers, this was big news. The *Times* ran six front-page stories, beginning January 28, 1944, even though the "news" was more than 1 year old. The first story, which led the paper and sported a six-column headline, recounted how the Japanese "barbarously tortured and cold-bloodedly starved to death and mercilessly murdered more than 5,200 Americans and many more times that number of Filipino soldiers on Bataan and Corregidor." The story also led the paper the following day, along with two other front-page stories on the atrocities. Numerous stories appeared on the jump page, including first-person accounts and descriptions of the American public's reaction. The *Times* ran two strong, lead editorials. The week in review led with five items based on the news, and ran a column describing how the military was "moved to reveal the real nature of the enemy."[20]

The government did not have a similar ban on stories about the treatment of the Jews in occupied Europe. Instead, the government's policy was not to suppress, but to downplay those stories.[21] This policy was most apparent in the agency specifically charged with providing information to the American public, the American press, and foreign nations – the Office of War Information (OWI). OWI was created in June 1942 out of a mishmash of 26 propaganda, intelligence, and information agencies. The executive order that created OWI gave the agency the authority to use press, radio, and motion pictures to facilitate understanding of the war effort, and to coordinate all the government's information activities.

Archibald MacLeish, a poet and the Librarian of Congress, who had headed one of the OWI's predecessor agencies, became OWI's domestic chief, whereas ardent New Dealer and playwright Robert Sherwood headed the foreign propaganda arm. Like many news organizations, the *Times* lost some of its top people to OWI. James Reston became the first chief of the British division, and Ferdinand Kuhn, the *Times'* former London bureau chief, was a regional division chief. Elmer Davis, a former *Times* reporter who had written a glowing in-house account of the *Times'* first 50 years, was OWI's director.

Davis, a Rhodes Scholar, joined the *Times* in 1914. After 10 years there, during which he wrote *History of the New York Times 1851–1921*, he left to become a freelance writer and novelist. An article he wrote during this period reveals a class-based anti-Semitism that might shed some light on his stewardship of OWI a decade later. For most of the article, "On the Gentility of Gentiles," published in the July 1933 *Harper's Magazine*, Davis railed against racially based anti-Semitism, but at one point he acknowledged that a mountain resort where he spent the summer led him to understand the basis for "a policy of rigorous exclusion."

> [T]he Hebrews who have chosen that part of the world for their summer resort are in the main the least pleasing specimens of their race. When you see the countryside and the market town overrun by fat women from the East Side clad in sweaters and dirty white linen shorts, the fatter the shorter, you return thankfully to the colony, a Gentile island in a Hebrew sea, and feel as if you and your neighbors were a little band of Greeks making a desperate last stand at Thermopylae against the engulfing hordes of the Orient. Naturally enough; those Jews are not our kind of people.

Davis then reassured, "they are not the Rosenblatts' kind of people either." The Rosenblatts – acquaintances who are "solid and settled persons" – by "most of the tests of congeniality, are our kind." As a good "Aryan Protestant," Davis advocated a policy position: "If we really believe that we are the salt of the earth we ought to welcome [middle-class reformed Jews or ex-Jews], assimilate them, instead of drawing a line on scientifically untenable grounds and driving them back into fellowship with people who are not like us at all."

In 1939, Davis joined CBS as a news analyst, and 2 years later began hosting his own nightly radio show with an audience of 12.5 million. As a Democrat and a liberal who was nonetheless pragmatic, Davis was considered a perfect choice to head the new agency, which ultimately would employ 10,000 people. As Clayton Laurie, who wrote a history of the agency, put it: Davis and his assistant "believed that OWI's job was to present the American perspective of the war in a clear, factual" and nonpartisan fashion, "using carefully selected news to convey the right message.... They sought to win the war with words."[22]

OWI's main weapon for winning the war was its pipeline to the media. "It was part of the philosophy of OWI that we furnished information to the press, radio, and other channels of communication," Elmer Davis wrote, "and supplemented it by direct communication to the public only when we though[t] the ordinary media would not give adequate coverage."[23] In a joint interview with Davis and Byron Price of the Office of Censorship, Arthur Krock, writing for the *Times* magazine, succinctly explained the difference between the two agencies. "Mr. Price says: 'We tell them what they cannot print.' Mr. Davis says: 'We give them stuff we hope they will print.'"[24]

Almost immediately upon its creation, OWI confronted the issue of whether "atrocity stories," as officials described them, should be among the "stuff" the agency would give the press to print.[iii] A predecessor agency had thrashed out the issue in the month before OWI was officially established. During a May 12, 1942 meeting, almost all the officials present endorsed the idea of using atrocity stories, with only John McCloy of the War Department expressing any hesitation. Archibald MacLeish summed up the discussion by saying "it would henceforth be the policy of the Government not to go easy on the use of atrocity material which would clearly show the barbarism and inhumanity of the systems under which our enemies operate." He warned against using "material which was fabricated

[iii] That the OWI officials continued to conceptualize the extermination campaign against the Jews as an "atrocity" throughout the war suggests limitations in their language or understanding, or both.

or trumped up in any way," sticking to "facts so carefully documented as to leave no doubt of their accuracy."[25] Soon after the meeting, OWI launched its campaign to draw attention to German reprisals against the residents of Lidice, Czechoslovakia, as well as against partisans and other innocent civilians in occupied countries. The Committee on War Information Policy, which included Davis and Price, as well as representatives of the various military branches, reached a similar consensus on the use of atrocity information over the next few months.[26]

That fall, OWI issued its own directives, again stating that atrocity stories could and should be used.[27] Leo Rosten, who years later gained fame as the author of popular books on the Yiddish language, was the OWI deputy director with responsibility for information on the enemy. Years after the war, Rosten wrote to the author of a textbook on public opinion to correct the statement that the debunking of World War I atrocity stories led British and American propagandists to not make use of Nazi atrocities during World War II.[28] Rosten enclosed three OWI directives that explained that propagandists should be aware of the difficulties in using such information, but should use it nonetheless. An exception was made if publication would "increase the suffering of prisoners now in the hands of fascist powers," which explained the ban on Japanese atrocity stories. One directive explicitly acknowledged that World War I's "fake propaganda" would complicate OWI's job in publicizing atrocities to the American public. "We must expect a certain amount of disbelief and resistance to true atrocity news," it stated. But the response should not be to avoid "legitimate and necessary news" that gives "a true picture of the enemy." Instead, the agency should stress that enemy atrocities are part of a plan and have a purpose. The directive listed nine such purposes, the eighth being "to exterminate literally certain 'inferior' peoples: *e.g.*, Jews, Poles, Greeks."[29] During the war, OWI followed these directives. In responding to a New York minister who was upset about the press' publication of a certain photograph in 1943, Rosten explained that the government and the press had a responsibility to present authenticated facts. "The truth about the conduct and action of the enemy we face is legitimate news and must legitimately be presented to the American public," he wrote.[30]

While OWI was willing to release information about atrocities, if cautiously, it had a different attitude toward Jewish atrocity stories. OWI officials considered themselves first and foremost propagandists whose job was not merely to disseminate information about the war effort, but to highlight events that would bolster it. News articles about German atrocities against civilians could be useful, if handled correctly. Articles specifically about atrocities against Jews, however, probably would not be helpful and might even be counterproductive at home and abroad. Too much attention on the plight of the Jews, OWI officials concluded, would contribute to Americans' fears that the war was being fought – and thus Allied soldiers were dying – to save the Jews.[31] They also assumed citizens in Axis countries, who had been steeped in anti-Semitism, would be no more sympathetic to propaganda about the Jews' suffering.

To support these assumptions, OWI officials relied on polls that indicated widespread anti-Semitism among the American public.[32] Intelligence officers also turned to journalists. In March 1942, as OWI was being organized, military intelligence sent detailed questionnaires to 17 American journalists who had been stationed in Axis-controlled countries and were then being detained at Bad Nauheim, a resort north of Frankfurt. (Because the Germans did not detain either George Axelsson or Guido Enderis, no *New York Times* correspondents filled out questionnaires.) The Jewish problem did not feature prominently in any of the journalists' responses, and they were not united on the stance that American propaganda should take. Some journalists, such as old Berlin hand Louis Lochner of the Associated Press, did not raise the issue. Others, such as his UP competitor, Frederick Oeschsner, advised that American propaganda "should indulge in no impassioned defenses of the Jews." A few journalists thought propaganda designed around the plight of the Jews might be useful. Paul Fisher of NBC suggested that the "barbaric pogroms against the Jews and the ruthless outrages committed by the S.S. in Poland and other occupied countries," be used in propaganda for "intellectuals," although in general he advised against using "anything which smacks of the Jewish angle or has a Jewish ring." Glen Stadler of UP believed that "figures on concentration camps, death rates in them and treatment of the Jews could be used" to "reveal the Gestapo as it really is." He did advise against using Jews, "however competent," to prepare propaganda for the German people, a view echoed by several journalists. From these replies, military intelligence made recommendations for an Allied propaganda strategy. "Vehement or sentimental defense of Jews," was one of 14 themes to be "carefully avoided." In contrast, "the denial of Christianity and repression of churches by the Nazis" was one of 20 themes to be emphasized.

That "the Semitic question be avoided" was one of five guiding themes for Allied propaganda.[33]

Whether because OWI officials actually relied on the questionnaires, or their assumptions merely corresponded with those of the responding journalists, OWI avoided the "Semitic question" – as World Jewish Congress (WJC) leaders learned in December 1942. Congress leaders had assumed OWI would play an important role in disseminating news about the German plan to murder all European Jews, which the State Department had just confirmed and the United Nations was about to denounce. When OWI director Davis sent a representative to see Stephen Wise in mid-December, WJC leaders were encouraged. OWI "was prepared to do all that it could to make the facts known concerning the massacres of the Jews," according to the minutes of a December 14 meeting during which the visit was discussed. But even then there seemed to be something of a quid pro quo: OWI had requested that Wise "in future action" to "the extent possible" include "the massacres of the other civilian populations" with that of the Jews. This led to a prolonged discussion among congress officials, some of whom expressed concern about any attempt to equate the massacre of the Jews with that of other civilian populations. Ultimately, they concluded that "the emphasis should be placed on the Jewish aspect," according to minutes of the meeting.[34]

Elmer Davis, however, seemingly did not want his agency to emphasize "the Jewish aspect." Soon after the relatively optimistic meeting in New York with an OWI representative, congress leaders had a discouraging encounter with the OWI boss. The day of the UN declaration's release, Wise, Nahum Goldmann, and another official traveled to Washington to talk with Davis, whom they found "cool," and mostly concerned that the declaration had been issued by the UN, not the State Department. They were no more impressed with Leo Rosten, who sat in on the meeting and whom the congress officials referred to as Davis' "Jewish collaborator." They were particularly concerned about Davis' and Rosten's conviction that emphasizing the Jewish victims would not make for good propaganda. "Leo Rostan [sic] added that, according to their experiences, the impression on the average American is much stronger if the question is not exclusively Jewish," their joint report on the meeting stated. "They had made Gollup [sic] polls on the matter. Conclusion – the effect is seven times stronger." Davis made clear that Rosten would be their contact person at OWI.[35]

In the weeks preceding the meeting, Rosten had already been busy ensuring the information OWI supplied to the press was nowhere near "exclusively Jewish." Upon hearing that the State Department had confirmed the "impending Nazi extermination of the Jews," Rosten told another OWI official that the agency's strategy should be to "urge that other groups – Poles, Serbs, Czechs, etc. – participate in any further information on Nazi treatment." Otherwise, the story would be "confused and misleading if it appears to be simply affecting the Jewish people."[36] When he prepared special informational material for news organizations to coincide with the tenth anniversary of the Nazis' ascension to power, Rosten avoided any such confusion. For a chronology of the decade's "more conspicuous dates and events," he included only one mention of Jewish persecution during the war years: on October 30, 1939, 50 religious Jews were burnt alive in a Polish synagogue. OWI sent 12,000 copies of "The Dark Decade" to newspapers, and Rosten arranged for six radio broadcasts and articles in *Colliers*, *Readers Digest*, *Life*, *Time*, and the *New Yorker*, among others.[37] The *New York Times* even used "Dark Decade" material 4 months later, to Rosten's delight. "See how much carry-over is possible when we service editors with material," he informed his boss.[38]

The United Nations' Joint Declaration on December 17 that confirmed the extermination campaign did not change Rosten's approach. When a New York state legislator wanted to introduce a resolution acknowledging the UN's statement and requesting presidential action, Rosten reminded him that the "crimes of the Nazis against the Jewish people often are duplicated by the most merciless suppression and extermination of non-Jewish people."[39]

In the OWI information he prepared, Rosten continued to deemphasize attacks on Jews. In January 1943, OWI sent out 43 pages of "radio background material," on "Our Enemies, the Nazis." There was only one mention of Jews, on page twenty-four. "The attack on the Jews is actually an attack on Christianity," it read. "Hitler duped many people by this ruse, using it as an opening wedge for his entire blitz of brutality. The Nazis kill Jews because they are Jews. But they also kill Poles because they are Poles, Slavs because they are Slavs, Greeks because they are Greeks . . . [ellipses in original]." The background material omitted any mention of mass murder, except to note that "Nazi atrocities and slaughter have been described in such detail, and with such justifiable rage, by qualified observers that all the civilized world is acquainted with this barbaric phase of Hitler's New Order."[40] Five months later, Rosten used a similar justification in urging an OWI colleague not to dwell on anti-Jewish persecution in a possible book of eyewitness accounts. The Jews' treatment is "well known (according to all our polls)" and mentioning it "tends to suggest that the Nazis exploit and murder *only* the Jews." Better to "emphasize the fate of businessmen, farmers, Catholics, Protestants, Poles, Greeks, etc. etc.," Rosten advised.[41]

He also urged public officials to emphasize the universality of the persecution in their public appearances, which they did. Secretary of the Interior Harold Ickes explained in a speech that the "attack on Jews is an attack on Christianity," and emphasized that Czechs, Danes, and Norwegians were also being murdered.[42] As OWI domestic bureau head MacLeish prepared for a March 1943 radio appearance, Rosten encouraged him to stress those points, as well as the theme that "the Jews are only *first* on the Nazis' rolls of terror and death." It "may seem like old stuff," Rosten acknowledged, but Americans' skepticism and "the relegation of atrocity news to the back pages of the newspapers," meant that the message about Nazi brutality could not be repeated "often and clearly enough," so long as the information "cut across religious lines and races lines and cultural lines."[43]

OWI's overseas propaganda took a similar approach – a fact that the WJC's Leon Kubowitzki noted with considerable chagrin. In July 1943, Kubowitzki complained to Wise and Goldmann that OWI's short wave broadcasts to Europe were "much too vague about the massacres of the Jewish population." The broadcasts contained general threats in retaliation for atrocities against the civilian population "but the horrible story of the way in which the Jewish population is being exterminated is not being told." Kubowitzki suggested taking the issue up with Robert Sherwood, head of the overseas branch.[44] The following month, he and James Wise, Stephen's son, met with one of Sherwood's deputies, James Barnes. Barnes, a distinguished journalist who had been the *Herald Tribune*'s Moscow bureau chief, Berlin correspondent and foreign editor, was considered one of the few OWI officials sympathetic to the Jews.[45] On Friday, August 20, 1943, Kubowitzki and the younger Wise discussed with Barnes how to inform citizens of occupied Europe about the extermination of European Jews. Barnes offered Kubowitzki advice on the best way to get OWI to make more of the story. "We must make it our business to have such items of information as we want the O.W.I. to release, first published by the American press or see to it that such information be first released by some outstanding American personality," Kubowitzki explained in a memo he wrote 4 days after the meeting. He and James Wise suggested that the congress appoint "a number of key men in various States, whose task it should be to have such reports and releases as we consider important printed in the influential publications of their respective regions." Once the articles were printed, "we should receive clippings to be handed over to Mr. Barnes." Kubowitzki personally recommended that a committee meet once a week to decide the stories to be released and to monitor press reaction.[46] This apparently never took place, at least in the formalized manner outlined.

Kubowitzki also wanted to persuade OWI that its rationale for minimizing the extermination of the Jews was wrong. Five days after meeting with Barnes, and on the eve of the American Jewish Conference, Kubowitzki drafted a memo urging OWI to drop leaflets and make broadcast to the German people with "the *facts* of the massacres committed by Germans on the Jews in Eastern Europe." The memo then addressed OWI's main objection to such droppings and broadcasts: that the news of massacres would, as Goebbels' claimed, so terrify both the Germans and citizens of occupied nations that they would never rise up against the Nazi government. This "psychosis of terror" argument did not hold up, Kubowitzki contended. "If the German Government were of the opinion that its hold on the German people would be strengthened by informing them of its crimes against the Jews, it would not be doing all it can to conceal these facts from them," he wrote. Such news would not dampen the enthusiasm of the partisans in occupied countries for a simple reason – they already knew. "The Underground constantly reports on these atrocities and is, moreover, one of the most reliable sources of information on the tragic extermination of Jews in Europe," he wrote.

Kubowitzki then tackled head on OWI's strategy of denouncing "the tragic fate of all the subject peoples of Europe" and not just Jews in order to avoid validating Hitler's racial distinctions. "This viewpoint is so remote from an understanding of the harsh and terrible world in which European Jewry agonizes that . . . the World Jewish Congress fails to grasp it," Kubowitzki wrote. "The special aspect of the Jewish plight, the fate for which the Jews have been singled out, cannot be concealed from the people of occupied Europe by an unrealistic approach."[47] Kubowitzki later claimed the memo did some good; the agency devoted more time in broadcasts to "authenticated material concerning the systematic annihilation of the Jews in Europe."[48] But the Congress, ultimately aided by the War Refugee Board, would have to continue to fight so the "fate of all the subject people" did not swallow up the Jews' tragedy.

Barnes would not be there to help. Along with his colleague, James Warburg, a member of the wealthy Jewish banking family, Barnes had been considered a maverick within OWI. At the end of 1942, Barnes and Warburg had been among the OWI officials who had challenged the official U.S. policy supporting the Vichy government, and particularly its administration in Algiers. By the summer of 1943, Barnes and Warburg were again in trouble. When Mussolini fell in 1943, an OWI broadcast suggested that the basic nature of the fascist regime would not change and included an "independent commentary" from John Durfee, who described Mussolini's replacement as "a moronic little king." The *Times*' Arthur Krock, who had begun monitoring OWI overseas broadcasts, pointed out in a front-page story and a column that OWI's position contravened State Department policy. He also noted gleefully that there was no "John Durfee." Barnes had written the commentary under a pseudonym, thus breaking agency promises to Congress to be "on the level" in its broadcasts. Krock later launched a broader attack, accusing OWI employees of conducting their own foreign policy, shaped according to "the personal and ideological preferences of Communists and their fellow travelers in this country."[49]

Elmer Davis, who in June had seen his domestic branch's budget slashed by almost two-thirds, did not want to anger Congress further. He ousted Barnes and Warburg from the agency.[50] From then on, OWI propaganda would be geared solely toward assuring as quick and uncomplicated a military victory as possible.[51] As would become even more evident in his fights with the War Refugee Board in 1944, Davis assumed worrying about the Jews would complicate victory.[52]

The *Times*' coverage tracked government policy in downplaying the plight of the Jews not because the newspaper had no choice, but because it was easier to do so. For one thing, journalistic convention tended to define news, at least partially, as what the government said and did. So if OWI issued release after release about the massacre at Lidice, it was more likely to become news than all the Jewish massacres that were not the subject of sustained government attention. In addition, the top *Times*men did not challenge the government's assumption that the Jews' fate should be downplayed because they tended to agree with it. Arthur Sulzberger had no trouble giving prominent display to articles about atrocities – as the *Times*' treatment of the news that the Japanese abused American soldiers on Bataan attests – and was even willing to challenge the government to publicize them more thoroughly. After a trip to the Pacific theater, Sulzberger told then Secretary of State Edward Stettinius, Jr., "some unbelievable stories with respect to Japanese atrocities which he had heard." Sulzberger "also made a strong point that he felt this Government was making a great mistake in not publicizing these atrocities," Stettinius informed the president.[53] But Sulzberger felt differently about atrocities involving Jews. He had long believed that the fate of the Jews should be linked to that of other oppressed people and never identified as a distinct tragedy. For both philosophical and tactical reasons, he was content that stories about the destruction of the Jews remain inside the newspaper. The other most powerful political actor at the *Times* was, if anything, even more inclined to ignore what was happening to the Jews.

Since 1931, Arthur Krock had headed the *Times* Washington bureau, wielding tremendous influence both inside and outside the paper. Within the *Times*, he ran his own fiefdom of 23 reporters, all of whom, at his insistence, called him "Mr. Krock." In the larger community, heading the capital's largest news bureau (aside from the wire services) and writing a column four times a week made Krock one of the country's most powerful journalists. In 1944, the *Saturday Review of Literature* polled 160 members of the Capitol press who concluded that Krock (with 51 votes) was the columnist with the greatest influence in Washington, followed by Drew Pearson (32 votes) and Walter Lippmann (19 votes).[54] "'The first thing we members of Congress do when we get up in the morning is to reach for The New York Times and read Krock," Senator Harry F. Byrd of Virginia told the *Saturday Evening Post* in July 1944. A 1939 poll of 200 correspondents indicated that more than 70% of them read four or five of the big Eastern morning newspapers each day, including the *New York Herald Tribune*, the *Washington Post*, and the *Baltimore Sun*, but 100% of them read the *New York Times* and Arthur Krock.[55]

Krock, who was born in 1886 in Glasgow, Kentucky, started his career as a reporter in Louisville and eventually became editorial manager of the *Louisville Courier Journal* and the *Louisville Times*. His social status never matched his professional success in Louisville's tradition-bound society, and he left the city to be an editorial writer at the *World* in New York. He joined an editorial board that included Walter Lippmann and Charles Merz, who would eventually head the *Times* editorial page. When Lippmann became the *World*'s editor, he and Krock had a falling out. Lippmann overheard Krock talking to the Dillon Read banking firm about a coming editorial that would likely affect certain stock prices. Lippman banished him from the editorial page.[56] Krock then moved to the *Times* in 1927, writing editorials and signed articles on politics. When the *Times* longtime Washington bureau chief died in 1931, Krock took over the post. He continued to write his column, which often harshly criticized FDR and the New Deal, and won Pulitzer Prizes in 1935 and 1938.

From the time he arrived in Washington, Krock was determined not to be excluded from the city's society as he had in Louisville. He courted Washington's establishment assiduously, helped by his courtly manners and conservative views. Yet, one obstacle seemingly threatened to stand in the way of his success – his Jewish origins. "Krock was a certified stuffed shirt," recalled Neil MacNeil, Jr., who worked at the *Times* in the 1940s and was the son of the paper's assistant night managing editor. "He was embarrassed of being Jewish. He had enormous social ambitions in Washington." So much so that MacNeil remembered Krock giving the coveted position of copy boy at the 1944 political convention to the daughter of a prominent socialite who had no other qualifications.[57]

Krock also lied about being Jewish. He said his father was Jewish, but his mother was not, which would have made him a Gentile. When that claim appeared in a July 1944, *Saturday Evening Post* profile, Krock's first cousin, Charles W. Morris, an attorney in Louisville, denied it. In a letter to Jacob Billikopf of the Jewish Federation of Charities, Morris said his grandparents, who were also Krock's maternal grandparents, were Jewish, and thus his mother was too. "'Krock's grandmother Mrs. Emanuel Morris (nee Henrietta Frank) never ate trafe [non-kosher food] in her 96 years,'" and his grandfather "'lived and died in the Jewish faith,'" Morris wrote of the grandparents with whom Krock lived for most of his boyhood. It was "Krock himself who told me that his mother was 'not Jewish'" on "two occasions in reply to pointed questions," the article's author, Matthew Josephson, told Billikopf, who had informed him of the inaccuracy. When Billikopf told Arthur Sulzberger about Krock's misrepresentations in the *Post* article, Sulzberger did not bite. "So far as Arthur Krock's parentage is concerned, I know nothing about it," Sulzberger replied curtly.[58]

Krock detested the *Post* articles and sent Sulzberger two letters correcting "numerous errors." Interestingly, the statement that his mother was Gentile was not among them.[59] In his memoirs, published in 1968 and 1973, when presumably it was easier to acknowledge Jewish roots, Krock wrote that all his ancestors were Jewish and hailed from German-ruled or "German principalities." He did not have a religious upbringing, his father being a "free thinker," and his mother's connection "with the ancestral faith was a seldom-observed formality." But Krock apparently never converted to Episcopalian, as another widely circulated story had it.[60] "I was brought up to make free choice of any creed or none," he said. "And, following my uninhibited inclination from earliest remembrances, I chose none."[61]

Krock may have been as worried about advancing within the *Times* as he was about conquering Washington society. *Saturday Post* author Josephson told Billikopf that he had "a well authenticated story" that around 1935 Sulzberger had told Krock he would not consider him as "editor-in-chief" of the *Times* because he was "afraid of what people would say if this Jewish-family [owned] newspaper" had a Jewish top editor. Josephson did not include the story in the article. "I did not want to expose A.K. as a 'bad Jew' and Sulzberger, as a hypocrite, at a time when Jews were having enough trouble," Josephson explained, mentioning that he too was Jewish. "The POST editors agreed with me."[62]

Whether Krock's religion or his conservative politics kept Sulzberger from appointing Krock editor-in-chief or editorial page editor (in the more common version of the story[63]) is hard to discern. In 1939, shortly after Merz received the job, Krock heard from then American Ambassador to Great Britain, Joseph P. Kennedy, that his religion indeed had stood in his way. Krock had championed Kennedy in his column, and Kennedy, returned the favor, letting Krock know he would be appointed ambassador before the incumbent ambassador, who was gravely ill, had died, and allowing Krock to use his Palm Beach villa while he was in London. In Kennedy's version of the story, Kennedy met with Sulzberger while the publisher was visiting London and asked him why Krock had not been named editor. Sulzberger explained that he "would be criticized if he appointed a Jew as Editor, since the ownership was in the hands of Jews."[64]

How Krock's discomfort with his Jewish origins affected his public position on the Jews cannot be ascertained directly for a simple reason. He never wrote about it. Of nearly 1,200 Krock columns published during the war, not one mentioned the Jews' persecution. While Sulzberger's editorials at least took up the issue, albeit infrequently and to universalize their plight, Krock did not mention it all. Nor did Krock express a view in internal *Times* communications. While Sulzberger fired off memos demanding to know the Administration's position on Zionism or countering the use of the dreaded term, "Jewish people," Krock played defense. He responded, mostly politely, to Sulzberger's requests, but did not stake out a position of his own. Again unlike his boss, Krock did not fret about Jews' status or suffering in private letters to other prominent Jews. Arthur Krock was silent on the topic, which of course was a statement in itself.

Where Krock stood can be seen mostly clearly from the company he kept. During the Roosevelt Administration, Krock allied himself with the conservative elements in the State Department, who erected bureaucratic obstacles to Jewish immigration and tried to suppress information about the Final Solution. He opposed State officials who identified with, as he put it, "PM, The New Republic, The Nation, the professional Jewish groups and the radical New Dealers." One incident that occurred in the critical summer of 1943 best illustrates both Krock's allegiances and his influence.

For years, a long-simmering feud between Secretary of State Cordell Hull and Undersecretary Sumner Welles had threatened to boil over. That summer it did. Hull often left his undersecretary in charge when he was ill and had to be away from Washington – which happened with increasing frequency during the war years. Yet, Hull grew frustrated and angry at the attention that Welles received from the press and from the president in his absence. (Sulzberger was among Welles' press confidantes.) By that summer, Hull was plotting to get rid of Welles, confirming for Senate Republicans rumors that Welles had once propositioned black Pullman porters on an overnight train ride.[iv]

The personality dispute also brought to the forefront tensions within the department over its policy toward the Jews, among other issues. Jewish groups saw Welles as their highest-ranking ally in State. Stephen Wise had

[iv] Hull later confided to Krock how he had managed to get rid of Welles by persuading the president that "a scandalous rumor about Welles was ready to explode in the Senate, 'blackening the President and the Department.'" Krock, 12/21/43, AK Collection, Box 60, SW Folder, PU.

turned to him the year before to obtain official confirmation of Riegner's news that the Germans planned to wipe out all Europe's Jews. During the first half of 1943, Welles had been pursuing small-scale rescue possibilities over the objections of some of his State colleagues.[65] Hull, however, tried to deflect charges that he favored Jewish interests (his wife actually had the religious lineage that Krock claimed – her father was Jewish and her mother was Christian[66]), and thus tended to defer to his personally chosen assistant secretary, Breckinridge Long. As liberal publications had been reporting for years, Long, who headed the visa division, had a well-known and well-deserved reputation as the embodiment of State's anti-Jewish policy.[67] That summer, the pressure on State mounted with the news of the murder of more than 3 million Jews, growing frustration over Great Britain's continued restrictions on immigration to Palestine, and the approach of the American Jewish Conference. As the pressure grew, so did the divisions within the department, especially over a bid to limit discussion of Palestine until after the war and the granting of licenses to finance rescue efforts.

A top *Times* Washington reporter, John Crider, got a whiff of rumblings within State, and wrote a story headlined, "Conflicts Impair State Department, President Is Told." The story, which appeared on the August 4 front page, presented a picture of State Department disorganization and discord, and described a "rivalry" between Hull and Welles. It did not delve into policy disputes, or the far more sensitive issue of Welles' homosexual predilections.[v] Krock, who had been out of town and had not seen the story before it ran, was furious. Krock had long been friendly with the secretary of state. When, at the start of his administration, Roosevelt offered Hull the post of secretary of commerce, the latter consulted with Krock who advised him to hold out for State. If Krock needed to talk to Hull during an international emergency, he could summon the secretary, who liked to retire at 9 P.M., by having a note slipped under his bedroom door.[68]

[v] Roosevelt had learned of the charges in 1940 after the FBI had investigated and confirmed them. Roosevelt had been convinced at the time that he could keep the information under wraps because the press would never print such stories. He may have been right. In 1944, Hull personally gave James Reston, who had written a column bemoaning Welles' departure, the FBI file containing the homosexual charges. Reston gave the information to Krock, who sent the file to the New York office, but nothing about the scandal appeared in the *Times*. Gellman, *Secret Affairs*, 352–3. Reston, *Deadline*, 103.

Krock believed Crider had been used by "the radicals" within the State Department, who had leaked the story to "show up the Department as inept, riddled by feuds and so forth." In a memo he later wrote to his deputy, Luther Huston, who had edited the story, Krock described Adolf Berle, assistant secretary of state, and Herbert Feis, economic adviser to State, as among the "radicals." Berle and Feis had been among the State officials considered sympathetic to the Jews.[69] (Feis was himself Jewish; Berle was a Congregationalist, but because of his name and appearance was often mistaken for a Jew.[70]) Berle had long pushed for more liberal interpretations of visa regulations over Long's objections.[71] Feis was then trying to keep alive proposals to funnel money for rescue, as State worked to squelch them. So Krock theorized that Berle and Feis had learned Roosevelt was to fire Welles, and had hoped to head that off by the leak to Crider. They wanted to "get rid of Hull and install Welles in his place, or anyone who agreed more nearly with" the liberal media, Jewish groups, and radical New Dealers.[72]

Although still on vacation, Krock decided he had to write a column to take the "heat" off Hull "that the story put on him. . . . Welles, of course, had immediately cited our story to the President as proof that Hull is congenitally incapable as the head of the Department." Krock's column "explained" that any problems within the State Department were the fault of Welles, who undercut Hull's authority, and the president, who allowed him to. "The State Department will function smoothly and effectively when the President permits the Secretary to be the real, undisputed head of a loyal staff," Krock concluded.[73]

Krock's column accomplished what he set out to do; he had "supplemented" Crider's story with the "facts," so the president could "go ahead with his sacrifice of Welles."[74] Krock wrote the August 25 front-page story that announced Welles' resignation and explained that the president had no choice but to accept it.[vi] Krock heralded Welles' departure, and in a column, pushed for Long's ascendancy to his vacated position. Long had been unfairly criticized, Krock said, "because of his course toward immigration, as an example."[75] Krock did not get his wish, however. Edward Stettinius, Jr., replaced Welles as undersecretary.

[vi] Gellman's insightful book on the episode, *Secret Affairs*, 341, concludes that Welles and his alleged allies were not plotting to depose Hull. If anyone was plotting, it was Hull.

From a few blocks away, another group of government officials was watching the discord with intense interest. After months of wrangling between Feis on one side and Long and his deputies on the other, State had in late June turned over to Treasury the question of approving licenses to release funds for the rescue of Jews in Rumania and France. "It is perfectly apparent to us from our dealings with the State Department on this issue that there is a very bitter fight going on in the State Department regarding the whole refugee question," Treasury General Counsel Randolph Paul wrote to Morgenthau on August 12. Paul, and other Treasury officials, were about to join the fray.[76]

Treasury had been drawn into the issue by the Allies' economic blockade of German-controlled countries, which was designed to reduce the funds available to Axis governments, but also thwarted relief efforts to Jews and others in Nazi-held territory. When the Allies allowed food shipments to Greece to fend off starvation there, Jewish groups seized on the example to press for similar exemptions to allow supplies to reach starving Jews. In the fall of 1942, Treasury granted a license to the American Jewish Joint Distribution Committee to send supplies to Polish ghettos. Treasury's involvement deepened after Cyrus Sulzberger's February 1943 story suggested that Rumania might accept money in exchange for 70,000 Jews. The possibility that Jews could be ransomed led the WJC to explore whether it could guarantee funds for rescue and relief efforts immediately, but pay up only after the war was over – thus avoiding the blockade.

When a divided State Department punted the issue to Treasury, John Pehle, foreign funds control director, and others, began investigating how to get money to Jews, yet keep it out of enemy hands. They quickly discovered that while they were looking for ways to approve the transfers, their State counterparts, with some exceptions, were looking for ways to deny them. The more Pehle, Paul, and Josiah DuBois, an assistant general counsel, probed, the more examples of State's obstructionism they encountered: the attempt to prevent Riegner in Switzerland from sending cables to Wise in New York; the effort to put off discussion of Palestine immigration until after the war; the objections to releasing Jewish refugees held in camps in Algiers; and the delaying of approvals to send relief packages from the American Jewish Joint Distribution Committee to Theresienstadt. Pehle, Paul, and DuBois, all young non-Jewish Treasury lawyers, decided it was not enough to support the current proposal for blocked accounts, which in itself was proving difficult as State continued to give them the runaround. The entire issue needed to be taken away from State officials, whom Paul would later describe as "indifferent, callous, and perhaps even hostile," and turned over to a separate agency that would be more sympathetic to rescue possibilities.[77]

As Treasury officials were maneuvering behind the scenes in the fall of 1943, Jewish organizations, particularly the Bergson Group, were increasing outside pressure. At a rally in early November, sponsored by the Emergency Committee to Save the Jewish People of Europe, Leon Henderson, formerly director of the Office of Price Administration, attacked the Allied governments for "moral cowardice in failing to meet 'the major political weapon of Nazi bestiality,' that is extermination of the Jews." As the *Times* reported, Henderson declared: "'This war issue has been avoided, submerged, postponed, played down and resisted with all the forms of political force available to powerful governments.'" A petition to establish an intergovernmental agency to save the Jews circulated at the rally.[78] The Bergson Group also decided to move beyond rallies and advertisements to push for resolutions in both the House and Senate, calling for the creation of an executive agency whose sole mission was to try to rescue European Jews.[79]

"Steps to Save Jews Urged in Congress," read the headline on the November 10 *Times* story that ran on page 19. "Measure in Both Houses Advocates Creating a Presidential Body to Act Now." As the House Foreign Affairs Committee held hearings on the resolution, the *Times* reported the testimony in inside stories – until December 11.[80] That day's front-page story ran across two columns at the top of the page – the most prominent display of any story about the Jews during the war, including the liberation of the Dachau and Buchenwald concentration camps a year and a half later. "580,000 Refugees Admitted to United States in Decade," declared the headline. The story described the previously secret testimony of Assistant Secretary of State Long before the committee. Long had personally sent a transcript of his testimony to Arthur Krock at the *Times*, which may account for its prominent treatment.[81] The move "was construed as intimation that Mr. Long's report had swung the committee into opposing" the bills that would establish a commission to try to rescue "the Jewish people of Europe,'" the *Times* explained high in the story.

The House indeed withdrew its resolution, House Foreign Affairs Committee Chairman Sol Bloom apparently convinced by Long's claim that the already existing Intergovernmental Committee on Refugees could negotiate with the Axis to rescue Jews. The Senate, however, did not, passing the resolution unanimously. Long's testimony drew sharp criticism, which, unlike his original statement, played out exclusively inside the *Times*. The very next day, Representative Emanuel Cellar challenged both Long's data and his sincerity. Long's statement "'drips with sympathy for the persecuted Jews, but the tears he sheds are crocodile,'" Cellar was quoted as saying in a *Times* story on page eight. "'I would like to ask him how many Jews were admitted during the last three years in comparison with the number seeking entrance to preserve life and dignity. It is not a proud record."

Two weeks later, in a page eleven story, the American Jewish Committee cited official U.S. Immigration and Naturalization Service (INS) numbers indicating the total number of Jews admitted was 166,843, not all of whom were refugees.[82] The INS officially disputed Long's numbers, but not until 2 months later and in a page 6 story.[83] Historians too have concluded that they "were grossly distorted."[84]

Long's gambit, however, may well have backfired, especially after the JTA printed a statement from the Intergovernmental Committee on Refugee's director that it had no authority to negotiate with the Axis. (The *Times*, which still did not subscribe to the JTA, did not carry that denial.) It gave additional ammunition to Treasury Department officials who were then preparing their indictment of the State Department. Two weeks later, on Christmas Day, Josiah DuBois was furiously drafting a document he had titled, "Report to the Secretary on the Acquiescence of This Government in the Murder of the Jews." Long's duplicity was the latest in a line that began with State's restrictive posture toward granting visas and had continued through its reluctance to find ways to transfer rescue funds to Europe. The document argued for a special government agency to save the remaining Jews of Europe. The proposal had a prominent backer, Secretary of Treasury Henry Morgenthau.

Although he did not have the religious commitment to assimilation of his friend Arthur Sulzberger, Morgenthau had been eager throughout his career to be recognized for his accomplishments, not his religion. He had thus distanced himself from organized Jewry. When Berlin rabbi Max Nussbaum met with Morgenthau, at Sulzberger's urging, in September 1940 to warn him about Hitler's plan to resettle Europe's Jews in Madagascar, Nussbaum found Morgenthau to be indifferent. "I had the feeling that the great political questions of the Jewish people all over the world interested Mr. Morgenthau only marginally," Nussbaum recalled, "and that Jewry – outside of the American sector – represented to him a world with which he does not identify and of which he prefers to speak in the third person." To Morgenthau, the "burning question" was whether there were Jewish spies in Germany.[85]

Three years later, after numerous appeals from Jewish groups who increasingly turned to the one Jewish member of the Roosevelt Cabinet, the treasury secretary, had begun to change. He knew responding to Jewish demands left him vulnerable to the criticism that he and Sulzberger feared – that he might be helping the Jews because he was one. "Let's call a spade a spade," he said during a December 17, 1943 meeting in his office.

> I am Secretary of the Treasury for one hundred and thirty-five million people, see? That is the way I think of myself; I represent all of them. But if Mr. Hamilton Fish [Congressman] was to go after me, he goes after me because I am a Jew. Let's use plain, simple language. He doesn't go after me because I am Secretary; he goes after me because he thinks that I have done something for the Jews because I am a Jew.[86]

Morgenthau "didn't want to stand out as a Jew, he wanted to stand out as Secretary of the Treasury," recalled John Pehle years later. Confronting the government's position toward Jews "was doubly hard I would think for him but he did it."[87]

Prodded by his staff of non-Jews, and by his secretary, Henrietta Klotz, who had been raised in an Orthodox Jewish home, Morgenthau became increasingly involved in the effort to save the Jews. DuBois considered one event pivotal in Morgenthau's transformation. Morgenthau met late on a Friday afternoon with a group of American rabbis trying to help 232 of their fellow rabbis in France whose Latin American visas had been declared invalid by the State Department. The passports were indeed forged, yet if the rabbis were not granted passage through the United States, they were doomed. An obviously shaken Morgenthau had to leave the room at one point and did not return for 10 minutes, DuBois recalled.

Morgenthau proceeded to try to get in touch with Secretary of State Hull and, when he was not in, Sumner Welles, who was also not there. DuBois, who said he was "very upset," took it upon himself to leak the story to Washington columnist Drew Pearson. Pearson made the State Department's denial of the rabbis' visas the subject of his regular Sunday night broadcast. The next day, Hull decided to recognize the visas. Morgenthau then called DuBois into his office to tell him the good news.

He said, I guess that broadcast last night had something to do with it. I said, it probably did. He said, I wonder who leaked that story. I said, well, someone who cared must have leaked it. That's all he said. He didn't ask me whether I'd leaked it, or anything else. But he had a pretty good idea, I think.

The story did not have a happy ending, however. By the time the State Department reversed itself, the rabbis had already been sent to their deaths.

As well as marking Morgenthau's "deep interest in the problem," DuBois took another important lesson from the incident – the press could be used as leverage. When the Treasury officials were about to present their report to the president, DuBois told Morgenthau that he could inform the president that if he did not act DuBois would "resign and release the report to the press."[88] Morgenthau too was prepared to resign if Roosevelt reacted negatively to the recommendation for a rescue agency. That proved unnecessary. The evidence in the report, which the secretary had given the less inflammatory title, "Personal Report to the President," was overwhelming. Coupled with Morgenthau's uncompromising stance and the threat of Congressional action, the president quickly agreed to issue an executive order creating the War Refugee Board. The secretaries of State, War, and Treasury would jointly head the new board, but in reality Treasury took control, with Pehle as its director. On January 22, 1944, Roosevelt signed the order.

A week later, Morgenthau called Sulzberger to complain about his newspaper's handling of stories about the board. Before getting to his complaint that the story announcing the board had appeared inside the *Times*, the secretary griped that two stories had not appeared at all: instructions to American diplomatic missions abroad on how to treat Jewish refugees, and the board's receipt of a $100,000 donation from the Hebrew Immigrant Aid Society (HIAS).

"Well, that's a God-damn crime, because I told them all I wanted to play that for all it was worth," Sulzberger said, reacting to the lack of a story on the mission instructions. He was no more pleased when Morgenthau informed him the *Herald Tribune* ran the HIAS story.

"The *Trib* carries the whole story – nothing in the *Times*. . . . Now that's pretty bad, Arthur," Morgenthau said.

"I was in the office last night, and I know what they were fighting with on the size of the paper, you see?" Sulzberger replied. "And, someone has just got to be down there with special interest watching every story. . . . It should have been in . . . because they know my particular interest in it . . . and it should have been there."

"Well, it looks as if some special interest kept it out," Morgethau said.

"Oh, no. No, that I'm sure of," Sulzberger said.

Morgenthau then raised the issue of the inside placement of the first War Refugee Board announcement. Sulzberger said he would look into it.[89]

He did. That afternoon memos flew among *Times* editors. James gently criticized MacNeil about the HIAS story. "Looking at it in retrospect, which I know is very easy, and also after a little needling may I say I think it would have been a good idea if we had had a little bit of this story in this morning," he wrote, attaching the *Tribune* article.[90]

For its part, the Washington bureau tried to explain why it had not made more of the release about U.S. diplomatic missions receiving new instructions, which at least in retrospect signaled a major change in U.S. government policy.[91] "That communique you mentioned was not put out by the White House and they knew nothing about it," the bureau's second-in-command, Luther Huston wrote James. "We have traced it to the Treasury, which put it out Thursday night under an 'Executive Office of the President' slug. It was put out late, as much of the Treasury stuff is, and appeared to the night desk here to be pretty routine stuff. [I] am sending [the] full text of the statement right away and will send a lead later."[92]

The next day, through Morgenthau's intervention with Sulzberger, the routine stuff had become a front-page story. "Roosevelt Board Is Negotiating to Save Refugees from Nazis," the headline read.

"Did you see where Sulzberger put this story on the front page of the *Times*, Sunday?" the secretary asked Pehle who was meeting with him in his office the following day.[93]

Sulzberger then wrote Morgenthau, enclosing the page one story. As for the omission of the mission instructions story, Sulzberger said that he had received "a very good answer," from his staff, "namely that there was nothing in the release which was not included in the original story." (The original story, however, did not mention the mission instructions specifically.) "I am sure you realize that the paper is extremely crowded these days – when there is more news than ever there is less newsprint on which to carry it," Sulzberger wrote. "May I suggest, therefore, in a very friendly manner 1) that those who prepare your releases bear this in mind and 2) that if there is anything of particular importance which is not apparent you ask one of your associates to phone me about it."[94]

The *Times* apparently was still not done making amends. On February 1, it ran an editorial, "A Beginning of Rescue," hailing the board's creation. Sticking to form, the editorial never mentioned Jews, preferring "persecuted minorities," and "Hitler's 16,000,000 homeless victims" – the language the War Refugee Board used as well. It also pointed out that rescue was a "difficult task" because it had to be "consistent with fighting and winning the war."[95] The following day, the *Times* ran another editorial, "United Jewish Appeal," describing the charity's urgent drive to raise $32 million for the 3 million Jews still alive in Europe.[96]

When prodded by an old friend holding a powerful position, Sulzberger was willing to put a story about the Jews' suffering on the front page. The *Times* did not initiate the coverage, and it placed the story, which referred to "Jews and other victims of Nazi aggression," at the bottom on the page. (The *Times* was in the midst of its all-out coverage of the horrors inflicted after the fall of Bataan.) Still, Sulzberger jolted a reluctant staff to treat the rescue of the Jews as something more than routine, inside fodder. The question, going into the war's last stages, was "would that interest last?"

9

"Final Phase of Supreme Tragedy Has Begun"

The War Refugee Board and the Destruction of Hungary's Jews

THE War Refugee Board's (WRB's) ability to save Jews and the *Times*' willingness to trumpet it were quickly tested. On March 20, 1944, 2 months after the WRB's founding, the Germans marched into Hungary. Until then, the 800,000 Jews who lived in Hungary or had found shelter there, had been relatively secure. The fascist Horthy government had allied itself with the Germans, enacted anti-Semitic laws, forced Jews into work battalions, and pushed thousands of them into Nazi territory in Eastern Poland. But the Hungarians had not deported hundreds of thousands to their deaths in Poland. With the German occupation, that was about to change.

In the month before the invasion, as WRB geared up its operation, the U.S. government seemed more willing to acknowledge the singular tragedy of European Jewry. In its initial announcement, the WRB had been careful to refer to "Jews and other victims of Nazi aggression," and had continued to prefer the term "refugees," as its very name indicated. The board's director, John Pehle, changed all references from "Jews" to "refugees" in a draft memorandum directed to State, for example, and removed a request for a breakdown between Jews and non-Jews.[1] But internally WRB officials signaled that their mission was to save Jews, and it was important to emphasize that. "The Nazis are singling out these people for murder solely because they are Jews," Josiah DuBois wrote in a February 22 memo. "We must make certain that we also single out our condemnation of this nefarious crime."[2]

The WRB also did not shy away from publicity about its mission to save Jews, both domestically and internationally. Concerned about public reaction to the board's activities, Pehle tapped Virginia Mannon, who had worked with him at Treasury, to spearhead the agency's public relations effort. In March, she reported some success: Pehle had made several radio speeches and three reporters were interviewing him for personality pieces.[3] The WRB encouraged news reports in which Jewish victims were featured prominently, including broadcasts on CBS, NBC, and the Blue Network. WRB also prepared a written script and a musical score to air on the popular "The Hall of Fame" show that Pehle hoped would "help our work of finding havens for the Jews we are rescuing from Hitler dominated regions of Europe."[4]

The WRB counted on the OWI to help disseminate its message abroad. Within weeks of being named refugee board director, Pehle met with his war information counterpart, Elmer Davis, to discuss the agency's handling of WRB material. Pehle found the OWI head to be "mildly cooperative." Yet, Davis would not assign an OWI staff person specifically to the WRB, although "we made clear to Elmer Davis the importance that we attached to the propaganda side of our program," Pehle recalled.[5] Pehle also noted that "Davis didn't seem too excited" about disseminating WRB information.[6] Soon after their meeting, however, OWI issued a directive at the end of February instructing its overseas operations to "use all available news pegs to emphasize, especially to the satellites, that the rescue of the Jews and other 'persecuted minorities' was U.S. government policy."[7]

Three weeks later, the Germans' last-ditch effort to destroy the sole intact Jewish community in Europe challenged that newfound commitment. In the first few days after the invasion of Hungary, it seemed as if the U.S. government's policy, and consequently the *Times* coverage, would continue to treat the impact on the Jews as a secondary story. As it had each previous time the Germans had occupied a country, the *Times* chronicled their arrival in a series of front-page stories, and what it might mean for the Jews in a line or two at the stories' end. Nor did the *Times* editorial, "Hitler Invades an Ally," mention the Jews.[8]

The WRB's efforts, however, soon became apparent. Even before the invasion, the WRB had been drafting a declaration for President Roosevelt that warned Germans of the repercussions of action against the Jews. After the secretaries of State, Treasury, and War signed off on a "very carefully crafted document," the president insisted that it be changed. Roosevelt believed the document put "too much emphasis on the Jewish situation," and that he should issue "only a statement" not a declaration.[9]

The reference to Jews was moved from the first to the fourth paragraph. Still, the resulting statement contained a strong condemnation of "one of the blackest crimes of all history . . . the wholesale systematic murder of the Jews of Europe."[10] The invasion of Hungary gave the statement greater urgency, as the president acknowledged when it was issued on March 24. He warned that "hundreds of thousands of Jews who, while living under persecution have at least found a haven from death in Hungary and the Balkans, are now threatened with annihilation."

The WRB seized upon the president's statement to put into effect what it considered its best strategy for saving Jews – convincing satellite governments and their citizens not to cooperate with the Nazis. (The WRB would later outline its propaganda goals to be to "terrify refugee oppressors, encourage potential refugee aid in enemy territory, and encourage Allies and neutrals to establish refugee havens.") Pehle told former *New York Times* reporter Frederick Kuhn, then an OWI official, that the effectiveness of the president's statement would depend on "the extent to which adequate publicity can be obtained for it, particularly in German controlled Europe." With OWI clearance, the board then cabled U.S. embassies and consuls in Berne, Stockholm, Lisbon, Madrid, Ankara, and Cairo to give "the utmost publicity" to the president's statement in local media.[11]

OWI unhesitatingly agreed to publicize the statement, but in internal communications the office instructed its overseas officials to give it a different emphasis. OWI propaganda should "stress the appeals rather than the threats," a confidential memo explained, and should give equal weight to "the Jewish problem" and the "problems of other refugees and sufferers." A cable from the office in London also stated that the agency's propaganda should not imply that the president's denunciation was limited to the persecution of the Jews, or "that it was especially aimed at it."[12] For the rest of the year, the OWI would have to be cajoled into aiming its propaganda at saving Jews.

The president's statement appeared on the *Times* front page the day after he made it. "Roosevelt Warns Germans on Jews," the unambiguous headline declared, even though the lead referred to "Jews and other victims of Nazi persecution." The *Times* ran an editorial that same day, which also suggested a change in the newspaper's approach. Although the editorial noted that the president's "vigorous statement" applied to the Japanese as well as the Nazis, it said that the timing was the result of Hitler's advance into the Balkans. The "full weight of the Nazi revenge" would be turned against refugees in those regions, the *Times* said, and "the most numerous among these are the Jews." It also urged that more be done to give them "havens of refuge." For the first time, the paper declared that "this task is as important as the winning of a battle." The editorial notably did not recommend any specific steps, saying it was hoping to learn of the government's plans.[13]

The WRB was in the process of formulating such plans. In February, it had sent Ira Hirschmann, a Bloomingdale's executive, to the Balkans to find a way to ferry Jews to safety. Greeting Hirschmann upon his arrival in Ankara were U.S. Ambassador Laurence Steinhardt and *Times* correspondent Joseph M. Levy. Steinhardt, a college classmate of Arthur Sulzberger's and fellow uptown Jew of German ancestry, had come into criticism for his refugee policy during his previous ambassadorship in Moscow.[i] But he was now poised to assist Hirschmann and the WRB. Also ready to help was the *Times*' Levy. Given his persistent problems receiving accreditation in the Middle East, Levy had been reassigned to Ankara at the beginning of 1944. When Sulzberger learned of Hirschmann's WRB assignment, he cabled Levy asking him to help the Bloomingdale's executive whom he knew because the department store was a major advertiser.[14]

Arthur Sulzberger and his editors continued to have misgivings about their correspondent. Their biggest concern seemed to be Levy's tendency to go beyond a strictly journalistic role. "Very frankly, there is no one around here who believes that Joe will not meddle in politics and I included myself in that statement," Arthur Sulzberger wrote. "Only when fishes stop swimming and men stop breathing will that particular miracle occur."[15] Levy clearly "meddled" in the Balkans, although his editors did not necessarily know the degree of his entanglement in Hirschmann's mission. In his memoirs, Hirschmann described Levy as his "right arm" for his "connections among Turkish politicians and police that were to prove indispensable."[16] Hirschmann did not spell out how Levy used those connections, but his diary makes clear that Hirschmann's interactions with

[i] On October 3, 1943, p. 6, *PM* published a story by I. F. Stone accusing Steinhardt of objecting to the grant of visas to "members of Laborite, Zionist and Moderately Socialist groups like the Polish Jewish Bund, even though they had already been approved by the State Dept." See also Transcript of Stone interview, 10/1/43, Laurence Steinhardt Papers, 1943, General Correspondence, Box 41, LC.

Levy were not solely those of a reporter and his source. They dined almost every day, sometimes twice per day. Hirschmann sought Levy's counsel on his increasingly acrimonious dealings with other rescue workers in Turkey, and Hirschmann and Levy often engaged in heated discussions about the envoy's strategy. One "stormy session" concerned Adolf Eichmann's offer to barter the lives of Hungarian Jews for 10,000 trucks and hundreds of tons of commodities. Conveyed through a German-born Jew, the gesture was top secret and highly controversial. Although Hirschmann did not explain what position Levy took, he described the reporter as "impulsive and disturbed" during their argument. Eventually they ate, talked, and resolved "the issue in my favor," Hirschmann noted. The *Times* never wrote about the offer, which did not go through.[ii]

Levy not only aided Hirschmann in his rescue mission, he also ensured that Hirschmann received positive, if not prominent, publicity. (None of Levy's stories appeared on the front page.) Levy had begun writing about the fate of the Jews as soon as he arrived in Ankara, describing the trip of the chief rabbi of Palestine to Turkey, which had become one of the only escape routes for Jews in southeastern Europe. When Hirschmann arrived, Levy wrote about it in commendatory language[iii] and continued to write inside stories lauding the WRB, particularly Hirschmann's role in it. In a story about Jewish refugees in Instanbul, some of whom had escaped from concentration camps, Levy wrote that the board through Hirschmann had "accomplished many great tasks that will alleviate the suffering of thousands in war-torn Europe."[17]

If Levy assisted Hirschmann with his job, Hirschmann also helped Levy with his. Levy, through his Hirschmann connection, was the only newspaper correspondent allowed to interview 152 Jewish refugees aboard a ship in Instanbul on its way to Palestine. The passengers included 120 children whose parents had been slain in Transniestria in Rumania, "the graveyard

[ii] *Times* Bureau Chief Raymond Daniell apparently abided by a request from "jewish sources" not to mention "proposed trade of trucks for jews lest it endanger lives hungarian jews." Other reporters, however, did not keep the confidence or obtained the information from another source. Daniell to James, 7/19/44, ELJ File, RD Folder, NYTCA. Tom Segev, *The Seventh Million: The Israelis and the Holocaust*, New York: Henry Holt and Company (1991), 93–4, explains that the British, as they had with the 1943 offer to barter for the lives of 70,000 Rumanian Jews, leaked the story to the press and effectively killed it. Like the Rumanian affair, the trucks-for-blood deal may not have come to fruition anyway.

[iii] The *Herald Tribune*'s similar story appeared on its front page.

of more than 150,000 Jewish men, women and children," Levy wrote. Levy's short story – eight paragraphs on page six – quickly described the experience of two children, a 5-year-old boy who had lived on grass and leaves in the woods where he had been left after his parents were killed, and an 11-year-old girl, who explained that her parents and two older sisters had all died of hunger and cold.[18]

Hirschmann's biggest publicity splash resulted from his own efforts in the States, not Levy's in Turkey. In mid-April, the WRB summoned Hirschmann home for what it described in its publicity as "urgent consultation." At least part of Hirschmann's domestic mission was to test the "free ports" rescue scheme. Like every other group that had tried to solve the Jewish crisis before the war and since it started, the WRB faced a vexing problem: where could it send Jews should they manage to escape? One possibility, which was first publicized by columnist Samuel Grafton in the *New York Post*, was to allow them to enter the United States for the duration of the war; their temporary status would mean they would not have to go through regular immigration procedures.[19] That April, the Roosevelt Administration had commissioned an Office of Public Opinion Research poll to determine the support among the American public for a proposal that would offer refuge until the war's end to people who have been persecuted by the Nazis and could make their way to the United States. Seventy percent favored the proposal in a poll considered reliable within seven or eight percentage points.

The administration was not completely reassured by the poll results. It also wanted to test the idea at a press conference.[20] Hirschmann and Pehle were designated to do so on April 18. As Hirschmann explained it to Steinhardt in Turkey, "some reporter was apparently tipped off to ask the question about 'Free Ports'" at a joint press conference. The response – that the administration was considering establishing free ports to admit "war refugees" – prompted front-page stories in the *Times* and elsewhere. The *Times* story explained that the refugees, who were never identified as Jews, would not be subject to immigration laws because they were not "technically" in the country. They would reside in free ports, just like "foreign goods, destined for reshipment to other countries" were housed in warehouses and were not subject to custom duties.[21]

Hirschmann was pleased with the *Herald Tribune*'s front-page story, which "quoted freely and so did the Jewish papers." He was less pleased with the *Times*, which "omitted most of my quotes and took an underhand 'crack' at the Free Port idea," presumably the comparison of refugees to "foreign goods." He complained to Arthur Sulzberger and his editors during a subsequent meeting, and Sulzberger "corrected" it with a favorable editorial.[22] The "'Free Ports' for Refugees" editorial, which endorsed the idea without mentioning Jews, appeared in the *Times* 3 weeks later.[23,iv]

Pehle considered the floating of the idea to the press a success, as he informed the president. Pehle cited the poll results, editorial endorsements in 29 newspapers, including the *Times*, and the support of individuals, such as Felix Frankfurter and Arthur Sulzberger. "It is significant that although there has been considerable publicity with respect to the 'free port' proposal," Pehle told the president, "no opposition to the proposal has been voiced by members of Congress or by the public."[24]

Pehle's and Hirschmann's press conference also produced a less positive outcome. As the *Times* reported it, Hirschmann said that "negotiations were almost complete" to allow the steamship, *Tari*, to carry 1,500 refugees from Constanza, Rumania, to Haifa, Palestine.[25] The *S.S. Tari*'s departure, however, depended on the Germans' grant of safe conduct, which they refused to do after Hirschmann's disclosure. The Germans apparently did not want to anger the Arabs by publicly permitting Jewish immigration to Palestine. The *Tari* and its 1,500 Jewish refugees never sailed.[26]

As the Americans were plotting to place thousands of Jews in free ports in the United States, the Germans were preparing to send hundreds of thousands of Hungarian Jews to their deaths in Poland. With an eye on the Russian advance to the east, the Germans moved quickly. Within 2 months of its invasion of Hungary, the Germans, assisted by the Hungarian government, imposed Nuremberg-like laws, confiscated Jewish property, organized a Jewish council, and moved Jews into ghettos.

[iv] Hirschmann had less success with the *Times* in a personal mission to bolster Ambassador Steinhardt's reputation, which Steinhardt apparently believed had been tarnished by *PM*'s criticism of the Russian visas. Sulzberger told Hirschmann that he could not use Hirschmann's quotes about Steinhardt's "priceless efforts on behalf of the refugees" because Steinhardt "'is too good a friend of mine.'" Hirschmann had more success plugging Steinhardt's role with various administration officials, the Jewish press, and even with *PM*, which lauded Steinhardt's refugee work in a column. Hirschmann to Steinhardt, 5/2/44; Steinhardt to Hirschmann, 5/13/44, Laurence A. Steinhardt Papers, Letter books, Box 82, LC; Hirschmann to Steinhardt, 6/1/44; Hirschmann to Steinhardt, 6/10/44, Laurence A. Steinhardt Papers, 1944, General Correspondence, Box 44, LC.

They then began deportations, as the *Times'* Levy was among the first outside observers to discover. "Distressing news reaching here from Hungary," David Schweitzer of the Hebrew Immigrant Aid Society in Beyoglu, Turkey, cabled his New York office on May 8. "Contact Ira Hirschmann who in receipt of cable from Joe Levy correspondent New York Times and with whom am in constant touch." HIAS's New York office then relayed the information to the WRB in Washington.[27]

Along with alerting Hirschmann, Levy had also filed a story to the *Times* in New York. Its transmission was delayed and did not appear until 2 days later, on May 10. "Jews in Hungary Fear Annihilation," read the headline on the page five story. "Although it may sound unbelievable, it is a fact that Hungary, where Jewish citizens were comparatively well treated until March 19, is now preparing for the annihilation of Hungarian Jews by the most fiendish methods," Levy's lead read. "The puppet Nazi government is completing plans and about to start the extermination of about 1,000,000 human beings." They were to meet the same fate as more than 5 million Jews, who had been "put to death in one form or another by the Germans," including in "gas chamber baths," the story said.

"Savage Blows Hit Jews in Hungary," read the headline on Levy's next story out of Hungary "The first act in a program of mass extermination of Jews in Hungary is over, and 80,000 Jews of the Carpathian provinces have already disappeared," read the lead of his May 18 story, which also appeared on page five. "They have been sent to murder camps in Poland." The news prompted a *Times* editorial, "The Jews of Hungary," that took the United Nations to task for not finding "adequate places of refuge," and concluded that the Allied nations remained the only hope for "these distressed people." It called for the United States and Britain to make "immediate and strong representations" that "the authors of these murders will be brought to justice."[28]

Some World Jewish Congress officials worried that Levy's articles contained too much information about specific rescue missions. Nahum Goldmann told Pehle that "the Levy articles in The New York Times might prove more hurtful than helpful." Even Leon Kubowitzki, long an advocate of publicity, called Pehle's deputy, Lawrence Lesser, when a Levy story appeared about the Germans' refusal to grant safe conduct to a ship that would take 1,350 Jewish orphans to Palestine.[29] "I think we might give serious consideration to taking the matter up with the New York Times or with Ambassador Steinhardt," Lesser wrote. It is not clear whether they did.[30]

Both the agency and Jewish groups, however, considered general publicity about the fate of the Hungarian Jews among their most promising tactics. Unlike news reports on specific rescue missions, they wanted more of it. "It is the opinion of the World Jewish Congress that there might be hope of saving the Hungarian Jews if the light of public attention were constantly focused on their treatment and movements," Kubowitzki wrote in a June 6 memorandum.[31] The Jewish Agency shared that assessment. As Levy reported the first deportations, Isaac Gruenbaum, head of the Jewish Agency's rescue committee, tried to interest the *Times* in an article he would write about the Hungarian Jews' perilous situation. Gruenbaum's interest, relayed through the *Times*' Jerusalem correspondent, Julian Meltzer, reached the Sunday editor, who said no thanks. Managing Editor James then cabled London: "Tell Meltzer we so crowded prefer pass up Gruenbaum article."[32] Meltzer instead wrote a news story that appeared May 20, laying out Gruenbaum's contention that if the Allies did not take "swift action" the "same process of extermination as occurred in Poland will befall" the 1.5 million Jews remaining in Hungary and Rumania.[33] The story appeared on page five, as did all previous ones – page five apparently having been designated for stories about the annihilation of Hungarian Jews.

A story that was about to break may have dictated the inside treatment.[34] The Allied invasion of Europe was imminent, as American journalists knew. On June 6, it happened. Allied forces landed on the beaches of Normandy, and began the slow drive to push the German army back into Germany. The invasion crowded out most but not all other front-page news. "Enraged Bull Kills 2 Brothers, Gores Neighbor on Long Island" read a front-page headline the day before the landing. Reports on a cabaret tax and an insurance law decision appeared on the same front page as the headline, "Allied Armies Land in France."[35] On June 9, along with the Allies' expansion of the Normandy beachheads, the front page included two political stories: a state party chairman's resignation and New Deal opponents' Southern strategy. On page five, the *Times* reported that 300,000 Jews in Hungary had been interned in camps and ghettos, forced to wear a yellow star, and allowed daily rations of "some fat and bread and nothing else."

A story about rescue did appear on the front page the very next day, although couched in a way that concealed the identity of the victims. The free ports proposal had finally come to fruition. One thousand "refugees from Italy" would be given "temporary sanctuary" at Fort Ontario, New York, the *Times* front page declared. The story, which never mentioned that most of those admitted would be Jews, quoted the president saying "this was the total number of refugees who would be brought to the United States." The *Times* endorsed the plan that same day on the editorial page (p. 14), again never mentioning Jews and emphasizing that "nothing in this proposal" seeks to evade the immigration laws or to disturb existing quotas. The president formally notified Congress of plans for the camp a few days later, which was also reported on the *Times* front page. The newspaper quoted the president saying that the Nazis' "insane desire to wipe out the Jewish race in Europe continues undiminished.'" In its own voice, the *Times* added that that was "but one example; many Christian groups also are being murdered." A week in review item, "Refuge for the Duration," also described those coming to Fort Ontario as "1,000 war refugees from Italy."[36,v]

At the same time a thousand Jews were allowed into the United States, it became clear what was happening to the hundreds of thousands of Jews being deported from Hungary to Poland – they were being sent to Auschwitz and killed immediately upon arrival. The *Times* had mentioned Auschwitz before, mostly by the Polish name of the town, Oswiecim, in which the camp was located, but briefly and vaguely.[37] Three months earlier, both the Polish Information Center, the exile government's propaganda agency in New York, and the WJC released reports to the press that for the first time described the extent of the slaughter taking place in Auschwitz. The Polish Information Center stated that the number of dead "certainly exceeds half a million, mostly Jews, both Polish and from other countries."[38] The WJC's report stated that smoke and an indescribable stench covered the whole district from the continual burning of bodies in "crematorium and on open pyres." The congress' report also described the liquidation of ghettos in Tarnow, Przemysl, Wilno, and Bialystok, among others, as well as naming the few ghettos and labor camps that still held Jews.[39] The *Times* carried neither report. It was not until the summer, just as

[v] The story subsequently sank deep into the newspaper. The refugees' arrival in New York City 2 months later was reported on page 13 (8/5/44), their arrival at Fort Ontario on page 29 (8/6/44), their welcome by presidential advisor Harold Ickes on page 17 (8/7/44), and their reaction to American life on page 15 (8/25/44). Contrast that with the arrival of British children escaping the bombing of London, which was often featured on the front page.

Hungarian Jews were arriving there, that *Times* readers got a detailed description of Auschwitz's horrors. On June 25, 1944, a page five story from London quoted Emanuel Scherer, a Jewish member of the Polish National Council, announcing that mass executions by gas were "taking place at the Oswiecim concentration camp," with Jews being gassed first, followed by war prisoners and invalids.

The Jewish Agency's Isaac Gruenbaum, a former journalist who had been born in Poland and immigrated to Palestine in 1933, believed more press coverage was needed. Upon learning that 450,000 Hungarian Jews had been deported to Silesia, he cabled Stephen Wise: "do utmost publicise above facts and organise effective steps by community."[40] Gruenbaum also decided to try to generate publicity on his own. On June 30, he initiated an interview with the *Times*' Meltzer in Jerusalem. Immediately after their talk, Meltzer cabled the London bureau: "authoritative information indicating that final phase supreme tragedy hungarian jewry now begun." Meltzer's wire was in the form of a story (except for the cablese shorthand) and was clearly intended for publication. Meltzer wired that by June 17, 400,000 Jews had already been sent to Poland "where tis supposed they already exterminated [with the] remaining 350,000 men women children expected [to] be put [to] death by july twentyfourth." Meltzer told London he obtained "these facts" from Gruenbaum who is "probably best informed person living palestine upon development among martyred jewish people." Melzter wrote that the destruction of Hungarian Jewry was being carried out "with greater speed than in case [of] other european jewries (apparently because they feared similar desperate defence as occurred with warsaw and other polish ghettoes year ago.)"[vi]

Meltzer then quoted Gruenbaum advocating what would prove to be the most hotly debated rescue plan at the time and subsequently, and yet one that Gruenbaum considered "the only possible" way to "deter such wholesale murders." He begged the Allies to consider bombing railway lines and highways leading to Poland and the "death factories." Around this time, his Jewish Agency colleagues were raising the issue with the British, as WRB officials were with the Americans; Gruenbaum apparently

[vi] A later *Times* story (8/4/44, 5) would reveal the brisk pace of the extermination. A Polish underground courier reported that when he left Poland 12 trainloads of Hungarian Jews were arriving every 24 hours at Auschwitz. The gassing time had decreased from 30 minutes to 15, and small children were being killed with bludgeons. The Auschwitz news appeared in the bottom three paragraphs of a story on the Polish underground's successes.

hoped he could use the press to increase pressure on the governments. In his interview with Meltzer, Gruenbaum pointed out that the Allies were already engaged in strategic bombing of communication lines, armaments plants, and petrol refineries. "When these death dealing areas, which have daily murder capacity of thousands [of] people, no longer exist, [it will] be difficult, perhaps impossible, for Germans to [carry out] their foul designs to [wipe out] hundreds of thousands of Jews [in the] next couple months," Meltzer quoted Gruenbaum.[41] The *Times* carried not a word of Gruenbaum's interview and never mentioned the proposal for bombing the death machinery.

Both the United States and Great Britain ultimately rejected the appeal to bomb the extermination centers and the routes to them. (The possible effectiveness of bombing has since sparked a heated controversy.[42]) Why the *Times* did not consider Gruenbaum's information newsworthy is not clear. Perhaps the *Times* considered the information too close to the type of military information the voluntary censorship code prohibited. Or perhaps a report by two Swiss relief organizations overshadowed Gruenbaum's news.[43] At the end of June, the church groups, one headed by the Reverend Paul Voght, released a detailed account of conditions in the Auschwitz and Birkenau camps. Daniel Brigham of the Berne bureau filed two stories based on what came to be known as the Voght report, about whose accuracy the *Times* seemingly had no reservations. "I certainly think we should use this [the Voght report]," James wrote Cable Editor Theodore Bernstein. Bernstein replied that he had not used the story the previous night because Brigham had indicated the story lacked some information. "I'm waiting to get it complete," Bernstein wrote, with a touch of annoyance. "I don't think we want to run a serial story on it all week."[44] The addition of Meltzer's story, which he sent that week, might have turned it into a "serial."

The *Times* ran two other stories instead. The first, on July 3, said that reports had confirmed the existence of "two 'extermination camps' where more than 1,715,000 Jewish refugees were put to death between April 15, 1942, and April 15, 1944." It listed the numbers of deaths by nationality, noting that "to this total must now be added Hungary's Jews," 30% of whom had died en route to the camps. The remaining Jews arrived at Auschwitz and Birkenau, where they were gassed in "fake bathing establishments handling 2,000 to 8,000 daily." Birkenau had about 50 crematoria that could burn 8 to 10 bodies at a time, the story said.

The *Times* ran another, more detailed Brigham story 3 days later. Through the experiences of "a group of well-to-do Hungarians from Budapest," it explained the reason for the high death rate en route to the camp. The Budapest Jews were dragged from their beds at 2 A.M., beaten, ordered to dress, and loaded into army trucks, the *Times* reported. After a few days in the ghetto at Wosice, they were put in a freight car that held 70 people, "with one bucket of water as 'supplies' for a trip that lasted ten days," to Silesia. "On arrival, only a few more than 4,000 of 5,000 who had left survived." Those refugees who were not put to death immediately were stripped, shaved, deloused, and then tattooed with identification numbers "'under the most primitive and inhumane conditions," the story said.

In case there was any doubt about the accuracy of that story, the *Times* carried on the same page British Foreign Secretary Anthony Eden's confirmation of the "widespread deportations and massacres of Hungarian Jews." The London story, which did not have a byline, also quoted the WJC's finding that 100,000 Hungarian Jews had been gassed at Oswiecim. "Between May 15 and 27, sixty-two railroad cars laden with Jewish children between the ages of 2 and 8 and six cars laden with Jewish adults passed daily through the Plaszow station near Cracow," the *Times* reported. "Information received by the World Jewish Congress leaves little doubt that the Germans are waging two wars – one against the enemies of Germany, the other against the Jews – and that, with Germany's defeat imminent, they are preparing to wipe out European Jewry."[45]

The *Times* responded to the Voght report in an editorial – the sixth of seven it ran that day. "It is almost impossible for a civilized mind to grasp the reality of figures given out this week as to the fate of Europe's Jews," the editorial, "No Peace with Butchers," said. It cited both the WJC's estimate of 4 million dead, and the Voght report's estimate of 1,715,000 killed in Auschwitz and Birkenau. It compared those figures "with some others that shock us: 3,000 or fewer killed by robot bombs in London; more than 56,000 American soldiers and sailors killed in action." The Jews in Europe, the *Times* concluded, were "dying for no crime and because of no military necessity." The *Times* called for "a hard and stern peace for all those in any Axis country who could have rebelled against their crimes and did not."[46]

Yet, the *Times* placed neither Auschwitz story on the front page. The first story appeared on page three, even though the front page featured five non-war-related stories, including "Simple Money Order Will Be Issued Soon" and Office of Price Administration "Raises Prices on Certain Items."[47] The second Auschwitz story ran on page six. At the same time, the deaths of other civilians warranted front-page treatment. Three days after the second Auschwitz story ran, accounts of the Germans' "cold-blooded massacres" of "virtually the entire populations" of the Greek village, Distomo, and the French town, Oradour-sur-Glace, appeared on the front.[48] Stories about robot bombs, that in the words of the *Times* editorial killed fewer than 3,000 people, routinely ran on the front page.[49]

That the Auschwitz story originated from the notoriously troublesome Berne bureau probably did not help, nor could the bureau be counted on for a follow-up. By 1944, the supposed German collaborator Jules Sauerwein was gone, but the remaining Berne bureau members, Brigham, Archambault, and Enderis, were at war with one another. Brigham accused Archambault of refusing to come into the office for months, and Archambault fired back that Brigham was just angry because he had tried to cut his expense account. The squabbling got so bad that in March James cabled: "Your private war isn't most important war and getting tiresome. If there had been proper regard for interest paper you two will have to get together and work together. Would like assurance now from you both will try to so Bureau there run for one purpose. If it fails in that it's useless."[50]

They apparently did not heed James' advice. In June, Brigham complained about Archambault and Enderis: "During the day-time I have to actually fight competition with the two old men, with whom I am supposed to collaborate, in order not only to keep my own sources of news but to get assigned a story – in my own office." When New York had to cable Brigham $250 for a trip to the frontier because Archambault had not left him any money, James tried again to make peace: "appreciate you fellows getting [on] better since situation getting critical and news is chief idea."[51] Shortly thereafter, Archambault's son Peter, who was within a few days of his twenty-fifth birthday, was lost at sea while flying a mission as an RAF pilot. Archambault accused Brigham of withholding the cable that informed him of his son's death.[52] The only thing that ended the feud was Archambault's return to Paris with his surviving son, after the city's liberation in August.

The editors then seemed to give up on Berne completely. Enderis, who by then was 72 and had suffered a slight stroke, was not coming into the office much, or producing much. Night Managing Editor Raymond McCaw suggested to James in August that "we bring Enderis home and turn him out to pasture. He would cost us a damn sight less money than he does sending up dispatches from Switzerland which we hardly ever use."[53] Plus, James had the same worries about Enderis' sympathies as he had at the beginning of the war. "Disappointed and concerned tone your goebbels story yesternight," James cabled Enderis in October 1944, about a story that suggested Germany would be able to hold off the Allied advance.[54] In November, Brigham complained about the 'decline' of Berne as an appreciated news center.[55,vii]

Yet throughout the summer and fall of 1944, the Berne bureau, along with London, continued to bear the brunt of reporting the Hungarian story. (In July 1944, the *Times* had again tried to send Levy to the Middle East theater, and he was again denied accreditation.[56] So he remained in the Balkans, but for whatever reason, did not file many stories.) In chillingly matter-of-fact terms, an unidentified Berne reporter tacked the following paragraph to the bottom of a story about an order to Budapest parents to evacuate their children younger than 14: "Other information says a trainload of 2,500 Jewish men, women and children was 'evacuated' from the Kassa 'concentration ghetto' Saturday night. If known schedules are adhered to, these victims will arrive in the Auschwitz and Birkenau camps by this week-end probably with previous knowledge of their fate. A German report just received in Zurich says 'railroad sidings have been constructed directly to the gassing halls in both establishments to expedite matters.'"[57]

If the WRB was unable to elevate the timely, detailed, horrific reports of the end of Hungarian Jewry to a front-page story, it was able to score some successes in overseas propaganda. It persuaded OWI to beam broadcasts to Hungary and other German satellite countries urging their citizens not to participate in the persecution of the Jews and to record the names of those who did. By the end of June, these efforts seemed to be having an effect. As refugee board official I. M. Weinstein told Pehle, "American propaganda to Hungary, particularly the stuff dealing with the Jewish situation, has made an impression on the fascists who control the government." He noted that in June "OWI played heavily" statements

[vii] Enderis was put out to pasture, and soon after the war ended Brigham was dismissed. Depressed over his son's death, Archambault asked to be, and was, assigned to South Africa. ELJ File, DB Folder, NYTCA.

condemning actions against the Jews in Hungary from the president and the U.S. Senate and House Foreign Relations Committee, and from prominent non-Jews, including Christian clergy.[58] (The *Times* columnist McCormick was identified as a "well-known American Roman Catholic" layperson who could make a personal private appeal to former Hungarian Prime Minister Imredy through the Vatican. Whether McCormick was ever asked to make such an appeal and whether she agreed could not be determined.[59])

In mid-July, the Hungarians suspended the deportations, as the *Times* reported on July 19 on page five. Secretary of State Hull noted the *Times* story and asked the WRB representative in Switzerland to confirm its accuracy.[60] The Hungarian government also promised to allow the Red Cross to provide relief to interned Jews, to let some children emigrate, and to give exit visas to all Jews with Palestine immigration certificates. Jewish Agency officials considered the "press campaign" an important element in changing the government's policy.[61] The conviction that the Nazis' days were numbered, especially since the invasion of Europe, and the assumption that Budapest might be bombed as part of Allied retaliation, also factored into the Horthy government's decision.[62] But as historian Monty Noam Penkower concludes, "world protest at the end of June played a major part in this dramatic reversal."[63] Auschwitz's gas chambers and crematoria had destroyed half of Hungary's Jews by the summer of 1944. The remaining half were spared, at least for awhile.

As the cataclysm of the Hungarian Jews unfolded, Arthur Sulzberger assumed the same posture he had since the 1930s: private maneuverings and public caution. Soon after Morgenthau had complained to the publisher about the *Times*' initial coverage of the WRB, Sulzberger appealed to the treasury secretary for assistance. Sulzberger wanted Morgenthau to meet with Dr. I. Steinberg who was trying to establish a "colony for Jews on non-political lines" in Australia, and possibly arrange for Steinberg to meet with Hull and the president as well. Morgenthau passed Sulzberger's letter on to Pehle who arranged to meet with Steinberg in Washington in March.[64] In mid-July, Sulzberger called again, this time about an attempt to rescue Hungarian Jews. Sulzberger had learned of a Hungarian living in Los Angeles who believed he could arrange to bribe a Gestapo leader in Budapest to prevent Jews from being deported to Poland. Sulzberger called Morgenthau about the Hungarian, Eugene Bogdanffy, and the treasury secretary again contacted Pehle. WRB officials took the offer very seriously, meeting several times with Bogdanffy, but the rescue scheme never materialized.[65]

That spring an unlikely source attacked the *Times* for its relative silence on the plight of the Jews. Former *Nation* editor Oswald Garrison Villard, a non-Jewish, anti-Zionist, published a book of press criticism that lambasted the newspaper's treatment of the news of European Jews.

> The only possible explanation [for the *Times*' handling of Jewish issues] is fear that its Jewish ownership will be held against it more frequently if it becomes a vigorous defender of the horribly ill-treated Jewish people. . . . If there ever was a case where the *Times* should have risen superior to fear of consequences it is this. For never were human beings more entitled to be defended and championed by a great organ of public opinion; certainly never have men and women anywhere been tortured and slaughtered in such numbers with less reason.[66]

Sulzberger did not respond to the charge directly, but he did have his consultant on Jewish issues, Bernard Richards, comment. In June, Richards wrote a letter to the editor of the *Jewish News* after it published a review of Villard's book. "Anyone who reads this paper [the *Times*] regularly would know that a close examination of its pages for the last few years would reveal hundreds of dispatches from Europe and other news stories and articles including a large number of editorials describing and condemning the indignities and cruelties to which our people have been subjected and demanded redress," Richards wrote in the letter the *News* printed. He acknowledged and deplored the "unfortunate controversy we have had with Mr. Sulzberger" over Zionism, but argued that the criticism should be "tempered" by the fact the *Times* published more news on Zionism and Jewish issues than any other newspaper in the United States. "A devoted Jewish newspaper like yours," Richards wrote, should not "repeat the loose and off-hand dictum of an eccentric goy [non-Jew] charging with anti-Semitism a great American newspaper."[67]

Sulzberger did respond privately to similar criticism from Pierre Van Paasen of the Emergency Committee to Save the Jewish People of Europe. "Mr. Van Paasen is in error if he speaks of The Times' indifference to the plight of the Jews, or of the people of any other faith or nation," Sulzberger wrote in March 1944 to a reader who had raised Van Paasen's criticism. "The point is, rather, on the part of the Zionists that because I, the publisher of The New York Times, happen to be a Jew, they expect to see that reflected in the columns of The Times through a one-sided approach to the question, and I am sure you will agree that should not happen."[68]

Sulzberger may not have softened his position on Zionists, but he had changed his views on one critical issue. In February 1944, the *Times* editorialized in favor of lifting the White Paper, which had limited Jewish immigration to Palestine and was set to expire at the end of March. "The increasingly desperate state of those of Jewish faith in Europe" meant immigration "on the most generous terms possible" should be allowed, the *Times* opined, without consideration of "the future political status of Palestine."[69] By October, Sulzberger and his critics were back on more familiar ground. The editorial page's unsigned "Topics of the Times" column attacked the proposal for a Jewish Brigade to fight with Allied forces, a variant on the earlier Jewish Army idea.[viii] The column demonstrated that the deaths of millions of Jews had not shaken the publisher's commitment to universal principles. The column, which provoked the by-now predictable round of condemnations,[70] fretted that such a brigade would "seriously misrepresent" most Jews.

> It can plaster them with the label of separatism. It can set up barriers between them and their non-Jewish fellow-citizens, or raise higher the barriers where unfortunately they already exist, as in the unhappy case of Poland. . . . It will be a plea of guilty to the long-standing charge that the Jew is a foreign body in the national organism. . . . It is hard to see how a Jewish brigade can fail to play into the hands of the enemies of the Jewish people. The hate-mongers who specialize in the international Jew will have a fine new text.[71]

If the *Times* reporting on the fate of the Jews in Hungary chronicled an ongoing tragedy, much of its coverage that year recorded tragedies that had already taken place. In short stories on the inside pages, the *Times* described cities without Jews. About half of Rome's 11,500 Jews had been deported during the 9-month German occupation, the *Times*' Herbert Matthews reported in a story that included effusive praise of the Vatican's efforts to save them. In Belgrade, only 20 of the city's 12,000 Jews were alive, the *Times* noted. In a similar, matter-of-fact tone, the *Times* explained how

viii The Jewish Brigade was formed in Italy in October 1944 and went into action against the Germans in March 1945, at which point the *Times* had a story on it (3/26/45, 8).

the largest Jewish community in Greece, 48,000 Jews from Salonika, had been sent to extermination camps in April 1943. The *Times* also described entire countries devoid of Jews. Of 90,000 Jews in Greece before the war, only 8,000 remained, the *Times* reported in a three-paragraph, page 14 story. Gone, too, were the Jews of the Netherlands, 180,000 of them had been "'completely wiped out' by the Nazis," the *Times* reported on page seven.[72]

Amidst the stories of destruction came a few of salvation, although they too appeared exclusively inside the *Times*. Belgian villagers had hidden Jews in their town for 4 years, as had residents of the German town of Aachen. In France, 5,000 orphans had been concealed in private homes and cloisters, and a few children from various parts of Europe had managed to escape to Palestine. The news that Bulgaria's 50,000 Jews had largely been spared appeared in three paragraphs on page 14, next to a similarly sized story about a war correspondent being slightly injured when the Japanese strafed a jeep in which he was riding on Saipan.[73]

The most important news about what had happened to the Jews during the previous 4 years came as the Soviets freed parts of their territory seized by the Germans in 1941. In a page eight story, the American Ambassador to the Soviet Union, W. Averell Harriman, confirmed that "German atrocities on the eastern front have not been and cannot be exaggerated." As the victims began to tell their stories, the *Times* included more first-person accounts. Abraham Sutskever, a poet and partisan, finally confirmed the massacre of Vilna's Jews that the *Times* had first reported with a qualifier in June 1942. Only 3,000 of Vilna's 80,000 Jews were alive, the story on page three stated, this time without qualification. Isador and Laura Hertz, a married couple in their early 20s, attested to the travails they endured as among the 2,000 to 3,000 Jews still alive in Lwow, once a Jewish community of 140,000. The Hertzses, whose only remaining family were "some cousins in New York," described how tens of thousands of Jews were murdered in a forest northeast of Lwow. A "21-year-old Jewish youth," told of escaping from the Warsaw ghetto and then smuggling guns back into it. W. B. Feinberg described the uprising in Sobibor, where he had been imprisoned for 17 months before escaping during the October 1943 rebellion.[74]

The story that had most impact, however, contained only the victims' silent testimony – the thousands of shoes and suitcases left behind by those murdered in the Maidanek extermination center. *Times* correspondent

William Lawrence, along with 30 other correspondents, arrived there at the end of August 1944.[ix] Almost 1 year earlier, Lawrence had been skeptical that a massacre had taken place at Babi Yar. Years later, he said his doubts evaporated when he arrived at the camp near Lublin, Poland. His August 30 story about Maidanek, headlined "Nazi Mass Killing Laid Bare in Camp," appeared in a one-column story in the middle of the front page.[x] Only one full paragraph and half of a sentence appeared on the front, but it was a devastating paragraph.

"I have just seen the most terrible place on the face of the earth," Lawrence wrote, "the German concentration camp at Maidanek, which was a veritable River Rouge for the production of death, in which it is estimated by Soviet and Polish authorities that as many as 1,500,000 persons from nearly every country in Europe were killed in the last three years." Lawrence then proceeded to describe what he had seen in and around Maidanek: gas chambers, five furnaces in which bodies were cremated, three of ten open mass graves with 368 partly decomposed bodies, a warehouse with tens of thousands of shoes, and another with suitcases, clothing, and other personal effects. "This is a place that must be seen to be believed," Lawrence wrote. "I have been present at numerous atrocity investigations in the Soviet Union, but never have I been confronted with such complete evidence, clearly establishing every allegation made by those investigating German crimes. After inspection of Maidanek, I am now prepared to believe any story of German atrocities, no matter how savage, cruel and depraved."

The story, however, had a significant omission. The one reference to Jews described those who entered the bath houses as "Jews, Poles, Russians and in fact representatives of a total of twenty-two nationalities." By now, almost 5 years into the war, readers knew enough to object. The *Times*

[ix] The Soviets also overran three other extermination camps that summer, Sobibor, Belzec and Treblinka, where at least 1.5 million Jews had been killed. The Germans had shut down all three camps at the end of 1943 and had tried to conceal the extermination operations by destroying buildings and burning any remaining bodies. Probably not understanding what they had found, the Soviets made no attempt to publicize what they had come across. Jon Bridgman, *The End of the Holocaust: The Liberation of the Camps*, Portland, Ore.: Aereopagitica Press (1990), 21–2.

[x] Other newspapers, including the *Atlanta Constitution* and *San Francisco Examiner*, ran stories about Maidanek on the front page. Lipstadt, *Beyond Belief*, 350n27. Mutual Network's New York station WOR broadcast its correspondent's eyewitness account on August 13, 1944. Fine, "Radio Coverage of the Holocaust," 160.

received several complaints about the story's failure to mention Jews, "it being alleged that two-thirds victims were Jewish," James wrote to Lawrence 2 weeks later, asking for an explanation. Lawrence replied that "through misunderstanding" the censors deleted "fact that most victims were Jews" from his lead, and that Maidanek was an "annihilation camp" for Jews and Slavs from subsequent references. Lawrence said he did not know that "until today."[75] Years later, Lawrence attributed the censor's action not to a "misunderstanding" but to anti-Semitism. "I descended hopping mad on the press office officials," he recalled. "I got a rather lame and halting explanation from the press officer on duty that some anti-Semites around the world might feel that if the victims were Jews, the murders were justified. This reflected, of course, the basic anti-Semitism of so many Russians.... Finally, the Soviet official allowed me to cable Mr. James that the reference to the Jews had been contained in my original dispatch and had been censored from it by mistake."[76,xi]

That the Soviet censor altered Lawrence's dispatch is plausible (although he or she apparently did not do a very good job; other newspapers and *Life* magazine carried accounts indicating most of the victims were Jews[77]). The Soviets often ignored Jewish victims.[78] Yet, on other occasions, the Soviets clearly identified victims as Jews, such as at Foreign Minister Molotoff's press conference on the Babi Yar massacre and in statements issued by the Soviet Embassy.[79] It may also be that Lawrence, from the perspective of 1972, the year in which his memoirs were published, overstated his own indignation three decades earlier. There was seemingly no attempt to correct or clarify the story. In previous, and even in subsequent stories, Lawrence was no more direct about the victims' identity.[80] When he had another chance to write about Maidanek a few months later for *True* magazine, he mentioned a majority of those killed were Jews only once and halfway through the article.[81]

The *Times* ran an editorial the day after Lawrence's Maidanek story appeared, but it focused more on the intensifying fight between the pro- and anti-Communist Poles than on the horrors the story revealed. The

[xi] Lawrence still detested the Moscow assignment. "We call the Metropole the 'Correspondents' Concentration Camp,' and I think in many ways a real concentration camp might be preferable because then one wouldn't indulge in idle dreams of trying to reason with your jailers," he wrote James on November 17. Lawrence finally left Moscow in February 1945. ELJ File, MB Folder, NYTCA.

Poles' behavior was "childish and inexcusable" in light of "some horrifying information," the *Times* opined. The editorial praised Lawrence as a "thorough and accurate correspondent," and urged both groups of Poles to unite. "It is civilization itself that is at stake. Over the graves of the Maidanek dead the common bond of humanity should surely draw all groups, all factions, all free nations together."[82] The *Times'* week in review did not consider the Maidanek discovery significant enough to include in the week's summary of the most important news events.

As the horrors of the Nazi past were unearthed in eastern Poland, Hungarian Jews still faced the horror of the Nazi present. In the days after the Horthy government had stopped the deportations to Poland, the WRB had scrambled to persuade diplomatic missions to expand their presence in Budapest and to shelter growing numbers of Jews. Raul Wallenberg's rescue of tens of thousands of Budapest Jews through the Swedish embassy was the most successful of these diplomatic interventions.[xii] In August, WRB director John Pehle seemed assured enough about the Hungarian Jews' position that he suggested the OWI turn its attention elsewhere. After crediting OWI's broadcasts with "softening the attitude of the Hungarian Government toward the 400,000 Jews still alive in that country," Pehle suggested its next round of broadcasts appeal to partisans to protect the Jews in France, the Low Countries, Czechoslovakia, and Poland. "We contemplate with dismay that the defeated German army and the guilt-ridden Gestapo will use their waning power to consummate Hitler's threat to make Europe 'Judenrein,'" he wrote to Davis on August 23.[83]

But Hungary's Jews were soon imperiled again. Afraid that a new Hungarian government would make a separate peace with the Allies, the Germans had moved into Budapest in late August and installed the head of the fascist Arrow Cross Party as prime minister. Adolf Eichmann, who had been in charge of the first deportations, was again allowed to move in on the remaining Jews, most of whom were in Budapest. On September 2, the *Times* signaled, in the last two paragraphs of a 13-paragraph story, "the start of a new wave of persecution of Hungarian Jews."[84]

So just 2 weeks after his reassuring letter, Pehle wrote Davis with growing alarm. The WRB director urged Davis to continue OWI's "vigorous

[xii] The *Times* reported on Wallenberg's "adventures" on April 26, 1945, p. 12, when the Swedish Consulate disclosed he had saved 20,000 Hungarian Jews.

broadcasts to Hungary" to head off Hungary's succumbing to German pressure to "resume the deportation of Jews to extermination centers."[85] After receiving a noncommittal response from Davis, Pehle wrote again, this time informing Davis that deportations of Hungarian Jews to Poland had resumed and urging that "broadcasts to Hungary during these crucial days include material designed to safeguard the lives of the Jews in that country." Not taking any chances, Pehle then wrote Secretary of State Hull enclosing a draft of a letter Hull might send to Davis stating that he agreed with the WRB's recommendation that OWI take "vigorous measures." Davis was not swayed, however, stating that "we have not found it advisable to start a special campaign to Hungary in the interest of the Jews." Davis explained that the "whole impact of our psychological warfare is now turned against Hungarian determination to stick it out with the Nazis," which if it persuaded the Hungarians to abandon the Germans would mean "the Jews in Hungary will be saved."[86]

Pehle's dispute with Davis over renewed broadcasts to Hungary was a prelude to a more significant run-in with OWI 2 months later. During the summer, the WRB had received, through its representative in Switzerland, Roswell McClelland, a summary of the testimony of two Slovakian Jews who had escaped from Auschwitz. In October, the board received the full reports in a diplomatic pouch. The reports were "convincing in a way in which other reports have not been," Pehle later wrote Hirschmann. "As you know it is not easy to believe such things take place but after reading these accounts one cannot refute the conclusion that such things do happen and are happening."[87] So Pehle, whose efforts to persuade the War Department to bomb Auschwitz's gas chambers and crematorium had been rebuffed, decided to release the reports to the press. To prepare the testimonies for publication, WRB staffers deleted the names of all living people. They considered removing references to Jews harming other Jews, but decided to leave the original text intact. They then wrote press releases to be sent to newspapers and radio stations, along with the reports. On November 16, the board told Leo Pinkus of the OWI's Foreign News Desk about its plans. Two days later, the board distributed the reports to the press, with instructions that the story be embargoed until Sunday, November 26, and sent 12 copies to Pinkus.

Upon learning of the press release, Davis on November 22 summoned Pehle to his office in the Social Security Building. There, Pehle, and two of his staff, met with Davis, and six of his staff. Davis started by asking

Pehle for the source of the reports. Pehle replied by reading excerpts from McClelland's cover letter vouching for their authenticity. "Mr. Davis' staff unanimously viewed with alarm the War Refugee Board's release of the reports," the WRB's Virginia Mannon, who attended the meeting, wrote that day in a memorandum to the files. Davis seemed particularly concerned that the WRB had flouted his authority, first by issuing the release without clearing it with OWI as required by a 1942 order, and second, by sending it to newspaper offices across the United States, not just to DC bureaus as it was supposed to, according to Mannon's memo. Davis was upset enough that Mannon referred sarcastically to "the enormity of the crimes which the WRB had perpetrated against the OWI." (Mannon implied that WRB's failure to get clearance was "unintentional," although Pehle later suggested to Hirschmann, with a wink and a nod, that the board may not have been quite that naive. "'Unfortunately'" he wrote putting the words in quotes, "the opposition didn't develop until the story had been released to the press for publication a week later, so nothing could be done to stop it."[88])

OWI staffers raised a variety of concerns, from whether anti-Semites might have planted the reports because of the references to Jews harming other Jews, to the fact that the reports concerned "a multiplicity of 'mean little things.'" The only common thread was a "fear of the reaction," although when asked, the OWI officials said they did not expect a negative press response, according to the memo. One even said he planned to use what he anticipated would be favorable editorials in overseas propaganda. Mannon wrote that Pehle "demolished their objections one by one," and mentioned that Treasury Secretary Morgenthau, among others, had not "felt any fears such as those voiced by OWI." She concluded: "At least three times Mr. Davis said the head of his Polish desk had read the reports carefully and had stated that the events in the reports might well have happened."[89] (Indeed, many OWI staffers, including one who would later claim that he opposed "the indiscriminate reporting" of inauthentic atrocity stories, received a constant flow of well-substantiated intelligence reports on the mass extermination of Jews.[90])

The next day, Davis wrote Pehle a testy letter suggesting that he send a "supplementary statement" to every paper that received the original release explaining that the board "was satisfied with the reliability of the channels" through which the report was received. Davis believed "this precaution appears the more necessary" once he realized the two Slovak refugees who provided it had held official positions in the Birkenau camp. "Several readers in this office" concluded that the Germans may have deliberately released the Slovakians because their information might "create contempt for the inmates," even "at the cost of including materials about atrocities committed by Germans." Pehle drafted a reply, noting that the "explanatory statement which we attached to all copies of the reports adequately describes their source and our view as to their credibility."[91] The WRB never sent any "supplementary statement."

In his study of World War II propaganda, Clayton D. Laurie concludes, based on this episode, that "Davis believed that news of the Holocaust would irreparably damage OWI's reputation for veracity and its credibility at a crucial juncture of the war. The audiences built up at home and abroad over two years could be lost permanently in an instant if presented with reports too fantastic to believed."[92] Yet, it seems just as likely that Davis' objection to releasing the Auschwitz reports was based more on their focus on Jewish victims, and less on their implausibility – not to mention his pique at WRB's bureaucratic slight.[93] For Davis seemingly had no objections to the widespread distribution of the Polish Labor Group's "Oswiecim, Camp of Death" booklet published in February 1944. It also described Auschwitz's horrors but, unlike the Slovakian Jews' reports, focused on the camps' "Polish backbone," rather than its "appendages – Czechs, Germans, Jews, Serbs and now Russians." In fact, Davis wrote the booklet's introduction.[94]

OWI was not the only government entity concerned about the Jewish nature of the story. A reporter for *Yank Magazine*, a government publication for servicemen, had been assigned to write about German atrocity stories "to show our soldiers the nature of their enemy." Pehle gave him the Auschwitz reports for December 1 publication and granted an interview on November 7. The reporter, Sgt. Richard Paul, called November 10 to say "that the New York editors had come to the conclusion that our reports were too Semitic and they had asked him to get a story from other sources." Virginia Mannon told Paul that "inasmuch as the whole Nazi extermination program was more than 90 percent Jewish, it was unlikely that he could get any stories that did not deal principally with Jews." After an unsuccessful appeal to Pentagon officials who had "a very negative attitude," Paul called Mannon again to say that "New York had asked him to try to get a less Jewish story." Mannon again told him she "could not help him." Paul then wrote a long memorandum arguing for publication of the reports, but the story was still held because, he was told, of latent anti-Semitism in the Army.[95]

Unlike *Yank*'s editors, OWI officials could not suppress the Auschwitz reports; WRB had already distributed them to the press. On Sunday, November 26, the *Times*, and many other American newspapers, ran the story on the front page. The *Times* story, which bore Washington reporter John Crider's byline, appeared at the very bottom of the page. (The *Herald Tribune* ran the story as the off-lead.) "It is a fact beyond denial that the Germans have deliberately and systematically murdered millions of innocent civilians – Jews and Christians alike – all over Europe," the story said on the front, quoting a WRB statement. Only inside was it clear that almost all those million and a half people were Jews. Most of the story, which filled an inside page except for ads, recounted the process of gassing the victims and disposing of their bodies. The *Times* never ran an editorial about the WRB reports, nor did it mention them in the week in review. From the entire active press corps, Pehle heard one expression of doubt – the *Times'* Crider had questioned the authenticity of the reports. On what basis is not known. A concerned Pehle had one of his staff check with the Czech Minister to see if "he had received similar reports," which he had not.[96]

There was another doubter. Oswald F. Schuette, who described himself as an "American war correspondent for three and one half years in the last war" – he had been a correspondent for the *Chicago Daily News* – challenged the authenticity of the report in two letters to Secretary of War Henry Stimson. His concern was that the reports were too detailed to believe that prisoners could recall so much with such precision. WRB drafted a reply that Stimson sent affirming the accuracy of the reports. But when Stimson, who apparently had not read the reports before, finally did, he cautioned Pehle to "be extraordinarily careful." Stimson worried that "it is so horrible that it will be sure to invite further inquiry by readers as to the care which we have taken to authenticate it." A good bureaucratic player, Pehle alerted Morgenthau to Schuette's and Stimson's concerns, while reiterating that the reports "contained only material about which there is no uncertainty either in the minds of the narrators or among the many qualified people who examined them in person."[97]

Overall, Pehle was pleased with the attention the reports received, noting that they were "getting big play in the press throughout the country."[98] The typical response to the Auschwitz reports seemed to be horror that such unimaginable events could be true, not doubt about their authenticity. "We don't want to believe. We don't want to think such horrible things can happen," wrote Lowell Mellett, a popular newspaper columnist who had been Roosevelt's special assistant on press relations. "We remember, too, that many atrocity tales during the last war turned out to be untrue." But he concluded: "The reports themselves seem completely convincing to any one who read them. The mass of detail given is calculated to overcome any doubts."

That seemed to be the case among the American people as well, according to the results of a Gallup poll recounted in the *Washington Post* on December 3, 1944. The poll found that 76% of those polled believed "stories that Germans have murdered many people in concentration camps." The poll, however, also attested to Americans' ignorance of the facts of the extermination campaign. Asked for their "best guess" as to the numbers killed, 27% said 100,000 or less and 12% said 100,000 to 1,000,000; only 12% guessed the correct number of more than 2 million. One-fourth of the respondents refused to guess.

If Pehle started the year credulous about OWI's intentions, by the end he was not. He had tried to persuade the Book of the Month Club to send the Auschwitz reports to its subscribers. After deciding the club would not distribute the reports, its president, Harry Scherman, contacted Clifton Fadiman and Rex Stout of the War Writers Board about other possible channels. "It seems that in the meantime they [Fadiman and Stout] have been having some discussion with an OWI representative about this very matter," Scherman explained to Pehle, "and reported that there appeared to be some doubt in Washington (just where it is centered, I don't know) that the distribution of such a pamphlet would not be 100% advisable." Pehle wrote back that given "the excellent press and radio coverage" the report received, he would not "push this matter further at this time." He did want to make one point: "With regard to the negative reaction of O.W.I., I hesitate to express myself in writing. You can be sure it has no adequate basis."[99]

In its first year, the WRB managed to change the tone of the government's policy to more forthrightly acknowledge what was happening to the Jews and to the Jews alone. Through rescue operations, such as Hirschmann's in Turkey and that of others in Lisbon, and through the encouragement of OWI broadcasts that helped forestall some deportations from Hungary, the board also managed to save several thousand Jews. Its efforts were, as Pehle conceded, too little, too late, but still far more than had been done before. That policy change was reflected in the *New York Times*' coverage. During 1944, the newspaper ran 12 front-page stories that concerned the Jews – more than any other year of the war. WRB actions prompted half of those stories, from the president's statement warning Germany not to harm the Jews in Hungary, to the "floating" and then introduction of the free ports idea, to the issuance of the Auschwitz reports.

The *Times* too changed, editorializing more frequently on the plight of the Jews, and stating more assertively that the victims were Jews. Indeed, one editorial was entitled, "The Jews of Hungary." Another, "Rumanian Tragedy," called for the Allied government to pressure Rumania to restore its Jews' rights and property. "This war will have been fought in vain if in its wake the old evils are allowed again to take root," it said. "Such action is only simple justice for the 270,000 who have suffered so much for no other reason than that they were Jews."[100]

But if the government's change was too little, too late, so was the *Times*'. Just 13 editorials mentioned the Jews' fate, out of nearly 3,000 published that year. None of the editorials was the lead, and several editorials still talked about refugees or a persecuted people, not Jews. Too many important stories were buried inside, including all Joseph Levy's stories about the destruction of Hungarian Jewry. Only 1 of the 12 front-page stories addressed the plight of Hungary's Jews, and then only in anticipation of what was to come, not in reaction to what did occur. In fact, of those 12 front-page stories, only that one – the president's warning on March 24 – clearly identified the primary victims as Jews. The others either did not mention Jews at all on the front – referring, for example, to "refugees from Italy" in the free ports story on June 10 or "persons from nearly every country in Europe" in the Maidanek story on August 30 – or mentioned Jews but only in conjunction with other "persecuted minorities."

Compared with other events, the *Times* still did not consider the extermination of the Jews to be terribly important. Neither mass murder at Maidanek nor at Auschwitz made it into the week in review highlights. On September 3, 1944, that section ran a full page of "Outstanding Events and Major Trends of the Second World War," presumably to coincide with the fifth anniversary of the war's commencement. It did not mention Jews.

Nor did Anne O'Hare McCormick's magazine piece in that same issue, "Europe's Five Black Years – and Now the Light."[101] A month later, the magazine published three articles that would seem to require some discussion of the Jewish issue, including an argument against a "soft peace" with Germany, but did not.[102] At the end of the year, the *Times* printed "Fifty Memorable Dates in the History of 1944." According to the *Times*, nothing memorable happened to the Jews in 1944.[103]

The WRB's rescue efforts and the *Times*' spotlight on them were not enough to save most of Hungary's Jews. Of nearly 800,000 Jews in Hungary at the beginning of 1944, only about 180,000 survived to the war's end. As the year came to a close, a *Times* story described Hungarian Jewry's final chapter. In early November, tens of thousands of Hungarian Jews were driven from Budapest toward the Austrian border in a "march of death," which the *Times* reported in December based on a survivor's account provided by the JTA. (Seven years after Arthur Sulzberger had ordered the *Times*' subscription cancelled, the newspaper was again receiving the JTA.) " 'Anyone who showed signs of a breakdown was immediately shot,' " the survivor, who had escaped to Switzerland, was quoted saying. " 'Wet through and through, our clothes torn to pieces, we had to spend nights sleeping along the roadside. Every two days we received a plate of watery soup and this was all.' " The story said that of 100,000 Jews who started the march, 75,000 reached the border. Only those fit for hard labor were taken across, the remaining Jews were driven into the woods to die of " 'disease, exposure and starvation.' "[104]

The final story, like almost all those that came before, appeared on page five of the *Times*. The day before, a story about the murder of hundreds of Belgian villagers by "Nazi thugs," made the front page.[105] A few days later, when the *Times* editorialized on the Germans' final spasm of violence in the face of defeat, it mentioned their "last-ditch defense" that resulted in the "sacrifice of Budapest," "the slaughter of American war prisoners," and the "murder of Russian truce emissaries." The editorial, "Unleashed Savagery," said nothing about the savagery of the death marches that were claiming the few remaining Jews.[106]

10

"Political Prisoners, Slave Laborers, and Civilians of Many Nationalities"

The Liberation of the Concentration Camps

In August 1945, a harrowing document landed on Arthur Sulzberger's desk. It described the wartime experiences of Elsbet Midas Gerst, a cousin of Erich Midas from Furth. The publisher had helped Erich, his wife Thea (Iphigene's cousin), and their young daughter immigrate to the United States 7 years earlier. The letter from Gerst to her parents and sisters had circulated among the Ochs relatives and someone had made sure Erich Midas' carefully translated version found its way to the *New York Times*.

Gerst and her husband had left Furth the same year as the Midases, escaping to the Netherlands – or so they thought. In July 1943, after the Gersts had spent 3 years living under harsh Nazi occupation, eight Gestapo men stormed their hiding place and Elsbet's excruciating odyssey began. After 3 weeks in a German prison, she was sent to Westerbork, a transit camp. A month later, Gerst, along with hundreds of others, was loaded into a cattle car, with one barrel for drinking water, and another as a toilet. It was August 24, 1943, her twenty-seventh birthday. The following night, the train arrived at Auschwitz.

One of 40 women to survive the selection process, Gerst was stripped, shaved, tattooed, dressed in dirty, torn clothes, and dumped in barracks with three tiers of beds. During her time in Auschwitz, Gerst underwent medical experiments and witnessed even worse conducted on others. "We were forced to see how other persons were hung, how parts of their bodies were cut off, how they were martyred with or without instruments," she wrote, "how some were driven to the electric wire, how little children were thrown into flames alive, and how lots of people were brought into the gas chambers while being beaten."

Gerst eventually was sent to a labor camp, where the inmates had to stand in line for roll call every morning and every evening for 3 or 4 hours. They went to work each morning surrounded by police dogs that the S.S. occasionally set loose on the prisoners. Only one thing kept her alive there, she wrote – her fanatical pursuit of cleanliness. She would sneak out of the barracks in the middle of the night to secretly wash herself with cold water in the freezing open air. With the Russians approaching, the Germans forced the inmates to leave the camp on January 18, 1945. For 3 days, they wandered through 5-foot high snow drifts without food or drink; anyone who did not march was shot. They were then loaded into an open coal car. "It was so cold in the cars that our overcoats froze to the bottom and our hair, so far as it was existent, froze together," Gerst wrote. The first night Gerst managed to grab a "beautiful thick" blanket that had slipped off an S.S. man and "that's the reason I didn't freeze to death." After a 10-day trip without food or toilet facilities, she arrived at Ravensbrueck at 10 at night. In the dark, Gerst managed to scavenge 10 times as much of her first meal as she was supposed to. She stayed there a month and was then transported to a factory where she subsisted on rations of a pint of water, a piece of turnip, and one slice of bread. Falling ill, she was taken to a hospital where she persuaded the nurses to allow her to remain once she had recovered.

After a 6-week hospital stay, Gerst was returned to the factory. "Then we heard after thirteen days, the Russians would come from the one side and the Americans from the other side to liberate us," she wrote, but "we still had thirteen days with hunger and misery and nobody really dared hope that liberation would come to us." It did. The Russians arrived in tanks and armored cars. The electric wire surrounding the camp was broken, and the inmates rushed to the S.S. post to gorge themselves on the food the Germans had left behind.

Once Gerst had recovered, the Red Cross provided transportation for her return to the Netherlands. In Amerongen on August 5, 1945, waiting for her husband who would never come, Gerst composed the letter that filled 18 typed pages. A few weeks later it arrived on Arthur Sulzberger's desk.

After reading the letter, the publisher sent a copy to the editor in charge of the *Times* magazine.[1]

As the Germans retreated in the face of the Soviet advance in the East and the British and American advance in the West, they abandoned the labor, concentration, and extermination camps where they had murdered millions of Jews, as well as Russian prisoners of war, Gypsies, and Poles. The liberating armies, dashing toward Germany, came across mounds of evidence of Nazi crimes. There was physical evidence in the form of partially standing gas chambers, still-smoldering crematoria, torture equipment of all descriptions, warehouses filled with hair and teeth and stolen possessions, and ground that still oozed blood and disgorged bones. There was also living evidence in the form of emaciated, broken, but still breathing bodies. About 100,000 Jews survived the camps; several hundred thousand more emerged from hidden cellars and deep forests, or returned from the far reaches of the Soviet Union. Each and every one had a story as dramatic, as painful, as horrifying, as Elsbet Gerst's.

Not far behind the soldiers, came the journalists, clutching pens and pointing cameras, seemingly ready to record the full horror of what the Germans had done to the Jews. Finally, stories such as Gerst's could be told to an eagerly awaiting public. At last in 1945, the full accounting could take place. But it was not to be. Although the press documented the scope and depth of Nazi depravity more fully than it had before, it continued to downplay its Jewish dimensions. Flipping through daily newspapers, including the *New York Times*, Americans read articles that described the revolting conditions in the camps and saw photographs of the dazed survivors amidst thousands of dead. Sitting in the darkness of first-run movie theaters, they watched newsreels of "piles of the dead," and "pitiful specimens of the 'living dead,'" taken moments after the camps had been liberated. That the Germans had committed crimes against humanity – in the words of the Nuremberg indictments issued later that year – struck Americans with terrifying clarity as the war in Europe ended. That the Germans had specifically committed crimes against the Jews was less clear. Only rarely were the living or the dead described as Jews, and never were their stories told except in the most truncated and fragmentary fashion. If anything, the confusion deepened over what had happened and to whom it had happened. The unique tragedy of the Jews did not emerge from the ashes of the liberated camps.

Even before correspondents arrived at the German concentration camps themselves, they had a strong indication of what had happened there and elsewhere from Allied and Axis soldiers, and from their own observations. Since 1943, as the Russians had reclaimed parts of their territory, journalists in the East had come across the sites and survivors of earlier massacres, from Babi Yar to Maidanek. In the last months of the war, as the Russians approached Berlin, they found more such scenes and many more eyewitnesses. It was also apparent that in the face of their impending defeat, the Germans had stepped up their killing of Jews.[i] "The Germans in Lithuania massacred 10,000 Jews in a Ghetto slaughter during one night and then burned the entire quarter before abandoning Kaunas," the *Times* reported in January 1945. The Germans had already killed 30,000 Jews in the ghetto there, the page 11 story explained, but 10,000 remained when the Germans had to retreat. So they "massed the survivors in a one-square-kilometer section of the Ghetto and machine-gunned them en masse."[2]

In February, one of the *Times*' roving correspondents, Harold Denny, came across captured German soldiers who provided confirmation of "German atrocities" that "might have been discounted as propagandist inventions." A corporal, who had been with the Rumanian Army and then joined a German S.S. division, recounted marching Jews from Bessarabia to Odessa, and machine gunning them at a spot where 15,000 people ultimately were slaughtered. The corporal, who "shows no emotion, no sense of guilt," also related being in a labor camp and at Gross Rosen, where he "worked on a detail that collected the dead and took the bodies to a cremating oven," Denny wrote in a page four story. Another German soldier described conditions in Sachsenhausen, near Berlin, that employed killing methods "so hideous that they cannot be indicated, and could have been conceived only by obscenely perverted minds." Finally, Denny described his interview with a German noncommissioned officer who had been in Brest-Litovsk in 1942, where 15,000 to 16,000 Jewish civilians had been killed in the year's last 4 months. In one incident, the officer witnessed the

[i] In one of his last acts before stepping down as WRB director, John Pehle continued to press OWI to step up its psychological warfare campaign to save Jews. "The policy of the central German authorities has, if anything grown even more ruthless," Pehle wrote OWI head Davis in January 1945. "Apparently it is the German policy to exterminate the Jews still alive in the face of Allied advances." Pehle received a noncommittal reply from Deputy Director Wallace Carroll: "Your suggestions will be carefully considered in preparing our German output." Pehle to Davis, 1/6/45; Carroll to Pehle, 1/12/45, WRB Papers, Box 33, FDRL.

police shooting 30 or 40 Jewish men, women, and children before graves they had dug themselves. Questioned by American soldiers about his reaction, the German's response was, as Denny described it: "He had not been shocked by that terrible scene. He had not been curious as to why they were being shot, nor wondered about the rightness of it, nor whether it violated humanity. His only regret was that these shootings were 'wasteful of manpower.'"[3]

That same month, the *Times*' William Lawrence traveled to Lodz, just before he was finally allowed to leave Moscow for his next assignment. There, 1,000 to 3,000 Polish political prisoners had just been murdered, the "climax of five and a half years of German occupation," he wrote in a page five story, "during which, it is estimated, 250,000 Jews were sent to slavery and probably death and 150,000 other Poles were sent as forced laborers to Germany." Lawrence wrote that along with eyewitness accounts, he had also "visually confirmed" much of the story. "All who see [evidence of atrocities] must be convinced that the enemy the United Nations are fighting knows no limits in brutal, savage destruction." Only 877 of Lodz's 250,000 Jews remained, he noted, 70,000 dead from starvation and tuberculosis, the remaining shipped to their deaths in Maidanek and Oswiecim.[4]

Lawrence never wrote about the liberation of Oswiecim, or Auschwitz, which occurred just a few days before he visited Lodz, although he knew of it. On January 27, the Russians arrived at the camp, where they found fewer than 2,000 survivors, almost all of them Jews. Most of the 58,000 Auschwitz inmates who had survived starvation, medical experimentation, disease, beatings, random executions, and the gas chambers, had been dragged, like Elsbet Gerst, to Germany with their escaping guards. Several thousand more died between the time the Germans fled and the Russians arrived. Having received word of Auschwitz's liberation, Lawrence asked the Polish Press Agency for information about it. In addition, the American Embassy informed him that about 4,000 prisoners were liberated, and that the Polish provisional government had sent "flour, fats, meal, soap and medicine" to the survivors.[5] But Lawrence apparently never did anything with the information. The only *Times* story to appear on the liberation of Auschwitz – whose detailed operations had been reported in two inside stories the previous summer and in a front-page story in November – was a two-paragraph brief from UP based on a *Pravda* report.[6]

Cyrus Sulzberger, who replaced Lawrence in February,[ii] also took an interest in Lodz. Sulzberger wrote a feature story about the "perfect ghetto" in Litzmannstadt (the German name for Lodz), which had a "Jewish fuehrer," 72-year-old Chaim Rumkowski. "His job was to assist the Gestapo in separating the sheep from the goats in the Nazis' sadistic slaughter process," Sulzberger wrote. The story described how the Germans provided lists of Jews for transport to what were called "special labor centers," but what everyone knew meant slaughter. When the name of Rumkowski's brother appeared on the list and the Germans refused to remove it, the ghetto leader asked to accompany him. "So Rumkowki left the 'perfect ghetto,'" the page four story concluded, "and reported for 'special labor' with his brother."[7]

As journalists haphazardly assembled the story of the Jews' fate in Eastern Europe from the people and places they encountered, Jewish relief organizations more systematically tallied the losses. In February, the WJC released a survey of 38 liberated Russian and Polish cities and found less than 1% of the Jews who had once lived there remained. There were just 1,878 Jews in Lublin, Vilna, Bialystock, and Kovno, which once had more than 200,000 Jews combined. "In some towns, as in Dvinsk, not a single Jew was found by the returning Soviet armies," according to the congress. The *Times* story appeared on page five.[8]

In the West, American correspondents accompanying the British or American armies also found few Jews. The American Jewish Joint Distribution Committee (JDC) estimated that only 1 million to 1.5 million of Europe's 6 million Jews were left on the continent, as the *Times* reported in February, including 20,000 out of 50,000 in Italy, 10,000 to 15,000 out of 140,000 in the Netherlands, and almost none of Germany's 600,000 Jews. In an earlier *Times* story, the JDC estimated that 10,000 French Jews had been shot or died in concentration camps; 127,000 had been deported, most of whom died in Polish extermination camps; 50,000 had immigrated legally or illegally; and some had gone into hiding. The *Times* Paris bureau, which was quickly reassembled after American troops liberated the city in August 1944, reported on the fate of some of those Jews. In September, Raymond Daniell, who had left London to follow the

[ii] Sulzberger had already been named chief foreign correspondent, but reluctantly agreed to return to Russia temporarily because he was the only *Times* reporter with the appropriate visa.

invasion and watch the Americans' progress in France, visited the city's Jewish quarter. About 100,000 Jews had once lived there and 90% of them had been deported, he wrote in a first-person story that described the Jews' deprivations. The *Times*, however, continued to absolve the French of anti-Semitic actions, placing all blame squarely on the Germans. David Anderson of the London bureau explained the Jews suffered a worse fate in France than their brethren in Belgium and the Netherlands because Vichy leader Petain "habitually left the handling of Jewish affairs to the Germans, who were likely to be ruthless." But Anderson also struck a note of reassurance: "Thoughtful Jews believe that some accounts of their life here [in Paris] during the occupation have been too pessimistic."[9]

It probably would have been impossible to describe any version of the Jews' wartime experiences as "too pessimistic" after visiting Struthof. The *Times*' Milton Bracker went there in early January 1945, after the American Seventh Army discovered a "German concentration camp" in Alsace. The *Times* ran five photographs of Struthof's guard posts, gas generator, and cremation victims' ashes and clothes. After the army studied camp records and concluded 15,000 of the 50,000 to 60,000 people in camp were killed, the *Times* ran a follow-up story. Bracker attested to the "gas-producing mechanism," "hooks" to hang men by their wrists, a dissecting table, and a fully equipped crematorium. "But that is perhaps the most incredible horror of this aspect of Hitler-outrages," he wrote, using words many journalists would echo in coming months. They are "too great to be believed even in the face of physical evidence."[10]

At Struthof, as at Maidanek and Vught, a transit camp the *Times* had written about in November, American journalists arrived after most inmates had been killed and the few survivors had been evacuated to camps in Germany. But by April, the Allies were in Germany; the Nazis had nowhere to go, and no time to destroy the camps or all their inhabitants. So as Allied soldiers penetrated deeper into the Reich, they overran relatively intact labor and concentration camps. In April, stories about what they found, first at Ohrdruf, then at Nordhausen, Langenstein, and climactically, at Buchenwald, Belsen, and Dachau, began to appear. What the soldiers found was: "ashes and arms and legs" near a "crude woodland crematory" at Ohrdruf; "3,000 living skeletons and 2,700 unburied bodies" at Nordhausen; inmates with "claylike pallor" and "bloodless bodies" dying at a rate of 20 a day at Langenstein; and "typhus, typhoid, tuberculosis, nakedness, starvation" at Belsen. What they did not find, at least according to the *Times* stories, were Jews. Ohrdruf's inmates were "European captives," and Nordhausen's were "Allied and political prisoners." Belsen held "persons . . . interned for political or 'criminal offenses,'" whereas Langenstein had "Polish, Russian, French, Belgian, Netherland and Czechoslovak inhabitants." In these initial liberation stories, Jews were mentioned only once. Several paragraphs into the story on Ohrdruf, the *Times* reported that those killed included "Poles, Czechs, Russians, Belgians, Frenchmen, German Jews and German political prisoners."[11]

Those first few liberation stories were typical of the *Times*' coverage, and that of the American press in general. (On this, more than any other story, American newspapers' reporting was strikingly similar; journalists reported the same events at the same time and cooperated to such a degree that the same people and stories often popped up in different publications.[12]) Although the *Times* and other American newspapers acknowledged the full horror of German atrocities, the coverage of the liberation of the camps[iii] did not, contrary to some accounts, fully illuminate the systematic campaign to obliterate the Jews. For one thing, the placement of the stories, at least in the *Times*, did not seem equal to the magnitude of what had occurred.[13] During April and May 1945, as the German concentration camps were liberated, there were only two front-page stories about their liberation, plus two additional stories run side by side on prisoner-of-war camps, and one three-paragraph brief on Germans being forced to bury "slave laborers and political prisoners."[14] None of these was the lead or even off-lead story.[iv] (The *Herald Tribune* ran 11 front-page stories on the camps' liberation during that same period, including two off-lead stories.) Of course, there was plenty of other news to report: President Roosevelt died on April 12, followed by Mussolini and Hitler, and Allied forces captured city after city within Germany. That the *Times* still had not grasped the mind-shattering importance of "German atrocities," however, was apparent later in the year. When the *Times* tallied 25 memorable dates in 1945, the liberation of concentration camps did not figure among them.[15]

[iii] As Tony Kushner, *The Holocaust and the Liberal Imagination*, Oxford: Blackwell (1994), and Zelizer, *Remembering to Forget*, correctly point out, "liberation" is a common and convenient way to describe the Allied troops' arrival at German concentration camps, but it conveys a celebratory moment that scarcely does justice to the experience.

[iv] The *Times* more regularly placed stories about Japanese atrocities on the front page. See 2/15/45, 8/6/45, 8/31/45, 9/1/45, 9/2/45, 9/6/45.

Along with the relatively restrained coverage, the fact that camp inmates were identified by their nationality or as political prisoners also tended to obscure the Jewish tragedy. Indeed, most of the inmates were not Jews. German camps held a higher proportion of political prisoners, common criminals, and forced workers than the camps in the East. In addition, fewer Jews survived to liberation. Still, Jews made up a significant portion of those in the German camps, at least 10% according to the best estimates, and a much higher percentage at some camps.[16] Plus, some journalists knew why there were so few Jews, and yet failed to integrate that information into their stories. Finally, even when Jews were mentioned, the reason they were imprisoned and murdered – because they were Jews – was not. So the nascent notion of genocide, of an attempt to destroy an entire religious, ethnic, or racial group, in this case a Jewish genocide, did not take hold.

Consider the *Times*' coverage of the liberation of Buchenwald, which received more attention than that of any other camp. Four days after the Eightieth Infantry Division reached the camp, the *Times* printed a small AP item announcing that the "young Americans" had "brought fresh air, hope and liberty to 21,000 miserable, sick and ragged men."[17] The same day the AP reporter toured the camp, the *Times*' own correspondent, Gene Currivan, arrived as German civilians from nearby Weimar viewed "the horror, brutality and human indecency." Currivan's story, which focused on the German civilians' reactions to the horrors, appeared the next day on the front page. "Nazi Death Factory Shocks Germans on Forced Tour," the headline read.

Tens of thousands of Jews had passed through Buchenwald, many of whom died there. But by the time of the last roll call, only 8,000 of the camp's 81,000 inmates were Jews, and at liberation, the number was even smaller because many Jews had been evacuated. Currivan did not highlight the Jews' history or presence in the camp. On the *Times* front page, camp inhabitants were "20,000 non-descript prisoners." Inside, they were variously described by profession (doctors, professors, scientists, statesmen, army officers, diplomats), by geographic origin (from all over Europe and Asia), or by position in the camp (slaves). Currivan mentioned Jews just twice in a 37-paragraph story that filled almost an entire inside page, exclusive of advertisements. In paragraph 21, Currivan quoted a 9-year-old Hungarian Jewish boy, Andor Gutman, who had been injected with typhus as part of an experiment. He said he had been in Buchenwald for 3 years. "'My father was killed and my mother was burned to death,'" the boy said "without any emotion." (The *Herald Tribune*'s front-page Buchenwald stories noted that most of the children in the camp were Jews, although it too did not mention Jews until many paragraphs into the story.[18]) In paragraphs 31, 32, and 33, Currivan recounted the 30,000 Jews who, when they could no longer work, had been sent from Buchenwald to Auschwitz to be killed.[19]

The next day, a *Times* editorial, "Buchenwald," described the camp as a "factory for death of political as well as military prisoners." The *Times* week in review item also said nothing about Jews. Nor did another item a week later, which described "Nazi Prison Camps" as holding "allied prisoners, internees and deported citizens," and "thousands of twisted and mutilated prisoners – political and military." The *Times* ran many follow-up stories on Buchenwald, particularly as military leaders, politicians, and journalists toured the camp at General Eisenhower's invitation. All the stories appeared inside, even one by Julius Ochs Adler, *Times* vice president and general manager and Iphigene's cousin, who represented the *Times* among a group of editors and publishers. His story, "Buchenwald Worse Than Battlefield," appeared on page six.[20] (Other newspapers, including the *Herald Tribune*, *St. Louis Post Dispatch*, and *Miami Herald*, featured the stories on the front.[21])

The coverage of the liberation of Dachau was similar. On May 1, the *Times* ran an AP story at the bottom of the front page that focused on "the furious battle" between "outraged American troops" and Dachau's "brutal garrison." The victorious divisions freed "32,000 tortured inmates." As in previous stories, those inmates were identified solely by nationality: "Frenchmen and Russians" grabbed weapons dropped by slain guards; "a Czech and a Pole working in the engine room" slew two Germans; and a nearby train was loaded with the bodies of "mostly Poles," who had starved to death trapped inside the cars. (Those "mostly Poles" were in fact all Jews who had been shipped to Dachau from Buchenwald in a last-ditch effort to complete the Final Solution.) The story never mentioned the Jews that made up about 10 percent of the camp's inmates, nor did a week in review item that followed.[22] That same day, the Associated Press provided a story that stated that 4,000 European Jews had been killed in a concentration camp near Landsberg and that almost all the survivors were Jews. The *Times* chose not to use it.[23]

Perhaps most telling was the *Times*' coverage of the liberation of Bergen-Belsen, whose name "has come to symbolize the horrors of the Holocaust" and whose photographic images "fixed indelibly on the Western consciousness the grim reality of the Final Solution."[24] Although liberated shortly after Buchenwald and weeks before Dachau, Belsen was never featured on the *Times* front page, perhaps because British, not American troops, were the liberators. As CBS's Edward R. Murrow, who had been set to go to Belsen, told a U.S. Army media coordinator: "'I am an American reporter for the American public, and I cannot go north to talk about the British occupying a camp. So I'll have to join the American correspondents [in Buchenwald].'"[25] Belsen's liberation also lacked a "hook" to elevate it to the front page, such as the reaction of ordinary Germans that was the focus of the Buchenwald front-page story, or the "furious battle" that was the centerpiece of the Dachau story.

Even more striking, the *Times*' five inside stories at the time of Belsen's liberation mentioned Jews only once, even though nearly 40,000 of its 55,000 surviving inmates were Jews, many of whom had lived through death marches from the East. The *Times* referred to "prisoners" or "the dead and the living dead" in stories about British troops' initial decision to skirt the camp because of fears of typhus, and their eventual entry and burial of thousands of bodies. The only story to mention Jews consisted of four paragraphs based on an interview with "a group of women who had been held in Belsen." (The women themselves were never identified as Jews, although 17,000 Jewish women were in Belsen when it was liberated.) Nor did the three photographs the *Times* published of Belsen – women and children in a crude hut, two women washing with water from a drain, and S.S. women carrying bodies to a mass grave – identify the inmates or the dead as Jews.[26] In fact, none of the captions for the 15 camp photographs that the *Times* ran in April mentioned Jews.[v]

Although the lack of any reference to Jews in the *Times*' Belsen stories may have been the most glaring omission, their absence in stories

[v] Like most newspapers, the *Times* turned to visual images to help convey the atrocities in a way that words could not. The photographs the *Times* chose to publish from those made available to the press by the U.S. and British military tended to be more circumspect than those used by other publications.

about Buchenwald and Dachau was also more a matter of emphasis than ignorance. (The JTA was able to find enough surviving Jews in both Buchenwald and Dachau to build stories around their experiences.[27]) The *Times*' Currivan knew that 30,000 Jews had been sent from Buchenwald to their deaths in Auschwitz; he said so in the story's penultimate paragraphs. He also knew that what had happened to Buchenwald's Jews was not an anomaly. The killing in the German prisons was "small-scale murder compared to what happened in Poland," Currivan wrote deep in a April 1 *Times* magazine piece on freed slave laborers. In those "concentration" camps, "all Jews were killed as soon as they arrived," he explained. "The customary procedure was to take Jews directly through to the lethal gas chambers and from there their bodies were reduced to dust at the crematory."

The American Congressmen, Army chiefs, and top editors and publishers who toured Buchenwald and Dachau shortly after they were liberated also realized why they found so few Jews. In a statement urging a strong policy on war criminals, the 18 editors and publishers who toured the camps, including the *Times*' Adler, declared: "By these tortures most of the Jews in prison camps had already been destroyed." In another news story, Gideon Seymour, executive editor of the *Minneapolis Star Journal*, was quoted: "'They just didn't waste any time on the Jews.... They put them to death.'" Another *Times* story indicated that Buchenwald prisoners told Sidney Silverman and another member of the British Parliament of "an even worse place" than their current camp, "Oswiecim in upper Silesia where 3,500,000 people were put to death."[28] In fact, the British delegation reported that "one of the statements made to us most frequently by prisoners" was that conditions in Eastern European camps were far worse.[29] Oswiecim was "'the most horrible of all,'" a one-paragraph brief quoted Anita Lasker, the niece of a former world chess champion who was forced to play in the camp's band.[30] A similar undercurrent ran through many liberation stories: what happened here was awful, beyond all imagining, but what occurred in the East, in Auschwitz, was worse.

Yet, the repeated refrain did not prompt a full-fledged examination of what happened at Auschwitz or other extermination centers. In April and May 1945, only two stories appeared in the *Times* about Auschwitz. The *Times* carried an AP story on page six that said 5 million Jews were killed at Oswiecim and attributed the information to the former president of the Hungarian Independent Democratic Party. Almost 1 month later, on the same day that the war in Europe officially ended, a *Times* story by Cyrus Sulzberger in Moscow put the Oswiecim death toll at 4 million. "The Germans thus accomplished with scientific efficiency the greatest incidence of mass murder in recorded history," he wrote in a page 12 story based on a report from the Soviet Union's Extraordinary State Commission investigating war crimes. (The *Herald Tribune* put the story on the front page and referred inside to the earlier accusation that 5 millions Jews had been killed there.) The *Times* story identified the victims exclusively by nationality.[31]

It has been suggested that American journalists' lack of familiarity with Auschwitz accounted for this failure to do more than a few perfunctory stories. But someone at the AP knew enough about Auschwitz to correct the figure of 5 million murdered Jews in its story. As soon as the lead provided that number, a lengthy paragraph in brackets noted differing numbers in a Polish Ministry of Information report and one from the International Church movement (the Voght report), which put the number of Jews killed in Oswiecim and Birkenau at the more accurate 1.7 million.

If the *Times*' liberation stories did not directly address why so few Jews were found alive in the camps, they were even more oblique about why so many Jews had been put there to begin with. The overwhelming impression was that those imprisoned in concentration camps had in some way or other challenged the Nazi regime. They were either "political prisoners" – Communists or others who had resisted Nazism – or "military prisoners," Allied combatants, or partisans. Acknowledging the presence of Jews, particularly Jewish children, threatened to disrupt the prevailing understanding. Instead, "Jew" became a variant of "political prisoner." The statement issued by the American editors and publishers who toured the camps is a prime example. The journalists described the inmates as "political prisoners, slave laborers and civilians of many nationalities," whose "only crime was that they disagreed or were suspected of disagreeing with the Nazi philosophy." The statement did mention the Jews as among "the most cruelly treated" in the camps. The next sentence quickly reasserted parity among the sufferers: "To the basic policy of brutality toward political prisoners there were, however, no significant exceptions." In that way, the unique tragedy of the Jews, and the emerging notion of genocide, were both obscured – a fact Jewish organizations at the time recognized. At a conference at the end of May called to help Polish Jewry, Israel Goldstein, president of the Zionist Organization of America, lamented: "'The world is not sufficiently aware that the victims of German atrocities were mostly Jews.'"[32]

There are many possible reasons why journalists took this tack, and few contemporaneous documents to help explain it. (Almost no memos or cables were found from this period in the *Times* archives.) Although the liberation period has provoked more commentary about the press coverage than any other aspect of the Holocaust, very little of it has addressed the invisibility of Jewish victims.[33] Journalists who had just visited the camps understandably focused on the overwhelming horror of what they witnessed and (less understandably) on their shock at discovering it.[34] Confronted with unprecedented atrocities and their own trauma, journalists were not inclined to reflect on whether their coverage adequately captured the nature of the victims and the reason for their demise. Some speculation is therefore required to explain why the German attempt to annihilate the Jews figured so minimally in liberation stories.

The most obvious explanation is that journalists based their accounts largely on information supplied by the Allied governments. Arriving at the camps often right behind the troops, reporters naturally would have turned to the military authorities to supply what seemed to be basic information, such as how many prisoners were in the camp and why they were there. For their part, government officials would have continued the wartime practice of universalizing the victims. Although the ostensible reasons for that practice had evaporated – the government no longer had to worry about pressure for rescue or the alienating effect of a war to save the Jews – the public information apparatus would not have been able to switch gears so quickly, even had it wanted to, and there is some indication that it did not want to. Much of the information about the camps came from military authorities who, throughout the war had resisted suggestions that they help European Jews,[35] and, if anything, had been more reluctant to publicize the plight of the Jews than their civilian counterparts. Recall *Yank Magazine*'s insistence that the WRB's Auschwitz reports have a "less Semitic" angle.[vi] At the end of March 1945, WRB and War Department representatives met to discuss the issuance of a joint Allied

[vi] When *Yank* finally published a story about German atrocities on May 18, 1945, it focused on American POWs and mentioned the extermination centers without explaining that their primary victims were Jews. Bendersky, *The "Jewish Threat"*, 346.

statement that promised "special consideration" for Germans who assisted "prisoners of war, civilian internees and stateless persons required to do labor for the German Reich." During the discussion at the Pentagon, one colonel objected to adding Jews to the statement. According to a WRB representative who was present, the colonel said "adding Jews would only weaken the statement" and "serve no useful purpose at all" because Jews were already in "a position to get a great deal of help from people on the scene." Other officials agreed that the word "Jew" should not be used in the statement, and the WRB settled for "persons detained by reasons of race, religion or political belief."[36]

Military officials most likely provided descriptions of the inmates that identified them by nationality, as political or military prisoners, or as slave laborers. At least some of the information must have appeared in press releases, or in other printed form, because at times the language used in disparate publications was not just similar, but identical. For example, the *Times* reported that those killed in Ohrdruf included "Poles, Czechs, Russians, Belgians, Frenchmen, German Jews and German political prisoners." The caption of a military photographer's pictures taken at Ohrdruf read: "'The 4,000 Ohrdruf victims are said to include Poles, Czechs, Russians, Belgians, Frenchmen, German Jews and German political prisoners.'"[37]

Of course, journalists were not bound to use the information the government supplied. In fact, unlike their coverage of other atrocity stories, which was almost completely dependent on government or other authoritative sources, journalists writing about Buchenwald, Belsen, and Dachau could rely on their own first-hand observations and eyewitness interviews. But after largely accepting government information throughout the war, reporters were unlikely to contest or correct it in the waning days. Besides, as they readily attested, journalists were physically revolted, emotionally traumatized, and intellectually confounded by what they saw. When military officials told them who was in the camps and why, they readily accepted and printed the information. They would take surety wherever they could get it.

In their search for "authoritative" sources, journalists may also have relied on the liberated prisoners for information. The ones who were well enough often took dignitaries and the press on tours of the camps. "Inevitably the biases of the guides entered into such presentations," explains Robert Abzug in his study of Americans' role in the camps' liberation, "especially in regard to rivalries between national groups and an endemic disdain for fellow prisoners who were Jews or Gypsies."[38] As the worst treated, and therefore, worst off group in the camps (along with Gypsies), the Jews tended to be the least capable of conducting such tours and establishing their presence.

The notion that the camps held political and military prisoners and slave laborers had an appeal apart from the availability of the sources offering it. It introduced a modicum of rationality into scenes so ghastly that they defied reason. "[I]t is the damndest, craziest, most insane thing that has ever happened to the world," one correspondent said, as related by an editor who had toured the camps. "You think you are awakening from a nightmare and then realize that you have not been sleeping. That what you saw actually happened – and is happening."[39] In this "maze of madness," the idea that concentration camps contained enemies of the regime supplied a rational explanation for the camps' existence, if not their contemptible incarnation. Locking up those who challenged a state's authority and threatened its existence was logical, if horrible. Forcing the citizens of conquered nations to replenish a depleted labor stock was sensible, if perverse. But murdering millions of people because they were Jews, and expending desperately needed resources to do it, was beyond comprehension. As Saul Friedlander suggests: "[T]he exterminations perpetrated by the Nazis are not an 'inversion of all values' (as would be the case if human beings were worked to death or killed for a very specific political aim), but represent an amorality beyond all categories of evil."[40] Journalists may not have been ready to understand this type of amorality.

The narrative mode that journalists adopted in the face of such horror also made them less likely to challenge the official story. As Barbie Zelizer persuasively argues in *Remembering to Forget: Holocaust Memory Through the Camera's Eye*, the journalistic approach that she calls bearing witness "undermined much of the interpretive work by which coverage is often fashioned." Because what they saw was too horrible to be believed, as they repeatedly wrote, reporters concentrated on persuading their audience of the truth of their accounts. That meant writing first-person, eyewitness stories that, according to Zelizer, "provided terse blow-by-blow chronicles that wandered little from the most obvious and concrete details of the scene at hand." The stories often took the form of a tour of the camps, "a topography of atrocity," describing the crematorium here, the stack of bodies there. "It had gallows, torture rooms, dissection rooms, modern crematoria, laboratories where fiendish experiments were made on living human beings and its sections where people were systematically starved to death," the *Times*' Gene Currivan wrote of Buchenwald. The strategy of bearing witness came at a cost. "In pitching the story so closely to the details of what they were seeing, many journalists did not regain sight of the larger picture," Zelizer explains. Among aspects of the larger picture that journalists overlooked – Jewish victimization and Jewish genocide.[41]

Even if they had had the impetus, many journalists covering the camps' liberation probably could not have grasped the larger picture. They arrived at the camps with the armies they were assigned to cover and had little, if any, understanding of what had happened to the Jews in the preceding 6 years. "Never a whisper about the existence of such a charnel house, of such awful treatment by one class of human beings of another, had reached me in all the years of war," British reporter Edwin Tetlow wrote of Bergen-Belsen.[42] Because the extermination of the Jews had never been considered an important enough story to assign someone to cover it regularly at the *Times* or most other papers, the journalists reporting the liberation of the camps were not the same ones who had written earlier stories. Neither Daniel Brigham of the Berne bureau, who wrote two detailed accounts of Auschwitz in the summer of 1944, nor John Crider of the DC bureau, who wrote about the WRB's report on Auschwitz in the fall of 1944, for example, covered the liberation of the camps.[vii] Reporters' newspapers may have published stories about the extermination of the Jews, but the correspondents covering the liberation had not written them (or apparently read them). Thus, many reporters did not have sufficient background to differentiate among political prisoners incarcerated as a threat to the Nazi regime, laborers forced to slave in German factories, and Jews imprisoned and murdered for being Jews.

Other journalists had the background, but of an outdated variety. A few of the old Berlin hands, including the AP's Louis Lochner and the *Chicago Tribune*'s Sigrid Schultz, returned to Europe to cover the victorious Allies' march through Germany. When they left Germany in 1941, concentration

[vii] Brigham did write about Terezin, or Theresiedstadt, one of the last places to be liberated. In June, he spent 2 days and nights in Terezin, whose remaining occupants had been saved at the last minute by the Russian advance. Brigham described jumping into an empty box car, which had never made its last trip taking 3,000 Jews to "the crematories in Oswiecim, Poland." 6/12/45, 6.

camps were largely for those who challenged the Nazi regime, although Jews, homosexuals, and others also passed through. Dachau was "Germany's most dreaded extermination camp," as the lead of the AP story on its liberation put it, and Buchenwald was "second only to . . . Dachau . . . as the world's worst atrocity center," as Currivan wrote in his liberation story. In the intervening years, the extermination centers of Treblinka and Auschwitz, where millions were deliberately and immediately murdered, eclipsed "concentration camps," such as Dachau and Buchenwald, where prisoners were worked and starved to death, but only occasionally killed outright. Yet, many reporters made the same mistake that the AP and Currivan did; perhaps they relied on the expertise of the former Berlin correspondents, or perhaps the concentration camp stories published in the 1930s made more of an impression than the inconspicuous and infrequent extermination camp stories published during the war.[viii]

Some of these returning journalists may have had another, possibly subconscious motivation. Many of those who had lived and worked in Germany, such as the AP's Lochner, had long argued that the Nazis did not represent the entirety of the German people. In the wake of Belsen and Buchenwald, those arguments were more necessary and far harder to make. Referring to concentration camp inmates as political prisoners made it easier to distinguish between the Nazis, the regime that locked people up in such horrible camps, and the German people, who as political prisoners were among those incarcerated. When the *Herald Tribune* refused to use what Editor Geoffrey Parsons, Jr., described as Lochner's series on "what his old German friend told him of conditions inside Germany," Lochner responded that he was "merely reporting what a responsible German claimed." He insisted that he had never "sympathized with the Nazis or militarists of any stripe," but he did admit to sympathy for the German people. "As to the charge that I make a distinction between the Nazis and the German people, or certain sections of them, I plead guilty now as always," he said. He offered the example of witnessing 40 "living skeletons" emerge from a Gestapo prison, including Dutch, Belgians, Russians, Poles, and two Germans. "I confess to having been sorry also for those two

[viii] The *Herald Tribune*'s Marguerite Higgins, who visited both Buchenwald and Dachau, did not make that mistake. She described Buchenwald as "the vilest of the various prisons yet liberated by the western Allied armies." Dachau was the "first and largest of the Nazi concentration camps." 4/18/45, 1, 4/21/45, 1.

German victims of Nazi cruelty and injustice. I think Jesus would also have been sorry for them."[43]

The journalistic tendency to overlook the Jews during the liberation of the camps thus resulted in large part from the terrible, chaotic conditions in which reporters found themselves. Unaware of the Jews' fate, or operating on outdated assumptions, overwhelmed by the appalling circumstances and under pressure to construct meaningful narratives from the insanity, they did not look past the official story. But even some journalists who did – who tried to grapple with the catastrophe's profound philosophical and moral dimensions – were strangely mute on the subject of the Jews. Take *Times*' roving correspondent Harold Denny. He had interviewed German soldiers who in unapologetic tones described their participation in the mass murder of Jews. He had visited Buchenwald and described the "calculated, mechanized murder" reserved for "truckloads of Jews." He even wrote a *Times* magazine article titled "'The World Must Not Forget,'" in which he suggested that genocide (although he did not use that term) shattered Western civilization's understanding of itself. Yet, when it came to identifying the targets of this cruel policy, Denny grew vague. Germany's motives were "the extermination of races which Hitlerian 'philosophy' classified as inferior and the enfeeblement of Germany's neighboring peoples."[44] Inferior races, neighboring peoples, not Jews.

In New York newsrooms far removed from the carnage, journalists who did not have to bear witness or churn out daily copy exhibited the same obliqueness in articles and editorials. In January 1945, a *Times* editorial assessing "Twelve Years of Hitler," referred to Jews once – not in elucidating "the millions of lives which he destroyed, not only in his military campaigns but in deliberate massacres, extended to the unborn, in order to exterminate or forever cripple the 'inferior' races in his path." Rather, the one reference to Jews came in presenting Hitler's claim that it was "all the fault of the 'international Jews and the Versailles Treaty.'" After Hitler's suicide, the *Times* again evaluated his impact in a week in review item that described the "civilian toll" – millions who died of disease and starvation, or were murdered in concentration and death camps – without referring to Jews. Nor were Jews mentioned in "A Chronology of the War in Europe: 100 Outstanding Dates," which appeared that same day. When Himmler chose the same fate as Hitler a month later, a sidebar to the main story credited him with conceiving of the "diabolical instruments of lethal chambers and mass shootings responsible for the deaths of millions of

Jews." Yet neither the main story, nor an editorial, "Himmler," mentioned Jews. In recounting his crimes, the *Times* editorial referred to "the efficient butchering of hundreds of thousands of people in concentration camps" and ordering "the massacre at Lidice."[45]

The *Times*, both deliberately and through happenstance, continued to bury the story of the Jewish genocide. The journalistic framework, which had been constructed as soon as the first Jews were persecuted in Germany, tended to perpetuate itself. Having never considered the Jews' persecution important enough to require its own reporter (and mistrusting the ones who had assigned themselves or who had fallen into the task), the *Times* did not have anyone with the requisite knowledge to send to the camps. Having rarely considered the Jews' persecution important enough to warrant front-page display, the *Times* had not laid the groundwork for regular war correspondents to understand what they were seeing. Having routinely accepted, if not encouraged, the government's practice of universalizing the victims of German atrocities, the *Times* could not have expected anything different from Belsen's and Buchenwald's new commandants.

Even more important, the institutional mind-set that initially conceived of the Jews as just one among many suffering peoples was still in place. The journalistic refrain from the concentration camps – the inmates included Poles, Russians, Czechs, French, Belgians, representatives of 22 nationalities, as well as German political prisoners – could have been lifted from *New York Times* editorials throughout the war. In September 1942, the *Times* opined that "the Jewish people stood in the front of the firing line," but they were soon followed by "an unnumbered multitude of other Germans," as well as Austrians, Czechs, Poles, and so on. In December 1942, a *Times* editorial described the European Jews as "The First to Suffer" on a long list, "which has since included people of other faiths and of many races – Czechs, Poles, Norwegians, Netherlanders, Belgians." In August 1943, the Jews again "came first," but were not alone "in this awful tabulation" of German atrocities. In June 1945, after the camps had been liberated and the *Times* acknowledged that 5 million Jews had been exterminated, the Jews were still the first to suffer. "Before the reign of the devil ended in Europe, the Germans had made it plain that there was no minority they would not exterminate if it impeded their plans," the *Times* opined. Then the *Times* explained one more time: "People of the Jewish faith came first but they were not to be the last."[46]

There was one final reason that the end-of-the-war press coverage did not mark a breakthrough in understanding what had happened to the Jews. The *Times*' coverage was almost completely devoid of individual Jewish survivors and their stories. In the articles that immediately followed the camps' liberation, the dead were presented as "dumps of unburied corpses in vast heaps" and the living as an undifferentiated, barely human mass. They were "human skeletons who had lost all likeness to anything human"; "human wrecks," "living skeletons," "wretched remnants," and "husks of men."[47] There were almost no quotes or comments from inmates that might have overcome the dehumanizing descriptions. As Tony Kushner argues in *The Holocaust and the Liberal Imagination* (p. 218), the emphasis on the crimes, not the victims, dovetailed with Allied postwar goals. "The objective of British and American governments in revealing the nature of the crimes of their enemy, had not been to focus on the victims of the Nazis (and especially not the Jews)," he writes, "but to emphasize the rightness of the war effort through the demonization of the German people."

In the dozens of *Times* liberation stories that appeared in April and May, only a handful of people were depicted as anything besides slaves, prisoners, or skeletons. When individuals were singled out, it was only to provide information about their experiences immediately prior to liberation, liberation itself, or general camp conditions. Pierro Gentil, a French political prisoner, described the liberation of a factory near Thekla, Germany. An Italian officer, who was not identified by name or any other identifying detail, told of his life as a slave laborer. One American POW, "a half-dead Polish Jew," and a "Dr. Rads, a Czechoslovak who worked in the hospital at Buchenwald," spoke to Julius Ochs Adler. Fayvel Grossman, a 43-year-old Jew from the Lodz ghetto, and Israel Kros, a 19-year-old from a little Lithuanian town, provided information about the hidden German factory in which they worked. Marcel Cadet, a 34-year-old Frenchman with an American wife, reconstructed the death march of 11,000 men from Buchenwald to the Czech border. In this, the Jews were no different than the non-Jews, whose individual stories were also ignored. Had reporters interviewed more inmates, including Jews, however, the story of the Jewish genocide might have emerged. The few Jews who were interviewed were clear on the reason for their imprisonment. Asked why he was in Buchenwald, an 8-year-old boy told the *Tribune*'s Marguerite Higgins, "I am Jewish."[48]

The extraordinary difficulties reporters had in conducting interviews partially explain why so few survivors were quoted. Journalists hesitated to approach inmates who were indeed "human wrecks" and "living skeletons," stinking from excrement and other filth, and suffering from any number of contagious diseases. In the middle of his Buchenwald story, Denny confessed, "I could not enter even for a moment any more barracks where men were rotting to death." People literally dropped dead as reporters watched. "As we went through the camp, we found dead persons every few yards," wrote the *Herald Tribune*'s Richard D. McMillan in his account of Belsen. "It was hard to tell sometimes, who was alive and who was dead. Some died as you looked."[49] A *Life* magazine photographer recalled one inmate who addressed him in German. "I couldn't understand what he said, and I shall never know, for he fell dead at my feet in the middle of his sentence." Other journalists reported vomiting or weeping, or peeking through their fingers like a child at a scary movie. Still others could not take it and demanded another assignment.[50]

Journalists' trepidation was understandable, perhaps even unavoidable.[ix] Normal journalistic practices, obtaining names and occupations, asking probing questions, did not apply. Tetlow of the Britsh newspaper, *Daily Mail*, recalled coming across a young girl sobbing uncontrollably in front of Belsen's gallows. "I stifled a professional urge to ask a question and, so wrung was I by pity for this child, that I did not even intrude by offering her banal words of consolation," he wrote.[51] Journalists' obsession with the immediate situation – what happened before, during, and after liberation – was also completely comprehensible. Staring into the abyss of Dachau, they wanted to know how the camp turned into a hell hole, not where the inmates came from, what their prewar lives were like, or even what had happened to them before they arrived there.

There were other avenues for reaching survivors, however. The WJC offered in a press release to make internees from Bergen-Belsen and other German concentration camps available to "relate their experience in the camp."[52] The release may have generated the *Times*' four-paragraph story

[ix] In his famous CBS broadcast from Buchenwald, Edward R. Murrow, however, included the names and occupations of several inmates. Chamberlin and Feldman, *Liberation of the Nazi Concentration Camps 1945*, 42–5.

on the group of women who survived Belsen and a longer one in the *Herald Tribune*,[53] but aside from the AP reporter who filed that brief story no other journalist seemed interested.

Even harder to explain is why the practice of ignoring survivors continued long after liberation. Throughout 1945, the *Times* covered the displaced persons (DP) camps that arose from the ruins of the concentration camps. Bergen-Belsen, which the British literally burned to the ground to prevent the spread of typhus, became the site of one of the largest DP camps. Most ex-slave laborers and former combatants returned to their homes within months of liberation, so the DP camps came to be inhabited primarily by Jews who had no home to which to return. Persecution and pogroms also drove Polish Jews over the border to the camps in Germany, which were administered by the British and American military. In the dozens of stories the *Times* published about the camps, especially after a controversy erupted over the American military's administration of them, almost no survivors were quoted.

At the end of August, for example, the *Times* did something it had never done before. At its own instigation, without a government report or an official statement to peg it to, the *Times* published a lengthy, front-page story about the condition of the Jews remaining in Europe. The story spread over two columns at the top of the front page and filled a full page (minus one ad) plus a quarter page inside. The main story, by Drew Middleton, explored the situation of Jews in Germany, the location of most of the DP camps. Different *Times* correspondents contributed reports on the Jews' status in Austria, Poland, Italy, and Spain, and in Germany outside the DP camps. Although the *Times* could not quite abandon its old ways – the story began "the Jews, the first of many minorities to be persecuted by fascism," and it tended to excuse faults in U.S. camp administration – the articles won praise from the usually critical Jewish press.[54]

In these six stories consisting of 131 paragraphs, only three survivors were quoted: Erich Zwilsky, a pharmacist whom the Russians appointed head of the Jewish hospital in Berlin; Ber Mark, a member of an organization of Polish Jews in the Soviet Union; and Rabbi Leopold Neuhaus, a special advisor to a military government detachment in Frankfort. The only reference to their wartime experience was to Neuhaus' "three years in the infamous concentration camp at Theresienstadt" and to Zwilsky's being allowed to remain in Berlin as "an essential practitioner." Nothing was said of Mark. Otherwise, all three men were quoted on prevailing camp conditions.[55]

The *Times*' lack of interest in survivor stories reflected the prevailing journalistic culture more than a particularized antipathy for the survivors' themselves.[x] Journalists gravitated toward official sources and official stories; officials made news, ordinary people did not. German officials, and then American and British ones, were subjects; the Jews were objects. If former prisoners had information no one else had, such as about conditions in individual factories or sites that the American military did not control, they were worth talking to. Otherwise, for the most part, they were not. These hierarchical notions also helped define the story. As the camps were liberated, the story was that the Germans murdered millions of people, not that millions of people had been murdered. So the thrust of the reporting was to document what the Germans had done, not to show to whom it had been done. In the postliberation period, the news changed but the reliance on officials held steady. The story became how the British and Americans would resolve the fate of the Jews stranded in DP camps. What the Jews thought, and certainly what had happened to them during the war, had little to do with that. So again there was no need to have Jews tell their stories.

As Zelizer argues, the anonymity, at least of the visual images, contributed to the public's understanding of the Nazis' transcendent evil. The German atrocities were presented and understood at the highest level of generality, that of evil run amok in the world.[56] But the mounds of corpses, the emaciated bodies, obscured more particularized stories, including that of the Jews, or any individual Jew. The liberation and postliberation coverage, instead of illuminating what went before, tended to blot it out. Millions were murdered, but who they were and how and why they died was almost completely lost. There was literally no *Times* story that followed a Jew from his or her prewar life, to a ghetto, and then to an extermination center, a death march, and a German concentration camp. Survivor testimony, as it is now commonly thought of, did not appear anywhere in the *New York Times* in 1945. So the American public may have grasped what atrocities meant, but not what an atrocity meant to one suffering person.

[x] It should be noted, however, that the *Times*' reporting of the Bataan death march in January 1944 did include extended narratives based on interviews with individual soldiers.

In August 1945, Arthur Sulzberger learned of one such story in Elsbet Midas Gerst's letter, which his extended family hoped the *Times* would find some way to use in the newspaper.

"You will be interested in this although I don't suppose there is any news value in it," Sulzberger said in the note he sent to magazine editor Markel along with the letter.

"This is quite a document but, unhappily, it is like a great many others that have come out of Europe," Markel replied, "and therefore I do not see what we can do with it."[57]

Neither, apparently, did the publisher. Gerst's story never appeared in the *Times*.

11

"Lessons from the Hitler Tragedy"

The Publisher and the Aftermath of War

When Arthur Sulzberger decided that Elsbet Midas Gerst's story did not have "news value," he had just returned from a tour of the "torture camps" in Germany, as he later put it. The concentration camps had been cleaned up since his wife's cousin and his business partner Julius Ochs Adler had been there in April. In August, there were no decomposing bodies or walking corpses, but the mass graves and crematoria ruins were still evident. A year later, Sulzberger returned to Germany and visited DP camps for both Jews and non-Jews. "I talked with these people whose past is filled with horror and whose future is filled with fear and doubt," he later said. "Their plight would move the hearts of men of stone."[1]

Seeing the camps and talking to DPs may have moved his heart, but those encounters did not alter his convictions. Arthur Sulzberger did not then, or ever, express regrets about the *Times*' coverage of what would come to be known as the Holocaust. He did not reconsider the philosophical stance that led him and his paper to downplay the extermination of the Jews. If anything, he came away from his postwar trips to Germany more convinced that he had been right and the organized Jewish community had been wrong.

At a synagogue in Chattanooga, founded by Iphigene's grandfather and supported by donations from her father, Sulzberger reaffirmed in an October 1946 speech the positions he had held during 6 years of Jewish persecution and 6 more years of Jewish annihilation. With a nod to his grandfather-in-law Isaac M. Wise ("founder of American Judaism") and his own "forebears" (warden and rabbi of Newport, Rhode Island's Hebrew Congregation), Sulzberger, on the occasion of the Mizpah Congregation's eightieth anniversary, evoked the tenets of Classical Reform Judaism. "I deplore the segregation of Jews, either on national or educational or any other than religious lines," he said. "Those of the

Jewish faith" should devote "the spiritual force that is their undiminished inheritance" to "securing freedom for every people everywhere."

Sulzberger acknowledged the suffering of the Jews in DP camps. Yet, they were "but a minor percentage of the total of displaced persons" and, thanks to the Zionists, received too much notice. "I take issue with the manner in which they have focused the attention of the world upon the question of the Jewish refugee," he said, "instead of using their great moral strength to plead the cause of all displaced persons." The Zionists also were to blame for much of European Jews' past and present problems. "It is my judgment that thousands now dead might be alive, and in Palestine as well, had there been through the past fifty years more emphasis upon George Washington's great conception [of religious tolerance] and less on statehood," Sulzberger declared. "By putting statehood first and refuge last the Zionists, in my judgment, have jeopardized both." They continued to do so by "the clamor for statehood." Those "unfortunate Jews of Europe's D.P. Camps" had become "helpless hostages for whom statehood has been made the only acceptable ransom." His distaste for Zionists as well as Zionism had not dissipated either. Sulzberger accused them of "coercive" economic pressure and "character assassination" to silence those who disagreed with them.[2]

Sulzberger's old antagonists reacted predictably to the speech, as he knew they would. "I stuck my neck out," Sulzberger commented in sending a copy to Hebrew University's Judah Magnes.[3] "You must be having a hard time defending me these days," he wrote to Bernard Richards, who was still on the *Times* payroll at a reduced $50 a month. Richards said he wanted to "deliver in person" his reaction to Sulzberger's speech in Chattanooga and another in New Orleans. "You may as well be prepared for the worst," Richards warned.[4]

As Sulzberger was beginning to realize, however, his real problem lay not with his enemies but with his former allies. Most American Jews, including confirmed anti-Zionists, had not had the same reaction to the Holocaust that he had.

At the beginning of 1945, the issue of Palestine threatened to continue to split the American Jewish community as it had throughout the war. Indeed, the fight seemed likely to reach a crescendo as Zionists and anti-Zionists contemplated the future of the European Jews who had managed to survive the conflagration. In February, Eliahu Dobkin, head of the Jewish Agency's immigration department, reeled off the grim statistics of "this holocaust of annihilation" in an interview with the *Times*' Julian Meltzer. Only 1.2 million European Jews had survived, Dobkin said, and most of them wanted to come to Palestine.[5] Zionists naturally wanted to ensure their immigration to help create a new state, but anti-Zionists had not resigned themselves to a Jewish homeland. They assumed the surviving Jews could return to their original homes, find some other place of refuge, or migrate to Palestine, but in small enough numbers to maintain the Arab majority.[6] "The most powerful and influential American groups hostile to Zionism are working as hard as they can and will continue to try to nullify our efforts," the Jewish Agency's Eliahu Elath observed during a mission to the United States.[7]

Arthur Sulzberger and his newspaper were among them. Instead of a Jewish homeland, Sulzberger, like his friend Judah Magnes, continued to advocate a binational state that would allow for greater immigration of DPs as long as the Jewish population did not overtake the Arab majority. In February 1945, the *Times* devoted almost its entire letters column to Magnes, who laid out a plan for a binational regime of Jews and Arabs.[8] Three weeks later, Anne O'Hare McCormick's "Abroad" column hailed an "Arab compromise" proposed by the foreign ministers of Arab states meeting in Cairo, similar to the Magnes proposal. It would allow 300,000 more Jews to immigrate to Palestine, and thus bring them to "parity" with the Moslem population.[9] McCormick had already explored the prospects for postwar Palestine in eight columns in January that Elath considered "rather unfriendly." (*The Jewish Morning Journal*, however, said the columns showed a "keen understanding of the Jewish problem and of Palestine.") Elath believed McCormick, whom he had met when she was in Palestine, had been "influenced by her talks with highly placed British officials" and "American representatives in the Middle East." Plus, Elath detected a "Christian undertone" which he believed made it "hard for her [as a devout Catholic] to accept the possibility of a Jewish state being set up in Palestine."[10]

Elath's June meeting with the *Times*' top editors, as well as Arthur Sulzberger, did not allay his concerns. During the first UN conference in San Francisco, McCormick arranged for Elath to lunch with her, Edwin James, Charles Merz, Lester Markel, and Sulzberger. During the lunch, Sulzberger, who often cited "'reliable information'" he had received from British sources, made clear where he and his newspaper stood. Elath noted that the editors "take the convenient course of agreeing with their boss on the question of Zionism and Palestine." Editorial Page Editor Merz in particular "went to great lengths to support Sulzberger's anti-Zionist views." (Even Felix Frankfurter thought Merz, whom he knew from their days at the *New Republic*, went too far, telling him that "you ought not to be victimized by Arthur Sulzberger's foolishness" on the subject of Zionism.[11]) Only Sunday Editor Markel defended lifting restrictions on Jewish immigration to Palestine. Elath talked to the Zionist Organization of America's Louis Lipsky about it later. "Lipsky feels that we have little chance of altering Sulzberger's anti-Zionist views because his mind is closed on the subject. Nevertheless, he urged me to keep up my contact with the paper's staff, especially with Markel."[12]

For his part, Sulzberger fretted over how to cover Palestine in the *Times* news columns. At first, he wanted Joseph Levy to do it; his nephew, the *Times* new chief foreign correspondent, did not. "Quite frankly, I feel that despite Joe's immense knowledge of the Middle East it would still be a good idea to keep him out of here – in Turkey – for the moment," Cyrus Sulzberger wrote Managing Editor James in January 1945 from Cairo where he was about to cover the trial of two Jews accused of killing the British resident minister in the Middle East. Cyrus repeated the long-standing complaints that Levy was "all too mixed in intrigue" and didn't "produce enough copy." Then he added: "Because the Palestine question is bound to boil up I think the New York Times would be in a better position having a non-Jewish reporter covering it no matter how objective a Jewish reporter might be."[13] He wanted Levy to stay in Turkey.

So did the British. Reminding Arthur Sulzberger of Levy's previous problems, Harold Butler of the British Embassy in Washington, DC, suggested that "these difficulties would be likely to recur" should Levy return to Cairo. Butler acknowledged that with the war over "the decision rests entirely in your hands"; still, he said, "we all attach a good deal of importance, as I am sure you will appreciate, to the maintenance of good relations."[14] Levy's recurring illness disarmed the issue when doctors ordered him to return to the States.[15] But Sulzberger was still not happy about the British response, which he suspected was more personal than political. In addition, unlike his nephew, the elder Sulzberger wanted Levy in the Middle East. "After all no one knows more about the Zionist problem than Levy," he wrote in August 1945, "and, unless I miss my guess, that situation is going to be full blown in a very short time."[16,i]

[i] By 1946, when Levy had recovered enough to return to foreign reporting, Sulzberger had lost confidence in him, convinced that he would "meddle in politics." Still, Sulzberger

Sulzberger was right. Within a month, Palestine would become a major front-page story that was covered by two non-Jewish reporters: Clifton Daniel, who had been in London during the war, and Gene Currivan, who had covered the liberation of the concentration camps.

During the summer after the European war's end, it became increasingly evident that the Jews in the DP camps could not simply be repatriated. Having been stripped of all possessions and having had their residences either destroyed or taken away, Jewish DPs, usually the sole survivors of their families, literally had no homes to which to return. The ones who did go home often met fierce anti-Semitism, especially in Poland, where the Poles tended to blame the Jews for Polish suffering under the Germans. The *Times* acknowledged the difficulty the Jews had in remaining in Europe in a July editorial, not unexpectedly titled, "Hitler's First Victims." The editorial noted Hitler's "one hideous achievement" – that only 1.25 million Jews remained in Europe – and acknowledged that even those few seemed unwilling to stay. "The feeling must be widespread among them that they cannot endure living in communities where they were so frightfully abused." Still, the editorial was primarily a plea to "solve the problem of religious discrimination" in Europe.[17]

Others, including some of the *Times*' own reporters, realized that ending "religious discrimination" was not the solution. The Allied governments, which were occupying Germany, had committed to religious neutrality, treating Jews and other Germans the same. Drew Middleton, a *Times* reporter in Germany, considered this folly and said so in his August front-page article on the Jews in Europe. Middleton explained that the Allied policy was "palpably unrealistic because the Jewish community is not strictly a religious group, and because, by implication it ignored the fact that it was the Jews – and not the Catholics and Lutherans – who were singled out by the Nazis for twelve years for physical extermination."[ii] A month later, a *Times* editorial called for "special attention" for Jewish survivors in the form of greater rations than German civilians.[18]

offered him a position in Los Angeles or Palestine, which Levy turned down. Sulzberger then decided to let him go. Sulzberger to Magnes, 6/11/46, Judah Magnes Papers, P3-218B, CAHJP.

[ii] The reality was even more complicated than that. Even within the category of DPs, Jews were in worse physical and mental condition and required more care. Abzug, *Inside the Vicious Heart*, 141–68.

But on the philosophical question of whether Jews were more than individuals with a certain faith, Arthur Sulzberger would not budge. "I do not believe Jews are a race. I do not believe that they are a people," he wrote in August 1945. Echoing language he had used before the war, Sulzberger declared that he saw "no more reason to reconstitute the Jews as a nation than the Angles, the Celts or the Saxons."[19] Even as Sulzberger reasserted his anti-Zionism, other Reform Jews of the Isaac Wise school seemed to be modifying their antistatehood stance. Julian Morgenstern, president of Hebrew Union College, which Wise founded, was quoted in the August *Jewish Post* of Indianapolis saying he was "not terrified" by the prospect of a Jewish state in Palestine, and had a "sympathetic understanding of Zionism."[20] The *Times* published a news story based on Morgenstern's comments. When *Jewish Post* columnist G. M. Cohen criticized the *Times* for not mentioning in its story that Morgenstern had changed his mind about Zionism – "since I know that Mr. Sulzberger personally handled the story," Cohen noted – Sulzberger denied that that was what Morgenstern meant. Had he, the *Times* would have acknowledged it. "Strangely enough, here on The New York Times we publish the news whether it happens to suit our opinions or not, and that is more than a good many periodicals can say," Sulzberger replied.

Sulzberger grew concerned about Morgenstern's possible defection, however, when another item appeared 2 months later in a syndicated column that ran in the Anglo-Jewish press. "I am wondering what has been done to set the record straight," Sulzberger inquired. Morgenstern replied 4 months later after recovering from a "rather severe attack of virus pneumonia." He said that "this is a complete mis-statement of my position" derived from the misrepresentations in the earlier interview with the *Jewish Post*. But Morgenstern chose not to do anything to correct the record. After 5 months, Morgenstern explained, he would prefer not to "revive the issue."[21]

Hebrew Union College delivered another jolt in November: it decided to award an honorary degree to Stephen S. Wise during a meeting that Iphigene Sulzberger, who was on the college's board of trustees, did not attend. "Would you be good enough to let me know for what reasons [Wise] was selected as a recipient of this honor," a rather testy Iphigene Sulzberger wrote Morgenstern. Wise had "been an outstanding figure in American – and world-Jewish life," Sheldon Blank responded, acting on behalf of the ailing Morgenstern. "And this weighed in his favor in spite of differences that may have made relations between this gentleman and the college authorities at times somewhat stormy."[22]

For his part, Stephen Wise was no more thrilled with the *Times*. The *Times* "is utterly unfair in its reports of the things I say and do," he wrote to James in January 1946. He was bitter about it. "I presume that I will have to continue for the little time that is left to me to endure the pins and pricks of the New York Times, which, it may interest you to learn, no longer comes to my home."[23] What set Wise off was a *Times* January 11 article describing Wise's attack on Lessing Rosenwald of the American Council for Judaism at an official hearing on the future of Palestine. The article also angered Milton Steinberg, rabbi at the Park Avenue Synagogue in Manhattan. A few months earlier, the *Times* had printed Steinberg's letter to the editor reacting to the newspaper's coverage of a Zionist rally at Madison Square Garden and an accompanying statement from Rosenwald.[24] After what he considered the patronizing description of Wise in the story about Rosenwald's testimony, Steinberg had had it. "I was furious with The Times for the way it handled your exposure of Lessing Rosenwald," he wrote Wise, "so furious that for that along with several other old scores I am asking our board next week to transfer our synagogue advertising to *The Tribune*. On that episode as on many others we get a much better deal from the straightforward Gentile than from a sick-souled, scared and tied-in-knots Jew." The synagogue board went along. Steinberg also promised that if "it isn't emotionally too taxing," he planned to preach a sermon on the theme, "The New York Times and Jewish News." He concluded: "All I can say is God protect us from that kind of Jew who publishes The Times."[25]

By 1946, even the most staunch anti-Zionists seemed to be changing their views. The American Jewish Committee, whose German-Jewish membership had long opposed Zionism, concluded that the DPs should be allowed to immigrate to Palestine and called on President Truman to support large-scale Jewish immigration. Lessing Rosenwald's brother and sister, who had originally agreed to his becoming head of the American Council for Judaism, publicly repudiated his position and, along with other relatives, donated $1 million to the UJA. Rosenwald's sister made her decision immediately upon returning from a trip to the DP camps.[26]

Binationalism was no more popular. In June, Sulzberger organized a dinner at the Hotel Pierre to seek support for Magnes' binational state and for "Jewish Arab cooperation."[27] Sulzberger invited 23 people, including some of the nation's most prominent Jews who had also been known for their opposition to Zionism: Herbert Lehman, Joseph Proskauer, Samuel Rosenman, Roger Straus, Herbert Bayard Swope, Edward Warburg, and Bernard Baruch. Only three people accepted Sulzberger's invitation, and the dinner was canceled.[28] Sulzberger continued to push binationalism through his reporters in Palestine. He urged Clifton Daniel to meet with Magnes. After the meeting, Daniel informed the publisher that the other two Middle East correspondents, Julian Meltzer and Gene Currivan, "had been made aware of your interest in his approach to the Palestine problem."[29]

The opposition to Zionism among American Jews continued to melt away. Joseph Proskauer, who had pushed the American Jewish Committee in more anti-Zionist directions when he became its president in January 1943, endorsed a Jewish state in Palestine as the only practical solution for the DP problem. By October 1946, there was so little opposition left that Jacob Fishman, a columnist for the *Jewish Morning Journal*, whom Richards considered "the most moderate and reasonable of the commentators," concluded that "all opposition" to a Jewish state "now centers in The New York Times." Fishman took Sulzberger to task for refusing to change his views in light of what had just happened to Europe's Jews. Sulzberger's father-in-law Adolph Ochs was an anti-Zionist, Fishman wrote, but "that was in a time when Jews here could not imagine such calamitous events as took place in Europe.... Ochs was a devoted Jew and would undoubtedly have gained some lessons from the Hitler tragedy." Even Richards conceded that the two articles that sparked Fishman's immediate concerns – one written by the Grand Mufti of Jerusalem who had allied with the Nazis and visited a death camp – were "painful to me." Sulzberger defended the use of the Mufti's article because he was "a news figure just as Hitler was." He reminded Richards: "The New York Times is a newspaper – not an organ for the Zionists' cause or for Jews, and I know you know that."[30]

Shortly thereafter, Sulzberger made his speech in Chattanooga, which could be considered his last stand. He made it with some fanfare, granting "special permission" to the American Council for Judaism to reprint "a substantial excerpt" in its bulletin. (After the ruckus over publishing the council's principles during the American Jewish Conference in 1943, Sulzberger never officially affiliated with the group, although he continued to support its goals and publicize its views.) A few months later, he tried to pin down another anti-Zionist on his evolving position. In April 1947, he wrote to Louis Finkelstein of the Jewish Theological Seminary of America, on whose board Sulzberger sat. (In 1940, Sulzberger had lobbied successfully for Finkelstein to become the Roosevelt Administration's liaison to the Jews rather than the Zionist Stephen Wise.) Sulzberger asked what Finkelstein meant when he was quoted saying, "we Zionists consider the establishment of a Jewish Palestine indispensable to a reformation of world culture." Finkelstein replied that he meant Zionism in the sense of a traditional Jewish tie to the Holy Land rather than in the political sense of the establishment of Palestine as a Jewish state. But Finkelstein asked that his letter to Sulzberger outlining his position on Zionism not be published, even though the *Hebrew Union College Monthly* was eager to include it.[31]

As the United Nations vote on creating a Jewish state loomed, Sulzberger stood almost alone among prominent American Jews in opposing it. "Anti-Zionist Judaism in the United States, Europe, and beyond appeared increasingly obsolete and dysfunctional, out of tune with the sense of mutual responsibility and consciousness of 'peoplehood' that now bound Israeli and Diaspora Jewry together in the post-Holocaust world," Robert S. Wistrich explains.[32] Sulzberger expressed his growing bitterness in a letter to his lawyer and friend, Edward S. Greenbaum: "Apparently if you are a Jew you have to contribute Jewishly, eat Jewishly, think Jewishly, part your hair Jewishly – everything for the sake of efficiency. Gosh, I'm sick." Sulzberger wrote again to Greenbaum: "Did you see the United Jewish Appeal advertisement in today's Times? And did you note that at least a part of the American Jewish Committee is now associated with the United Jewish Appeal. So, too, is the Jewish Telegraphic Agency. The only thing I miss is the Jewish Chiropractors' Society. In other words J E W is to be the common denominator for everything we do. God help us!"[33]

As a Jewish state became more likely, Sulzberger in essence gave up, first on fighting Zionism, then on Judaism. In 1947, he wrote Morris Lazaron, founder of the American Council for Judaism, that "the only solution" he could see to the situation in Palestine was to "partition the Holy Land and give the Zionists complete freedom in the section which was under their jurisdiction." They could then admit "all Jewish D.P.'s" and "it would be their economic problem." He would have British soldiers patrol the boundary lines, shooting Jews who crossed into the Arab section and Arabs who crossed into the Jewish section. "I was told by some of my associates that that would make a Jewish State and my answer was 'Okay if it does.' It is not what I would have wanted in the beginning, but in a practical world I see no other way out."[34]

When the United Nations recommended partition of Palestine in 1947, with one part dedicated to a Jewish state, the *Times* supported it as a way to buttress the still fragile international organization. But the *Times* did not endorse Israel's Declaration of Independence in May 1948, and the editorial page was never allowed to refer to the "Jewish state."[35] "I have a feeling of kinship for my fellow Jews when the question of Judaism is involved," Sulzberger wrote the August after Israel had come into being. "I feel a deep sense of tragedy for the suffering of refugees. But when a national state is the issue, I feel no closer to the state of Israel than I do to Britain or China."[36] He lost interest in the American Council for Judaism, concluding that the establishment of the State of Israel and the waning of Zionist intolerance for other viewpoints "spells the beginning of the end" for the organization. He never visited Israel, canceling a planned trip after becoming incensed at a Ben-Gurion speech before the World Zionist Conference in December 1960.[37]

As his Reform friends abandoned anti-Zionism, Sulzberger abandoned Reform and ultimately Judaism. "There are only some Jews who insist on rituals. I consider myself a Jew and I don't," Sulzberger wrote in April 1948. "In fact, I know of no difference in my way of life than in that of any Unitarian."[38] He ended his membership in the old Spanish Portuguese synagogue his forefathers founded because the congregation sang Hatikva at a gathering, and resigned as a trustee of Emanu-El.[39]

By 1959, he ended his subscription to the *Menorah Journal*, a traditional Reform publication that his father had supported before him. "Frankly, I've become less and less interested in formalized faiths of any kind and find an inclination to support those things that unite rather than those that separate," he wrote explaining his cancellation. He did, however, make a one-time gift of $250 to the Menorah Association, on the theory that "if someone needs a formal faith . . . you make a lot of sense." He made clear, however, that he did not, attaching a "private memorandum," in which he concluded: "If I am faithful to my fellow man, I'll take my chances with the Lord, even if I do not go on every Sabbath to hear His virtues extolled."[40]

In November 1959, he wrote a rambling disquisition questioning the meaning of life:

> I hate any and all formalism. The more rigid it is, the worse it is, and the more crimes and stupidities have been done in its name. Reform Judaism doesn't demand much, but too much contact with it has drawn me far away from it. . . . But religion to my way of thinking is not learning to be a child of God but rather learning how to live with man, and I think I do that of and for myself.

So by all rights, Sulzberger, who had proclaimed years earlier that those who no longer had Jewish faith "cease to be Jews, whether or not the world permits them to make that decision," should no longer have considered himself a Jew. But Sulzberger was not quite willing to make that leap. Four years later he wrote to his children: "I know nothing of God and consequently look to Him for nothing. I call myself a Jew because they have been picked on and I want to help. Besides, the faith is less demanding than the others I know."[41]

Arthur Sulzberger died on December 11, 1968, and was buried after a ceremony at Temple Emanu-El. Among other tributes, his wife established an Arthur Hays Sulzberger Scholarship in his memory at Hebrew University in Jerusalem.[42]

Conclusion

"The Horrible Story Was Not Told"

It was a typical day in the war's fifth year when the anguished cry of the remnants of Polish Jewry reached the *New York Times* buried in a routine, page four item about a relatively inconsequential parliamentary debate. The *Times* editors handled the "last voice from the abyss" in Poland as they had hundreds of similar stories before and the hundreds that would come after. They dropped it inside the newspaper with a tiny headline and no follow-up, a gesture that probably went unnoticed and unchallenged by all the *New York Times* journalists who came in contact with the story.

The dismissive treatment of Polish Jewry's last cry reveals a seemingly incomprehensible chasm between the journalists' response and the information they received. When confronted with the facts of mass murder, journalists reacted as if they had no understanding of what those facts meant. This gap between knowing and understanding is undoubtedly unique to these particular people and that particular place, and thus is best understood through detailed narrative such as the one in the preceding pages. But the chasm so evident at the *Times* reflects a larger problem, one that has bedeviled scholars grappling with the role of bystanders to the Holocaust, those who watched while others murdered or were murdered. "Various recent studies dealing with the 'terrible secret' stress in diverse ways the simultaneity of considerable knowledge of the facts and of a no less massive inability or refusal to transform these facts into integrated understanding," Saul Friedlander writes.[1]

To researchers, the problem is both perplexing and perturbing, for the lack of understanding is often cited as the primary reason for the witnesses' inaction. "Writing on bystanders to the Holocaust conveys a persistent and depressing theme – disbelief in reports of mass murder, widespread indifference and unwillingness to break established patterns to help the Jews," explains Michael Marrus in *The Holocaust in History*.[2]

It is therefore important to explore this credibility problem, as it has been called,[3] within a general framework, without losing sight of the particular ways in which it was expressed at the *New York Times*. The goal is to describe the competing currents of information, attitudes, and approaches that circulated throughout the news organization, and suggest reasons why some came to the surface, while others remained submerged.

The credibility problem affected all the bystanders, including the Allied governments, the Jews in America, Great Britain and Palestine, relief organizations, churches, and the media, but it affected them all in different ways. The press' position in relation to the problem is particularly interesting, and particularly difficult to untangle, because journalists were both affected by their own credibility problem and contributed to the credibility problem of others. They had to assess information in the face of questions about reliability, believability, and salience, and they simultaneously influenced others' judgments on those issues. The way the press presented the facts of the Holocaust helped shape public understanding and contributed to the complex interplay between the government and Jewish groups who were trying to spur a political response to the tragedy.

For journalists, the credibility problem involved four interrelated processes: receiving information, assessing its believability, determining its importance, and relying on it to take action.[i] Despite initial scholarly and other claims to the contrary, a consensus has emerged over the last two decades that information about first the persecution and then the destruction of European Jewry reached Allied nations, including members of the press, throughout the war. Because of its long-time dedication to international news, the *New York Times* was a prime recipient of this information. As we saw in Chapters 2, 3, and 4, during the 2 years before the United States and Germany went to war, the *Times* acquired information about Jews in Axis-controlled countries mostly from its correspondents on the scene (or those of the wire services) who used ordinary newsgathering techniques: first-hand observations, authoritative interviews, official government statements and edicts, local newspapers, and the reports of interested organizations.

[i] This is a reformulation of Yehuda Bauer's delineation of the stages of knowing required for action to more closely fit a journalistic framework. *The Holocaust in Historical Perspective*, Seattle: University of Washington Press (1978), 18.

For the most part, these sources provided a timely and accurate picture of the increasingly severe economic and social measures taken against the Jews in Germany; in the countries Germany occupied, such as France and the Netherlands; and in the countries it allied with, such as Rumania and Hungary. The *Times* also knew that hundreds of thousands of Jews were deported from these countries and transported in sealed cattle cars with only a few possessions to Poland. What happened to them once they got there was harder to discover because Poland, like the Soviet territories Germany conquered in 1941, was closed to all but a few journalists. Still, in 1940 and 1941, the *Times* learned of the establishment of filthy, crowded ghettos that imprisoned hundreds of thousands of Polish Jews, as well as those deported from the West, tens of thousands of whom died from disease and starvation. The information came from official German statements published in the German and Polish press; the Polish exile government in London, which had an extensive underground in the homeland; and Jewish groups who managed to learn of conditions from those who escaped and from citizens of neutral countries. At the end of 1941, the Soviet government and foreign journalists provided sporadic reports of massacres in eastern Poland and the former Soviet territories, which, with a few exceptions, were vague and unsubstantiated.

Once America joined the war, the *Times* could no longer rely on the first-hand reporting of its own correspondents for news from occupied Europe; it had to depend on the second-hand sources it had been using for information from Poland – exile governments, Jewish groups, German and local newspapers, and, to a lesser extent, the Allied governments. As we saw in Chapters 5 and 6, those sources provided information in 1942 and 1943 about the establishment of extermination centers in Poland within 5 months of their beginning operation, the shipment of Jews from Polish ghettos and the rest of occupied Europe to those centers where they were killed upon arrival in specially designed gas chambers, and a plan to destroy all Europe's Jews in this fashion. By the end of 1943, as the Soviets reclaimed areas where massacres had occurred during the prior 2 years, *Times* reporters again gleaned information from first-hand observations and eyewitness interviews with victims, and eventually with perpetrators. This reporting climaxed with the liberation of extermination camps in the East, and concentration and labor camps in the West, discussed in Chapter 10.

The information the *Times* received through routine journalistic channels was augmented by what its publisher learned from his personal ties to

German Jews and the Jewish community generally. Before the war, Arthur Sulzberger became involved with German-Jewish families trying to emigrate and with various schemes to find refugee havens outside Palestine. On the eve of war, Sulzberger met with Leo Baeck, the chief rabbi of Berlin. In 1940, he worked to save his Jewish Bucharest correspondent under siege in German-allied Rumania and learned from Max Nussbaum about the fate of the Jews the rabbi had just left behind in Germany. In 1941, he followed the plight of a relative in the Gurs concentration camp and assisted other acquaintances as they maneuvered through the U.S. immigration labyrinth. In 1942 and 1943, he became entangled in fights within the Jewish community over Palestine as a haven for European Jews. In 1944, he explored rescue schemes with the WRB. In 1945, he learned of the travails of one woman from his wife's ancestral home and visited the liberated camps. This information often did not find its way directly into the *Times*, but influenced the behind-the-scenes understanding of events.

In theory, more and better information about what was happening to Europe's Jews could have eliminated or reduced the credibility problem. Had journalists toured Auschwitz in 1943, for example, questions about believability and importance might have quickly evaporated. Yet, the *New York Times* received a steady stream of information, as did other American and British media, so a lack of data cannot be at the core of the credibility problem.

This leads to the next step in the process: was that information believed? Scholars taking up the credibility problem face a strong temptation to explain bystanders' responses by assuming they received information about the annihilation of the Jews but did not believe it. Quick conclusions of this kind, however, risk the dangerous circle of using the lack of response as evidence of nonbelief and then relying on nonbelief to explain the lack of response. This study of the *New York Times* journalists' role helps break this circle precisely because the response available to journalists differed from those facing groups more likely to attempt rescue.

Considering bystanders' different goals is essential because typically people do not assess information or believe or disbelieve in the abstract; they consider information's validity in terms of what they plan to do with it. To make sense of the sentence – "bystanders received information about the annihilation of the Jews but did not believe it" – it is necessary to include "and therefore they did what?" The answer to that reflects back on the nature of belief. Here the position of journalists differed from that of other bystanders to the Holocaust, who might have been formulating, or fending off, rescue schemes. Journalists would have assessed the credibility of information for essentially two purposes: to decide whether to include the information in the newspaper (or broadcast) and, if so, where to put it.[ii] In other words, journalists who received information about the Holocaust had to decide first: do I believe this information in order to include it in my newspaper? If the answer is yes, do I believe it enough to put it on the front page? (Certainly, other factors affect decisions about what stories to use and where to locate them in the newspaper, but the purpose here is to consider the role that the believability of the information played in those decisions. The other issues are taken up later.)

The answers to questions about inclusion and placement turn on what is meant by believing information. At its most basic level, journalists disbelieve information they either know to be untrue or consider lacking in foundation, such as an unsubstantiated rumor. The utterance – "I don't believe it, it's not true" – captures this sense of disbelief. Journalists would have discounted entirely information they did not believe, or considered, in 1940s parlance, "a fake." Given that nearly 1,200 stories appeared in the *Times* about the fate of European Jews, including many specifically about the Final Solution, it can be assumed the journalists did not discredit the information entirely.

Walter Laqueur and others have suggested that disbelief, although of a different kind, also played a role in determining story placement. This sense of disbelief is more akin to the utterance, "I don't believe it, I don't think it's true." In discussing this sense of disbelief, commentators have focused almost exclusively on reports of mass murder, and often within a limited time frame, late 1941 and 1942. Laqueur selects one *Times* story – a June 30, 1942, page seven story, based on a WJC press conference – to illustrate the broader point. Journalists did not necessarily deny the truth of information they received about the death of 1 million Jews, he argues, they just were not sure whether it was true. "Quite likely the stories contained some truth," Laqueur speculates the editors reasoned, "but probably it was exaggerated." That uncertainty might not have been strong

[ii] This description oversimplifies the journalistic response. Assessments of the credibility of information also affect how reporters frame information within stories, how editors respond in terms of requiring additional information, and the interaction between reporters and editors. In the context of the believability of information about the Holocaust, however, those factors were of lesser importance.

enough to keep the story out of the newspaper altogether, he theorizes, but it might have been enough to keep it off the front page.

Because editors often have some degree of uncertainty about all but the most straightforward stories, including many they decide to put on the front page, it is important to ask: did editors have reason to be particularly uncertain about this story, to assume there was a fairly good chance it was not true at all? Was there some reason, in other words, for editors to respond: "I don't believe it, I don't think it's true." Two primary hypotheses have been offered. For one, wildly differing estimates of the numbers killed appeared during the war, "no doubt leading many to suspend judgment on the facts and suspect exaggeration," Peter Novick suggests.[4] For another, journalists who had been banished from Poland and the former Soviet territories had not witnessed the massacres. Editors could not count on their first-hand observations to verify what had occurred. Yet, reporters do not witness many of the events they write about. In this case, as in many others, journalists relied on secondary sources for their information, primarily the Soviet government, Polish government-in-exile and Jewish groups. So the next question is: was there a reason to doubt these sources, to believe they were not providing reliable information? The most frequent answer is that skepticism bred by World War I atrocity stories, and perhaps aggravated by the uses to which atrocities stories were put during the Spanish Civil War, made journalists dubious about stories of mass execution, particularly when coming from groups that might be seen as furthering propaganda goals. *Times* London Bureau Chief Raymond Daniell, for example, discounted the news value of Polish exile government releases in 1940 because he assumed they contained propaganda.

Within the *Times*, uncertainty about the sources and nature of the information about mass murder surfaced from time to time. Perhaps that is what Edwin James meant when he cabled his Stockholm correspondent in June 1942 about an account of 60,000 Jews slain in Vilna: "lots skepticism here reyour Vilna story." Or that may have been what concerned George Axelsson 2 weeks later when he wrote that figures on Jewish massacres "permit any conclusion one wants to make from 100,000 to 1,500,000." Or maybe that is why Moscow correspondent William Lawrence, escorted to Kiev by Soviet officials, hesitated to believe that 50,000 Jews had been slaughtered there. Undoubtedly, doubts were in the air. In a July 1943 story about a Polish government press conference called to reveal "a new high" for the murder toll in Poland of 3,200,000, including 1,800,000 Jews, *Times*' London correspondent Milton Bracker described a revealing exchange between a journalist and Wiadyslaw Banaczyk, the Polish Minister of Home Affairs. "Not only the statistics but the methods of slaughter detailed by M. Banaczyk – including the kicking to death of small children – were so appalling," Bracker wrote, "as to draw from a British reporter at the press conference a question as to the basis for the 'assumptions' M. Banaczyk was making."[5] Faced with such "assumptions," some editors probably figured that putting certain stories inside, rather than on the front, was a safer bet.

Yet, that was not the only, or necessarily, a common response. The *Times*' Bracker, for example, seemed satisfied with the answer Polish Minister Banaczyk gave to the dubious journalist. "The Minister was not in the least annoyed by the query," Bracker reported. "He simply explained that the Polish underground system had a special statistical section engaged in primarily compiling the black deeds for which some day the Nazi regime will have to answer. Moreover, it was obvious that even if the toll were only a fraction of the figure given, it would still be safe to charge the Nazis with a virtually unparalleled campaign of extermination." In other news stories and editorials, *Times* journalists directly confronted doubts over reports of mass murders that might have arisen because of World War I atrocity stories and differing estimates of the dead. In a January 1942 editorial prompted by Soviet Foreign Minister Molotoff's press conference on murders in the former Soviet territories, the *Times* explained that even though the number of dead "is not likely to be accurate to the last digit, the Nazis themselves have prepared us to believe the charges." The German government during the previous world war, "had sufficient respect for civilization to try most anxiously to refute atrocity charges," the *Times* continued. By contrast, "the Hitler regime is the result of a deliberate, long-continued program of atrocities," and its leader "would not hesitate to exterminate the whole Russian nation if he could."[6]

In fact, James' cable about the June 1942 story on the Vilna massacre is the only documented instance of a *Times* editor expressing such doubts. In that case, the reporter insisted the information was true, providing substantial backup for his position. Only two other stories, the estimates of Jewish massacres by Axelsson, and the Babi Yar visit by Lawrence, suggested doubts about the information the journalists reported. In both cases, as with the Vilna story, the journalists' reservations were incorporated into the story. In many other stories, reporters expressed no such doubts and indicated that the information came from "reliable sources."

Whatever doubts *Times* journalists may have had about questionable numbers from unreliable sources, these probably lessened after December 1942. At that time, the 11 Allied countries, known collectively as the United Nations, issued an official statement confirming the ongoing extermination campaign that had already killed 2 million people. The *Times* editorial page signaled that this meant there was no longer any basis for disbelief. "For [the United Nations] statement is not an outcry of the victims themselves to which many thought it possible to close their ears on the ground that it might be a special plea, subject to doubt," the *Times* opined in December 1942. "It is the official statement of their own Governments, based on officially established facts." If disbelief had been the primary basis for consigning stories about mass murders to the inside of the newspaper, at that point, in the face of "officially established facts," the coverage should have changed. It did not – in 1942, nine front-page *Times* stories concerned the Jews compared with seven in 1943 – suggesting that journalists "thinking it was not true," did not alone make the Holocaust an inside story.

Perhaps another form of disbelief, one that could not be quelled by "official confirmation," crept into the *Times*' placement decisions. For the people who lived through the Holocaust "it was a totally new reality that was unfolding before their shocked eyes and paralyzed minds," Yehuda Bauer explains. "It was literally unbelievable, because it was unexpected and unprecedented."[7] The utterance – "I don't believe it, it's hard to imagine it to be true" – expresses this sense of disbelief. Accompanying that notion of disbelief may have been another that also affected bystanders' reactions to news of the Holocaust. Even if they acknowledged mass murder was taking place on an unprecedented scale for unfathomable reasons, this argument goes, at some level they could not accept it.[8] "I don't believe it, I don't want it to be true" – conveys this meaning of disbelief, a psychological reaction most commonly referred to as denial. The response stems from both the event itself – hideous torment intentionally inflicted upon millions of innocent people – and what it meant about human behavior and civilized society's ability to control mankind's worst impulses. "The [World Jewish] Congress never succeeded in breaking through the crust of skepticism, the refusal to believe that human beings could be so inhuman," Leon Kubowitzki wrote in 1948. "People could not be persuaded that the Germans were really bent upon wiping out all the Jews, every one of them, and that they would find accomplices in every nation; that even in Western Europe they would find fellow hunters of little children for delivery to death.... The death struggle in which the Jewish people were engaged was not only incredible to the human mind; it was also incomprehensible."[9]

Both the sense that the Holocaust was too hard and too terrible to imagine pervaded the bystanders' (as well as the victims') response, as has been amply documented. As was the case with the more ordinary understandings of disbelief, however, it is important to distinguish among bystanders to more fully understand the reaction.[iii] Individuals varied greatly in how difficult they found it to accept the terrible news from Europe. For those personally affected, including Jewish leaders or Jews in Palestine who had family trapped in Europe, denial was a particularly powerful psychological response, especially in light of their own powerlessness. Jewish Agency leader Isaac Gruenbaum epitomizes this response, as Dina Porot describes it: "The fact that [Gruenbaum], who had been an admired leader of Polish Jewry, was now watching its destruction from a safe place surely increased his inability to accept the bitter news at face value. Another reason, surely, was the knowledge that one of his sons, Eliezer, had been deported, probably to the camp in Buchenwald or in Birkenau...."[10] Of course, some Jewish leaders did face the reality, including Kubowitzki and, later, Gruenbaum, who pressed for rescue measures such as bombing the death camps.

Journalists too would have found it hard to imagine such unprecedented horror and would not have willingly accepted its terrifying implications. Journalists' claims that each new government statement was "the first official confirmation" of the Final Solution, and the repeated refrain of "too terrible to be believed" upon encountering the liberated concentration camps – which Deborah Lipstadt documents so well – bespeak journalists' deep desire not to want to believe the information they received, and their refusal to do so, even in the face of strong evidence. That *Times* internal documents do not contain these profound reservations does not mean much; such internalized and elusive sentiments are not easily conveyed in office memoranda. Still, denial was probably a less potent force

[iii] The issue here concerns only those bystanders who received and attempted to process information about the Holocaust, not those who were, or chose to remain, ignorant, even though such ignorance may be another form of denial.

for most mainstream American journalists who were not likely to feel the same acute, personal pain as other primarily Jewish bystanders.[iv] Journalists obviously struggled with it, fluctuating between belief and disbelief. "The barbarities we have witnessed and heard of in the past four years are too nightmarish to be real," *Times* columnist Anne O'Hare McCormick wrote in March 1943. "We read of helpless human creatures thrown into the streets to die or dumped into swamps and forests or executed en masse when that seems the easiest way to get rid of them, but the ordinary mind can't take in such pictures." Journalists' resistance reflected an ongoing, philosophical crisis, however, not a settled, ready rationale for placing news stories about those pictures inside the newspaper. Indeed, McCormick, after acknowledging the difficulty, insisted that the nightmarish pictures had to be believed. "Yet they represent dreadful realities," she continued. "There is not the slightest question that the persecution of the Jews has reached its awful climax in a campaign to wipe them out of Europe."[11]

One final point should be mentioned before leaving the issue of believability. Discussions of the credibility problem tend to center on whether bystanders believed information about the extermination campaign, not whether they believed information about events leading up to and proceeding simultaneously with the Final Solution. The reason for that emphasis is clear. Almost no one doubted that European Jews faced the most extreme forms of state-sponsored discrimination (German Jews were not allowed to stroll; everywhere they had to wear a star), economic deprivation (homes, possessions, livelihoods all taken away), and inhuman brutalization (hundreds of thousands shipped in closed cattle cars to imprisonment in filthy, disease-ridden ghettos). Hundreds of those stories appeared in the *Times*, almost none of them were subject to any doubts, and yet not one of them appeared on the *New York Times*' front page. Within a journalistic framework, that seems almost as difficult to understand as why the murder of millions would not be on the front page.

One consequence of focusing on the Final Solution is that, by implication, it seems to address the other conundrum. If Auschwitz was not on the front page, then of course "lesser events," short of the Final Solution, would not be either. But that assumption reflects a misunderstanding of the historical context and the journalistic process. Gulie Ne'eman Arad

[iv] Journalists who worked for the Jewish press often had personal ties to Europe, which made their responses more akin to the experience of Jewish leaders. See, for example, Marie Syrkin, "Reactions to the News of the Holocaust," *Midstream*, May 1968, 62–4.

criticizes the historiography of the Holocaust in general for the tendency to analyze all Nazi era events "within the closed referential framework of its catastrophic ending." She argues that "whatever preceded the industrial killing, however horrific, has come to be accepted within the bounds of the normal. Viewed through the distorting prism of Auschwitz, the events of the preceding years are shifted out of historical focus."[12] Stories about deportations from Stettin in 1940, pogroms in Rumania and "Aryanization" in France in 1941, and incarceration in sealed ghettos in early 1942, for example, would not have been measured against the "moral signifier" of Auschwitz; when those stories appeared, Auschwitz was just one of many atrocious labor camps in Poland. They would have been found wanting on their own terms, not in relation to the Final Solution, and not because they were not believed.

Another possibility is that those stories were in some vital sense incomplete without an understanding of where those events were leading. Michael Marrus points out that there were "significant gaps" in the information bystanders received, particularly in 1942. "Even the best informed had no real sense of the assembly-line organization by which so many hundreds of thousands met their deaths in Polish camps," Marrus explains. "Even an attentive reading of the reports from Poland yielded only a partial view of the Holocaust and conveyed little sense of its historical uniqueness."[13] Yet, for journalists (and Marrus does not speak specifically of them) that should not have mattered as much. Journalists almost always encounter information with "significant gaps"; that is the nature of the journalistic enterprise, which is often described as the first draft of history. In other words, just because journalists did not know exactly where thousands of French Jews were going when they were deported in the summer of 1942, or what would happen to them once they got there, should not in and of itself have kept that story off the front page. Doubts about the believability of the information the press received about the Jews during the war thus played a role in the handling of the news but was not dispositive. Another step in the process was critical to the credibility problem as applied to journalists.

Along with receiving and believing information, the credibility problem also turns on determinations of the information's importance. It is unlikely someone would act on information he or she considered unimportant, even if it had been received and believed. If bystanders to the Holocaust did not consider the fate of European Jews important, they would not act to help even if they knew and believed what was happening to them. That the bystanders never made saving European Jews a priority lies at the heart of the credibility problem for some scholars. The endangered Jews were not citizens of either Great Britain or the United States, and thus lay outside those countries' sphere of concern, they argue.[14] American Jews, who were at least concerned about their brethren, could not alter their government's priorities because of their own disunity, organizational ineffectiveness, and perception of political powerlessness.[15] In addition, American Jews often put their interest in thriving in American society ahead of helping those in Europe.[16] Thus, Europe's Jews were not important enough to any of the bystanders to take major actions to help them.

That the *New York Times* and other newspapers did not consider what was happening to the Jews important is to some extent self-evident. Because only 44 front-page stories that had anything to do with Jews, a little more than half of which directly concerned their fate in Europe, appeared during the war, the *Times* obviously did not perceive the news to be important, or at least not as important as the other approximately 24,000 stories it put on page one. The reasons for that determination, however, are not at all obvious. As with believability, some currents pushed journalists to conclude the information did not have much value, whereas other currents suggested it did.

To some extent, journalists' priorities mirrored those of other bystanders. During the war years, the war itself dominated the minds of most Americans. Their sons were fighting and dying, and all Americans faced the terrifying prospect of living under Nazi domination. "Unless we keep that in mind," Peter Novick admonishes, "we will never understand how the Holocaust came to be swallowed up in the larger carnage surrounding it."[17] As was true of other powerful institutions, American newspapers' constituency, or in media parlance, audience, did not include European Jews, or very many American Jews for that matter. (In this, the *Times*, with its Jewish audience, Jewish editors and reporters, and Jewish ownership, differed from other publications, as is discussed later.) It is therefore not surprising that editors considered the Jews' fate unworthy of the front page, especially given so many other pressing concerns. For 6 years, the world war dominated the news like no event before or since: ship battles in the Pacific, air fights over Britain, hand-to-hand combat in the cities of the Soviet Union. Harried editors had to sort through the stories, while planning maps and charting future coverage. A *Washington*

Post editor, for example, told representatives of the Bergson Group, who had come to the newspaper to complain about its coverage, of his irritation with their visit. "[S]uch important and decisive things are going on, things that will shape the future of the whole world," an October 12, 1944 memo records Managing Editor Alexander Jones saying, "and he is being bothered and annoyed with such unimportant, irrelevant matters as ours."[18]

Military news certainly diminished the importance of what was happening to the Jews in the minds of most American journalists. Yet, it does not fully explain why almost all the stories about their destruction appeared inside. Relative lulls in the fighting, such as the winter of 1940's "phony war," did not generate a number of front-page stories about the Jews. In addition, even in the midst of all-important war news, stories about bulls goring Long Island brothers and gas ration coupons lacking registration numbers found their way to the front page of the *Times* and other newspapers. About half of the 12 to 15 stories on a typical *Times* front page concerned something other than military news. It may be, however, that those stories (brothers gored on Long Island, gas rationing) were perceived as a different beast entirely and not judged in relation to the global conflict. The Jews' persecution was judged in relation to the conflict and found to be of lesser significance, because of their numbers (9 million compared with hundreds of millions of people caught up in the conflagration) and the supposed reason for their persecution. Before the war, and during its first 2 years, the press portrayed their persecution as part of the Nazis' quest for domination of first Germany and then other Axis countries. The Jews were considered convenient scapegoats, not the targets of unbridled anti-Semitism. So news about the Jews was perceived as a footnote to a larger narrative that fit comfortably on an inside page alongside continuations of front-page European stories.

During the war's first 2 years, the *Times* made decisions that tended to reinforce this initial assessment. The most important was the decision to maintain its existing network of foreign correspondents to cover occupied Europe, some of whom had questionable affinities and limited abilities. The *Times*' stars went to London, and later to European or Pacific battlefields with American troops; the second string watched "Fortress Europe." These correspondents, even given their weaknesses, did not impede the flow of information about the Jews to the *Times* – although better, more determined reporters would likely have produced more and better information. But perhaps because of their long residences, the foreign correspondents tended to shape the information to reflect the interests of the countries they were covering. The *Times* Berlin bureau chief, Guido Enderis, out of some combination of sympathy for the regime and reluctance to rock the boat, tended to blunt coverage of the Nazis' most extreme anti-Semitic actions. The reporters who had helped keep his pro-German inclinations in check were gone soon after the war began. In France, Lansing Warren and Gaston Archambault perceived events through a French lens that tended to glorify the Vichy government and rationalize its anti-Semitic actions. Long-time correspondents in Poland and Rumania never had a chance to reflect their countries' perspectives; Jerzy Szapiro and Eugen Kovacs had to flee because they were Jews.

Having second-string reporters covering occupied Europe affected not only how the information was presented, but also how that information was perceived by editors in New York. Editors did not think highly of some of these reporters. Daniel Brigham in Berne was prone to make mistakes. Ralph Parker in Moscow was pro-Soviet. Percy Knauth and Brooks Peters in Berlin were young and untested, whereas Enderis was too protective of the Nazis. Ray Brock in the Balkans was a rabble rouser. Fighting among reporters in Berne and Stockholm did not enhance their reputations with their editors. Given these perceptions, editors would be less likely to put their stories on page one, although they sometimes did. Once war broke out, the strapped Berlin bureau tended to leave stories about the Jews to the wire services, which also made them less likely to appear on the front. Only one reporter covering occupied Europe had the clout to elevate stories to the front page because he wrote them, but Cyrus Sulzberger was not inclined to write about what was happening to the Jews.

Editors might also have considered stories about the persecution of European Jews to be "old news," too familiar to be worthy of the front page.[19] But what was happening to the Jews was not old news in the sense that journalists were repeating previously disclosed information. Each time an Axis country tightened its repressive laws, each time German, or Dutch, or Belgian Jews were shipped to Poland, each time a ghetto was sealed with Jews inside, new information was revealed. Indeed, the addition of new information to an already established story line often makes the article more, not less, newsworthy. Editors may have lumped together all the separate, new events and discounted them as just more Jewish persecution. But if they did, it would have been because they had already consigned "Jewish persecution" to the category of relatively, unimportant inside news, not because they had evaluated each new bit of information and found it to be "old news."

In 1942, what was happening to the Jews could not be dismissed as just more Jewish persecution. The extermination centers had gone into operation in Poland, and the Einsatzgruppen's murderous onslaught in the Soviet territories had claimed at least 1 million Jews. Yet, at the same time, the war's "larger carnage" had grown, too, and engulfed the United States. In the wake of Pearl Harbor, American forces beat a steady retreat in the Pacific. The German drive in the Soviet Union met ferocious resistance that left millions of Russians, including civilians, dead. The killing of millions of Jews could have been lost in the midst of this apocalyptic news. Indeed, some stories, particularly out of the Soviet Union, did not differentiate the Jewish dead from the Russian, Ukrainian, or Polish dead. Nor did they specify the method of their execution. Editors might have considered news of the deaths of "from 100,000 to 1,500,000" Jews, as Axelsson put it, to be the unfortunate, but not unusual, collateral damage of war.

Yet, throughout the latter half of 1942 and into 1943, Jewish organizations, particularly the WJC, struggled to establish that the Jews' deaths were not just collateral damage, that Jews were dying because Germans, often in collaboration with the local population, murdered them in a systematic campaign to rid the world of Jews. Many stories inside the *Times* said just that and included the places, dates, and methods of their deaths. They also described the deaths as unprecedented, or as the "greatest mass murder in history." Still journalists did not think this news consistently warranted the front page.

Several factors might explain this. First, questions of believability likely became entangled in assessments of importance. To recognize the importance of the mass murder of Jews amidst so much mayhem, editors might have had to believe that they were dying in a specific extermination campaign, the element of the story that was the most subject to doubt. In other words, belief was necessary to validate importance. But that cuts the other way as well. If journalists believed Jews were dying in an extermination campaign, as some said they did, including the editors of the *New York Times*, then they also should have been able to recognize the importance of the story, and have placed it in on the front page more regularly. That did not happen.

The sources journalists relied on for information about the extermination campaign might also have figured in the editors' calculations. Journalists assess newsworthiness based on the perceived stature of the source, as well as the value of the event itself. It may have been that the Jewish groups and exile governments who disclosed the Final Solution were not so much considered untrustworthy as less newsworthy than other sources of information, particularly Allied government sources. In fact, 20 of the 44 stories that appeared on the *New York Times*' front page about the Jews originated with Allied governments or individual Allied officials.[v] But official statements were few and far between and so, not surprisingly, was the front-page coverage.

This too is an important but not all-encompassing explanation for the press response. The press had enough information, even without Allied government statements, to play the Holocaust as a front-page story. It did not because its judgment of newsworthiness coincided with that of the government. At some level, journalists, like other bystanders, did not recognize the importance of what was happening to the Jews because it was not happening to them, or to their readers, or to a group they or (they assumed) their readers could identify with.[vi] (Liberal journalists, such as those at *PM*, the *New Republic*, and the *Nation*, were an exception.) "Editors cabled from oh-so-gentle America: 'Our readers are tired of horror stories. Cable only those of death rolls unusually large or deaths themselves unusually gruesome,'" wrote Raymond Arthur Davis, who reported from Eastern Europe in 1944 and 1945. "Such stories could always be written on the basis of the experiences of the Jews. But, alas, the editors then cabled: 'Jewish atrocity stories are not acceptable news material.' Ah, America, America!"[20]

Most journalists, it seems, did not so much acknowledge the Jews' destruction, and then discount its importance; they determined as a matter

[v] The American government's strong and high-level condemnation of Kristallnacht in November 1938, along with first-hand descriptions from its reporters on the scene, helps to explain why that event received sustained, front-page coverage in the *Times* and other American newspapers.

[vi] This attitude reflects a long-standing, deep-seated news value, sometimes referred to as proximity, meaning the closer, either geographically or emotionally, an event is to readers, the more newsworthy it is.

of the first order that the Jews' fate had relatively little news value no matter what had happened to them. Questions about believability, from the prosaic to the profound, made it easier to maintain that indifference. But that indifference also made it less likely that journalists would seek to resolve their doubts by aggressively pursuing the truth. Unless they had an ethnic identification (like the Jewish press) or an ideological impetus (like the liberal press' fight against fascism), most American journalists simply did not focus on what was happening to the Jews.

But the *New York Times* did. For conventional journalistic reasons – its extensive network of foreign correspondents, its commitment to international news, its larger number of pages for news, and its substantial Jewish audience who identified to some extent with the plight of their European brethren – the *Times* had more reasons than most American newspapers to pay attention to what was happening to Europe's Jews. In addition, the *Times*' publisher, who set the tone for his newspaper,[vii] identified with the plight of European Jews, as evidenced by his efforts to help distant relatives, a Bucharest correspondent, and total strangers; by his support of refugee havens in the Dominican Republic and Australia, and rescue schemes in Hungary; and by his intense, if acrimonious, involvement in the American Jewish community.

Yet, Arthur Hays Sulzberger had reasons he did not want his public pronouncements to match his private gestures, why he did not want his newspaper to recognize fully and forthrightly the significance of what was happening to the Jews. Philosophically, he considered singling out Jews to be a concession to Hitler's racial views and a contravention of his Reform Jewish convictions that the Jews were not a race or a people. To retreat from that ideal would have meant acknowledging that his place in America and his identity as an American were not as secure as he resolutely asserted. Although other Jews might have felt torn between their roles as Americans and their roles as Jews – between supporting their nation's leaders and maintaining ties to their community – Sulzberger professed no such conflict. America, as he repeatedly stated, came first. Besides, Sulzberger maintained that the only hope for European Jews was

[vii] In this, he seemingly differed from another prominent Jewish publisher, Eugene Meyer of the *Washington Post*. Managing Editor Jones apparently told the Bergson representatives: "There is no use in writing to Meyer because Meyer is out of the whole incident. He, Jones, is the one responsible for it." 10/17/44 memo, Palestine Statehood Committee, Reel #1, YU.

if their plight could be linked to that of other groups, because, as he said repeatedly, a minority could not save itself. His idealism (Jews should not be recognized as a separate group) and his pragmatism (Jews could not be saved as Jews) meshed perfectly. That particularly potent combination also made him less likely to alter his convictions throughout the war and even afterward. So his newspaper's opinion page published editorials about refugees, about persecution in Poland, about mass slaughter in Russia, and even about the Warsaw ghetto uprising, that never referred to Jews. His newspaper, when it ran front-page stories, described refugees seeking shelter, Frenchmen facing confiscation, or civilians dying in German camps, without making clear the refugees, Frenchmen, and civilians were mostly Jews. Only six stories during the war both described the Jews' plight and acknowledged that Jews were the primary victims on the front page. The Protestant-owned *New York Herald Tribune*, although its coverage was neither copious nor conspicuous, was less circumspect about the identity of the victims.

But here, too, the currents did not run in one direction. The United Nations' declaration confirming the extermination campaign appeared on the *Times*' front page, as did a story that recognized "one of the blackest crimes of all history . . . the wholesale systematic murder of the Jews of Europe." An editorial declared the task of saving them "as important as the winning of a battle." These stories and statements appeared most often in 1944 when the creation of the WRB gave official sanction to the effort to save European Jews. For all his philosophical and practical pronouncements, it may be that Arthur Sulzberger was not so much reluctant to recognize the suffering of his fellow Jews, as hesitant to lead his fellow citizens to that recognition. An intriguing 1947 *Commentary* article discusses the "guest-in-the-house theory of Jewish existence in the Diaspora," as applied to the *New York Times*' Ochs and his son-in-law successor. The author, Louis Berg, was not referring to the *Times*' Holocaust coverage, but his analysis may apply nonetheless.

> These otherwise excellent and able people have defaulted on the kind of leadership in this democracy that their probity and responsibility might entitle them to. Being cautious Jews, they cannot be bold Americans. No household could ask for more proper guests, no lord for better stewards. They make excellent public servants, obeying all the rules, leaning backwards to exonerate themselves from the charge of originality or pathfinding. But, by the same token, they cannot lead. . . . 'What will the Gentile say?' is hardly a slogan by which a people may express itself, or contribute its particular

> and useful genius to others. Too great a desire to please leads often to impotence – in politics as in love. How long, one wonders, will it take these particular Yahudim to believe in their heart of hearts what they so stubbornly profess to believe – that America means liberty and equality for all men, even Jews.[21]

The irony is that the *Times* was reluctant to lead for the same reason that the government and the press looked to it for leadership – its Jewish ownership.

The final step in the credibility problem is bystanders' willingness to rely on information received, believed, and valued to take action. Indeed, the credibility problem seeks primarily to explain bystanders' inaction, rather than to illuminate their actions. It is not necessary here to explore rescue possibilities except within one context – how the perception that nothing could be done, whether justified or not, may have affected bystanders' other judgments. In this sense, the last step in the credibility problem – relying on information to take action – flips back to affect assessments of believability and importance. Bystanders not only needed to believe and value information to take action, this argument goes, they also had to be able to foresee a possible course of action to be willing to believe and value information. If nothing could be done to save Jews, it was probably easier for bystanders to continue to disbelieve information or reject its salience than to accept their own powerlessness.[viii]

As with the previous processes, however, the last stage will vary depending on the bystanders' position. In this case, a key variable might be the action that would have been expected of bystanders had they acknowledged Jews were being exterminated. Government leaders who acknowledged the extermination campaign, for example, might have felt pressured to develop military and other strategies to rescue Jews. Jewish leaders who accepted news of the Holocaust might have felt obliged to mobilize the masses and prod a vast, intransigent bureaucracy. Given the difficulty of both tasks, some bystanders might have opted for denial. Determined not to be deterred from the singular goal of winning the war as quickly as possible, Allied officials, from Roosevelt and Churchill on down, probably found it easier, psychologically and practically, to cast doubt on the

[viii] This problem probably had a particularly strong impact among the Jews in Palestine, who were both more distraught because of personal ties to Europe's Jews and more dispirited because their weakness challenged the Zionist ideal. See Porot, *The Blue and the Yellow Stars of David*, and Segev, *The Seventh Million*.

possibility that a Holocaust was taking place than admit they were not going to try to stop it. Faced with the difficulty of devising and advocating a rescue strategy, many Jewish leaders probably clung to the possibility that the information about the Holocaust was not to be trusted. Yet, the process also might have worked in reverse. Government officials who believed that an extermination campaign was taking place and considered it important, such as Henry Morgenthau and John Pehle, were better able to envision and thus implement rescue strategies. Jewish leaders, such as Leon Kubowitzki, who accepted the news and cared deeply about it, advocated passionately for action.

Journalists again are situated differently from other bystanders. Journalists who believed the information in the thousand or so stories produced did not have to implement, or try to have implemented, some kind of rescue strategy. Their challenge: to decide to place a story on page one, instead of inside the newspaper, or write an editorial or column, rather than remain silent, or include a reference to the Jews in one of the highlights of the week, year, or war in review that ran periodically. Seen in this way, journalists faced a far less formidable challenge than either government or Jewish leaders, and thus had fewer grounds for inaction. The actions they could have taken were completely within their own power.

That description of journalists' possibilities, however, may frame the issue too narrowly. It may be, as Deborah Lipstadt argues, that the same sense of hopelessness that afflicted other bystanders also hobbled journalists. Lisptadt attributes the "practice of burying the information," to journalists' "dispassion, if not indifference," which she assumes stemmed from the perception that "nothing could be done and therefore there was no point in even talking about it." Conversely, as Lipstadt also points out, news organizations with a liberal orientation, such as the *New Republic*, the *Nation*, and *PM*, not only ardently advocated rescue measures, but also provided more, and more prominent, news coverage. For journalists, as well as for other bystanders, the ability to perceive possibilities for action might have affected judgments about believability and importance. Those who perceived that there were possibilities for action may have been more likely to believe and value information. Those who believed and valued information may have been more likely to conceive and entertain courses of action.

Yet, as Lipstadt notes at another point, objective journalists, like those at the *Times* and most mainstream news organizations, were not supposed to consider the potential impact on public policy in making news judgments. "The press does not decide how it will treat a story on the basis of whether attention to a topic will effect a change in policy," Lipstadt explains.[22] Certainly, the *New York Times* night editors would not consciously have concluded that they might as well put stories about the Jews' suffering on the inside pages because nothing could be done for them anyway. They would have been offended at the very notion. In the words of Neil MacNeil: "The flow of news would have been the determining factor."

The Allies' ultimate ability to save Jews therefore should have played less of a role in affecting journalists' actions than that of other bystanders. It may have played some role, however. Whatever the principle, the *Times* in practice used its news pages to rally support for various policy objectives. The newspaper, for example, had no reservations about writing news stories to drum up support for the American Red Cross, on whose board the publisher served. Other concrete, accomplishable objectives, such as changing immigration laws to allow British children to escape German bombs, generated many news stories and editorials. So did, though to a lesser extent, the prospect of a Dominican Republic refugee haven during the early stages of the war (a pet project of Arthur Sulzberger), and free ports at the end of the war. Without clear policy goals, it might have been harder to generate consistent front-page stories and numerous, enthusiastic editorials. By the same token, Sulzberger did not endorse certain policy options, such as loosening immigration quotas, that may have been available. Sulzberger's aversion to the solution advocated most vocally and vociferously by Jewish groups, a Jewish homeland in Palestine, might have dampened the newspaper's ability to rally around any rescue effort.

Throughout the war, the processes of receiving information, assessing its believability, determining its importance, and relying on it to take action interacted in exceedingly complex ways within individual bystanders and within communities of bystanders. At each stage of the process, there were also interactions among bystanders – the press, the U.S. government, American Jewish groups, and the American public. The press received and assessed information about the Holocaust, which it then disseminated to other bystanders who in turn received, believed or disbelieved, and valued it. The U.S. government, American Jewish groups, and the American public then took action, making statements, organizing protests, or attending rallies – or not. That in turn generated new information about the statement or the rally, for example, which the press received, and assessed for believability and importance. Depending on those assessments, the press would disseminate the new information, and the process would start all over again. At the same time, multiple players were jockeying behind-the-scenes to influence how the information would be disseminated. In this way, journalists were not simply affected by the credibility problem, they also played a crucial role in defining its terms. In other words, they played a crucial role in constructing the gap between knowing and understanding that affected bystanders' responses to the Holocaust.

The feedback loop can be illustrated with two examples. Consider the Roosevelt Administration's efforts to implement the free ports proposal in 1944. The plan allowed Jewish refugees to enter the United States outside regular immigration channels and stay for the duration of the war. Officials of the newly created WRB embraced the idea, which a *New York Post* columnist initially pushed.[ix] But the administration did not just take action and establish free ports. It orchestrated the presentation and dissemination of information about the proposal, engaging the press and the public in the process; the press then presented and disseminated the information back to the public and the administration in a way that helped shape the government's ultimate action.

Initially, the administration commissioned a poll. The poll described the proposal to respondents in the most innocuous terms possible, seemingly dictating, or at least forcefully directing, the positive outcome.[x] This suggests two things. First, that the administration (or at least some officials within the administration) were less interested in an objective reading of public sentiment, than in obtaining a particular reading of public sentiment. That in turns suggests less genuine concern about public

[ix] The creation of the refugee board was itself an example of this interaction, although an even more complex one.

[x] Respondents were asked: "It has been proposed that our government offer now [sic] temporary protection and refuge to those people in Europe who have been persecuted by the Nazis but have escaped, and are now homeless, and could save themselves by coming here. The plan proposes that these people would be kept in special camps in this country for the duration of the war. They would not be allowed to have jobs outside the camps. When the war is over, they would all be returned to their native lands. Would you approve or disapprove of this plan?" Of those responding, 70% approved, 23% disapproved, and 7% had no opinion. Cantril to Niles, 4/14/44, DN Papers, Box 25, BU.

reaction, and more concern for other administration officials' response. Indeed, Secretary of War Henry Stimson had been opposing havens and only reluctantly came around to support the proposal.[23] In either case, the public's "attitude" was not one-dimensionally affecting public actions. Various administration officials were helping construct a public response to produce a desired outcome.

The press also played a part. The administration next "floated" the idea at a press conference, having WRB officials mention the proposal was under consideration in response to a question. The administration even planted the question with a reporter. As anticipated (but not assured), the press disseminated the information about the free ports idea. One WRB official continued to try to influence the presentation of the news by meeting with the *Times*' Sulzberger and his top editors. The public presumably received (meaning read in the newspaper) and assessed the information, and in the case of several prominent individuals, including Felix Frankfurter and Arthur Sulzberger, acted in response to it. They made statements in favor of the proposal. Others, namely isolationist Congressmen, did not act to condemn it, which was also significant. WRB officials then used the public response they had helped shape to justify government action, which the president took a month and a half later when he announced 1,000 refugees would be housed in Fort Ontario, New York, until the war's end.

The process was not one way; the *Times* chose if, and how, to disseminate the information. WRB officials spoke about many issues at the press conference; the *Times* chose to lead with free ports. The *Times* described the free port residents as "1,000 refugees from Italy," which probably comported with the administration's preferred language but need not have. It chose supportive but not overwhelmingly enthusiastic language to describe the proposal in editorials. The *Times*, in effect, dropped the issue by not pressing Congress and the president to create more free ports, and by reporting the arrival of the refugees a few months later deep inside the paper. The administration contributed to the subdued coverage by having presidential advisor Harold Ickes, rather than Roosevelt himself or the secretary of state, greet the refugees. Had the press done things differently, had it ignored or condemned the proposal, for example, the government might have abandoned the free ports idea at the outset. Or, had the press continued to push the idea, splashing photos of the refugees' arrival on the front page and writing heartrending stories about their escape, the government might have decided to allow many more refugees to enter the United States.

Consider another example. In the summer of 1943, the WJC's Leon Kubowitzki wanted to get the OWI to change the way it distributed information about what was happening to Europe's Jews, particularly in broadcasts to European countries. "There are only general threats and warnings concerning the atrocities of which the civilian population in general is the victim," he complained, "but the horrible story of the way in which the Jewish population is being exterminated is not being told." Kubowitzki faced a problem. When he approached OWI, he was told by sympathetic officials that the agency would not act differently unless the information had first appeared in the American press. Indeed, when a Congressman, who had received constituent letters complaining that accounts of Axis executions and tortures were "fakes," OWI compiled a list of 18 "authenticated" atrocities, all drawn from American newspapers, 14 from the *New York Times*.[24] But the press, as has been seen, looked to government to help it determine how to play "the horrible story"; if the government did not distribute the information, the press tended to display it less prominently.

The reasons the government and the press were inclined to downplay the horrible story also tended to be mutually reinforcing. The government relied on the press, among other indicators, to help it discern public sentiment. It used systematic analyses of the content of newspapers, and to a lesser extent radio broadcasts,[25] as well as the judgment of individual reporters. When the U.S. government plotted its "propaganda strategy" for the occupied countries shortly after its entry into the war, it turned to journalists who had covered Germany, France, and Rumania for advice. The journalists told them not to push the Semitic angle for fear of alienating the citizens of Axis countries.[xi] The OWI relied on similar rationales

[xi] There are some indications that the press might have been more likely than other groups to perceive anti-Semitism as a powerful force. After the war, the Truman Administration convened panels of opinion leaders, including clergy, small businessmen, housewives, and editors, to determine attitudes toward immigration. It found the editors to be the "least likely of any panel to report unqualified approval," not because they or their newspapers opposed immigration but because of their perceptions of "public opinion as they have observed it." Of those who opposed greater immigration, almost two-fifths indicated that that point of view was "equated with or conditioned by feelings against Jews." "Opinions about Immigration," Preliminary Report, 10/21/46, Correspondence Panels, GIS, Bureau of the Budget, DN Papers, BU.

for not emphasizing Jewish persecution in domestic releases, referring to polls suggesting widespread anti-Semitism in the United States. Americans would not see the Jews' suffering as grounds for identification, the officials assumed, but as the basis for alienation. The result would be not sympathy for the Jews, but hostility to the war. The prewar experience, in which isolationists and anti-Semites accentuated the Jews' supposed role in dragging America into a European war, tended to shape these assumptions, at least in the minds of opinion makers.[26] The press in turn took official silence as an indication that the Jews' plight was not that important or that too much attention to it would jeopardize the war effort, further justifying their news judgments to play the story inside. The Roosevelt Administration, which, since its inception had assigned a government agency to index 425 newspapers daily, then used the lack of prominent news stories to confirm its judgment that the public was not interested and to justify its lack of response.

But neither the press nor the government really knew how much the public's anti-Semitic sentiment, which no doubt existed, might affect Americans' attitude toward the news that Jews were being mass murdered. Antipathy toward Jews in the United States or Great Britain might not necessarily translate into antipathy for European Jews. In his study of the responses of ordinary American and British citizens to news of the extermination of the Jews, Tony Kushner concludes that "in its most basic and common form, there could be dislike of Jews at home and sympathy for the Jews abroad." Nor was it clear that such anti-Semitism would necessarily reflect negatively on rescue efforts. Anti-Semitism was strongest in the spring of 1944, as American anxieties about the coming invasion of Europe and resulting American deaths peaked.[27] But at that point, "the efforts and success of those sympathetic to the plight of the Jews in the worlds of organized labour, the churches and American Jewry also peaked," Kushner explains. He concludes that "the relationship between state policy and public sentiment was extremely complex and cannot be explained by simplistic notions of the existence or absence of antisemitism."[28]

Even if domestic anti-Semitism carried over to European Jews, it still was not clear how that might have affected Americans' attitudes toward the war effort. Polls taken during the war did not try to measure how news of the Jews' destruction, whatever the depth of anti-Semitic fervor, affected public support for the war.[29] Before December 1941, Jews were suspected of trying to draw the United States into war, but those concerns likely dissipated after Pearl Harbor. The American Council of Public Affairs, made up of distinguished academics, concluded in January 1943 that American public opinion swung decisively in favor of war after Pearl Harbor and was based on detailed information that led to an understanding of the "fundamental issues of the war."[30] Charles Stember concludes in *Jews in the Mind of America* (p. 110): "In the end, the United States' entry into the war placed the nation squarely on the side of Hitler's victims and among the avowed opponents of anti-Semitism."

That is not to say, given lingering anti-Semitism, that Americans might not have turned against the war if they had become convinced their sons were dying to save Jews. But the assumption that any emphasis on the Jews would alienate the American public, which seemed to animate much of the American government's public relations response, was not self-evident. After Pearl Harbor, why would learning that Germans were murdering millions of Jews lead Americans to believe the war was being fought to save them? If it did, why would that automatically translate into negative feelings toward the war effort? Even assuming that was Americans' instinctive reaction, it still was not clear whether those concerns could have been alleviated depending on how the government and/or the press disseminated information.[xii] It might have been possible to generate sympathy for some victims (Jewish children perhaps), or trumpet all the other reasons for fighting the Nazis, or reiterate that the government's only goal was winning the war quickly, or even describe limited rescue efforts so as to blunt possible objections.

That is not to suggest that there was no basis for believing that the mass murder of Jews would make for poor propaganda. The point is the government, and the press, were governed by something more like a hunch, than strong evidence of an inevitable, overwhelming negative public response. OWI officials may have believed that too much publicity about the Jews would have created a backlash, or they may have found it

[xii] OWI, in fact, countered one anti-Semitic charge – that American Jews shirked military duty – by encouraging the press to publish stories about Jewish military heroes. See Rosten to Luce, 3/19/43; Rosten to Cowles, 4/14/43, RG208/75/232, NA; Rosten to O'Connor, 1/9/43, RG208/75/233, NA.

easier to believe that it would than to figure out whether it was true, or figure out if and how it could be changed.[xiii]

The point of both the free ports and OWI examples is that public opinion was not a fixed, immovable barrier that hemmed in policy makers or journalists. Different information presented in different ways elicited different responses. The examples also indicate that the press played a critical role in disseminating information, and thus in shaping public understanding, which in turn influenced public action. Had information been distributed differently, different understandings may have been created, leading to different actions. The chasm between knowing and acting might have been, if not bridged, at least narrowed. The gap reflected not fixed polarities, but fluctuating perceptions constructed from the individual choices of many actors.

As a result, how the press in general and the *New York Times* in particular told "the horrible story" mattered. It mattered because it affected what the public knew or did not know. Most Americans learned of European Jews' fate from the mass media, and most of them seemingly did not know about the Holocaust as it was happening. "The public almost certainly was not aware at first how large a proportion of the victims had been Jews," Charles Stember concludes. "Even by the end of the war, when Hitler's policy of systematic murder probably was generally known in the country, the public does not seem to have realized the extent to which Jews were special targets of his wrath."[31] Other scholars have concluded that the way the press disseminated the information left the public largely in the dark. "One reason ordinary Americans were not more responsive to the plight of the European Jews was that very many (probably a majority) were unaware of Hitler's extermination program until well into 1944 or later," David Wyman argues. "The information was not readily available to the public, because the mass media treated the systematic murder of millions of Jews as though it were minor news."[32] Lipstadt echoes that assessment: "[T]he press bears a great measure of responsibility for the public's skepticism and ignorance of the scope of the wartime tragedy."[33]

[xiii] In this, the government's public relations arm was like its military wing. Bendersky in *The "Jewish Threat,"* 347, criticizes the American Army not for inaccurate calculations of the military costs of helping Jews, but for its unwillingness to even undertake such calculations.

The *New York Times* contributed to the public's ignorance. Because the *Times* and other publications did not feature what was happening to European Jews *as Jews* on its front page, or write about their fate repeatedly in hard-hitting editorials, or highlight their plight in magazine articles or in retrospectives, the information likely was lost amid a barrage of world-shattering news. The *Times*' tendency to not identify the victims as Jews and to link their fate with that of other suffering peoples made it even harder to recognize "the extent to which the Jews were special targets of [Hitler's] wrath." Because of where and how the information was presented, most Americans might not have received news about the Holocaust in a way that suggested the information was believable and significant, or just as likely, may not have received it at all.[xiv] Even if information about what was happening to the Jews had been presented more directly, Americans may still have not grasped the dimensions of the tragedy. Studies of the response to news of the Holocaust in three small cities suggest that even among Jews, who would have received information from the Jewish press, other concerns tended to be paramount.[34,xv] It may also be that, given the difficulties of representing the Holocaust experience that Saul Friedlander, among others, have identified, news stories could never have transmitted the information effectively. But without the story being regularly and prominently displayed in the mainstream press, there was not much chance Americans could have understood the Holocaust's importance, however it was depicted.

The *Times*' coverage also mattered because other bystanders, particularly the American government, American Jewish groups, and the rest of

[xiv] During the war, the Gallup organization took three polls that tried to measure the American public's knowledge of German atrocities, but only the first, taken in January 1943, specifically asked about Jews. That poll is often cited as proof that Americans did not believe news about the extermination of the Jews. But the way the poll question was phrased as much as invited skepticism: "It is said that 2 million Jews have been killed in Europe since the war began – Do you think that is true or just a rumor?" Still, 48% of those asked said they believed it was true, 28% said it was a rumor, and 24% had no opinion. George H. Gallup, *The Gallup Poll: Public Opinion, 1935–1971*, New York: Random House (1972).

[xv] Alex Grobman, "What Did They Know?" 351, suggests that it was not enough for American Jews to read about attacks on the Jews in the Jewish press. "It was particularly important for the atrocities committed again the Jews to be publicly acknowledged in the American press, since many Jews became skeptical about their veracity if they were not."

the American press, took cues from the *New York Times*. Among major American newspapers, the *Times* was unique in the information it received, how it disseminated the news, and to whom. Recall how carefully government officials and Jewish leaders followed the news in the *Times*, not only to be informed themselves, but also to discover what information other bystanders were receiving. The *Times* was one actor, although by no means the only one, that might have been able to help bring the facts about the extermination of the Jews to public consciousness. But the full story of European Jewry's destruction remained below the surface, only emerging now and then in a diluted and fractured form. The swirling currents of disbelief, of other concerns, of hopelessness, of other people's pain, of conflicts about recognizing your own people's pain, swamped the news. In the process, the *Times* helped to drown out the last cry from the abyss.

Appendix A

Key Individuals

Abt-Peissak, Eugen, Elizabeth, and Clark	German refugees, Iphigene Sulzberger's cousins whom the family helped establish in States
Adler, Julius Ochs	*New York Times* Vice President and General Manager
Altmann, Josef, Betti, and children	Sulzberger cousins in Wiesbaden, Germany, whom Arthur Hays Sulzberger declined to help emigrate
Archambault, Gaston H.	*New York Times* Correspondent (Paris, Vichy, Berne) and French native who tended to support Vichy government
Axelsson, George	*New York Times* Correspondent (Paris, Berlin, Stockholm)
Barnes, James	U.S. Office of War Information official
Bergson, Peter	Palestinian Jew who came to the States to lobby for a Jewish Army to fight Nazis, and to help save European Jewry
Berle, Adolf	U.S. Assistant Secretary of State
Bernstein, Theodore	*New York Times* Cable Editor, handled all foreign news during war, including news of Jewish persecution
Billikopf, Jacob	Jewish Federation of Charities head, Arthur Sulzberger friend
Birchall, Frederick T.	*New York Times* Chief European Correspondent who reported from Germany, previously Acting Managing Editor

Bracker, Milton	*New York Times* Correspondent (London, North Africa, Rome)
Brigham, Daniel	*New York Times* Correspondent (Paris, Vichy, Berne)
Brock, Ray	*New York Times* Correspondent (Ankara) and critic of *Times*' Middle East reporting
Catledge, Turner	*New York Times* Correspondent (Washington, DC), Assistant Managing Editor (New York)
Crider, John	*New York Times* Correspondent (Washington, DC)
Currivan, Gene	*New York Times* Correspondent (London, Germany, Jerusalem)
Daniel, Clifton	*New York Times* Correspondent (London, Jerusalem)
Daniell, Raymond	*New York Times* Bureau Chief (London), married to London correspondent Tania Long Daniell
Daniell, Tania Long	*New York Times* Correspondent (London), married to London Bureau Chief Raymond Daniell and daughter of Berlin bureau Correspondent Robert Crozier Long
Davis, Elmer	U.S. Office of War Information Director, in charge of government propaganda efforts, tended to discourage propaganda about Jews' persecution
Denny, Harold	*New York Times* Correspondent (roving)
DuBois, Josiah	U.S. Treasury Assistant General Counsel, helped to create government agency whose mission was to rescue European Jews
Eden, Anthony	British Foreign Secretary
Elath, Eliahu	Jewish Agency official (Ankara)
Enderis, Guido	*New York Times* Bureau Chief (Berlin), Correspondent (Berne), considered sympathetic to Nazi regime

Feis, Herbert	U.S. Department of State, Economic Advisor
Frankfurter, Felix	U.S. Supreme Court Justice
Gerst, Elsbet Midas	Auschwitz survivor
Geyde, G. E. R.	*New York Times* Correspondent (Prague, Moscow)
Goldmann, Nahum	World Jewish Congress official (New York)
Gruenbaum, Isaac	Jewish Agency official (Jerusalem) who tried to persuade *Times* to publicize campaign to have Allies bomb death camps
Higgins, Marguerite	*New York Herald Tribune* Correspondent (Germany)
Hirschmann, Ira	U.S. War Refugee Board envoy (Turkey) who arranged rescue missions in 1944; friend of Arthur Hays Sulzberger
Hull, Cordell	U.S. Secretary of State
Huston, Luther	*New York Times* Deputy Bureau Chief (Washington, DC)
Irvin, Warren	*New York Times* Correspondent (New York, Geneva)
James, Edwin L.	*New York Times* Managing Editor, former Bureau Chief (Paris), who influenced coverage through control of staff
Knauth, Percy	*New York Times* Correspondent (Berlin)
Kovacs, Eugen	*New York Times* Correspondent (Bucharest), a Jew, who fled Rumania because of persecution
Krock, Arthur	*New York Times* Bureau Chief (Washington, DC) and conservative columnist who allied with State Department officials opposing immigration and assistance to Jews
Kubowitzki, A. Leon	World Jewish Congress official (New York), former Belgian lawyer who pushed to publicize European Jews' plight
Landau, Jacob	Jewish Telegraph Agency Editor

Lawrence, William	*New York Times* Correspondent (Washington, DC, Moscow) who provided on-site accounts of Babi Yar massacre, Maidanek death camp
Lazaron, Morris S.	Baltimore rabbi, American Council for Judaism founder, friend of Arthur Hays Sulzberger, opposed Jewish state in Palestine, argued that refugees should return to nations of origin
Levinthal, Louis	Judge, Zionist Organization of America official
Levy, Joseph M.	*New York Times* Correspondent (Cairo, Jerusalem, Ankara) who crossed British officials in Middle East, covered deportation of Jews from Hungary
Lichtheim, Richard	Jewish Agency official (Geneva) who pushed to publicize European Jewry's fate
Lochner, Louis	Associated Press Correspondent (Berlin)
Long, Breckinridge	U.S. Assistant Secretary of State in charge of visas who opposed greater immigration
Long, Robert Crozier	*New York Times* Financial Correspondent (Berlin)
MacDonald, James	*New York Times* Correspondent (London)
MacLeish, Archibald	U.S. Office of War Information Domestic Chief
MacNeil, Neil	*New York Times* Assistant Night Managing Editor, as part of the bullpen controlled the newspaper at night, personally decided the stories that would appear on front page
MacNeil, Neil, Jr.	*New York Times* Correspondent (New York) and son of Assistant Night Managing Editor Neil MacNeil; later became *Time* magazine's congressional correspondent
Magnes, Judah	New York City rabbi, Hebrew University President, friend of Arthur Hays Sulzberger,

	advocate of binational state of Jews, Arabs in Palestine
Mannon, Virginia	U.S. War Refugee Board official in charge of publicity
Markel, Lester	*New York Times* Sunday Editor
Matthews, Herbert	*New York Times* Correspondent (Spain, Rome)
McCaw, Raymond	*New York Times* Night Managing Editor, as part of the bullpen controlled the newspaper at night
McCormick, Anne O'Hare	*New York Times* columnist, specialized in foreign policy
McDonald, James G.	League of Nations' High Commissioner for Refugees, *New York Times* Editorial Page Writer
Meltzer, Julian	*New York Times* Correspondent (Jerusalem)
Merz, Charles	*New York Times* Editorial Page Editor, agreed with Publisher Arthur Hays Sulzberger, who named him to post, on newspaper's editorial positions, deferred to Sulzberger on Jewish issues
Meyer, Margarete Midas	German refugee, Iphigene Sulzberger's cousin whom Sulzbergers helped to immigrate to the United States
Midas, Erich and Thea	German refugees, Iphigene Sulzberger's cousins whom Sulzbergers helped to immigrate to the United States
Midas, Joseph and Emilie	German refugees whom Sulzbergers helped to immigrate to the United States
Morgenthau, Henry, Jr.	U.S. Secretary of the Treasury, friend of Arthur Hays Sulzberger, overcame initial reluctance to become involved in Jewish issues by supporting War Refugee Board
Neumann, Emanuel	Zionist activist and public relations expert

Nussbaum, Max and Ruth	German refugees who alerted Arthur Hays Sulzberger to position of Jews in Germany
Ochs, Adolph	*New York Times* Publisher, 1896–1935
Oechsner, Frederick	United Press Correspondent (Berlin)
Parker, Ralph	*New York Times* Correspondent (Moscow), wrote many stories of German massacres in Soviet territories based on eyewitness accounts
Paul, Randolph	U.S. Treasury General Counsel who pushed for government agency to help Jews
Pehle, John	U.S. War Refugee Board Director
Peters, C. Brooks	*New York Times* Correspondent (Berlin)
Philip, Percy J.	*New York Times* Bureau Chief (Paris)
Phillips, Ruby	*New York Times* Correspondent (Havana)
Price, Byron	U.S. Office of Censorship Director
Proskauer, Joseph	American Jewish Committee official
Reston, James	*New York Times* Correspondent (London, Washington, DC), assistant to Arthur Hays Sulzberger
Richards, Bernard	Jewish Information Bureau official whom Arthur Hays Sulzberger hired to advise him on Jewish issues
Riegner, Gerhart	World Jewish Congress official (Geneva), learned of German plan to exterminate all European Jews in 1942
Rosenwald, Lessing	American Council for Judaism official who opposed Jewish state in Palestine, argued that refugees should return to nations of origin
Rosten, Leo	U.S. Office of War Information Deputy Director, prepared government propaganda on "the nature of the enemy" that deliberately downplayed the Nazis' Jewish victims

Sauerwein, Jules	*New York Times* Correspondent (Paris, Berne), considered a German collaborator
Schultz, Sigrid	*Chicago Tribune* Correspondent (Berlin)
Schwarz, Daniel	*New York Times* Sunday editor
Schwarzbart, Ignacy	Polish National Council member, one of Council's two Jewish members who first learned of and publicized the extermination campaign in Poland
Sedgwick, Alexander C.	*New York Times* Correspondent (Middle East), considered sympathetic to British interests in Palestine
Sherwood, Robert	U.S. Office of War Information Foreign Chief
Silver, Abba Hillel	Cleveland rabbi, American Zionist Emergency Council head, accused the *Times* and Publisher Arthur Hays Sulzberger of anti-Zionist bias in reporting news
Steinberg, Milton	New York City rabbi, Park Avenue Synagogue, accused the *Times* and Publisher Arthur Hays Sulzberger of anti-Zionist bias in reporting news
Steinhardt, Laurence	U.S. Ambassador (Moscow, Ankara), friend of Arthur Hays Sulzberger, criticized for handling of visas for Jews in Moscow, considered more helpful to rescue efforts in Turkey
Sulzberger, Iphigene Ochs	Part-owner, *New York Times*, daughter of Publisher Adolph Ochs, wife of Publisher Arthur Hays Sulzberger, shared their orientation that considered Jews solely a religious group, opposed a Jewish state
Sulzberger, Arthur Hays	*New York Times* Publisher who dictated the newspaper's editorial direction, particularly on issues involving Jews

Sulzberger, Bertha	German refugee, Arthur Hays Sulzberger's cousin by marriage whom he helped to leave a concentration camp in France
Sulzberger, Cyrus L.	*New York Times* Correspondent (Southern Europe, Moscow, Middle East, Chief Foreign), nephew of Arthur Hays Sulzberger, shared his uncle's assimilationist orientation, not particularly interested in fate of Jews in countries he covered
Sulzberger, David Hays	Arthur Hays Sulzberger's brother who was involved in various Jewish organizations helping refugees
Sulzberger, Ernest	German refugee, Arthur Hays Sulzberger's cousin whom he helped to immigrate to the United States
Sulzberger, Fritz and Else	German refugees, Arthur Hays Sulzberger's cousins, whom he helped establish themselves in the United States
Sulzberger, Paul	German refugee, Arthur Hays Sulzberger's cousin, whom he declined to help emigrate
Szapiro, Jerzy	*New York Times* Correspondent (Warsaw, Paris, London)
Szoszkes, Henryk	Refugee, former Warsaw banker who provided information on Jews in Poland
Tetlow, Edwin	*Daily Mail* Correspondent (Germany)
Tolischus, Otto	*New York Times* Correspondent (Berlin, Tokyo) whose tough approach to Nazi regime helped balance the Berlin bureau chief's more sympathetic stance
Valery, Bernard	*New York Times* Correspondent (Stockholm)
Villard, Oswald Garrison	*Nation* Editor who criticized *Times*' unwillingness to defend Jews
Warburg, James	U.S. Office of War Information official

Warren, Lansing	*New York Times* Correspondent (Paris, Vichy) who tended to support Vichy government, including its administration of concentration camps
Welles, Sumner	U.S. Undersecretary of State, known as one of State officials sympathetic to Jews
Wise, Isaac M.	Rabbi, Iphigene Ochs Sulzberger's maternal grandfather, founder of American Reform movement, who considered Jews solely a religious group, not a race or people, who should integrate into the countries where they lived, opposed a Jewish state
Wise, Stephen S.	New York City rabbi, head of World Jewish Congress who led American Jews' mostly unsuccessful effort to rescue their European brethren, often came into conflict with the *Times*
Wolsey, Louis	Detroit rabbi, American Council for Judaism founder who opposed Jewish state in Palestine, argued that refugees should return to nations of origin
Zinn, Louis	Iphigene Sulzberger's cousin who committed suicide after being released from German concentration camp
Zygielbojm, Szmul	One of two Jewish members of the Polish National Council who first learned of and publicized the extermination campaign in Poland; committed suicide to protest world's indifference to Jews' fate

Appendix B

Key Institutions

Jewish Organizations

American Council for Judaism: Anti-Zionist Reform rabbis organized the council in 1942 in response to what they perceived to be Reform's movement away from the Judaism-as-a-religion-only principles of Reform founder Isaac M. Wise. The council expanded to include laymen, such as *Times* publisher and Wise's grandson-in-law Arthur Hays Sulzberger, who helped write the group's founding statement and served briefly as a vice president. The group was stridently anti-Zionist and even after the Holocaust insisted that Jews remain in their countries of origin, including Poland and Germany. Sulzberger officially broke with the group in 1943, but continued to support it behind the scenes until the founding of the state of Israel in 1948. Among its religious leaders were founders, Rabbis **Morris S. Lazaron** and **Louis Wolsey**. **Lessing Rosenwald**, scion of the Sears Roebuck fortune, served as lay president.

American Jewish Committee: The committee was founded in 1906 by well-to-do American Jews, mostly of German background, including several of *Times* publisher Arthur Hays Sulzberger's relatives. Because its membership included men of wealth and social prestige, the committee had influence within the American government. It shunned public protests, preferring behind-the-scenes negotiation to affect U.S. policy. The group did not support the idea of a Jewish state and thus often found itself in conflict with other Jewish groups. **Maurice Wertheim** served as president at the beginning of World War II and was succeeded by lawyer **Joseph Proskauer** in 1943.

American Jewish Conference: An assembly of major Jewish organizations formed in 1943 to develop a unified position on wartime and postwar issues. The group sponsored a conference in the late summer of

1943 that was supposed to hammer out American Jewry's policy positions. When conference delegates passed a resolution endorsing a Jewish state, however, several constituent organizations, including the American Jewish Committee, bolted. The conference was never able to a achieve unity on either the wartime issue of how to save European Jews or the postwar issue of immigration to a Jewish state.

American Zionist Emergency Council: Several Zionist organizations, including the Zionist Organization of America and Hadassah, organized AZEC in 1942 to serve as their political action and public relations arm. (The group was originally known as the **American Emergency Committee for Zionist Affairs**.) It initially waged an effective grassroots campaign pushing for greater immigration to Palestine and the eventual creation of a Jewish commonwealth there. Fighting between its two powerful leaders, Rabbi **Abba Hillel Silver** and Rabbi **Stephen S. Wise**, limited the group's influence, particularly after Silver quit the organization at the end of 1944 as a result of the power struggle.

Emergency Committee to Save the Jewish People of Europe: A group of Palestine Jews, who had originally come to the United States to lobby for a separate Jewish Army, formed the Emergency Committee in late 1942 upon confirmation of the news of Germany's extermination campaign. Led by **Peter Bergson** and more commonly referred to as the Bergson Group, the organization sponsored newspaper advertisements, including many in the *New York Times,* lobbied Congressional leaders and the Roosevelt Administration, and held public rallies. The Emergency Committee's public campaign helped to push the administration to create the War Refugee Board, but established Jewish organizations accepted neither its tactics nor its leaders.

Joint Emergency Committee on European Jewish Affairs: In the wake of the news that Germany was determined to destroy European Jewry, representatives of major Jewish organizations, including the World Jewish Congress and the American Jewish Committee, met periodically to try to coordinate the American Jewish community's response to the unfolding tragedy. The representatives were known at first as the Temporary Committee and then reconstituted as the Joint Emergency Committee in March 1943. Given his other important posts in Jewish organizations, including president of the World Jewish Congress and vice president of the Zionist Organization of America, Rabbi **Stephen S. Wise** was the unofficial leader of this group.

Jewish Agency: The Jewish Agency, led by **David Ben-Gurion**, was the quasigovernmental organization of the Jews in Palestine. Its representatives were engaged in various attempts to rescue European Jews. Among them were **Eliahu Elath**, its political director who was in Turkey in 1941; **Isaac Gruenbaum**, who headed its rescue committee; and **Richard Lichtheim**, its representative in Geneva who worked closely with the World Jewish Congress' Gerhart Riegner.

World Jewish Congress: The congress was founded in 1936 to serve as a worldwide umbrella organization for Jewish organizations in different countries and to counter attacks on Jewish economic and political rights. During World War II, its headquarters moved from Geneva to New York City, where its largest affiliate, the **American Jewish Congress**, was based. Middle- and lower-class Jews of East European origin had founded the American Jewish Congress in 1922 as an alternative to the uppercrust, German-dominated American Jewish Committee. During the war, Rabbi **Stephen S. Wise** headed both the World Jewish Congress and the American Jewish Congress. **Nahum Goldmann** chaired the WJC's administrative committee, while **A. Leon Kubowitzki** headed its European Affairs section. **Gerhart Riegner**, who served as the group's representative in Geneva, was instrumental in getting news of the extermination campaign to the West.

U.S. Government

Office of Censorship: Established shortly after the attack on Pearl Harbor, the office censored communications between the United States and foreign countries, including the mail, and asked the domestic press to voluntarily censor itself. It issued a code listing the type of information that should not be published. **Byron Price**, the Associated Press' executive news editor who was on leave from the wire service, headed the office. The military also engaged in censorship but under separate authority. To receive accreditation in military theaters, which was required to enter those areas, war correspondents had to agree to submit their copy to military censors.

Office of War Information: OWI was created in June 1942 with the authority to use press, radio, and motion pictures to facilitate understanding of the war effort, and to coordinate all the government's information activities. **Elmer Davis**, a former *Times* reporter and CBS radio commentator, served as director. **Archibald MacLeish**, a poet and the Librarian of Congress who had headed one of the OWI's predecessor agencies, became OWI's domestic chief, while ardent New Dealer and playwright **Robert Sherwood** headed the foreign propaganda arm. **Leo Rosten**, the OWI deputy director with responsibility for information on the enemy, supervised propaganda about German atrocities and was the official OWI contact for Jewish organizations. **James Barnes**, who had been the *Herald Tribune*'s Moscow bureau chief, Berlin correspondent, and foreign editor, and **James Warburg**, a member of the wealthy Jewish banking family, were considered among the few OWI officials sympathetic to European Jews' plight.

State Department: Secretary of State **Cordell Hull** tended to defer to his personally chosen assistant secretary, **Breckinridge Long** on issues involving immigration of Jews to the United States and other rescue issues. Long, who headed the visa division, had a well-known and well-deserved reputation as the embodiment of State's anti-Jewish policy. Jewish groups saw Undersecretary of State **Sumner Welles** as their highest-ranking ally in State, but Hull forced Welles to resign in the summer of 1943. **Adolf Berle**, assistant secretary of state, and **Herbert Feis**, economic adviser to State, were also among the State officials considered sympathetic to the Jews.

Treasury Department: As the only Jew in the Roosevelt Cabinet, Secretary of the Treasury **Henry Morgenthau, Jr.**, often found himself being asked to help European Jews. Until 1943, he and his department had not been deeply involved in the issue. But then **John Pehle**, foreign funds control director, began exploring ways to circumvent the Allies' economic blockade of German-controlled countries to provide relief to Jews and others in Nazi-held territory. Along with General Counsel **Randolph Paul** and Assistant General Counsel **Josiah DuBois**, Pehle discovered many examples of the State Department's unwillingness to assist European Jews. The young non-Jewish Treasury lawyers then pushed Secretary Morgenthau to wrestle the entire issue away from State officials. Helped by outside pressure from Congress and Jewish groups, particularly the Emergency Committee to Save the Jewish People of Europe, Morgenthau was able to convince Roosevelt to establish the War Refugee Board in January 1944.

War Refugee Board: In January 1944, President Roosevelt signed the executive order establishing the War Refugee Board, a U.S. government agency whose mission was to try to save Jews and other persecuted minorities. The Secretaries of State, War, and Treasury jointly headed the board, but in reality Treasury took control, with Treasury's **John Pehle** as its director. Pehle tapped **Virginia Mannon**, who had worked with him at Treasury, to spearhead the agency's public relations effort. Among other rescue efforts, **Ira Hirschmann**, a Bloomingdale's executive, was sent to the Balkans in February 1944, to find a way to ferry Jews from Europe to safety.

Appendix C

List of Wartime Front-Page Stories Concerning Jewish Issues

1939

October 31: "Nazi Tortures Detailed by Britain; Concentration Camp Horrors Told"

1940

January 19: "Kin of Boston Man Found by Pope in Warsaw; Other Agencies Long Unable to Aid Tailor"

January 31: "Dominican Haven Set Up for Exiles: Trujillo Signs Contract to Put 500 Families on Land Which He Has Given Personally"

February 29: "Palestine Curbs Jews' Land Buying; British Bans Purchases in Big Area, Limits Them in Another – Jewish Agency Defiant"

March 2: "Vatican Post Goes to Jew as Italy's Ban Is Imposed"

August 1: "France to Seize Fortunes of Rothschild, Louis-Dreyfus and Other Noted Exiles"

November 26: "Refugee Ship Off Palestine Sunk by Blast; Casualties Feared Among 1, 771 Homeless"

1941

January 9: "U.S. Refuses French Plea to Take Refugees; Reich Curb Called Bar to Orderly Emigration"

March 13: "Last Sea Route from Lisbon to U.S. Stops Ticket Sale to Refugees"

May 7: "Nazis Held Ready to Crush Serb Guerillas and Jews"

June 18: "U.S. Bars Refugees with Kin in Reich; Charges Threat to Torture Relatives Force Immigrants to Become Espionage Spies"

August 22: "Zone in Paris Is Encircled For a Round-Up by Police"
November 9: "Berlin Dean Held; Prayed for Jews"
December 14: "100 Hostages Shot by Nazis in France"

1942

June 14: "258 Jews Reported Slain in Berlin for Bomb Plot at Anti-Red Exhibit"
July 15: "2 Die in Marseille in Bastille Parade"
July 22: "Nazi Punishment Seen by Roosevelt; Says Hitler Will be Held to 'Strict Accountability' – Churchill Greets Rally"
August 6: "Pope Is Said to Plead for Jews Listed for Removal from France"
August 22: "President Warns Atrocities of Axis Will be Avenged"
September 16: "Hull Warns Vichy on Labor Draft; Condemns Deportations of Jews"
September 18: "Laval Interns a Catholic Leader In Wake of Church Plea for Jews"
September 20: "Pope Has Long Talk with Taylor; Move to Aid Jews in France Seen"
December 18: "11 Allies Condemn Nazi War on Jews"

1943

March 2: "Save Doomed Jews, Huge Rally Pleads"
April 20: "Refugee Aid Linked to Victory in War"
April 22: "Secret Polish Radio Asks Aid, Cut Off"
August 31: "Rescue at Once of Europe's Jews Demanded at Conference Here"
September 2: "Opening of Palestine as Homeland Demanded by Jewish Conference"
October 17: "Pope Said to Help in Ransoming Jews"
December 11: "580,000 Refugees Admitted to United States in Decade"

1944

January 30: "Roosevelt Board Is Negotiating to Save Refugees from Nazis"
March 5: "Marshall Opposes Vote on Palestine"
March 6: "Senate Expected to Defer Vote on Palestine Immigration Issue"

March 10: "Roosevelt Backs Palestine Plan As Homeland for Refugee Jews"
March 25: "Roosevelt Warns Germans On Jews"
April 19: "'Free Ports' to Admit Refugees May Be Set Up Under U.S. Plan"
June 10: "1,000 Refugees Will Enter, To be Housed at Fort Ontario"
June 13: "President Predicts Murder Orgy by Nazis to Wipe Out Minorities"
August 30: "Nazi Mass Killings Laid Bare at Camps"
October 20: "Dewey Backs State Department in Warning Nazis Over Murders"
November 13: "Foe Put Nurseries Inside Death Camp; Fairy-Tale Settings to House Children of Internees Are Found at Holland Prison"
November 26: "U.S. Board Bares Atrocity Details Told by Witnesses at Polish Camps"

1945

April 18: "Nazi Death Factory Shocks Germans on a Forced Tour"
May 1: "Dachau Captured by Americans Who Kill Guards, Liberate 32,000"

Notes

Introduction

1. This includes all inside stories detailing how the Germans or German allies treated the Jews during the war where the stories specifically state that Jews are involved, or where their involvement is apparent from the context. Stories that mention civilian massacres in Poland or the Soviet Union, for example, are excluded if they do not state explicitly that Jews were among the victims. Stories about American Jewish organizations or events in Palestine were only counted among the inside stories if they touched on German actions. Stories that dealt mainly with other topics, such as the German invasion of Hungary, were included if at least two paragraphs mentioned what was happening to the Jews. Front-page stories about Palestine and other events that involved Jews, even if Jews were not explicitly mentioned in the text, were included to provide a fuller picture of the *Times*' editorial priorities.
2. Richard Breitman, *Official Secrets: What the Nazis Planned, What the British and Americans Knew*, New York: Hill and Wang (1998); Henry L. Feingold, *The Politics of Rescue: The Roosevelt Administration and the Holocaust, 1938–1945*, New York: Holocaust Library (1980); Saul Friedman, *No Haven for the Oppressed: United States Policy Toward Jewish Refugees, 1938–1945*, Detroit: Wayne State University Press (1973); Martin Gilbert, *Auschwitz and the Allies*, New York: Holt, Rinehart and Winston (1981); Monty Noam Penkower, *The Jews Were Expendable: Free World Diplomacy and the Holocaust*, Urbana: University of Illinois Press (1983); and David S. Wyman, *The Abandonment of the Jews, America and the Holocaust, 1941–1945*, New York: Pantheon (1984).
3. Boston: Little Brown and Company (1980), 74. See also Deborah Lipstadt, *Beyond Belief: The American Press and the Coming of the Holocaust*, New York: The Free Press (1986), 272.
4. See, for example, "Nazis Envisage Chattel Slavery for People of Conquered Nations," 12/6/40, 1; "800 Reported Dead in French Riots," 11/12/43, 1; and "London Hears Hitler Is Dying," 4/12/45, 1.
5. David Engel, *Facing a Holocaust: The Polish Government-in-Exile and the Jews, 1943–1945*, Chapel Hill: The University of North Carolina Press (1993), 15.

6. *Politics of Rescue*, 321.
7. Joyce Fine, "American Radio Coverage of the Holocaust," *Simon Wiesenthal Center Annual* 5 (1988): 145–65. See also Jean Seaton, "Reporting Atrocities: The BBC and the Holocaust," in Jean Seaton and Ben Pimlott, eds., *The Media in British Politics*, Brookfield, Vt.: Gower Publishing Co. (1987), and Jeremy D. Harris, "Broadcasting the Massacres: An Analysis of the BBC's Contemporary Coverage of the Holocaust," *Yad Vashem Studies* 25 (1996): 65–98.
8. See Anthony Bosnick, "America and the Jews: 1933–1948," *America* 177:15 (November 15, 1997) 23–7; Arlene Rossen Cardozo, "American Magazine Coverage of the Nazi Death Camp Era," *Journalism Quarterly* 60(4) (1983): 717–8; and Robert Ross, *So It Was True: The American Protestant Press and the Nazi Persecution of the Jews*, Minneapolis: University of Minnesota Press (1980).
9. See Yehuda Bauer, "When Did They Know?" *Midstream* 14(4) (1968): 51–9; Alex Grobman, "What Did They Know? The American Jewish Press and the Holocaust," *American Jewish Historical Quarterly* 68(3) (1979): 327–52; and Haskel Lookstein, *Were We Our Brothers' Keepers? The Public Response of American Jews to the Holocaust, 1938–1944*, New York: Vintage (1985).
10. Variations on these explanations can be found in Laqueur, *The Terrible Secret*; Lipdstadt, *Beyond Belief*; Wyman, *The Abandonment of the Jews*; Barbie Zelizer, *Remembering to Forget: Holocaust Memory Through the Camera's Eye*, Chicago: University of Chicago Press (1998); and Peter Novick, *The Holocaust in American Life*, Boston: Houghton Mifflin Company (1999). Novick also offers the following argument for why "American newspapers published relatively little about the ongoing Holocaust" (p. 23): "News is event-, not process-oriented: bombing raids, invasions, and naval battles are the stuff of news, not delayed, often hearsay accounts of the wheels of the murder machine grinding relentlessly on." But of course the Holocaust too involved "events," the deportation of Jews from a particular town, the liquidation of a particular ghetto, an uprising at a particular concentration camp, reports of which were for the most part neither delayed nor based on hearsay.
11. Phillip Knightly, *The First Casualty: From the Crimea to Vietnam: The War Correspondent as Hero, Propagandist, and Myth Maker*, New York: Harcourt Brace Jovanovich (1975), 192–216, describes the propaganda uses of Spanish Civil War atrocities, and Zelizer, *Remembering to Forget*, makes the connection to journalistic doubts about reports of the Holocaust. Seaton, "Reporting Atrocities," argues that the political uses made of atrocity stories in Spain, Abyssinia, and Palestine affected the BBC coverage.
12. 6/27/42, 5.
13. See, for example, "Germans Execute 70 at Bordeaux," 9/23/42, 1; "72 Dutch Anti-Nazis Shot," 5/5/42, 1; and "Nazis Kill 10 Hostages in Norway after Proclaiming an Emergency," 10/7/42, 1.
14. 3/13/42, 8. This was even the contemporaneous academic understanding. See Vernon McKenzie, "Atrocities in World War II – What We Can Believe," *Journalism Quarterly* 19 (September 1942): 268–76.

15. This includes part-time correspondents who had a variety of financial arrangements with the paper, from receiving a retainer to being paid "by space," or the amount they wrote.
16. David Halberstam, *The Powers That Be*, New York: Alfred A. Knopf (1979), 183.
17. Richard Kluger, *The Paper: The Life and Death of the New York Herald Tribune*, New York: Alfred A. Knopf (1986), 301–3.
18. *NYT*, 5/6/41, 1.
19. See for example, 9/10/44, 1.
20. Oswald Garrison Villard, *The Disappearing Daily: Chapters in American Newspaper Evolution*, New York: Alfred A. Knopf (1944), 78.
21. *Beyond Belief*, 220.
22. Halberstam, *The Powers That Be*, 213. The New York Times Company Archives does not have records of the demographic breakdown of the *Times*' readership in the late 1930s and 1940s. Kluger, *The Paper*, 385, also notes that the *Herald Tribune* had a large and growing Jewish audience in the 1930s.
23. In an e-mail to the author, dated 10/16/02, Jason Maleski, a student at West Chester University, described finding his grandmother's clippings.
24. *The Political World of American Zionism*, Detroit: Wayne State University Press (1961), 35.
25. Matthew Josephson, "Typewriter Statesman," *Saturday Evening Post* 216:5 (7/29/44), 9.
26. Meinholtz to James, no date, mid-1943, ELJ File, RD Folder, NYTCA.
27. *Jewish Power: Inside the American Jewish Establishment*, Reading, Mass.: Addison-Wesley Publishing Co. (1996), 300–1.
28. H. G. Nicholas, ed., *Washington Dispatches 1941–1945: Weekly Political Reports from the British Embassy*, Chicago: University of Chicago Press (1981), 437–8.
29. When the World Jewish Congress, for example, issued press releases on war crimes in 1945, nine of 12 excerpts in its file were from the *Times*. MSS 361/C119/13, AJA. When the Office of War Information compiled a list of 18 news stories about enemy atrocities, 14 were from the *New York Times*. Colby to Clark, 9/22/44; Tinsley to Colby, Davis to Johnson, 10/3/44, 9/22/44, OWI, News Bureau, Office of the Chief, General Subjects Files, Box 975, NA. See also Morgenthau Diaries, FDRL.
30. Hull to Sulzberger, 1/6/43, AHS File, CH Folder, NYTCA.
31. Frankfurter to Sulzberger, 12/30/40, FF Papers, Reel #64, LC. See also Frankfurter to Sulzberger, 1/16/53, FF Papers, Reel #102, LC.
32. Eliahu Elath, *Zionism at the UN: A Diary of the First Days*, Philadelphia: Jewish Publication Society of America (1976), 301.
33. Box 66.13, Cable from London, 8/12/43, Box 3.2 (translated by Zbigniew Stancyzk), Polish Information Center Papers, HI.
34. Herbert L. Matthews, *A World in Revolution: A Newspaperman's Memoir*, New York: Charles Scribner's Sons (1971), 113.
35. Josephson, "Typewriter Statesman," 9.

36. Leo C. Rosten, *The Washington Correspondents*, New York: Harcourt, Brace and Company (1937), 171.
37. Lipstadt, *Beyond Belief*, 171.
38. Transcript of videotaped interview (unaired) for *Holocaust: The Untold Story*, Freedom Forum Productions, courtesy of producer Colette Fox. Beichman offered the anecdote to illustrate why the "most important failure" of coverage of the Holocaust was "that of *The New York Times*," but in subsequent e-mails to Fox, dated 1/5/01 and 1/9/01, he argued strongly that the *Times* should not be singled out for criticism. Transcript and e-mails in the author's possession.
39. *The Disappearing Daily*, 78.
40. *The Abandonment of the Jews*, 323.
41. David S. Wyman and Rafael Medoff, *A Race Against Death: Peter Bergson, America, and the Holocaust*, New York: The New Press (2002), 75.
42. Talese, *The Kingdom and the Power*, 114.

Chapter 1

1. 11/22/39 memo, ELJ File, JTA Folder, NYTCA.
2. Sulzberger to Brown, 12/1/41; Brown to Sulzberger, 12/2/41; AHS File, JJ Folder, NYTCA; Wise to Slomovitz, 3/17/37, SSW Papers, Reel 74-53, AJHS.
3. Even news organizations that were not controlled by Jews faced charges that they were. In 1938, the American Jewish Committee moved quickly to quell rumors that the nation's two largest news services, the Associated Press and the United Press, "were so largely owned and controlled by Jewish money that a distorted picture of the atrocities perpetrated against Jews in foreign countries was presented to American readers." Buell to Waldman, 9/29/38, Bernstein to Schneiderman, 9/30/38, Waldman to Buell, 10/3/38, American Jewish Committee Collection, Gen-10, Box 231, Press/Mass Media 1938–62 Folder, YIVO.
4. Enderis to James, 7/19/33; Enderis to James, 2/2/34; Enderis to James, 1/16/36, ELJ File, BB Folder, NYTCA.
5. Geyde to Sulzberger, 2/1/36, AHS File, JJ Folder, NYTCA.
6. 1/31/34, ELJ File, Anti-Semitism Folder, NYTCA.
7. See Charles H. Stember, *Jews in the Mind of America*, New York: Basic Books (1966), and Leonard Dinnerstein, *Antisemitism in America*, New York: Oxford University Press (1994).
8. Sulzberger to his children, 8/31/62, AHS File, JJ Folder, NYTCA.
9. Sulzberger to Morgenthau, 7/12/38, Morgenthau diaries, Reel #36, Diary #134, FDRL.
10. See Stephen Birmingham, "Does a Zionist Conspiracy Control the Media?" *More* 6 (July/August 1976): 15; Max Frankel, *The Times of My Life and My Life with the* Times, New York: Random House (1999), 399; Goldberg, *Jewish Power*, 301; Joseph Goulden, *A. M. Rosenthal and His Times*, Seacaucus, N.J.: Lyle Stuart Inc. (1988), 38, and Nan Robertson *The Girls in the Balcony*, New York: Random House (1992), 221.

11. See Ronald Steel, *Walter Lippmann and the American Century*, Boston: Little Brown and Company (1980).
12. Talese in *The Kingdom and the Power*, 71–2, points out that reporters who believed their bylines were changed to mask their Jewishness could not prove it and were better off keeping their theory to themselves.
13. AHS File, JJ Folder, NYTCA.
14. Meyer Berger, *The Story of the New York Times 1851–1951*, New York: Simon and Schuster (1951), 243; Tifft and Jones, *The Trust,* 110; Iphigene Ochs Sulzberger, *Memoirs of Iphigene Ochs Sulzberger of* The New York Times *Family*, New York: Dodd Mead & Co. (1981), 107.
15. 1937 unpublished essay, AS Papers, Series II, Folder 47, YU; Louis Rapoport, *Shake Heaven and Earth: Peter Bergson and the Struggle to Rescue the Jews of Europe*, Jerusalem: Gefen Publishing House (1999), 190.
16. 12/15/59, sent 8/31/62; *Congress Weekly*, 11/20/42, AHS File, JJ Folder, NYTCA; I. Sulzberger, *Memoirs,* 110.
17. James G. Heller, *Isaac M. Wise: His Life, Work and Thought*, New York: The Union of American Hebrew Congregations (1965); Robert Wistrich, Zionism and Its Jewish Assimilationist Circle, 1897–1948, *Jewish Social Studies* 4 (Winter 1998): 88; Naomi Wiener Cohen, The Reaction of Reform Judaism in America to Political Zionism, 1897–1922, *Publications of the American Jewish Historical Society* 21 (June 1951): 365, 372, 383.
18. *Ibid.*
19. Iphigene Molony Bettman, 5/3/64 interview, AJA.
20. Gerald Johnson, *An Honorable Titan: A Biographical Study of Adolph S. Ochs*, Westport, Conn.: Greenwood Press Publishers (1946), 260–1; Morgenstern to I. Sulzberger, 1/5/45, Morgenstern Correspondence, AJA; Talese, *The Kingdom and the Power,* 205.
21. Sulzberger to Rosenberg, 6/7/43, MSS 31/6/15, AJA.
22. 11/30, revised in 1934, AHS File, JJ Folder, NYTCA.
23. Sulzberger to Reigelman, 11/2/54, *Ibid.*
24. I. Sulzberger to Steinhardt, 1/6/42, Laurence Steinhardt Papers, 1942 General Correspondence, Box 35, LC.
25. Richard Shepard, *The Paper's Papers: A Reporter's Journey Through the Archives of* The New York Times, New York: Random House (1996), 303.
26. The claim apparently originated with two columnists who wrote at the time of Frankfurter's nomination that Sulzberger led a delegation of Jewish leaders to urge Franklin Roosevelt not to nominate Frankfurter because it would aggravate anti-Semitism. A year after the supposed incident, however, Sulzberger lunched with Roosevelt at the White House. "I said to the President that, while he knew I had not led a delegation to see him," Sulzberger wrote of the conversation, "I was glad to add that I had never entertained any thought of doing so." 12/28/39, AHS File, FDR Folder, NYTCA. Right after the column was printed, he told his friend, Jacob Billikopf of the Jewish Federation of Charities, the same thing. Billikopf to Sulzberger, 11/4/38, MSS 13/29/2, AJA. Still, the story that Sulzberger led

such a delegation has been repeated many times over. (See, for example, Richard Breitman and Alan M. Kraut, *American Refugee Policy and European Jewry, 1933–1945*, Bloomington: Indiana University Press (1987), 106; Goldberg, *Jewish Power,* 279; Peter Grose, *Israel in the Mind of America*, New York: Alfred A. Knopf (1983), 226; and Michael E. Parrish, *Felix Frankfurter and His Times: The Reform Years*, New York: The Free Press (1982), 276.) Of the many authors who have related this story, only Dinnerstein, *Antisemitism in America*, 125, and Henry Feingold, 'Courage First and Intelligence Second': The American Secular Elite, Roosevelt and the Failure to Rescue, *American Jewish History*, 72 (June 1983), provide a source. Feingold's reference is to Joseph P. Lash's introduction to *The Diaries of Felix Frankfurter*, New York: W. W. Norton & Company, Inc. (1975), 64, which does not mention Sulzberger. Dinnerstein, too, cites secondary sources and a few primary sources, but when he cites primary sources it is to the descriptive text not original documents. See Max Freedman, ed., *Roosevelt and Frankfurter, Their Correspondence, 1928–1945*, Boston: Little Brown & Co. (1967), 481–2. Sulzberger did apparently tell Henry Morgenthau, Sr. that he opposed the nomination, and the elder Morgenthau then spoke with FDR aide Tom Corcoran. Frankfurter, for his part, did not consider this much better. "It is clear that he [Sulzberger] didn't do it directly but got someone who is even more influential perhaps than he is to do it for him," Frankfurter wrote to Billikopf soon after his nomination. Billlikopf to Frankfurter, undated; Frankfurter to Billikopf, 11/15/38, FF Papers, Reel #14, LC.

27. 12/28/39 memo, AHS File, FDR Folder, NYTCA.
28. See, for example, Levinthal to Silver, 10/25/43, AS Papers, Series I, Folder 102, YU; Steinberg to Wise, 1/25/46, Milton Steinberg Papers, Box 20/3, AJHS; and Frankfurter to Merz, 4/27/47, FF Papers, Reel #50, LC.
29. *An Honorable Titan*, 298.
30. Adolph Ochs File, Genealogy Folder, NYTCA.
31. *The Story of* The New York Times, 400.
32. Sulzberger to Sherwood, 4/19/49, Robert E. Sherwood Collection, bmsAm 1947 (793) Houghton Library, HU.
33. *The Storm Breaks,* New York: Viking Press (1940), 329.
34. Shepard, *The Paper's Papers*, 302.
35. Sulzberger to Morgenthau, 10/18/39, Henry Morgenthau, Jr. Correspondence, Box 277, FDRL.
36. Krock to Sulzberger, 11/3/38, AHS File, JJ Folder, NYTCA.
37. See Marc Dollinger, *Quest for Inclusion: Jews and Liberalism in Modern America*, Princeton, N.J.: Princeton University Press (2000).
38. Sulzberger to Haas, 8/2/38, AHS File, JJ Folder, NYTCA. See also Sulzberger to Billikopf, 1/5/39, MSS 13/29/2, AJA.
39. Sulzberger to Sherwood, 4/19/49, Robert E. Sherwood Collection, bmsAm 1947 (793) Houghton Library, HU. Whether Sulzberger took that line consistently is disputed. Former *Nation* editor Oswald Garrison Villard in *The Disappearing Daily*, 82, noted that Sulzberger's attendance at every editorial conference

inhibited his editorial writers and contributed to an editorial page that "withholds its fire, not in order to see the whites of the enemy's eyes, but to observe the whereabouts of the largest battalions." See also Seldes to Villard, 5/15/44, Oswald Garrison Villard Collection, bMS Am 1323, Box 105, Houghton Library, HU.

40. Sulzberger to Ochs, 2/21/31, AHS File, CM Folder, NYTCA.
41. *Times Talk*, 5/18/56.
42. Sulzberger to Sherwood, 4/19/49, Robert E. Sherwood Collection, bmsAm 1947 (793) Houghton Library, HU.
43. Author interview, 11/18/01.
44. Merz to Lang, 5/15/44, ELJ File, CM Folder, NYTCA.
45. James to Morrison, 10/19/33; James to Mulitsky, 10/16/33, ELJ File, Anti-Semitism Folder, NYTCA.
46. James to Sulzberger, 3/16/36; Sulzberger to Nathan, 4/6/36, AHS File, JJ Folder, NYTCA.
47. Sulzberger to McDonald, 2/1/36, AHS File, JGM Folder, NYTCA.
48. Ronald Brownstein, The *New York Times* on Nazism (1933–39), *Midstream* 4 (April 1980): 14–9, 18.
49. 2/18/39, 14.
50. Sulzberger to McDonald, 7/28/34, AHS File, JGM Folder, NYTCA; Sulzberger memos, 9/37, Sulzberger to Strunsky, 7/7/36; Duranty to Sulzberger, 7/25/36; Sulzberger to Duranty, 8/9/36, AHS File, JJ Folder, NYTCA.
51. I. Sulzberger, *Memoirs*, 223.
52. Selig Adler, Franklin Roosevelt and Zionism – The Wartime Record, *Judaism* (Summer 1972): 270.
53. Yehuda Bauer, *American Jewry and the Holocaust: The American Jewish Joint Distribution Committee, 1939–1945*, Detroit: Wayne State University Press (1981), 201.
54. 4/28/40, Rotogravure, 4; and 12/15/40, Rotogravure, 7.
55. F. Sulzberger to A. Sulzberger, 1/27/38; S. Sulzberger to A. Sulzberger, 10/10/37, AHS File, FMS Folder, NYTCA.
56. Margarete Midas Meyer, author interview, 7/1/01.
57. T. Midas to I. Sulzberger, 3/15/38, AHS File, EJM Folder, NYTCA.
58. E. Midas to Birchall, 6/5/38, AHS File, FTB Folder, NYTCA.
59. I. Sulzberger, *Memoirs*, 193–4. She puts the number of relatives "my aunts, cousin Julius, and Arthur and me" sponsored at 25 or 30, but references to only 14 such affidavits, not all relatives, could be found in the *Times* archives.
60. A. Sulzberger to F. Sulzberger, 3/11/38; F. Sulzberger to A. Sulzberger, 8/18/38; A. Sulzberger to F. Sulzberger, 8/29/38; A. Sulzberger to F. Sulzberger 8/22/38; F. Sulzberger to A. Sulzberger, 6/8/40; A. Sulzberger to Oppenheimer, 7/26/39; AHS File, FMS Folder, NYTCA.
61. Julius Ochs Adler File, Mr. and Mrs. Eugen Peissak Folder, NYTCA.
62. AHS File, Abt Family Folder, NYTCA.
63. Sulzberger Genealogy, AJA.
64. A. Sulzberger to B. Sulzberger, 7/21/38, AHS File, Refugees Folder; E. Sulzberger to A. Sulzberger, 8/9/38; A. Sulzberger to E. Sulzberger, 8/9/38; E.

Sulzberger to A. Sulzberger, 8/29/38; E. Sulzberger to A. Sulzberger secretary, 9/1/38; P. Sulzberger to A. Sulzberger, 9/9/41; A. Sulzberger to P. Sulzberger, 10/20/41; P. Sulzberger to A. Sulzberger, 11/23/41, AHS File, EPS Folder, NYTCA. See also MS 250, Paul Sulzberger, "Situation, 1941 of Jewish Persecution," 12/30/41, Leo Baeck Institute.

65. Clark Abt, Interview, 7/30/01; Sulzberger to James, 12/12/36, AHS File, Abt Family Folder, NYTCA.
66. Lochner to Sulzberger, 1/19/39; James to Sulzberger, 1/31/39; Sulzberger to Lochner, 2/10/39; Lochner to Sulzberger, 2/27/39; Pelz to Sulzberger, 6/14/41, AHS File, Walter and Edith Pelz Folder, NYTCA. See also Walter and Edith Pelz Collection, AR 10116, Leo Baeck Institute.
67. Teutsch to A. Sulzberger, 12/16/38, AHS File, Refugees Folder, NYTCA.
68. A. Sulzberger to E. Sulzberger, 7/10/36; E. Sulzberger to A. Sulzberger, 12/15/39; Brown to E. Sulzberger, 12/18/39, AHS File, EPS Folder, NYTCA.
69. A. Sulzberger to Einstein, 5/29/34; D. Sulzberger to A. Sulzberger, 7/9/34; A. Sulzberger to D. Sulzberger, 7/10/34; A. Sulzberger to D. Sulzberger, 7/13/34; D. Sulzberger to A. Sulzberger, 7/17/34; A. Sulzberger to D. Sulzberger, 7/20/34. AHS File, Refugees Folder NYTCA.
70. Sulzberger to Hirschmann, 11/22/35, *Ibid.*
71. 3/20/39, 17.
72. Feingold, *The Politics of Rescue*, 69–70.
73. Sulzberger to Lehman, 3/16/39, Special File, AHS, Lehman Papers, CU.
74. 2/37, AS Papers, Series II, Folder 47, YU. See also, Sulzberger to Goldman, 4/23/37, MSS 31/6/15, AJA; Sulzberger to Billikopf, 1/5/39, MSS 13/29/2, AJA.
75. 2/37, AS Papers, Series II, Folder 47, YU.
76. Sulzberger to Magnes, 9/11/35, AHS File, Hebrew University Folder, NYTCA.
77. Sulzberger to Lehman, 3/16/39, Special File, AHS, Lehman Papers, CU.
78. Sulzberger to Hoffmann, 11/9/39, AHS File, Refugees Folder, NYTCA.
79. 5/11/39, 1; 5/18/39, 24.
80. See for example, 3/1/39, 6; 3/2/39, 11; and 3/11/39, 8.
81. 6/2/39, 1.
82. 6/8/39, 24; 6/9/39, 20.
83. See, for example, 6/2/39, 5; 6/3/39, 4; 6/7/39, 11; and 7/2/39, 7.
84. 6/4/39, 34.
85. 6/8/39, 10.
86. 6/22/39, 1.
87. 6/11/39, E5.
88. Sulzberger to Merz, 8/13/39, AHS File, CM Folder, NYTCA.
89. 9/13/39, 5.
90. 10/7/39, 5.
91. 10/22/39, 36; 10/25/39, 2; and 11/4/39, 2.
92. 11/5/39, 30; 11/20/39, 6; 11/20/39, 7; and 11/6/39, 7.
93. 10/22/39, 33; 11/16/39, 22; 11/30/39, 20. This pattern continued over the next year. The *Times* ran four more editorials on conditions in Poland in 1940 without

ever mentioning what was happening to the Jews. 1/24/40, 20; 1/29/40, 14; 1/30/40, 18; 11/27/40, 22.

94. Sulzberger to Morgenthau, 4/27/34, Henry Morgenthau, Jr. Correspondence, Box 277, FDRL.
95. Sulzberger to Morgenthau, 10/18/39, *Ibid.*
96. 12/28/39, AHS File, FDR Folder, NYTCA.
97. Sulzberger to Ochs, 7/26/33; McCaw to James, 7/31/35; Sulzberger to James, 9/28/36; James to Sulzberger, 4/26/37; Sulzberger to James, 7/12/37, ELJ File, JTA Folder, NYTCA.
98. "History and Origin of the Jewish Telegraphic Agency and Associated Agencies," 5/20/48, 54, and "Report to the Board of Directors and Committee on Work of Jewish Telegraphic Agency," 5/38, 10, JTA Collection, AJHS.
99. James to Wishengrad, 1/15/40, ELJ File, JTA Folder, NYTCA.
100. Sulzberger to Landau, 1/7/36, AHS File, JJ Folder, NYTCA.

Chapter 2

1. Morgenthau Diaries, Reel #83, Diary 300, FDRL.
2. Max Nussbaum, 9/40 memorandum, copy provided to author by Ruth Nussbaum.
3. Wise to McDonald, 9/30/40; McDonald to Wise, 10/3/40, JGM Collection, General Correspondence, SSW File, CU.
4. James to Finch, 4/6/35; Birchall to James, 2/26/36, ELJ File, BB Folder, NYTCA.
5. Lipstadt, *Beyond Belief*, 24.
6. Louis Lochner, Interview, 3/2/68, Oral History, Louis P. Lochner Papers, Box 11, WSHS.
7. Enderis to James, 7/2/35, ELJ File, BB Folder, NYTCA.
8. Ronald Brownstein, "The *New York Times* on Nazism (1933–39)," *Midstream* 4 (April 1980): 14–9, 15.
9. Birchall to James, 4/4/34, ELJ File, BB Folder, NYTCA.
10. Talese, *The Kingdom and the Power*, 43–4.
11. Sulzberger, *Times Talk*, 3/12/55, AHS File, FTB Folder, NYTCA.
12. Shepard, *The Paper's Papers*, 304.
13. Lipstadt, *Beyond Belief*, 16, 51–2.
14. Sulzberger to Birchall, 3/9/33; Birchall to Sulzberger, 3/21/33, AHS File, FTB Folder, NYTCA.
15. See Brownstein, "The *New York Times* on Nazism."
16. Birchall to James, 4/20/34; James to Sulzberger 5/2/34, ELJ File, BB Folder, NYTCA.
17. George Seldes, *Freedom of the Press*, New York: Garden City Publishing Co. (1937), 207.
18. Sulzberger to Birchall, 5/1/34, AHS File, FTB Folder, NYTCA.
19. Birchall to Sulzberger, 3/15/34, ELJ File, BB Folder, NYTCA.

20. Birchall to Adler, 4/30/34, World Wide Photo, 8/19/34, AHS File, BB Folder, NYTCA.
21. Birchall memo, 5/11/35; Bolgar to Birchall, 1/5/35; Birchall to James, 5/7/35; Birchall to Sulzberger, 5/16/35; Birchall to James, 10/23/35; Hall to Sulzberger, Adler, 10/25/35, ELJ File, BB Folder, NYTCA.
22. C. B. Conger, one of United Press' Berlin correspondents, had lived in Germany from 1920 to 1925 before returning to Europe as a reporter in 1940. Fellow UP correspondent Frederick Oechsner had lived in Germany and Central Europe for more than 12 years. Louis Lochner of the Associated Press lived in Germany for 21 years and had married a German woman. None of them, however, came close to Enderis' more than 30 years in Germany.
23. Birchall to Sulzberger, 4/20/32, AHS File, BB Folder, NYTCA.
24. *Berlin Diary: The Journal of a Foreign Correspondent 1934–1941*, New York: Alfred A. Knopf (1941), 42.
25. Sulzberger to James, 4/5/38, 12/9/38, ELJ File, BB Folder, NYTCA.
26. Birchall to Sulzberger, 7/19/33; Sulzberger to Birchall, 7/22/33, AHS File, BB Folder, NYTCA.
27. 9/2/34, E5.
28. Enderis to James, 9/27/34, AHS File, BB Folder, NYTCA.
29. James to Sulzberger, 3/2/36; Sulzberger to James, 3/4/36, *Ibid.*
30. Birchall to James, 4/4/34, ELJ File, BB Folder, NYTCA.
31. Birchall to Sulzberger, 2/10/36, AHS File, FTB Folder, NYTCA. See also Birchall to James, 12/30/35; Birchall to James, 1/2/36, ELJ File, BB Folder, NYTCA.
32. Neil MacNeil, *Without Fear or Favor*, New York: Harcourt, Brace and Company (1940), 129.
33. Tolischus to Birchall, 12/37, marked "not sent," Otto D. Tolischus Papers, WSHS.
34. 3/6/38, 4E.
35. Enderis to James, 3/19/38, ELJ File, BB Folder, NYTCA.
36. James memo, 10/23/40; James to Markel, 4/6/38; Markel to James, 4/6/38, *Ibid.*
37. Cohn to Sulzberger, 5/13/33; Sulzberger to Maes, 5/15/33; James to Birchall, 7/4/33; James to Birchall, 7/5/33; James to Birchall, 8/3/33, ELJ File, BB Folder, NYTCA. See also, James to Berlin, 7/8/33; Enderis to James, 7/11/33; James to Enderis, 9/17/35; James to Enderis, 11/12/35; James to Enderis, 9/26/36; James to Enderis, 5/17/37, *Ibid.*
38. James to Enderis, no date; Birchall to James, 7/17/36; Enderis to James, no date, *Ibid.*
39. Bienstock to Lincoln, 8/30/34; Enderis to Birchall, 9/15/34, *Ibid.*
40. 2/26/39, 1; James to Enderis, 2/26/39; Enderis to James, 2/28/39; James to Enderis, 3/4/39; ELJ File, BB Folder, NYTCA; 3/4/39, 2, 3/6/39, 2, Lochner to Thompson, 3/7/39, Louis P. Lochner Collection, Box 1, WSHS; Enderis to Birchall, 5/30/39, AHS File, BB Folder, NYTCA.

41. Birchall to James, 9/11/39; Enderis to James, 11/15/39; Enderis to James, 11/17/39; Pisnan, 12/7/39; James to Enderis, 12/12/39; James to Berlin, 10/22/39, ELJ File, BB Folder, NYTCA; 12/19/39, 9.
42. The memo's author is identified as a "Berlin correspondent," but because it was sent from Oslo where Tolischus was at the time, he is unquestionably the writer. Morgenthau to Roosevelt, 4/20/40, Morgenthau Correspondence, Box 277, FDRL.
43. Clark Abt, Interview, 7/30/01; Birchall, *The Storm Breaks*, 328; Sulzberger to Birchall, 9/24/40, AHS File, FTB Folder, NYTCA; *NYT* 3/7/55, 28.
44. ELJ, Address to Teachers, Times Hall, 2/21/45, NYTCA.
45. CLS File, 1939–1940, NYTCA.
46. MacNeil, *Without Fear or Favor*, 53.
47. James Reston, *Deadline: A Memoir*, New York: Random House (1991), 88; M. Bracker to V. Bracker, 1/16/43, 1/14/43, Milton and Virginia Bracker Papers, Folder 9, WSHS.
48. Daniell to Sulzberger, 12/42, AHS File, London Bureau Folder, NYTCA.
49. 7/2/40, 20, 7/11/40, 18, 7/15/40 14, 7/22/40, 16, 7/24/40, 20, 7/26/40, 16, 7/27/40, 12, 8/2/40, 14, 8/8/40, 18.
50. 8/2/40, 8/8/40, 8/9/40, 7/14/40, Rotogravure section, 7/25/40, 5, 7/30/40, 3, 8/11/40, 25, 8/13/40, 3, 8/25/40, magazine 6.
51. Harrison Salisbury, *Without Fear or Favor: The New York Times and Its Times*, New York: Times Books (1980), 453–4.
52. Irvin to Sulzberger, 9/6/40, AHS File, BB Folder, NYTCA.
53. Irvin to Schultz, 7/8/42, Sigrid Schultz Papers, Box 11, WSHS.
54. Birchall to James, 1/14/36, ELJ File, BB Folder, NYTCA.
55. James to Sulzberger, 9/25/40, AHS File, BB Folder, NYTCA.
56. Sulzberger to Irvin, 9/26/40, *Ibid.*
57. Sulzberger to Merz, 8/13/39, AHS File, CM Folder, NYTCA.
58. Irvin to Schultz, 7/8/42, Sigrid Schultz Papers, Box 11, WSHS.
59. M. Bracker to V. Bracker, 1/16/43, Milton and Virginia Bracker Papers, Folder 9, WSHS.
60. James 10/23/40, AHS File, BB Folder, NYTCA.
61. 4/12/43.
62. *Deadline*, 78.
63. Enderis to James, 1/22/41; James to Enderis, 2/13/41; Enderis to James, 2/13/41; Enderis to James, 2/14/41, ELJ File, BB Folder, NYTCA; 2/14/41, 5.
64. Interview with Ruth Nussbaum 6/11/01.
65. New York: Dodd, Mead & Co. (1942), 238–45.
66. Boston: Little, Brown and Company (1942).
67. New York: Alfred A. Knopf (1946). New York: Reynal & Hitchcock, (1940), 107, 115, 336.
68. 1/7/40, 47, 1/14/40, 31, 8/3/40, 2.
69. 4/3/41, 4, 9/29/41, 5, 10/11/41, 4, 11/16/41, 17.
70. *Germany in Defeat*, viii.
71. *NYT*, 1/21/95, 12.

72. *What About Germany?*, 359.
73. 8/4/41, 3.
74. 9/7/41, 14, 9/21/41, 9, 9/23/41, 9, 10/13/41, 13.
75. 10/16/41, 6, 10/18/41, 4, 10/26/41, 5.
76. Lipstadt, *Beyond Belief*, 136.
77. 2/14/40, 10, 2/22/40, 5.
78. 3/5/40, 6.
79. 3/28/40, 6.
80. *NYT*, 1/6/40, 12.
81. 8/3/40, 2, 8/8/40, 11, 2/4/41, 5.
82. 2/20/41, 8.
83. JTA Collection, Box 1, "Report to the board of directors" Folder, AJHS.
84. James to Enderis, 2/18/41, ELJ File, BB Folder, NYTCA.
85. 2/28/41, 4.
86. 10/18/41, 4, 10/22/41, 11.
87. 10/28/41, 10, 10/30/41, 6.
88. 10/30/41, 6.
89. *NYT*, 8/20/66.
90. See 10/24/41, 7, 11/4/41, 12.
91. 11/2/41, 24.
92. *This Is the Enemy*, 128–39.
93. 11/23/41, 26.
94. James to Enderis, 11/15/41, ELJ File, BB Folder, NYTCA.
95. 11/14/41, 11.
96. Other *Times* reporters were not so fortunate. Rome correspondents, Herbert Matthews and Camille Cianfarra, were arrested there. *NYT*, 12/11/41, 6, 12/12/41, 7. Roving correspondent Harold Denny was captured in Libya in 1941 and was held by the Axis for 6 months. *NYT*, 7/4/45, 13.
97. Brigham to James, 12/15/41; Clark to James, 12/16/41; James to Brigham, 12/18/41; 12/[date unclear], Enderis to James; Daniell, 8/21/45, ELJ File, BB Folder, NYTCA.

Chapter 3

1. F. Sulzberger to A. Sulzberger, 10/29/40, AHS File, FMS Folder, NYTCA.
2. A. Sulzberger to F. Sulzberger, 10/29/40; A. Sulzberger to James, 10/30/40, AHS File, FMS Folder, NYTCA.
3. 11/3/40, 21.
4. Matthews, *A World in Revolution*, 63.
5. *NYT*, 6/4/40, 1.
6. *NYT Magazine*, 4/2/44, 8.
7. Philip to James, 6/24/40, AHS File, Percy Philip Folder, NYTCA.
8. Michael R. Marrus and Robert O. Paxton, *Vichy France and the Jews*, Stanford, Calif.: Stanford University Press (1995), 14–5.

9. Archaumbault to James, 7/17/40, ELJ File, GHA Folder, NYTCA.
10. James to Krock, 8/5/44, ELJ File, Lansing Warren Folder, NYTCA.
11. 7/19/40, 8.
12. 10/3/40, 7, 10/8/40, 3.
13. 10/10/40, 10, 11/1/40, 5, 1/15/41, 7.
14. 8/1/40, 1, 8/2/40, 8.
15. 8/28/40, 4,10/2/40, 8, 10/18/40, 5.
16. 10/19/40, 2.
17. Lipstadt, *Beyond Belief*, 147.
18. 12/19/40, 24, 12/22/40, E4, 1/19/41, magazine, 5.
19. FIS, Special Directive, France VI, 3/28/42, OWI, Historian, Subject File/41–46, Box 8, FIS Directives/42, NA.
20. Special Report, 3/6/42, NDD745015, NA.
21. Marrus and Paxton, *Vichy France and the Jews*, 165.
22. 9/10/40, 25, Marrus and Paxton, *Vichy France and the Jews*, 10.
23. A. Sulzberger to D. Sulzberger, 1/23/40; A. Sulzberger to F. Sulzberger, 3/6/40; A. Sulzberger to F. Sulzberger, 3/18/40; F. Sulzberger to A. Sulzberger, 11/26/40, AHS File, FMS Folder, NYTCA.
24. 11/9/40, 5.
25. Tifft and Jones, *The Trust*, 220; Raick to Chabry, 11/18/40, AHS File, FMS Folder, NYTCA.
26. 11/22/40, 3.
27. 12/5/40, 16, 12/8/40, 46.
28. 2/23/41, 13.
29. The Stuttgart consuls were particularly strict with Jewish applicants. Bat-Ami Zucker, *In Search of Refuge: Jews and US Consuls in Nazi Germany 1933–1941*, London: Vallentine Mitchell (2001), 177.
30. For a discussion of the difficulties that the Berlin consul imposed on Jewish visa applicants, see *Ibid.*, 173–8.
31. Interview, Ruth Nussbaum, 6/11/01; Max Nussbaum, 9/40 memo, given to the author by Ruth Nussbaum.
32. 2/11/41, 7.
33. The *New Republic*, 4/28/41, 6/16/41, 6/23/41, 8/18/41, The *Nation*, 7/19/41.
34. 3/2/41, 35, 3/15/41, 1.
35. Raick to Chabry, 11/18/40; A. Sulzberger to F. Sulzberger, 11/22/40; A. Sulzberger to Krock, 11/19/40; Krock to A. Sulzberger, 11/22/40; Sulzberger to Corn Exchange Bank Trust Co, 12/12/40, AHS File, FMS Folder, NYTCA.
36. Chabry to Raick, 12/7/40; F. Sulzberger to A. Sulzberger, 11/26/40, AHS File, FMS Folder, NYTCA.
37. 1/26/41, 24.
38. 2/7/41, 4, 2/16/41, 13, 2/24/41, 7.
39. 12/1/40, 6, 12/19/40, 16, 1/9/41, 1.
40. 1/10/41, 11.
41. 1/11/41, 7.

42. Marrus and Paxton, *Vichy France and the Jews*, 112, argue that the Germans encouraged emigration of Jews as a general principle until the fall of 1941, but left Vichy free to formulate its own policy on Jewish emigration.
43. 1/12/41, 8.
44. Brown to A. Sulzberger, 1/6/41; A. Sulzberger to E. Sulzberger, 1/7/41; Brown to Phillips, 1/31/41; Phillips to Brown, 3/17/41, AHS File, FMS Folder, NYTCA.
45. F. Sulzberger to Safford, 3/20/41; Safford to F. Sulzberger, 3/21/41, *Ibid.*
46. 3/24/41, 6.
47. Marrus and Paxton, *Vichy France and the Jews*, 171–5.
48. 3/29/41, 2.
49. 4/7/41, 16, 4/9/41, 24.
50. Marrus and Paxton, *Vichy France and the Jews*, 173–4.
51. 3/30/41, 25.
52. 4/27/41, 12.
53. 4/30/41, 7, 5/4/41, Rotogravure section, 2.
54. 5/3/41, 4.
55. Bauer, *American Jewry and the Holocaust*, 156.
56. 3/8/41, 4.
57. 3/31/41, 5.
58. *Vichy France and the Jews*, 175.
59. *Gedenkbuch: Opfer der Verfolgung der Juden unter der nationalsozialistischen Gewaltherrschaft in Deutschland, 1933–1945*, Frankfurt/Main: J. Weisbecker (1986), and Sulzberger Genealogy, AJA.
60. 6/18/41, 1. Lipstadt, *Beyond Belief*, 128–9, makes a persuasive case that the press' trumpeting of the spy threat presented by German refugees laid the groundwork for the State Department policy.
61. 6/26/41, 22.
62. Lipstadt, *Beyond Belief*, 130.
63. David Wyman, *Paper Walls: America and the Refugee Crisis, 1938–1941*, Amherst: University of Massachusetts Press (1968), 197–8
64. *NYT*, 7/14/41, 4.
65. McDonald to Sulzberger, 8/15/41, JGM Collection, General Correspondence, Arthur Sulzberger, CU.
66. *Paper Walls*, 194. See also Zucker, *In Search of Refuge*, 153–5.
67. F. Sulzberger to Brown, 8/13/41; Brown to Phillips, 4/7/41; Brown to F. Sulzberger, 8/21/41, AHS File, FMS Folder, NYTCA.
68. E. Midas to I. Sulzberger, 1/2/39, AHS File, EJM Folder, NYTCA.
69. Interview with Margarete Midas Meyer, 7/1/01.
70. E. Midas to A. Sulzberger, 4/23/41; A. Sulzberger to E. Midas, 5/1/41, AHS File, EJM Folder, NYTCA.
71. Wyman, *Paper Walls*, 197.
72. McDonald to Merz, 9/26/41, JGM Collection, General Correspondence "M," CU.
73. Wyman, *Paper Walls*, 199.

74. Interview, Margarete Midas Meyer, 7/1/01.
75. Warren to E. Midas 3/26/42; A. Sulzberger to Warren, 3/30/42; Coulter to A. Sulzberger, 4/10/42; A. Sulzberger to Clark, 4/17/42; Clark to A. Sulzberger, 4/21/42; E. Midas to A. Sulzberger, 6/5/42; E. Midas to A. Sulzberger, 8/3/42; A. Sulzberger to Hull, 8/4/42, AHS File, EJM Folder, NYTCA.
76. F. Sulzberger to A. Sulzberger, 2/7/42; A. Sulzberger to F. Sulzberger, 2/11/42, AHS File, FMS Folder, NYTCA.
77. 2/4/41, 1, 2/8/41, 3, 3/9/41, 5.
78. 3/30/41, 2, 4/1/41, 9, 4/22/41, 9.
79. 5/15/41, 5, 6/14/41, 5.
80. 6/15/41, 11, 6/22/41, 14, 6/25/41, 7, 6/28/41, 4.
81. Lipstadt, *Beyond Belief*, 149. In addition to the *Tribune*, Lipstadt cites articles in the *Charleston Mail, Schenectady Union Star, Miami Herald, Dubuque* (Iowa) *Telegraph Herald*, and *Augusta Herald*, but does not give the pages on which the articles appeared.
82. 8/18/41, 5, 8/27/41, 4.
83. There were also front-page stories on 8/29/41, 9/17/41, and 9/22/41.
84. 8/3/41, 8/4/41, 5.
85. 8/22/41, 1, 5.
86. 8/23/41, 1, 12.
87. See, for example, McCormick to Roosevelt, 5/21/41, PPF 675, FDRL; Day by Day, The Pare Lorentz Chronology, FDRL.
88. 8/18/41, 12. Roosevelt often used his conversations with McCormick to test new ideas that would be mentioned in her columns but would not be attributed to the president. Betty Houchin Winfield, *FDR and the News Media*, Urbana, Ill.: University of Illinois Press (1990), 63.
89. 8/24/41, 1, 9/9/41, 4, 10/12/41, 14.
90. Marrus and Paxton, *Vichy France and the Jews*, 223.
91. 10/22/41, 10/24/41, 10/25/41.
92. *Vichy France and the Jews*, 225.
93. 9/2/41, 6.
94. 10/4/41, 3.
95. 10/9/41, 5.
96. *Vichy France and the Jews*, 225.
97. 12/3/41, 10, 12/10/41, 7.
98. *NYT Magazine*, 4/2/44, 8, 4/23/44, 8.
99. 9/5/42, 3.

Chapter 4

1. Elath, *Zionism at the UN*, 42–4. See also, Dina Porat, *The Blue and the Yellow Stars of David: The Zionist Leadership in Palestine and the Holocaust 1939–1945*, Cambridge, Mass: Harvard University Press (1990), 120.
2. Salisbury, *Without Fear or Favor*, 455.

3. Tifft and Jones, *The Trust*, 209–10.
4. A. Sulzberger, 6/19/35, AHS File, Leo Sulzberger Folder, NYTCA.
5. C. Sulzberger, *A Long Row of Candles: Memoirs and Diaries, 1934–1954*, New York: Macmillan (1969), 1.
6. *Ibid.*, 28–30.
7. C. Sulzberger to Birchall, 8/3/39; Birchall to James, 8/16/39; Birchall to C. Sulzberger, 8/21/39; Birchall to James, 8/21/39; James to Birchall, 8/23/39; Birchall to James, 8/26/39; C. Sulzberger to New York, 9/3/39; Birchall to James, 9/6/39, ELJ File, CLS Folder, NYTCA.
8. *A Long Row of Candles*, 89, 124.
9. A. Sulzberger to James, 10/27/39; James to A. Sulzberger, 9/29/41; Lang to James, 9/30/41, ELJ File, CLS Folder, NYTCA.
10. A. Sulzberger 7/3/41; A. Sulzberger to Krock, 7/16/41; Krock to A. Sulzberger, 7/17/41; Sedgwick to A. Sulzberger, 10/30/41, AHS File, CLS Folder, NYTCA
11. James to Clark, 3/16/42; Huston to James, 3/16/42; ELJ File, CLS Folder, NYTCA. James to A. Sulzberger, 5/12/42, CLS File, ELJ Folder, NYTCA.
12. Welles to A. Sulzberger, 8/20/43, Sumner Welles Papers, Box 92/4, FDRL.
13. A. Sulzberger to C. Sulzberger, 8/24/43; A. Sulzberger, 9/4/43; Hull to A. Sulzberger, 9/8/43; Berle to A. Sulzberger, 9/29/43; Berle to A. Sulzberger, 10/15/43, AHS File, CLS Folder, NYTCA.
14. Tifft and Jones, *The Trust*, 210.
15. Author interview, 11/18/01.
16. Bernstein to James, 1/23/44; James to C. Sulzberger, 1/24/44; C. Sulzberger to James, no date, ELJ File, CLS Folder, NYTCA.
17. *My Life and* The Times, New York: Harper & Row (1971), 192.
18. *A Long Row of Candles*, 104.
19. Massacres of Jews occurred throughout the region, as documented in Radu Ionanid, *The Holocaust in Romania: The Destruction of Jews and Gypsies Under the Antonescu Regime, 1940–1944*, Chicago: Ivan R. Dee (2000), 37–43.
20. 8/9/40, 7.
21. 9/10/40, 6; C. Sulzberger to James, undated cable, ELJ File, EK Folder, NYTCA; 10/1/40, 8.
22. Kovacs to A. Sulzberger, 9/29/40, ELJ File, EK Folder, NYTCA.
23. Clark to James, 10/5/40, *Ibid.*
24. 10/12/40, 1.
25. Kovacs to James, 10/19/40; Huston to James, 10/21/40; James to Sulzberger, 10/21/40; Kovacs to James, 11/8/40; James to Kovacs, 2/8/43; Huston to James, 2/8/43; Kovacs to James, 2/9/43; James to Kovacs, 10/15/43, ELJ File, EK Folder, NYTCA.
26. 12/5/40, 6, 3/28/41, 6, 7/11/41, 3, 10/23/41, 8.
27. See also *NYT*, 12/5/40, 7, describing a "pogrom of large proportions" launched by the Moldavian Iron Guard, and *NYT*, 12/23/40, 7, describing daily acts of cruelty against Jews "whose bodies are being found shattered by involuntary falls from windows."

28. Ionanid, *The Holocaust in Romania*, 61.
29. See Robert St. John, "Reporting the Romanian Pogrom of 1940/41," in Robert Moses Shapiro, ed., *Why Didn't the Press Shout? American and International Journalism During the Holocaust*, Jersey City, N.J.: Ktav Publishing House (2003), 87–107.
30. Grobman, "What Did They Know?" 339–40. "Kosher slaughtering" of Jews did indeed take place, as did the cutting off of women's breasts. Ionanid, *The Holocaust in Romania*, 58.
31. See, for example, 2/17/40, 3, 7/2/40, 4, 8/17/40, 2, 9/6/40, 8, 9/8/40, 45, 9/17/40, 7, 10/9/40, 4, 12/21/40, 4.
32. 5/2/41, 4, 5/5/41, 3, 5/11/41, 1.
33. James to Daniell, 9/29/39, ELJ File, Jerzy Szapiro Folder, NYTCA.
34. I. Sulzberger, *Memoirs*, 136–7.
35. *NYT*, 6/2/62.
36. Dariusz Stola, "Early News of the Holocaust from Poland," *Holocaust and Genocide Studies* (1997) 11: 1–27, 3.
37. David Engel, *In the Shadow of Auschwitz: The Polish Government-in-Exile and the Jews 1939–1942*, Chapel Hill: University of North Carolina Press (1987), 170–1.
38. Szapiro's *New York Times* obituary, 6/2/62, said he had "headed the press service of the exiled Polish Government and was editor of The Polish Daily." This seems to be a bit of obit hyperbole. Szapiro co-directed the paper for a month in the summer of 1940. Piotr Wrobe "*Dziennik Polski*" (The Polish Daily), The Official Organ of the 'Polish Government-in-Exile, and the Holocaust 1940–1945' in Shapiro, *Why Didn't the Press Shout?* 507–34, 570. A perusal of the files of the Poland Ministerstwo Informacji and Ministerstwo Spraw Zagranicznych did not find Szapiro listed among the employees of either the exile government's Information Ministry, the Foreign Affairs Ministry, or, the *Polish Daily* after that. The only internal reference to Szapiro was among those to invite to a party. He apparently did freelance work for the exile government. Poland Ministerstwo Informacji Papers, Box 19.4, HI.
39. Daniell to James, 8/10/40; Daniell to James, 8/30/40, ELJ File, Jerzy Szapiro Folder, NYTCA.
40. 1/23/40, 5. See also 1/5/40, 8, 1/6/40, 2.
41. 1/7/40, 36. See also 1/15/40, 8.
42. JTA Collection, Box 1, "Report to the board of directors" Folder, AJHS.
43. 3/16/40, 3.
44. 10/13/40, 38.
45. 1/7/42, 8, 11/ 26/40, 8, 12/15/40, 7, 3/1/42, 28.
46. Bauer, *American Jewry and the Holocaust*, 187.
47. Shepard, *The Paper's Papers*, 305.
48. Sulzberger to Hoover, 9/13/41; Lang to James, 9/13/41, AHS File, Herbert Hoover Folder, NYTCA.
49. 9/14/41, 31.

50. "Report on Conditions in Poland as of December 1941," Office of War Information, Overseas Branch, Bureau of Overseas Intelligence, Central File, Box 304, NA.
51. Yehuda Bauer, *Jewish Reactions to the Holocaust*, Tel-Aviv: MOD Books (1989).
52. In addition to the *Times* stories mentioned elsewhere in the chapter, see 1/14/42, 6, 6/16/42, 6, 1/3/43, magazine, 7.
53. Grobman, "What Did They Know?" 342–3.
54. Laqueur, *The Terrible Secret*, 67.
55. Lichtheim to Lourie, 10/5/42, MSS 361/D92/1, AJA.
56. Batt to Sulzberger, 10/20/41, AHS File, CLS Folder, NYTCA.
57. There is a rich body of work describing the difficulties of reporting from the Soviet Union, including Harrison Salisbury, *To Moscow and Beyond: A Reporter's Narrative*, New York: Harper (1960), Nicholas Daniloff, *Two Lives, One Russia*, Boston: Houghton Mifflin (1988), and David Remnick, *Lenin's Tomb: The Last Days of the Soviet Empire*, New York: Vintage Books (1991).
58. James to Sulzberger, 3/10/39, ELJ File, G. E. R. Geyde Folder, NYTCA.
59. Duranty, who was the *Times*' Moscow correspondent from 1921 to 1934, gave up his post to write books and lecture, although he agreed to spend 3 or 4 months per year in Russia for the *Times* for a $5,000 retainer. In retrospect, Duranty has become a controversial figure, who has been described as at the least pro-Bolshevik and at the worst a Stalinist agent. Salisbury, *The New York Times and Its Times*, 462–6.
60. Sulzberger to Steinhardt, 4/8/40; Sulzberger to Steinhardt, 5/27/40, Laurence A. Steinhardt Papers, General Correspondence, Box 34, LC.
61. 9/11/40, 8, 9/13/40, 4, 9/14/40, 6.
62. C. Sulzberger to A. Sulzberger, 10/3/41, AHS File, CLS Folder, NYTCA.
63. *A Long Row of Candles*, 155.
64. *Deadline*, 117.
65. 1/5/42, 3, 1/12/42, 6, 12/8/41, 18.
66. *The Paper's Papers*, 169.
67. *A Long Row of Candles*, xvi. See also *NYT*, 9/21/93, B9.
68. *Germany Will Try It Again*, 185–6.
69. 10/15/41.
70. *This Is the Enemy*, 136.
71. Progress Report, JTA, Overseas News Agency, February 1942, JTA Collection, Box 1, "Report to the board of directors" Folder, AJHS.
72. Progress Report #2, JTA and ONA, January 1943, *Ibid.* The *Times* still did not subscribe to the JTA as of 3/19/44, the last subscription list available. The *Times* did pick up another JTA-sponsored news agency, the Overseas News Agency (ONA), beginning in January 1943. The JTA started ONA in 1939, apparently with Sulzberger's explicit approval. 12/5/38, JTA board meeting minutes, AS Papers, Roll 42, Folder 1031, YU. ONA was staffed exclusively by non-Jewish journalists in the hope that they could function more effectively and the agency

itself would not be saddled with the Jewish label. I. Landau to Council of Jewish Federations and Welfare Fund Bulletin, 9/30/40, AS Papers, Roll 100, Folder 2, YU.

73. Breitman, *Official Secrets*, 99–100.
74. JTA Collection, Box 1, "Report to the board of directors" Folder, AJHS.
75. Engel, *In the Shadow of Auschwitz*, 174–5, and Stola, "Early News of the Holocaust from Poland," 2.
76. JTA Collection, Box 1, "Report to the board of directors" Folder, AJHS.
77. Stola, "Early News of the Holocaust from Poland," 5, 4, and Breitman, *Official Secrets*, 99–100.
78. Grobman, "What Did They Know?" 342.
79. 10/26/41, 6
80. Breitman, *Official Secrets*, 63–5.
81. 3/14/42, 7.
82. *Terrible Secret*, 68.
83. Grobman, "What Did They Know?" 343.
84. Lipstadt, *Beyond Belief*, 150–1, *NYT* 1/7/42, 8, *NYHT* 1/7/42, 1.
85. 1/8/42, 7.
86. 1/8/42, 20.
87. 3/27/42, 8.
88. 11/20/41, 2.
89. 5/18/42, 4. For other examples of *Times* stories in which the nature of the victims is ambiguous, see 11/12/41, 10, 1/28/42, 4.
90. 5/24/42, E1.
91. "Study of War Propaganda," 3/6/42, NND745015, NA.
92. Lipstadt, *Beyond Belief*, 159–60, 327.

Chapter 5

1. Survey on the Rescue Activities of the World Jewish Congress 1940–1944, MSS 361/A68/2, AJA.
2. See 1/27/42, 12, 4/2/42, 8.
3. Lichtheim to Lauterbach, 5/13/42, MSS 361/C174/2, AJA.
4. Stola, "Early News of the Holocaust in Poland," 6.
5. *Auschwitz and the Allies*, 40.
6. Stola, "Early News of the Holocaust in Poland," 6.
7. 6/13/42, 7.
8. Brigham to James, 6/15/42, ELJ File, BV Folder, NYTCA.
9. James to Valery, 6/16/42; Valery to James, 6/20/42; Valery to James, 6/21/42, *Ibid.*
10. 1/17/42, 1, 1/19/42, 1, 1/23/42, 7, 1/24/42, 1, 1/25/42, 28, 3/1/42, magazine, 9, 5/3/42, 3.
11. Axelsson to James, 6/20/42, ELJ File, BV Folder, NYTCA.
12. Lipstadt, *Beyond Belief*, 164–7.

13. 7/7/42, 3.
14. Axelsson to James, 11/12/42; James to Valery, 11/16/42; Valery to James, 2/26/43, ELJ File, BV Folder, NYTCA.
15. *Beyond Belief*, 174.
16. Brigham to James, 6/19/44, ELJ File, DB Folder, NYTCA; McCaw to James, 8/8/44, ELJ File, JML Folder, NYTCA.
17. *A World in Revolution*, 57–8.
18. Sauerwein to James, 7/25/40, ELJ File, JSS Folder, NYTCA; Sauerwein to Sulzberger, 3/25/41, AHS File, JSS Folder, NYTCA; James to Wales, 11/23/45, ELJ File, JSS Folder, NYTCA.
19. Archambault to James, 8/31/42, ELJ File, GHA Folder, NYTCA; James to Wales, 11/23/45; James to Sulzberger, 10/19/45, ELJ File, JSS Folder, NYTCA.
20. C. Sulzberger to A. Sulzberger, James, 10/5/42, CLS File, NYTCA.
21. Daniell to James, 11/29/44, ELJ File, DB Folder, NYTCA.
22. 1/2/42, 4, 2/8/42, 4E.
23. 4/15/42, 20.
24. 9/6/42, 14.
25. 9/9/42, 9, 9/11/42, 4, 9/18/42, 1.
26. 8/27/42, 3, 9/2/42, 5, 9/3/42, 5, 9/5/42, 3.
27. 9/20/42, 1.
28. Susan Zuccotti, *Under His Very Windows: The Vatican and the Holocaust in Italy*, New Haven: Yale University Press (2000), 93–112.
29. Marrus and Paxton, *Vichy France and the Jews*, 269.
30. *Ibid.*, 277.
31. 9/14/42, 1, 9/15/42, 22, 9/16/42, 1, 22, 9/20/42, E2.
32. 8/7/42, 18, 9/18/42, 22.
33. 10/3/42, 10/21/42, 10/23/42.
34. *Official Secrets*, 138.
35. Lichtheim to Lauterbach, 5/13/42, MSS 361/C174/2, AJA.
36. Shub to Robinson, 7/14/42, MSS 361/C89/7, AJA.
37. "A Few Remarks About the Jewish Attitude in this War," MSS 361/D92/1, AJA.
38. Kubowitzki to Wise, etc., 8/21/42, MSS 361/ D97/1, AJA.
39. 8/22/42, 1.
40. Kubowitzki to Wise, etc., 8/26/42; Caplan, Boraisha to Kubowitzki, 8/28/42, MSS 361/D97/1, AJA.
41. Wise to Slonim, 10/29/40, Reel 74–54; Wise to Slomovitz, 9/8/42, Reel 74–53, SSW Papers, AJHS.
42. Received, 9/4/42, MSS 361/D92/3; Barou, Easterman to S. Wise, 9/18/42, MSS 361/A13/11; Tartakower to S. Wise, etc. 10/5/42, MSS 361/D92/1, AJA.
43. Gilbert, *Auschwitz and the Allies*, 71.
44. Kubowitzki to Wise, etc., 9/29/42, MSS 361/D97/1, and "Advisory Council on European Jewish Affairs," 10/28/42, MSS 361/D93/1, AJA.
45. Lichtheim, Riegner, 10/22/42, MSS 361/ D92/1, AJA.
46. Penkower, *The Jews were Expendable*, 72.

47. Kubowitzki to Wertheim, 11/24/42, MSS 361/D92/1, AJA.
48. Penkower, *The Jews Were Expendable*, 79.
49. Grose, *Israel in the Mind of America*, 126–7.
50. Lipstadt, *Beyond Belief*, 180–3.
51. 12/2/42, 24.
52. See 12/2/42, 7, 12, 12/3/42, 10.
53. Kubowitzki to Wise, 12/4/42, MSS 361/D92/2, AJA.
54. Breitman, *Official Secrets*, 152.
55. *Complete Presidential Press Conferences of Franklin D. Roosevelt*, New York: De Capo Press (1972).
56. Joint Report, submitted to the Meeting of the Planning Committee, 12/17/42, MSS 361/D92/2, AJA.
57. MSS 361/D92/2, AJA.
58. "Proposals," 12/10/42, 12/14/42, Minutes of Special Committee on European Situation Meeting, *Ibid.*
59. 12/14/42, Minutes of Special Committee on European Situation Meeting, *Ibid.*
60. Law to Easterman, 12/16/42, MSS 361/A11/13, AJA.
61. The document has neither a date nor an author but based on the *Times* stories it refers to, it was written in late fall 1942. Given that it was found in Kubowitzki's files and reflects his obsession with the *Times*, he is most likely the author. MSS 361/D92/1, AJA.
62. "Activities of the American Jewish Congress and the World Jewish Congress with Respect to the Hitler Program of Exterminating the Jews," undated, MSS 361/D92/1; Brodetzky to Wise, etc., MSS 361/A11/13; Wise to Rubenstein, 1/25/43, MSS 361/ A11/13, AJA.
63. "Activities of the American Jewish Congress and the World Jewish Congress with Respect to the Hitler Program of Exterminating the Jews," undated, MSS 361/D92/1, AJA.
64. Shultz to Wise, etc., 12/29/42, MSS 361/A11/13; Planning Committee Meeting Minutes, 12/29/42, MSS 361/D92/2, AJA.
65. 12/22/42, MSS 361/D92/2, AJA.
66. 12/28/42, 1E.
67. 1/19/43, 18, 1/24/43, 26.
68. MSS 361/D92/2, AJA.
69. 2/4/43,10.
70. 1/19/43, MSS 361/A11/13, AJA.
71. MSS 361/C171/ 6, AJA.

Chapter 6

1. 3/21/43, 10, 4/12/43, 5, 4/1/43, 2, 6/23/43, 6, 11/8/43, 6, 7/27/43, 9, 8/27/43, 7, 3/24/43, 8, 10/10/43, 35, 11/12/43, 4, 12/1/43, 6, 8/8/43, 11, 11/29/43, 3, 12/6/43, 10, 12/26/43, 19.
2. *NYT*, 12/4/51, 1.

3. *Deadline*, 122–3.
4. *The Kingdom and the Power*, 68–74, 44–7.
5. That James and Arthur Sulzberger made most of the editorial staff decisions is apparent from their correspondence. Sulzberger was directly involved in hiring and assigning journalists to foreign posts, including part-time correspondents in out-of-the-way capitals. See AHS File, ELJ Folder, and ELJ, AHS Folder, NYTCA.
6. *A World in Revolution*, 58, 61–2.
7. *Memoirs: Sixty Years on the Firing Line*, New York: Funk & Wagnalls (1968), 87–8.
8. *My Life and The Times*, 161–2.
9. Address to Teachers, 2/21/45, ELJ & Family File, General Folder, NYTCA.
10. *My Life and The Times*, 162; McCaw to James, 9/7/44; McCaw to James, 7/11/44, ELJ File, RM Folder, NYTCA.
11. MacNeil, *Without Fear or Favor*, 67–8, 82–3; 4/11/45, MacNeil speech, "The Newspaper – Its Making and Its Meaning," ELJ File, NM Folder, NYTCA; *NYT*, 6/24/72, 28.
12. MacNeil, *Without Fear or Favor*, 21–7; Neil MacNeil Jr., 10/25/01, letter to author.
13. MacNeil, *Without Fear or Favor*, 94–5, 99–100; 4/11/45, MacNeil speech, "The Newspaper – Its Making and Its Meaning," ELJ File, NM Folder, NYTCA.
14. ELJ File, Ralph Parker Folder, NYTCA; Lawrence to James, 12/15/43; Lawrence to James, 2/19/44; Sulzberger to James, 1/21/44; Lawrence to James, 4/20/44; Sulzberger to James, 4/22/44; James to Parker, 6/14/44, ELJ File, MB Folder, NYTCA; Salisbury, *Without Fear or Favor*, 508.
15. 5/7/41, 7, 5/15/43, 6.
16. 6/4/43, 7.
17. 9/25/43, 6.
18. 10/26/43, 8.
19. New York: Charles Scribner's Sons (1944), 40, 16, 35, 47–8, 128, 132.
20. The *Times*' account of the report mentioned the similar plight of the Jews in Poland, but only in the second-day story, and then briefly and far into the story. That emphasis reflected the priorities in the report itself.
21. 1/23/40, 1/29/40, 1/30/40, 3/8/40, 6, 12/5/42. See also, 11/20/40, 7/7/41, 1/3/42.
22. 1/19/40, 11/9/41, 8/6/42, 9/18/42, 9/20/42, 6/11/43, 10/17/43.
23. James to Birchall, 6/18/37, ELJ File, BB Folder, NYTCA. The reference to "thousands of them now facing trial" seems to be an exaggeration. The number was closer to 300.
24. Matthews, *A World in Revolution*, 20–40; Talese, *The Kingdom and the Power*, 71; Salisbury, *Without Fear or Favor*, 452–3; Knightley, *The First Casualty*, 199–201; McCaw to James, 2/23/39; McCaw to James, 5/8/39, ELJ File, RM Folder, NYTCA.
25. Office of War Information, Washington News Division, Sample News Stories, 3/23/42, Box 2852, 1/30/42, 2/1/42, 2/9/42, 2/16/42, Box 2850, 2/20/42, Box 2853, 3/22/42, 3/28/42, Box 2854, NA.

26. 2/4/40, 4E.
27. Feingold, "'Courage First and Intelligence Second'".
28. Gay Talese, *The Kingdom and the Power*, 70; Steinhardt to Hirschmann, 5/2/44, Laurence A. Steinhardt Collection, Letterbooks, Box 82, LC; Hirschmann to Steinhardt, 6/1/44; Hirschmann to Steinhardt, 6/10/44, Laurence A. Steinhardt Collection, 1944 General Correspondence, Box 44, LC; Talese, *Ibid.*
29. Like many theories about the *Times*, it is not easy to decipher the origins of the idea that the newspaper was edited by Catholics. Talese, *The Kingdom and the Power*, 70, may have been referring to the "high percentage of [Roman Catholic] editors in the newsroom," rather than the religion of the top editors in particular, although he did imply that McCaw was Catholic, and reporter Herbert Matthews, *A World in Revolution*, 20, stated it directly. A Presbyterian minister presided at McCaw's funeral, however. *NYT*, 3/26/59. Salisbury, *Without Fear or Favor*, 253, said James was Catholic, but his funeral services were held at the Methodist Christ Church on Park Avenue. *NYT*, 12/7/51. Fellow *Times*men knew Bernstein was Jewish.
30. Author interview, 10/11/01.
31. *NYT*, 12/31/69; Matthews, *A World in Revolution*, 20.
32. MacNeil, *Without Fear or Favor*, 48; Matthews, *Ibid.*; Salisbury, *Without Fear or Favor*, 453n.
33. Dinnerstein, *Antisemitism in America*, 112–22; *Tablet*, 12/8/38, 11, as quoted in Patrick J. McNamara, "A Study of the Editorial Policy of the Brooklyn *Tablet* under Patrick F. Scanlan, 1917–1968," master's thesis, Department of History, St. John's University, New York, 4/15/94. See also Charles R. Morr, *American Catholic: The Saints and Sinners Who Built America's Most Powerful Church*, New York: Times Books (1997), 250–4; Bosnick, "America and the Jews."
34. 6/11/42, 1, 7/13/42, 1, 6/12/42, 20, 6/27/42, 12, 6/30/42, 20, 7/14/42, 18, 6/14/42, E2.
35. 5/29/42, 5/30/42, 6/5/42, 6/19/42. All four stories had Daniel Brigham's byline.
36. Lipstadt, *Beyond Belief*, 172–3, suggested that one reason this story appeared on the front page was that it came from "'various trustworthy sources' in Berlin," rather than the victims who were "less credible" sources. But as Lipstadt herself points out, the sources were not official and the article's author, George Axelsson, explicitly doubted parts of their story. In addition, in looking at all the *Times* stories on the Holocaust that appeared during the war years, no pattern could be discerned in the treatment of stories from the "perpetrators," as Lipstadt labeled them, and from the victims. Her second explanation – that the 258 deaths "was entirely within the realm of 'reason,'" while the death of millions was not – is more plausible. Yet, it does not explain why the deaths of 258 Jews, in and of itself, would be a front-page story.
37. 1/27/43.
38. 8/3/42.
39. See, for example, 9/23/42, 5/5/42, 10/7/42.

40. 1/5/42, 2/8/42, 2/15/42, 4/23/42, 5/26/42, 7/15/42, 9/19/42, 9/23/42, 1/27/43, 3/9/43, 11/12/43. See Chapter 3 for a discussion of the *Times*' coverage of resistance and reprisals in France in 1941.
41. 8/16/42, 10/7/42, 3/29/43.
42. 4/5/43.
43. Office of War Information, Washington News Division, Sample News Stories, 3/13/42, 3/19/42, 2/21/42, 3/23/42, Box 2852, 2/25/42, 3/9/42, Box 2853, NA; Herrick to Bernstein, 6/11/42, Office of War Information, Office of Facts and Figures, File of Director, 1941–1942, Lidice Mass Murder Campaign, NA; Office of War Information, Records of the Office of the Director, Records of the Director, 1942–1945, Monthly Reports, 1942–43, NA.
44. 6/12/42, 20, 6/30/42, 20, 7/13/42, 1, 7/14/42, 18, 8/22/42, 1, 6/10/43, 20, 3/14/44, 18.
45. MSS 361/D92/1, AJA.
46. Author interview, Marylea Meyersohn, 9/20/01; Talese, *The Kingdom and the Power*, 140–1.
47. Editorial, *The Jerusalem Post*, 12/15/91, Opinion Section.
48. *Kingdom and the Power*, 68.
49. MacNeil Jr., letter to author, 10/25/01.
50. *Without Fear or Favor*, 367.
51. Catledge, *My Life and The Times*, 189; Polish Information Center Papers, Box 48.2, "Profiles of Journals," 2/43, HI.
52. *My Life and The Times*, 189.
53. *Ibid.*, 163. James to McCaw, 6/15/39; McCaw to James, 3/20/44; James to McCaw 6/27/40, ELJ File, RM Folder, NYTCA.

Chapter 7

1. Sulzberger to Krock, 12/24/42, AK Collection, Box 56, 1927–49 Folder, PU.
2. Halperin, *The Political World of American Zionism*, 75–80.
3. Sulzberger to Morgenthau, undated; Morgenthau to Sulzberger, received, 5/14/40, Henry Morgenthau Jr. Correspondence, Box 93, FDRL.
4. Halperin, *The Political World of American Zionism*, 379, fn46; Sulzberger to Montor, 2/26/41, AHS File, MSL Folder, NYTCA. See also Sulzberger to Lazaron, 1/17/42, MSS 71/8/10, AJA.
5. Neumann to Silver, 1/30/42, AS Papers, Series II, Folder 6, YU.
6. Minutes of Meeting of the Public Relations Committee, AECZA, 1/26/42, AS Papers, Series II, Folder 28, YU; Sulzberger to Richards, 1/30/42, BGR Collection, Box 9, JTS.
7. Hull to Sulzberger, 1/30/42, AHS File, CH Folder, NYTCA; Adler, "Franklin D. Roosevelt and Zionism, 273; Sulzberger to Welles, 2/10/42; Welles to Sulzberger, 2/11/42, SW Papers, Box 84/13, FDRL; Buss to Sulzberger, 4/8/42, ELJ File, JML Folder, NYTCA.
8. *New Palestine*, 10/17/41.

9. Bernard Wasserstein, *Britain and the Jews of Europe 1939–45*, New York: Oxford University Press (1979), 143–56.
10. Minutes of the Meeting of the Zionist Organization of America National Administrative Council, 3/8/42, Report of the AECZA, AS Papers, Series II, Folder 109, YU.
11. Minutes of the Meeting of Office Committee, AECZA, 3/13/42, AS Papers, Series II, Folder 28, YU; Minutes of the ZOA Executive Committee Meeting, 4/26/42, Report of the Emergency Committee, AS Papers, Series II, Folder 109, YU.
12. Minutes of the Meeting of the Zionist Organization of America National Administrative Council, 3/8/42, AS Papers, Series II, Folder 109, YU.
13. Halperin, *The Political World of American Zionism*, 81.
14. Lazaron to Sulzberger, 4/28/41; Lazaron to Sulzberger, 5/14/41, MSS 71/8/10, AJA; Sulzberger to Lazaron, 4/30/41, AHS File, MSL Folder, NYTCA.
15. Lazaron to Sulzberger, 11/9/41; Sulzberger to Lazaron, 11/14/41, AHS File, MSL Folder, NYTCA; Sulzberger to Lazaron, 12/26/41, MSS 71/8/10, AJA; Menahem Kaufman, *An Ambiguous Partnership: Non-Zionists and Zionists in America, 1939–48*, Detroit: Wayne State University Press (1991), 78.
16. Monty Noam Penkower, "The Genesis of the American Council for Judaism: A Quest for Identity in World War II," *American Jewish History* 86:2 (June 1998), 167–94, 180.
17. Sulzberger to Lazaron, 6/2/42; Lazaron to Sulzberger, 6/4/42, MSS 71/8/10, AJA.
18. Sulzberger to Lazaron, 6/29/42; Sulzberger to Lazaron, 6/25/42, *Ibid.*
19. 8/30/42; Lazaron to Sulzberger, 8/26/42, MSS 15/3/7, AJA; Sulzberger to Lazaron, 9/17/42; Philipson to Lazaron, 9/17/42, MSS 71/8/10, AJA.
20. 9/21/42.
21. Sulzberger to Magnes, 12/4/42; Sulzberger to Magnes, 12/15/42, JLM Papers, P3/215, CAHJP.
22. Sulzberger to Lazaron, 9/17/42, MSS 71/8/10, AJA; Sulzberger to Welles, 10/21/42, SW Papers, Box 84/13, FDRL; Sulzberger to Krock, 5/23/48, AK Collection, Box 56, 1927–49 Folder, PU.
23. Minutes of Office Committee Meeting, AECZA, AS Papers, 11/10/42, Series II, Folder 28, YU.
24. Frank to Sulzberger, 11/17/42; Sulzberger to Frank, 11/18/42, Group 222/IV/70/889, YU; Sulzberger to Lazaron, 11/12/42; Sulzberger to Lazaron, 11/25/42, MSS 71/8/10, AJA.
25. *Congress Weekly* 11/20/42, AHS File, JJ Folder, NYTCA.
26. Sulzberger to Welles, 11/11/42; Welles to Sulzberger, 11/13/42, SW Papers, Box 84/19, FDRL.
27. Sulzberger to Hull, 12/6/42, MSS 71/8/10, AJA; Hull to Sulzberger, 12/22/42, AHS File, CH Folder, NYTCA.
28. Sulzberger to Schulman, 12/28/42, AHS File, JJ Folder, NYTCA.
29. Sulzberger to Willen, 11/26/42, *Ibid.*
30. 11/15/42, E10.

31. 12/2/42, 14; Sulzberger to Schulman, 12/28/42, AHS File, JJ, Folder, NYTCA.
32. Penkower, "The Genesis of the American Council for Judaism," 187; Halperin, *The Political World of American Zionism*, 87.
33. Shpiro, *From Philanthropy to Activism: The Political Transformation of American Zionism in the Holocaust Years 1933–1945*, Oxford: Pergamon Press (1994), 129; Thomas A. Kolsky, *Jews Against Zionism: The American Council for Judaism, 1942–1948*, Philadelphia: Temple University Press (1990), 62; Hexter to Sulzberger, 12/21/42, AHS File, ACJ Folder, NYTCA.
34. *The Political World of American Zionism*, 100–1.
35. Sulzberger to Levinthal, 1/23/43; Levinthal to Frankfurter, 2/9/43; Frankfurter to Morgenthau, undated, Morgenthau Correspondence, Box 101, FDRL.
36. Sulzberger to Lazaron, 1/18/43, AHS File, MSL Folder, NYTCA.
37. In 1942 and 1943, the *Times* ran nine advertisements for the group, although only after it eliminated "inflammatory, exaggerated and misleading statements, some of which have gone a little too far in attacking the policy of the British government." Hall to Gannon, 1/14/44; Sulzberger to Alfange, 1/14/44, AHS File, JJ Folder, NYTCA.
38. Easterman to Miller, 3/1/43, MSS 361/D92/3, AJA; Berlin, 2/24/43, AS Papers, Series II, Folder 64, YU.
39. 2/13/43, 5.
40. Porot, *The Blue and the Yellow Stars of David*, 169, 174.
41. 3/3/43, 22.
42. 3/8/43, MSS 361/D92/3, AJA.
43. 3/10/43, 12, 3/31/43, 12, 3/23/43, 4, 8, 4/18/43, 11, 3/24/43, 5. Other newspapers afforded the "We Will Never Die" rally more attention, including the *Washington Post* and the *New York Herald Tribune*.
44. See *NYT* 4/18/43, 30, and 4/19/43, 4. Shultz to Wise, etc., 4/16/43, MSS 361/D92/3, AJA; 4/19/43, 18.
45. 4/20/43, 1, 4/22/43, 10, 4/23/43, 9, 4/24/43, 2, 4/25/43, 19, 4/25/43, 2E, 5/2/43, 17.
46. Penkower, *The Jews Were Expendable*, 113; Rothschild to Rosten, 4/21/43, RG 208/75/233, NA; 5/2/43, 48.
47. *NYT*, 4/20/65; Arthur A. Goren, ed., *Dissenter in Zion: From the Writings of Judah L. Magnes*, Cambridge, Mass.: Harvard University Press (1982), 436, fn4.
48. Sulzberger to James, 8/27/40; Sulzberger to Butler, 5/16/45, ELJ File, JML Folder, NYTCA.
49. See ELJ File, JML Folder; Author interview, 11/18/01.
50. James to A. Sulzberger, 10/18/48, ELJ File, JM Folder, NYTCA.
51. Butler to Sulzberger, 5/4/45, ELJ File, JML Folder, NYTCA.
52. C. Sulzberger to James, 11/7/42; A. Sulzberger to Bracken, 11/23/42, CLS File, NYTCA.
53. Silver to Sulzberger, 11/9/43, AS Papers, Series I, Folder 1310, YU. See also Monty Noam Penkower, *The Holocaust and Israel Reborn*, Urbana: University of Illinois Press (1994), 145–76.

54. Sedgwick to Sulzberger, 10/30/41, AHS File, CLS Folder, NYTCA; Sedgwick to Catledge, 6/19/46, ELJ File, ACS Folder, NYTCA.
55. 8/13/43, 7, 9/26/43, 33. See also 8/15/43, 29, 8/23/43, 10, 9/14/43, 7, 9/24/43, 7, 9/25/43, 5, 9/28/43, 7, 9/30/43, 5.
56. Friedrich to Neumann, 8/25/43; Neumann to Friedrich, 8/27/43, AS Papers, Series I, Folder 106, YU; Nicholas, *Washington Dispatches*, 239–40.
57. Shertok to Silver, 9/13/43, AS Papers, Series II, Folder 65, YU.
58. 8/15/43, 29, 9/27/43, 7, 10/7/43, 11.
59. 9/15/43, Milton Steinberg Papers, Box 20/3, AJHS; Sulzberger to Silver, 12/21/43, "not sent," AHS File, PZ Folder, NYTCA.
60. Sedgwick to Sulzberger, 11/29/43; Sedgwick to Sulzberger, 12/21/43, AHS File, PZ Folder, NYTCA.
61. C. Sulzberger to James, A. Sulzberger, 11/18/43. James to Brock, 3/8/44; Brock to James, 3/21/44, ELJ File, RB Folder, NYTCA. See also, Berger, *The Story of The New York Times*, 446. Military authorities routinely refused credentials to journalists considered "suspect." Richard W. Steele, "News of the 'Good War': World War II News Management, *Journalism Quarterly* 62 (Winter 1985): 703–16, 783.
62. Bendersky, *The "Jewish Threat"*, 325–6; Monty Noam Penkower, "American Jewry and the Holocaust: From Biltmore to the American Jewish Conference," *Jewish Social Studies* (Spring 1985): 95–114, 102.
63. Sulzberger to Lazaron, 11/25/42, MSS 71/8/10, AJA; Sulzberger to Silver, 11/2/43, AS Papers, Series I, Folder 1310, YU; Sulzberger to Rosenberg, 6/7/43, MSS 31/ 6/15, AJA.
64. Lazaron to Sulzberger, 4/15/43; Sulzberger to Lazaron, 4/17/43; Sulzberger to Rosenwald 4/17/43, MSS 71/8/10, AJA; Sulzberger to Meyer, 8/7/45, Annie Nathan Meyer Collection, AJA; Sulzberger to Rosenwald, 4/28/43; Sulzberger to Rosenwald, 5/24/43; Sulzberger to Rosenwald, 5/25/43, AHS File, ACJ Folder, NYTCA.
65. Sulzberger to Goldman, 11/15/43, MSS 31/6/15, AJA. See also Sulzberger to Lazaron, 9/8/43, AHS File, ACJ Folder, NYTCA. Sulzberger to Meyer, 8/7/45, Annie Nathan Meyer Collection, AJA; Sulzberger to Rosenwald, 1/30/52, AHS File, ACJ Folder, NYTCA.
66. Jan Karksi Papers, "Raport p. Karskiego z pobytu w U.S.A.," Boxes 1.7, 2.3, HI.
67. 7/21/43, 13, 7/22/43, 7, 7/23/43, 11, 7/26/43, 19, 7/27/43, 9, 8/27/43, 7.
68. 8/28/43, 10; *NYHT*, 8/28/43, 1, 10.
69. Penkower, "American Jewry and the Holocaust," 104; Doreen Bierbrier, "The American Zionist Emergency Council: An Analysis of a Pressure Group," *American Jewish Historical Quarterly* (September 1970): 82–105; 8/30/43, 6; Sulzberger to Lazaron, 9/8/43, AHS File, ACJ Folder, NYTCA.
70. James to Sulzberger, 9/1/43, *Ibid*; Lazaron to Sulzberger, 9/18/43, AHS File, JLM Folder, NYTCA.
71. *NYT*, 9/1/43, 12. The *Times*' account corresponds with the transcript of the 8/31/43 session of the American Jewish Conference. MSS 361/8, AJA.

72. Sulzberger to Horwitz, 10/26/47; Sulzberger to Arsht, 3/30/61, 4/5/61, 4/12/61, 4/13/61, AHS File, ACJ Folder, NYTCA.
73. 9/2/43, 1.
74. 9/4/43, 2e.
75. 9/11/43, 8.
76. 9/12/43, 12.
77. Sulzberger to Krock, 9/11/43; Sulzberger to Krock, 9/13/43; Krock to Sulzberger, 9/13/43; Sulzberger to Krock 9/14/43; Krock to Sulzberger, 9/18/43, AHS File, PZ Folder, NYTCA.
78. Feingold, "'Courage First and Intelligence Second"; *NYT*, 10/25/43, 17.
79. 9/15/43, Milton Steinberg Papers, Box 20/3, AJHS.
80. *NYT*, 10/29/43, 14; Levinthal to Silver, 10/25/43; Silver to Levinthal, 11/12/43, AS Papers, Series I, Folder 102, YU.
81. Sulzberger to Silver, 11/2/43; Silver to Sulzberger, 11/9/43, AS Papers, Series I, Folder 1310, YU.
82. Lazaron to Sulzberger, 9/13/43; Sulzberger to Lazaron, 9/15/43; Sulzberger to Lazaron, 11/6/43, AHS File, MSL Folder, NYTCA.
83. Dryfoos to Sulzberger, 11/4/43; Dryfoos to Sulzberger, 11/5/43, AHS File, PZ Folder, NYTCA; Jenks to Sulzberger, 12/6/43, BGR Collection, Box 9, JTS.
84. Sulzberger to Nelson, 11/3/43, AHS File, BGR Folder, NYTCA.
85. Richards to Asher, 6/8/44, Box 9; Richards to Slomovitz, 5/28/56, Box 8, BGR Collection, JTS.
86. Montor to Silver, 11/11/43; Montor to Silver, 12/6/43, AS Papers, Series II, Folder 91, YU.
87. Monsky to Montor, 12/3/43, AS Papers, Series I, Folder 105, YU; Dryfoos to Sulzberger, 12/8/43, BGR Collection, Box 9, JTS.
88. Sulzberger to Silver, marked not sent, 12/21/43, AHS File, PZ Folder, NYTCA.
89. 10/28/43, 22.
90. Richards to Sulzberger, 1/6/44; Sulzberger to Richards, 1/7/44, AHS File, BGR Folder, NYTCA; Sulzberger to Billikopf, 1/8/44, MSS 13/29/2, AJA.
91. Sulzberger to Kallen, 1/11/45; Kallen to Sulzberger, 1/15/45; Sulzberger to Kallen, 1/16/45; Sulzberger to Kallen, 1/30/45, AHS File, JJ, NYTCA.
92. Rosenberg to Sulzberger, 1/19/44, JLM Papers, P3–250G, CAHJP; Sulzberger to Rosenberg, 1/27/44, MSS 31/6/15, AJA.
93. Sulzberger to Marks, 1/31/44, AHS File, ACJ Folder, NYTCA.

Chapter 8

1. Morgenthau Diaries, 1/29/44, Roll 202, #698, FDRL.
2. Tifft and Jones, *The Trust*, 171.
3. Sulzberger to James, Krock, 11/9/40, AHS File, FDR Folder, NYTCA.
4. Pare Lorentz Chronology, FDRL.

5. Roosevelt to Sulzberger, 5/9/40; Sulzberger to Roosevelt, 5/10/40, Presidential Papers Folder 675, FDRL.
6. Sulzberger to Morgenthau, 4/13/44, Morgenthau Correspondence, Box 277, FDRL.
7. Welles to Sulzberger, 7/13/42; Sulzberger to Welles, 7/18/42; Welles to Roosevelt, 7/22/42; Duggan to Welles, 5/12/42; Welles to Duggan, 5/15/42, SW Papers, Box 84/13, FDRL.
8. Sulzberger to Roosevelt, 2/24/41, AHS File, FDR Folder, NYTCA.
9. Draft of book chapter, "In the Newspapers," 9/20/45, Lester Markel Collection, Box 16, WSHS.
10. 11/21/41, 16.
11. Sulzberger to Krock, 12/9/41, AK Collection, Box 56, 1927–49 Folder, PU.
12. *NYT*, 12/20/41, 9, 1/15/42, 12, 1/19/42, 16.
13. Price to James, 1/1/44; James to Price, 1/5/44; James to Price, 11/23/43; Price to James, 11/25/43; James to Howard, 2/18/43; Howard to James, 2/19/43, ELJ File, Censorship Folder, NYTCA. See also Martin Walker, *Powers of the Press*, New York: The Pilgrim Press (1982), 22–3, and Michael S. Sweeney, *Secrets of Victory: The Office of Censorship and the American Press and Radio in World War II*, Chapel Hill: The University of North Carolina Press (2001), 156–60. *NYT*, 6/25/44, E3.
14. Lockhart to James, 11/10/43; Sulzberger to Crider, etc., 11/11/43, AK Collection, Box 56, 1927–49 Folder, PU.
15. Sweeney, *Secrets of Victory*, 142–4, 66–70.
16. McCaw to James, 3/29/42; McCaw to Huston, 11/13/41, AHS File, Censorship Folder, NYTCA.
17. 1/7/42, 18.
18. Knightley, *The First Casualty*, 278.
19. "Special Directive on Handling of Stories of Japanese Atrocities," 1/44, OWI, Director of Overseas Operations, Area Policy File, Box 110, NA.
20. 1/28/44, 1, 6, 1/29/44, 1, 2, 5, 12, 1/30/44, 1, 28, 29, 30, E1, E2, 2/1/44, 1, 10, 18.
21. Many fine books have grappled with the reasons for this government policy, including Breitman, *Official Secrets*; Feingold, *The Politics of Rescue*; Friedman, *No Haven for the Oppressed*; Gilbert, *Auschwitz and the Allies*; Penkower, *The Jews Were Expendable*; and Wyman, *The Abandonment of the Jews*.
22. *The Propaganda Warriors*, University Press of Kansas (1996), 117.
23. OWI, Historian, Draft, Historical Reports, 1941–1948, Report to the President, 6/13/42, 9/15/45, Box 3, NA.
24. 8/16/42, 3. The division was not nearly as clear as either director suggested, although it does accurately capture the differences in their offices' missions. See Sweeney, *Secrets of Victory*, 93–9, for a discussion of their conflicts.
25. Brigham to MacLeish, 6/19/42, OWI, Records of the Office of the Director and Predecessor Agencies, Box 12, "Crimes and Atrocities, various agencies, 1942–1944," NA.

26. Minutes, Committee on War Information Policy, 7/29/42; Minutes, Committee on War Information Policy, 9/2/42, OWI, Records of the Office of the Director, Box I, NA.
27. Laurie, *The Propaganda Warriors*, 180–1, concludes that OWI hesitated to release "World War I-style 'atrocity propaganda,'" including "news associated with the Holocaust," because it might damage "OWI's reputation for sober truthfulness." Laurie's claim seems to be based on one episode, OWI's reaction to the War Refugee Board's release of a report on the Auschwitz extermination camp, which is discussed in Chapter 9, rather than a sustained study of the agency's approach throughout the war.
28. Rosten to Albig, 6/8/61, LCR Papers, HI.
29. Cowles, "Interpretation of Enemy Atrocities," Domestic Branch, OWI, 2/18/43, LCR Papers, HI. See also MacLeish, Basic Policy Directive No. 1, "The Nature of the Enemy," 10/5/42, and Cowles, "Policy Directive on 'Hate' Propaganda," 4/9/43, OWI, Domestic Branch, LCR Papers, HI.
30. Rosten to Rice, 3/8/43, RG208/75/233, NA. See also, Clark to Arrengton, 1/13/44, OWI, News Bureau, Office of the Chief, General Subjects File, Box 975, NA; OWI, Domestic Branch, Information Guide, The Enemy, Sheet 6, 4/43, LCR Papers, Box 74, BU.
31. Penkower, *The Jews Were Expendable*, 295. The British had similar concerns. See Seaton, "Reporting atrocities"; Harris, "Broadcasting the Massacres"; and Wasserstein, *Britain and the Jews of Europe*.
32. "In 1943, OWI correspondents said anti-Semitism was 'widely reported to be strong and definitely on the increase,'" according to OWI Bureau of Special Services reports. "Opinions About Immigration," Preliminary Report, 10/21/46, Bureau of the Budget, DN Papers, BU.
33. "Study of War Propaganda," 3/6/42, NDD745015, NA. See also Breitman, *Officials Secrets*, 124–7.
34. Special Committee on European Situation, Meeting, 12/14/42, MSS 361/D92/2, AJA.
35. Joint Report, submitted to the Meeting of the Planning Committee, 12/17/42, *Ibid.*
36. Rosten to Arthur Sweetzer, 12/1/42, RG208/75/233, NA.
37. Cowles, 12/7/42, LCR Papers, Box 73, BU.
38. Rosten to Cowles, 4/14/43, RG208/75/232, NA.
39. Rosten to Farbstein, 2/16/43, RG208/75/233, NA.
40. 1/12/43, LCR Papers, Box 74, BU.
41. Rosten to Sweetser, 6/14/43, RG208/75/233, NA.
42. RG208/75/233, NA.
43. Rosten to Farbstein, 2/16/43; Rosten to MacLeish, 2/22/43, *Ibid.*
44. Kubowitzki to Wise, Goldmann, 7/2/43, MSS 361/D97/3, AJA.
45. Morgenthau Diaries, 1/26/44, Roll 202, #696, FDRL.
46. Kubowitzki to Shultz, 8/24/43, MSS 361/D97/3, AJA.

47. 8/25/43, MSS 361/D97/3, AJA.
48. "Survey on the Rescue Activities of the World Jewish Congress 1940–1944," MSS 361/A68/2, AJA. See also Penkower, *The Jews Were Expendable*, 296.
49. Allan M. Winkler, *Politics of Propaganda: The Office of War Information 1942–1945*, New Haven: Yale University Press (1978), 93–9, 96; Laurie, *The Propaganda Warriors*, 176–8.
50. Nicholas, *Washington Dispatches*, 316.
51. Winkler, *Politics of Propaganda*, 110.
52. Breitman and Kraut, *American Refugee Policy and European Jewry*, 180–1.
53. Stettinius, Memo for the President, 1/2/45, Presidential Papers File 675, FDRL.
54. Nicholas, *Washington Dispatches*, 435.
55. Josephson, "Typewriter Statesman," 9.
56. Steel, *Walter Lippmann and the American Century*, 200.
57. Author interview, 10/10/01.
58. Sulzberger to Billikopf, 9/11/44, MSS 13/29/2, AJA.
59. Krock to Sulzberger, 7/24/44; Krock to Sulzberger, 7/31/44, AK Collection, Box 56, 1927–49 Folder, PU.
60. See Edwin Diamond, *Behind the Times: Inside the New New York Times*, New York: Villard Books (1993), 43, and Tifft and Jones, *The Trust*, 175–6.
61. Krock, *Memoirs: Sixty Years on the Firing Line*, New York: Funk & Wagnalls (1968), xii, 80–1; Krock, *Myself When Young: Growing Up in the 1890's*, Boston: Little Brown and Company (1973).
62. Josephson to Billikopf, 10/21/44; Billikopf to Josephson, 10/25/44, FF Papers, Reel #14, LC.
63. Halberstam, *The Powers That Be*, 216.
64. Kennedy to Krock, 10/10/41, AK Collection, Box 56, 1927–49 Folder, PU.
65. Breitman, *Official Secrets*, 176–86.
66. Irwin F. Gellman, *Secret Affairs: Franklin Roosevelt, Cordell Hull, and Sumner Welles*, Baltimore: The Johns Hopkins University Press (1995), 98–9, 209.
67. See, for example, *PM*, 2/11/41, 7; the *New Republic*, 8/18/41; and the *Nation*, 5/20/39, 12/28/40, and 7/19/41.
68. Josephson, "Typewriter Statesman," 42. Krock did not include either episode when he told Sulzberger of 15 mistakes Josephson had made in his two-part series. Krock to Sulzberger, 7/24/44; Krock to Sulzberger, 7/31/44, AK Collection Box 56, PU.
69. Zucker, *In Search of Refuge*, 174.
70. Jordan A. Schwarz, *Liberal: Adolf A. Berle and the Vision of an American Era*, New York: The Free Press (1987).
71. Breitman and Kraut, *American Refugee Policy and European Jewry*, 160.
72. Krock to Huston, 8/19/43; Huston to Krock, 8/19/43; Krock to Huston, 8/19/43, AK Collection, Box 29, Luther Huston Folder, PU. Krock, 12/21/43, AK Collection, Box 60, SW Folder, PU.
73. 8/6/43, 14.

74. Krock to Huston, 8/19/43; Huston to Krock, 8/19/43; Krock to Huston, 8/19/43, AK Collection, Box 29, Luther Huston Folder, PU.
75. 8/29/43, 4E.
76. Paul to Morgenthau, 8/12/43, Morgenthau Diaries, Reel #199, FDRL.
77. See Penkower, *The Jews Were Expendable*, 122–47, for a description of the creation of the War Refugee Board.
78. 11/1/43, 5.
79. Penkower, *The Jews Were Expendable*, 137.
80. 11/20/43, 6, 11/25/43, 31, 12/3/43, 4, 12/7/43, 4.
81. Breckinridge Long Papers, Subject File, State Department, 1939–1944, Box 202, LC.
82. 12/27/43, 11. See also *NYT*, 1/3/44, 9.
83. 2/19/44, 6.
84. Breitman and Kraut, *American Refugee Policy and European Jewry*, 144.
85. Max Nussbaum, 9/40 memo, copy given to author by Ruth Nussbaum.
86. 12/17/43, Morgenthau Diaries, Roll 200, FDRL.
87. Interview with Pehle, 1979, Henry Morgenthau III Papers, FDRL.
88. Interview with DuBois, *Ibid*. See also Breitman and Kraut, *American Refugee Policy and European Jewry*, 199–200.
89. Morgenthau Diaries, 1/29/44, Roll 202, #698, FDRL.
90. James to MacNeil, 1/29/44, ELJ File, NM Folder, NYTCA.
91. Penkower, *The Jews Were Expendable*, 142.
92. Huston to James, 1/29/44, AHS File, Henry Morgenthau, Jr., Folder, NYTCA.
93. Morgenthau Diaries, 1/31/44, Roll 202, #698, FDRL.
94. Sulzberger to Morgenthau, 1/31/44; Morgenthau to Sulzberger, 2/3/44, Morgenthau Diaries, Roll 203, #700, FDRL.
95. 2/1/44, 18.
96. 2/2/44, 20.

Chapter 9

1. Abrahamson to Pehle, etc., 4/24/44; Abrahamson to Warren, 4/24/44, WRB Papers, Box 26, FDRL.
2. 2/22/44, Box 33, WRB Papers, FDRL.
3. Pehle to Mannon, 12/20/44, Box 53; Mannon to Pinkus, 3/30/44, Box 50, WRB Papers, FDRL.
4. See Quincy Howe's CBS broadcast in February 1944, Douglas Edward's CBS broadcast in May 1944, Raymond Gram Swing's broadcast on the Blue Network in April 1944, and H. R. Baukhage's interview with Pehle on NBC in May. Pehle to Green, 4/7/44, WRB Papers, Box 22, FDRL.
5. Pehle memorandum, 2/14/44, WRB Papers, Box 50, FDRL.
6. "Report of Accomplishments for Week of February 14–19, 1944" Box 1, Ira Hirschmann Papers, FDRL.
7. Central Directive, 2/24–3/2/44, WRB Papers, Box 22, FDRL.

8. 3/21/44, 1, 4, 3/22/44, 1, 12, 18.
9. Stettinius to Early, 3/8/44, Palestine Statehood Committee Papers, YU. Pehle memorandum, 3/9/44, WRB Papers, Box 33, FDRL.
10. Breitman, *Official Secrets*, 202–3.
11. Katz to Cowan, 4/1/44, Box 50; Pehle to Kuhn, 3/24/44, WRB Ankara Cable No. 13, 3/24/44, WRB Papers, Box 33, FDRL.
12. Thomson to Control Desk, New York, 3/24/44, OWI Papers, Division of Overseas Operations, Policy Subject File, Box 116, NA. See also Breitman, *Official Secrets*, 203.
13. 3/25/44, 1, 14.
14. Hirschmann, *Caution to the Winds*, New York: David McKay Company Inc. (1962), 136.
15. Sulzberger to Magnes, 6/11/46, P3–218B, CAHJP.
16. *Caution to the Winds*, 139.
17. 2/13/44, 10, 2/20/44, 11, 4/11/44, 2.
18. 5/4/44, 6.
19. Pehle to Grafton, 6/9/44, WRB Papers, Box 22, FDRL.
20. Cantril to Niles, 4/14/44, DN Papers, Box 25, BU.
21. 4/19/44, 1.
22. Hirchmann to Steinhardt, 6/10/44, Laurence A. Steinhardt Papers, 1944, General Correspondence, Box 44, LC.
23. 5/4/44, 18.
24. Pehle to Roosevelt, 5/18/44, DN Papers, Box 25, BU.
25. 4/19/44, 1.
26. Episodes such as this have led to conflicting views of Hirschmann's effectiveness. Bauer, *American Jewry and the Holocaust*, 405–6, considered Hirschmann a "flamboyant figure," whose penchant for "self-dramatization" sabotaged his rescue efforts. Bernard Wasserstein, "The Myth of Jewish Silence," *Midstream* XXVI:7 (August/September 1980), 14, echoed that view. But Penkower, *The Jews Were Expendable*, 181, concluded: "Hirschmann's determination, his bold initiatives strengthened by Pehle in Washington and Steinhardt in Ankara, brought dramatic change." That is a view largely shared by Henry Feingold, *Bearing Witness: How America and Its Jews Responded to the Holocaust*, Syracuse: Syracuse University Press, 141–68.
27. 5/8/44, Abrahamson to Pehle, 5/10/44, WRB Papers, Box 34, FDRL.
28. 5/19/44, 18.
29. 5/22/44, 5.
30. Lesser to Pehle, 5/22/44, WRB Papers, Box 29, FDRL.
31. WRB Papers, Box 34, FDRL.
32. Meltzer to James, 5/19/44, ELJ File, RD Folder; James to Markel, 5/19/44; James to Daniell, 5/22/44, ELJ File, JM Folder, NYTCA.
33. 5/20/44, 5.
34. Wyman, *The Abandonment of the Jews*, 323.
35. 6/5/44, 6/6/44.

36. 6/13/44, 6/18/44, 2E.
37. 3/30/41, 9, 5/21/41, 9, 6/18/41, 9, 11/25/42, 10, 3/8/43, 5.
38. Cable from London, 9/16/43, Box 3.3; Cable from London, 3/21/44, Box 3.9, Polish Information Center Papers, HI.
39. Kubowitzki to Teller, 3/8/44, reports attached, MSS 361/G1/2, AJA.
40. Gruenbaum to Wise, 6/27/44, 8570/34, CZA.
41. Meltzer to London, 6/30/44, 8510/34, CZA.
42. See, for example, Michael J. Neufeld and Michael Berenbaum, eds., *The Bombing of Auschwitz: Should the Allies Have Attempted It?* New York: St. Martin's Press (2000).
43. See Teveth Shabtai, *Ben-Gurion and the Holocaust*, New York: Harcourt Brace & Co. (1996), 208–9.
44. James to Bernstein, undated memo, ELJ File, DB Folder, NYTCA.
45. 7/6/44, 6.
46. 7/8/44, 10.
47. 7/3/44, 3.
48. 7/9/44.
49. 7/20/44, 8/4/44. See also, a magazine article on life in London "under the persistent barrage of robot bombs." 7/30/44, 8.
50. James to Brigham, Archambault, 3/17/44, ELJ File, GHA Folder, NYTCA.
51. Brigham to James, 6/19/44; James to Archambault, 8/25/44, ELJ File, DB Folder, NYTCA.
52. Archambault to James, 9/19/44, ELJ File, GHA Folder, NYTCA.
53. McCaw to James, 8/8/44, ELJ File, JML Folder, NYTCA.
54. James to Enderis, 10/8/44, ELJ File, Guido Enderis Folder, NYTCA.
55. Brigham to James, 11/18/44, ELJ File, DB Folder, NYTCA.
56. James to C. Sulzberger, 7/14/44, CLS File, ELJ Folder; Huston to James, 7/14/44, ELJ File, JML Folder, NYTCA.
57. 7/13/44, 3.
58. Weinstein to Pehle, 6/29/44, WRB Papers, Box 35, FDRL.
59. Standish to Lesser, 6/21/44, WRB Papers, Box 34, FDRL.
60. 7/22/44, WRB Papers, Box 58, FDRL.
61. Silberschein to Neustadt, 7/19/44, S26/1251, CZA.
62. Feingold, *Bearing Witness*.
63. *The Jews Were Expendable*, 194.
64. Sulzberger to Morgenthau, 2/2/44; Pehle to Steinberg, 2/8/44; Pehle to Sulzberger, 2/8/44; Sulzberger to Pehle, 2/11/44; Steinberg to Pehle, 3/5/44, WRB Papers, Box 26, FDRL.
65. WRB Papers, Box 70, FDRL.
66. *The Disappearing Daily*, 86.
67. Richards to Slomovitz, 6/29/44, BGR Collection, Box 8, JTS.
68. Sulzberger to Whitney, 10/21/44, AHS File, PZ Folder, NYTCA.
69. 2/12/44, 12.

70. Richards to Sulzberger, 10/2/44, BGR Collection, Box 9, JTS; Manson to Silver, 10/6/44, AS Papers, Roll 7, Folder 153, YU.
71. 9/29/44, 20.
72. 7/9/44, 18, 11/18/44, 4, 5/1/44, 5, 11/29/44, 14, 2/18/44, 7.
73. 9/20/44, 3, 10/27/44, 10, 11/29/44, 14.
74. 10/27/44, 8, 4/15/44, 3, 3/29/44, 2, 11/7/44, 16, 9/4/44, 9.
75. James to Lawrence, 9/14/44; Lawrence to James, 9/15/44, ELJ File, MB Folder, NYTCA.
76. Lawrence, *Six Presidents, Too Many Wars*, 100–1.
77. Lipstadt, *Beyond Belief*, 253–4.
78. See *NYT*, 5/8/44, 8.
79. Office of Strategic Services, Research and Analysis Branch, "A Statistical Analysis of Soviet Atrocity Charges," 7/4/44, MSS 361/C174/7, AJA.
80. See 8/13/44, magazine, 22, 10/6/44, 6.
81. APT786 1944, John Hay Library, Brown University.
82. 8/31/44, 16.
83. Pehle to Davis, 8/23/44, WRB Papers, Box 33, FDRL.
84. 9/2/44, 6.
85. Pehle to Davis, 9/4/44, WRB Papers, Box 33, FDRL.
86. Davis to Pehle, 9/7/44; Pehle to Davis, 9/12/44; Pehle to Hull, 9/13/44, WRB Papers, Box 33, FDRL; Davis to Pehle, 9/14/44, WRB Papers, Box 35, FDRL.
87. Pehle to Hirschmann, 11/28/44, WRB Papers, Box 6, FDRL.
88. *Ibid.*
89. Mannon, Memorandum to Files, 11/22/44, WRB Papers, Box 6, FDRL.
90. See Wallace Carroll, *Persuade or Perish*, Boston: Houghton Mifflin (1948), 238; Instanbul to Carroll, 5/22/44; Istanbul to Carroll, 5/23/44, Director of Overseas Operations, Area Policy Files, Box 109, NA; Krzyzanoswki to Carroll, 7/24/44; Krzyzanoswki to Carroll, 8/2/44, OWI, Overseas Branch, Bureau of Overseas Intelligence, Central Files, Box 304, NA.
91. Davis to Pehle, 11/23/44; Mannon, Memorandum to Files, 11/27/44; Pehle to Davis, not dated, not sent, WRB Papers, Box 6, FDRL.
92. *The Propaganda Warriors*, 180–1.
93. Laqueur, *The Terrible Secret*, 91.
94. Krzyzanowski to Davis, 8/7/44 OWI, Overseas Branch, Bureau of Overseas Intelligence, Central Files, Box 304, NA; Polish Information Center, Box 71.13, HI.
95. Mannon to Pehle, 11/44, WRB Papers, Box 34, FDRL.
96. Mannon to Pehle, 12/15/44, WRB Papers, Box 6, FDRL.
97. Schuette to Stimson, 11/28/44; Stimson to Schuette, undated; McCloy to Friedman, 12/1/44; Schuette to Stimson, 12/18/44; McCloy to Pehle, 12/27/44; Pehle to Morgenthau, 12/30/44, WRB Papers, Box 6, FDRL.
98. Pehle to Hirschmann, 11/28/44, WRB Papers, Box 6, FDRL. For examples of "the big play," see Lipstadt, *Beyond Belief*, 263–5.

99. Scherman to Pehle, 12/13/44; Pehle to Scherman, 12/19/44, WRB Papers, Box 6, FDRL.
100. 11/4/44, 14.
101. 9/3/44, 4E, magazine, 5.
102. 10/1/44, magazine, 5, 8, and 13.
103. 12/30/44, E5.
104. 12/29/44, 5.
105. 12/28/44, 1.
106. 1/2/45, 18.

Chapter 10

1. AHS File, EJM Folder, NYTCA.
2. 1/4/45.
3. 2/17/45.
4. 2/5/45.
5. Kennan to Secretary of State, 2/9/45, WRB Papers, Box 6, FDRL.
6. 2/3/45, 2.
7. 3/17/45.
8. 2/19/45.
9. 2/17/45, 8, 1/11/45, 8, 9/4/44, 5, 9/24/44, 12. See also 9/17/44, magazine, 8.
10. 12/18/44, 3, 1/1/45, 5.
11. 11/13/44, 1, 4/9/45, 5, 4/15/45, 9, 4/17/45, 4, 4/19/45, 4, 4/9/45, 5, 4/15/45, 9, 4/16/45, 13, 4/17/45, 4, 4/9/45, 5.
12. Zelizer, *Remembering to Forget*, 63, attributes the similarity to journalists' reliance on each other to confirm "what they were seeing, both for themselves and their reading public."
13. Other newspapers were somewhat more inclined to run these stories on the front page. See Lipstadt, *Beyond Belief*, 255–8.
14. 4/18/45, 5/1/45, 4/4/45, 4/20/45.
15. 12/30/45, 2E.
16. Bridgman, *The End of the Holocaust*, 57.
17. 4/17/45, 4.
18. 4/18/45, 4/21/45, 4/22/45, 4/23/45.
19. 4/18/45, 1.
20. 4/19/45, 26, 4/22/45, 13, E1, 4/23/45, 5, 4/26/45, 12, 4/27/45, 3, 4/28/45, 6.
21. Lipstadt, *Beyond Belief*, 255.
22. 5/6/45, E2.
23. *The Washington Post* bundled the stories together and ran them side by side on its 5/1/45 front page.
24. Bridgman, *The End of the Holocaust*, 33, 77, 30.
25. Brewster Chamberlin and Marcia Feldman, eds., *Liberation of the Nazi Concentration Camps 1945: Eyewitness Accounts of the Liberators*, Washington, DC: United States Holocaust Memorial Council (1987), 46.

26. 4/16/45, 13, 4/19/45, 4, 4/21/45, 5, 4/25/45, 3, 4/26/45, 12, 4/29/45, 20.
27. See Haskel Lookstein, "The Public Response of American Jews to the Liberation of European Jewry, January–May 1945," in Shapiro, *Why Didn't the Press Shout*, 127–47, 130.
28. 5/6/45, 8, 5/9/45, 17, 4/23/45, 5.
29. Kushner, *The Holocaust and the Liberal Imagination*, 215.
30. 4/29/45, 20.
31. 4/12/45, 6, 5/8/45, 12.
32. 4/22/45, 13, 5/6/45, 8, 5/28/45, 7.
33. See, for example, Martha Gelhorn, *The Face of War*, New York: Atlantic Monthly Press (1988); Antoinette May, *Witness to War: A Biography of Marguerite Higgins*, New York: Beaufort Books Inc. (1983); and Edwin Tetlow, *As It Happened: A Journalist Looks Back*, London: Peter Owen (1990).
34. Lipstadt, *Beyond Belief*, 273.
35. Bendersky, *The "Jewish Threat,"* 287–347.
36. Hodel, 3/20/45, WRB Papers, Box 33, FDRL.
37. Lawrence Douglas, *Memory of Judgment: Making Law and History in the Trials of the Holocaust*, New Haven: Yale University Press (2001), 62, quotes that phrase from the narration of the *Nazi Concentration Camp* film shown during the Nuremberg trial. Telford Taylor, *The Anatomy of the Nuremberg Trials: A Personal Memoir*, New York: Alfred A. Knopf (1992), 186, explains that the narration was lifted directly from military photographer's captions.
38. *Inside the Vicious Heart: Americans and the Liberation of Nazi Concentration Camps*, New York: Oxford University Press (1985), 127–8.
39. Lipstadt, *Beyond Belief*, 273.
40. *Memory, History and the Extermination of the Jews of Europe*, Bloomington: Indiana University Press (1993), 107.
41. 54–5, 61–81.
42. *As It Happened*, 76.
43. Parsons to Kennedy, 3/20/45; Kennedy to Parsons, 3/22/45; Cooper to Lochner, 3/27/45; Lochner to Cooper, 4/6/45; Lochner to King, 4/20/45; Louis Lochner Papers, Box 1, WSHS. Lochner's diary during this period includes only one reference to the liberated camps, and many to the fate of his German friends and his interest in redeeming the German people. Louis Lochner Papers, Box 11, WSHS. Sigrid Schultz of the *Chicago Tribune* had a similar response. Schultz to her mother, 4/20/45, Sigrid Schultz Papers, Box 44, WSHS.
44. 5/6/45, magazine, 8.
45. 1/30/45, 18, 5/6/45, E1, E5, 5/25/45, 1, 8, 18.
46. 9/12/42, 12, 12/2/42, 14, 8/28/43, 10, 6/19/45, 18.
47. 4/19/45, 4, 4/18/45, 8, 4/15/45, 9, 4/20/45, 3, 4/18/45, 6.
48. 4/22/45, 12, 4/1/45, magazine 5, 4/28/45, 6, 5/20/45, 7, 4/30/45, 5, 4/18/45, 14.
49. *NYT* 4/20/45, 3, *HT* 4/21/45, 3.
50. Zelizer, *Remembering to Forget*, 73, 82.

51. *As It Happened*, 77.
52. MSS 361/C163/3, AJA.
53. 4/25/45, 8.
54. Richards to Sulzberger, 9/4/45, AHS File, BGR Folder, NYTCA.
55. 8/26/45.
56. Zelizer, *Remembering to Forget*, 126.
57. Sulzberger to Markel, 9/4/45; Markel to Sulzberger, 9/6/45, AHS File, EJM Folder, NYTCA.

Chapter 11

1. AHS speech, Box 9, BGR Collection, JTS.
2. *Ibid.*
3. Sulzberger to Magnes, 11/4/46, JLM Papers, P3-218B, CAHJP.
4. Sulzberger to Richards, 1/24/47; Richards to Sulzberger, 1/30/47, AHS File, BGR Folder, NYTCA.
5. 2/11/45, 10.
6. See, for example, Elmer Berger, *The Jewish Dilemma*, New York: The Devin-Adair Company (1945).
7. *Zionism at the UN*, 63.
8. 2/17/45, 12.
9. 3/12/45, 18.
10. Elath, *Zionism at the UN*, 61.
11. Frankfurter to Merz, 4/27/47, FF Papers, Reel #50, LC.
12. Elath, *Zionism at the UN*, 315–7.
13. C. Sulzberger to James, 1/4/45, CLS File, ELJ Folder, NYTCA.
14. Butler to A. Sulzberger, 5/4/45, ELJ File, JML Folder, NYTCA.
15. James to C. Sulzberger, 6/21/45, ELJ File, CLS Folder, NYTCA; James to Butler, 6/25/45, ELJ File, JML Folder, NYTCA.
16. A. Sulzberger to Butler, 8/22/45, ELJ File, JML Folder, NYTCA. See also A. Sulzberger to Butler, 5/16/45, ELJ File, JML Folder, NYTCA.
17. 7/18/45, 26.
18. 10/1/45, 18.
19. Sulzberger to Fondiller, 8/1/45, AHS File, PZ Folder, NYTCA.
20. 8/18/45, 11.
21. Sulzberger to Cohen, 8/30/45, AHS File, PZ Folder, NYTCA; Sulzberger to Morgenstern, 10/26/45; Morgenstern to Sulzberger, 2/11/46, Hebrew Union College Collection, Morgenstern Correspondence, AJA.
22. I. Sulzberger to Morgenstern, 11/6/45; Blank to I. Sulzberger, 11/8/45, *Ibid.*
23. Wise to James, 1/8/46, SSW Papers, Box 80, Reel 74–53, AJHS.
24. 10/7/45, 8E.
25. Steinberg to Wise, 1/25/46; Steinberg to Godwin, 2/5/46, Milton Steinberg Papers, Box 20/3, AJHS.

26. Kaufman, *An Ambiguous Partnership*, 201.
27. Sulzberger to Magnes, 6/6/46, JLM Papers, P3/218B, CAHJP.
28. June 1946, AHS File, PZ Folder, NYTCA.
29. Daniel to Sulzberger, 11/3/46, AHS File, PZ Folder, NYTCA.
30. Richards to Sulzberger, 10/8/46; Sulzberger to Richards, 10/11/46, AHS File, BGR Folder, NYTCA.
31. Sulzberger to Finkelstein, 4/14/47; Finkelstein to Sulzberger, 4/30/47; Sulzberger to Rothman, 5/8/47; Rothman to Sulzberger, 5/12/47; Sulzberger to Rothman, 5/14/47; Sulzberger to Rothman, 7/11/47, Sulzberger-Finkelstein Papers, AJA.
32. "Zionism and Its Jewish 'Assimilationist' Circle," 100–1.
33. Sulzberger to Greenbaum, 3/19/47; Sulzberger to Greenbaum, 4/13/48, AHS File, JJ Folder, NYTCA.
34. Sulzberger to Lazaron, 4/22/47, MSS 71/8/10, AJA.
35. Tifft and Jones, *The Trust*, 237–8.
36. Sulzberger to Frank, 8/2/48, BGR Collection, Box 9, JTS.
37. Sulzberger to Sussman, 12/4/58; Sulzberger to Arsht, 3/30/61, AHS File, ACJ Folder, NYTCA.
38. Sulzberger to Miles, 4/30/48, AHS File, JJ Folder, NYTCA.
39. Sulzberger to children, 8/31/62, AHS File, JJ Folder, NYTCA.
40. Sulzberger to Hurwitz, 1/13/59; Sulzberger to Hurwitz, 1/26/61, MSS 2/57/17, AJA.
41. Sulzberger, 11/29/59; Sulzberger, 9/10/63, AHS File, JJ Folder, NYTCA.
42. AHS File, Hebrew University Folder, NYTCA.

Conclusion

1. *Memory, History and the Extermination of the Jews of Europe*, 107.
2. Hanover, N.H.: University Press of New England (1987), 156.
3. Feingold, *The Politics of Rescue*, 326.
4. *The Holocaust in American Life*, 22.
5. 7/27/43, 9.
6. 1/8/42, 20.
7. *Holocaust in Historical Perspective*, 7.
8. Most scholars who have researched the role of the bystanders have observed some manifestation of this form of disbelief. See, for example, Gilbert, *Auschwitz and the Allies*; Laqueur, *The Terrible Secret*; and Lipstadt, *Beyond Belief.*
9. World Jewish Congress, *Unity in Dispersion: A History of the World Jewish Congress*, New York: World Jewish Congress (1948), 195.
10. *The Blue and the Yellow Stars of David*, 38.
11. 3/3/43, 22.
12. "Rereading an Unsettling Past: American Jews during the Nazi Era," in Alvin H. Rosenfeld, ed., *Thinking about the Holocaust: After Half a Century*, Bloomington:

Indiana University Press (1997), 184. Arad's primary interest is in explaining why there should be more scholarly attention focused on the Nazi period prior to establishment of extermination centers.

13. *The Holocaust in History*, 161.
14. See, in particular, Feingold, *The Politics of Rescue*, and Wasserstein, *Great Britain and the Jews of Europe*.
15. See Aaron Berman, *Nazism, the Jews, and American Zionism, 1933–1948*, Detroit: Wayne State University (1990); Seymour Maxwell Finger, *American Jewry During the Holocaust*, New York: Holmes & Meier Publishers Inc. (1984); Lookstein, *Were We Our Brothers' Keepers?*; and Rafael Medoff, *The Deafening Silence*, New York: Shapolsky Publishers (1987).
16. See Dollinger, *Quest for Inclusion*.
17. *The Holocaust in American Life*, 20.
18. Palestine Statehood Committee Papers, Reel #1,YU.
19. Lipstadt, *Beyond Belief*, 141.
20. *Odyssey Through Hell*, New York: L. B. Fischer (1946), 11.
21. "The Americanism of Adolph S. Ochs: A Guest in the House," *Commentary* 3:1 (January 1947): 67–72, 70–2.
22. *Beyond Belief*, 274–5, 239.
23. Bendersky, *The "Jewish Threat,"* 336–7.
24. Colby to Clark, 9/22/44; Tinsley to Colby, 10/3/44; Davis to Johnson, 9/22/44, OWI, News Bureau, Office of the Chief, General Subjects Files, Box 975, NA
25. For a detailed discussion of how the Roosevelt Administration and the president in particular used the press to gauge public sentiment, see Laurel Leff "News of the Holocaust: Why FDR Didn't Tell and the Press Didn't Ask," *Hakirah: A Journal of Jewish and Ethnic Studies*, (January 2005).
26. Dollinger, *Quest for Inclusion*, 73–6.
27. Ben Halpern, "Anti-Semitism in the Perspective of Jewish History," in Stember, *Jews in the Mind of America*.
28. *The Holocaust and the Liberal Imagination*, 272.
29. For a discussion of the Roosevelt Administration's inattention to this issue, see Leff, "News of the Holocaust." See also American Jewish Committee Collection, Gen-10, Box 8, Anti-Semitism Polls Folder, YIVO.
30. Cowles to Deputies, Bureau Chief of OWI Domestic Branch, 1/18/43, RG208/75/232, NA.
31. *Jews in the Mind of America*, 41.
32. *The Abandonment of the Jews*, 321.
33. *Beyond Belief*, 244.
34. Abraham J. Karp, *Haven and Home: A History of the Jews in America*, New York: Schocken Books (1985), 294–9, 299; Kenneth Wolk, "New Haven and Waterbury, Connecticut Jewish Communities' Public Response to the Holocaust 1938–44," Ph.D. dissertation, May 1995.

Index